THE LANAHAN READINGS

in

CIVIL RIGHTS

and

CIVIL LIBERTIES

Third Edition

Other Books by David M. O'Brien

Judges on Judging: Views from the Bench, Third Edition (*editor*)

Animal Sacrifice and Religious Freedom: Church of the Lukumi Babalu Aye v. City of Hialeah

To Dream of Dreams:
Religious Freedom and Constitutional Politics in Postwar Japan

Storm Center: The Supreme Court in American Politics, Eighth Edition

Constitutional Law and Politics:
Struggles for Power and Governmental Accountability, Seventh Edition

Constitutional Law and Politics:
Civil Rights and Civil Liberties, Seventh Edition

Supreme Court Watch (Annual)

Abortion and American Politics (*co-author*)

Judicial Roulette

What Process Is Due? Courts and Science-Policy Disputes

The Politics of Technology Assessment:
Institutions, Processes and Policy Disputes (*co-editor*)

Views from the Bench: The Judiciary and Constitutional Politics (*co-editor*)

Judicial Independence in the Age of Democracy: Critical Perspectives from Around the World (*co-editor*)

The Public's Right to Know:
The Supreme Court and the First Amendment

Privacy, Law, and Public Policy

THE LANAHAN READINGS

in

CIVIL RIGHTS

and

CIVIL LIBERTIES

Third Edition

———

Edited by
David M. O'Brien
Leone Reaves and George W. Spicer Professor
University of Virginia

LANAHAN PUBLISHERS, INC.

Baltimore

The text of this book was composed in Bembo
with display type set in Garamond and Bernhard Modern.
Composition by BYTHEWAY PUBLISHING SERVICES.
Manufacturing by VICTOR GRAPHICS, INC.

ISBN-10 1-930398-14-X
ISBN-13 978-1-930398-14-6

LANAHAN PUBLISHERS, INC.
324 Hawthorne Road, Baltimore, MD 21210
1-866-345-1949 [Toll Free]
LANAHAN@AOL.COM
WWW.LANAHANPUBLISHERS.COM

1   2   3   4   5   6   7   8   9   0

CONTENTS

Introduction   xiii

PART ONE

The Supreme Court and the Construction of Civil Rights and Liberties

1. *The Federalist No. 78* ALEXANDER HAMILTON
   [The classic defense of the establishment of a
   federal judiciary and its role in interpreting the
   Constitution: 1788]   3

2. *Constitutional Interpretation: A Contemporary Ratification*
   JUSTICE WILLIAM J. BRENNAN, JR.
   [Reflections on interpreting and applying the
   Constitution and the Bill of Rights to
   contemporary controversies: 1985]   9

3. *Originalism: The Lesser Evil* JUSTICE ANTONIN SCALIA
   [Countering the jurisprudence of judges like
   Justice Brennan, a defense of basing the
   interpretation of the Constitution and Bill of
   Rights on the "original understanding" of those
   documents: 1989]   20

4. *Our Democratic Constitution* JUSTICE STEPHEN G. BREYER
   [Advocating a pragmatic or consequentialist
   approach to interpreting the Constitution and
   the Bill of Rights in order to promote "active
   liberty": 2002]   29

PART TWO

Due Process In Historical Perspective

5. *The Path of Due Process of Law* WALTON H. HAMILTON
   [The development of a "liberty of contract" in
   historical perspective: 1938]   47

6. *Economic Due Process and the Supreme Court:*
   An Exhumation and Reburial
   ROBERT G. McCLOSKEY
   [A political scientist looks at the Court's post-
   1937 problematic "double standard" concerning
   civil rights and economic rights: 1962]   64

7. *The Nationalization of the Bill of Rights in Perspective*
   RICHARD C. CORTNER
   [An examination of the bases for the Court's
   "due process revolution": 1981]   77

8. *Due Process, Government Inaction, and Private Wrongs*
   DAVID A. STRAUSS
   [A legal scholar critically assesses the Supreme
   Court's rejection of broader claims of
   substantive and procedural due process: 1989]   93

PART THREE

Freedom of Expression

9. *The System of Freedom of Expression* THOMAS I. EMERSON
   [The basic normative principles and liberal
   justifications underlying an expansive
   protection of freedom of speech and press: 1970]   109

10. *Arguing the "Pentagon Papers" Case* ERWIN N. GRISWOLD
    [An insider's account of the "Pentagon
    Papers" case during the heated and
    controversial war in Vietnam: 1992]   114

11. *Defending Pornography* NADINE STROSSEN
    [A former ACLU president defends First
    Amendment protections against claims to
    greater gender equality: 1995]   125

12. *Communication and the Capitalist Culture*
    RONALD K. L. COLLINS and DAVID M. SKOVER
    [The manipulations of mass commercial
    communications' sound-bites and advertising's
    provocative images versus James Madison's ideal
    of deliberative debate and individual self-
    determination: 1996]   130

                         PART FOUR
                         ─────────

                   Freedom of Religion

13. *Habits of the Heart* ROBERT N. BELLAH and OTHERS
    [A team of sociologists reports on
    individualism and religious pluralism
    and argues that Americans find fulfillment
    in religious communities that historically
    have unified, rather than divided, support
    for religious freedom and a civic religion:
    1985]   139

14. *Culture Wars: The Struggle to Define America*
    JAMES DAVIDSON HUNTER
    [Sociologist Hunter examines the emerging
    alliances of religious groups and their
    battles over family, art, education, and law:
    1991]   149

15. *Blasphemy* LEONARD W. LEVY
    [An historian considers blasphemy and its
    protection under the First Amendment: 1993]   162

PART FIVE

The Rights of the Accused and Criminal Justice

16. *Security Versus Civil Liberties* JUDGE RICHARD A. POSNER
[A judge considers the tradeoff between
security and liberty in the aftermath of the
terrorist attacks of September 11, 2001, and
the "war against international terrorism": 2001]   171

17. *Terrorism and the Constitution*
DAVID COLE and JAMES X. DEMPSEY
[An argument in defense of civil rights and
civil liberties against claims of national
security: 2006]   175

18. *Mapp* v. *Ohio and the Fourth Amendment*
PRISCILLA H. MACHADO ZOTTI
[A political scientist tells the story behind the
Supreme Court case that extended the Fourth
Amendment's exclusionary rule to state as
well as federal courts: 2005]   181

19. *Fourth Amendment First Principles* AKHIL REED AMAR
[A legal scholar critically examines recent
Court rulings on "unreasonable searches and
seizures" and argues that the Court should
abandon the "exclusionary rule": 1997]   192

20. *Blind Spot: Racial Profiling, Meet Your Alter Ego:
Affirmative Action* RANDALL KENNEDY
[A legal scholar juxtaposes the controversies over
racial profiling and affirmative action: 2002]   215

21. *Homicide: A Year on the Killing Streets* DAVID SIMON
[Journalist-writer Simon takes a hard look at
police questioning "outside of *Miranda*" in
real interrogation rooms: 1991]   218

22. *Gideon's Trumpet* ANTHONY LEWIS
[The classic story of *Gideon v. Wainwright* and
the right to counsel in state courts: 1964]   226

23. *Search and Destroy: African-American Males in the Criminal Justice System* JEROME G. MILLER
[How the "war on drugs" and the "war on crime" has a disproportionate impact on African-Americans: 1996]   233

PART SIX

Capital Punishment

24. *Witness to Another Execution* SUSAN BLAUSTEIN
[A journalist's meditations before and after witnessing an execution: 1994]   245

25. *For Capital Punishment: Crime and the Morality of the Death Penalty* WALTER BERNS
[Why those who commit heinously cruel crimes ought to be executed: 1979]   257

26. *Capital Punishment: The Inevitability of Caprice and Mistake* CHARLES L. BLACK, JR.
[The argument against capital punishment because of the inevitability of mistakes: 1974]   263

27. *The Broken Machinery of Death* ALAN BERLOW
[Places recent moratoriums on executions and the current debate over capital punishment in historical and political perspective: 2001]   268

PART SEVEN

The Quest for Social Equality and Personal Liberty

28. *Simple Justice: The History of* Brown v. Board of Education RICHARD KLUGER
[An historical and political perspective on the landmark school desegregation case: 1977]   275

29. *Dismantling Desegregation: The Quiet Reversal of*
    Brown v. Board of Education
    GARY ORFIELD and SUSAN E. EATON
    [How the Rehnquist Court's rulings and
    contemporary housing patterns are returning
    the nation to systems of increasingly
    segregated schools: 1996]   282

30. *The Equality Crisis: Some Reflections on Culture,*
    Courts, and Feminism WENDY W. WILLIAMS
    [A legal scholar's review of the Court's
    application of the Fourteenth Amendment's
    equal protection clause to claims of gender
    discrimination: 1982]   293

31. *Speaking in a Judicial Voice: Reflections on*
    Roe v. Wade JUSTICE RUTH BADER GINSBURG
    [Reflections on *Roe v. Wade* and the quest
    for gender equality in the courts prior to the
    author's appointment to the Supreme Court:
    1992]   304

32. *Sex, Death, and the Courts* RONALD DWORKIN
    [A legal scholar draws parallels between a
    woman's right to abortion and homosexuals'
    claims against discrimination and a person's
    right to physician-assisted suicide: 1996]   312

33. *Sexual Harassment and the Ironies of the 1964*
    Civil Rights Act DAVID M. O'BRIEN
    [The story of how the 1964 Civil Rights Act
    came to apply to heterosexual and
    homosexual harassment in the workplace: 2002]   327

34. *Rethinking the Civil Rights and Civil Liberties*
    Revolution MICHAEL J. KLARMAN
    [Is the Court leading the struggle to advance
    civil rights and liberties or merely validating
    emerging national political consensus?: 1996]   339

Contents

35. *Constitutional Futurology, or What Are Courts Good For?*
    JEFFREY ROSEN
    [A legal scholar argues that courts are the
    most democratic branch and serve America in
    defending basic civil rights and liberties:
    2006]   346

Permissions and Acknowledgments   355

INTRODUCTION

CONTROVERSIES OVER civil rights and liberties are, obviously, not confined to opinions of the Supreme Court and justices' exchanges of concurring and dissenting opinions. Neither are the Court's decisions, as Justice Harlan F. Stone put it, "like babies, brought by storks." Since the Court is not a self-starter and must await the arrival of "actual cases or controversies," its annual docket of cases presents windows of opportunity to decide cases that register often vexing political controversies abroad in the land. Even though the modern Court has virtually complete discretion over which cases it decides, the justices can run, for a term or more, but ultimately they cannot hide from the most divisive issues dividing the country at any given time, whether school desegregation, women's rights, homosexual rights, or the "right to die." In short, the business of the Court reflects social and economic changes, as well as broader cultural movements, whether brought by individuals or interest groups, state or federal governments, or challenges to new or old laws and practices.

Moreover, the Court's rulings, even a series of rulings, on the most divisive controversies do not lay them to rest. Major controversies over civil rights and liberties, such as those over the integration of schools and abortion, tend to carry over from one generation to another, frequently becoming transformed in the process due to larger generational and socio-economic changes that shift the legal and political landscape or on-going debate. New critical perspectives challenge "old" ways of thinking. The "modern" constitutional legal theory of free speech and press (circa 1960s and 1970s), for instance, has been profoundly challenged by some feminists, critical-race theorists, and communitarians on the left and the right. In short, controversies over civil rights and liberties register more than contrasting judicial philosophies within the Court, they reflect larger political conflicts, philosophical disagreements, historical changes, and multidimensional contexts that require interdisciplinary study on multiple levels of analysis.

This LANAHAN reader aims to put major constitutional controversies over civil rights and liberties and the role of the Supreme Court in

American politics into interdisciplinary and critical perspective. It does so by collecting essays by leading historians, political scientists, sociologists, and legal scholars, as well as practitioners, justices, and journalists. In different ways and on different levels of analysis, these readings provide unique narratives, insightful analyses, compelling data, and critical perspectives on some of the major controversies over civil rights and liberties confronting the Court and the country.

The first edition of this LANAHAN reader came about because students in my civil rights and civil liberties courses wanted to read the "opinions" of others in addition to those of the Court. I was delighted to learn from my publisher that there were other such students all over the country who also wanted to read the "opinions" of others — and did so when their instructors assigned the first edition. This interest and the evolving mix of new topics and opinions (see below) prompted a second edition and now this third edition. As before, those teaching new courses on the introduction to law may find that their students will be willing to apply their new understanding of the law to the great issues raised in this reader. And for the many law and society courses, and for even the occasional American government class, this third edition offers an even more diverse commentary on the societal, political, and legal issues of the day. Let's look at these issues:

Part One provides contrasting perspectives on constitutional interpretation and the role of the Supreme Court in constructing and enforcing civil rights and liberties. It begins with Alexander Hamilton's classic defense of the establishment of the Supreme Court and federal judiciary in *Federalist* No. 78. Notably, he argued that the judiciary was "the least dangerous branch" because it has "neither FORCE nor WILL." That selection is followed by excerpts from a lecture by Justice William J. Brennan, Jr., an influential liberal on the Court in the latter half of the twentieth century. He contends the Constitution must be interpreted as "a living document" — interpreted in light of changing conditions and contemporary controversies. By contrast, conservative Justice Antonin Scalia counters that the interpretation of the Constitution and Bill of Rights should be based on the "original understanding" of those documents. Finally, Justice Stephen Breyer finds both textualism and a jurisprudence of "originalism" inadequate. Instead, he advocates a pragmatic or consequentialist approach in order to promote "active liberty."

Part Two, then, turns to one of the most fundamental concepts in constitutional law and politics, namely, in Justice Benjamin Cardozo's words, that "majestic generality": "due process of law." The four selections here provide diverse and historical perspectives on the critical question:

"What process is due?" They also illuminate how that question has been answered in different ways, at different times, by different Courts, but invariably stirring political controversy. Historian Walton H. Hamilton narrates the story of how the Supreme Court in the late nineteenth and early twentieth century came to enforce the doctrine of a "liberty of contract" as a substantive, yet unenumerated, right protected by the Fourteenth Amendment's due process clause. That doctrine and interpretation of due process, as identified with *Lochner v. New York* (1905), in striking down progressive economic legislation, precipitated the constitutional crisis of 1937 and the Court's repudiation of economic substantive due process.

After abandoning the doctrine of economic substantive due process, the Court gradually assumed a "guardianship" role in advancing civil rights and liberties, notably, by extending to the states under the Fourteenth Amendment's due process clause the substantive and procedural guarantees of the Bill of Rights. The so-called nationalization of the Bill of Rights, along with some unenumerated rights, like the right to privacy in *Griswold v. Connecticut* (1965) and *Roe v. Wade* (1973), also created a constitutional "double standard" — in the Court's deferring to legislative regulation of economic interests while giving heightened scrutiny to claims of civil rights and liberties — that remains controversial. Political scientist Robert G. McCloskey examines the Court's post-1937 "double standard" and finds it problematic, though he would not have the Court return to the days of *Lochner*'s enforcement of a philosophy of laissez-fair economics. Another political scientist, Richard C. Cortner, takes up the Court's nationalization of the Bill of Rights and, specifically, the "due process revolution" forged under Chief Justice Earl Warren (1953–1969). In doing so, he highlights the profound consequences for American politics of the Court's post-1937 expansive interpretation of the due process protection afforded civil rights and liberties.

One of the consequences of the Court's "due process revolution" has been that conservative politicians since the 1960s have attacked the Court for "judicial activism" in handing down rulings like *Griswold v. Connecticut* (1965) and *Roe v. Wade* (1973) on the right of privacy, much as liberals attacked the pre-1937 Court for enforcing *Lochner*'s "liberty of contract." A series of Republican presidents from 1970 to 2008 — Richard M. Nixon, Ronald Reagan, George H. W. Bush, and George W. Bush, gradually transformed the Court through their appointment of conservative justices. As a result, the Court was much less willing to expand the protection afforded by the Fourteenth Amendment's due process clause. Legal scholar David A. Strauss critically illuminates the Court's recent rejection of broader claims to substantive and procedural due process in decisions like *DeShaney v. Winnebago County Department of Social Services* (1989), rejecting a due process claim to government protection from private wrongs and injuries.

Part Three addresses controversies over freedom of speech and press. Thomas I. Emerson's essay lays out some of the basic normative principles and liberal justifications for an expansive interpretation of the First Amendment's protection for freedom of speech and press. Former Solicitor General Erwin N. Griswold, then, provides insight into the background of his arguing the landmark no prior restraint "Pentagon Papers" case in *New York Times, Co. v. United States* (1971). In the following essay, the president of the American Civil Liberties Union, Nadine Strossen, defends liberty against the claims of some contemporary feminists and communitarians who would refashion the First Amendment's protection for free speech and press. Finally, Ronald K. L. Collins and David M. Skover call into question accepted First Amendment principles by pointing to the disjunction between First Amendment theory and contemporary trends in mass commercial communications and popular culture. Whereas the freedom of speech and press is typically defended as instrumental to deliberative democracy and self-governance, Collins and Skover contend that mass commercial communications primarily aim to manipulate consumers and their economic choices. In other words, "the market place of ideas" is dominated by Madison Avenue's advertising sound-bites and provocative images, not governed by James Madison's ideal of deliberative debate and individual self-determination.

Part Four takes up controversies over freedom from and to religious exercise. In an excerpt from their highly acclaimed *Habits of the Heart*, Robert N. Bellah and his colleagues argue that religious communities unify, more than divide, Americans. But in the following essay, sociologist James Davidson Hunter argues contrariwise that new alliances among religious groups are in fact producing a growing "culture war" over the family, art, eduction, and the law. Historian Leonard W. Levy, then, argues that blasphemy of religious figures, symbols, and sacred texts should (and largely does) receive full protection under the First Amendment.

Part Five turns to the rights of the accused and criminal justice. Judge Richard A. Posner offers historical and legal perspectives on the tradeoffs between security and liberty that must be made in the aftermath of the September 11, 2001, international terrorist attacks on the World Trade Center in New York City and the Pentagon in Virginia. Judge Posner argues for a pragmatic balancing of individuals' liberty versus interests in national security. In contrast, David Cole and James X. Dempsey counter that liberty and the guarantees of the Bill of Rights should be defended especially in times of perceived national emergency. Political scientist Priscilla H. Machado Zotti then tells the story behind the Supreme Court's landmark ruling in *Mapp v. Ohio* on the Fourth Amendment's exclusionary rule, which required the exclusion of evidence obtained from illegal searches and seizures at trial in state courts, no less than federal courts. Yale Law School professor Akhil Reed Amar, however, criticizes the Court's rulings on the Fourth Amendment's guarantee against "unreasonable searches and seizures," in addition to offering some provocative proposals for reform. Yet another view is offered by Harvard Law School professor Randall Kennedy, who juxtaposes the controversies over racial profiling and affirmative action. Journalist–writer David Simon then describes a routine police interrogation, drawing the reader into the psychological experience of both the interrogator and the suspect, and illuminating how police may circumvent the Court's rulings on the Fifth Amendment's privilege against self-incrimination. That selection is followed by an excerpt from the *New York Times* reporter Anthony Lewis's awarding-winning book *Gideon's Trumpet*, in which he tells the story of the watershed Sixth Amendment ruling on the right to counsel in *Gideon v. Wainwright* (1963). This section concludes with Jerome G. Miller's perspective as a former corrections official on how the "war on drugs" and the "war on crime" has had a disproportionate impact on African-American males.

Part Six provides three perspectives on capital punishment and the increasing number of annual executions as a result of recent Court rulings. Journalist Susan Blaustein recounts her visit to Huntsville, Texas, where that state's executions take place. Blaustein offers her observations on the town, its people, death row, and witnessing an execution. Her article is followed by two others, arguing for and against capital punishment. Walter Berns takes the position that not only does the death penalty not violate the Eighth Amendment ban on "cruel and unusual punishments," but that the execution of those who commit heinously cruel and unusual crimes satisfies society's anger and demand for moral retribution. In contrast, Charles L. Black, Jr., counters that the arbitrariness and capriciousness of the criminal process and capital punishment system, as well as the inevitability of mistakes, renders the imposition of death sentences constitutionally indefensible. Finally, Allan Berlow discusses how the current debate over capital punishment is changing course and places it in historical and political perspective.

Part Seven focuses on contemporary struggles over the quest for social equality and personal liberty, as well as the underlying tensions between equality and liberty. The first two selections provide historical and political perspectives on the controversy over the integration of public schools, sparked by the landmark school desegregation ruling in *Brown v. Board of Education* (1954). An excerpt from Richard Kluger's seminal work *Simple Justice*, details how the Court came to decide *Brown*. Political scientist Gary Orfield, in turn, examines the consequences of the changing composition of the high bench and the Court's recent rulings on integration efforts. He contends that, along with contemporary housing patterns, they are returning the country to systems of increasingly segregated schools.

The struggle over gender equality has been the subject of several Court rulings. Law school professor Wendy W. Williams reviews the Court's application of the Fourteenth Amendment equal protection clause to claims of gender discrimination and reflects, more generally, on equality, feminism, and American culture. The struggle for judicial recognition of gender discrimination was, of course, led in the 1970s by now Supreme Court Justice Ruth Bader Ginsburg. In her article, Ginsburg offers critical reflections on *Roe v. Wade* and the quest for gender equality in the courts.

The following reading deals with two of the most contentious contemporary controversies over personal autonomy, namely, claims to homosexual rights and to a "right to die." Law school professor Ronald Dworkin argues that, just as a woman's right to choose an abortion was recognized in *Roe v. Wade* as a fundamental liberty, so too homosexuals' claims against discrimination, in cases like *Romer v. Evans* (1996), and those of terminally-ill patients to physician-assisted suicide are constitutionally defensible claims to personal autonomy and liberty.

The book concludes with three selections that address the roles of Congress, the executive branch, the courts, and interest groups in defining and protecting civil rights and liberties. My selection tells the ironic story of how the 1964 Civil Rights Act came to forbid heterosexual and homosexual harassment in the workplace as a result of federal agencies, courts, interest groups, and individuals' taking its provisions seriously and interpreting them in unanticipated ways. In a provocative essay, Law School professor Michael J. Klarman challenges the "conventional wisdom" that the Supreme Court is in the forefront of struggles to advance civil rights and liberties. To the contrary, Klarman claims that the Court is generally behind the times and merely validates an established or emerging national political consensus when deciding cases like *Brown v. Board of Education* and *Roe v. Wade*, among many other controversial rulings on civil rights and liberties. Finally, journalist and law school professor Jeffrey Rosen argues that courts serve democracy by engaging the President, Congress, and the American people in a constitutional dialogue over the construction of civil rights and liberties.

THE LANAHAN READINGS

in

CIVIL RIGHTS

and

CIVIL LIBERTIES

Third Edition

PART ONE

The Supreme Court and the Construction of Civil Rights and Civil Liberties

THE UNITED STATES CONSTITUTION ARTICLE III

The judicial Power of the United States shall be vested in one supreme Court, and in such inferior Courts as the Congress may from time to time ordain and establish. . . .

The judicial Power shall extend to all Cases, in Law and Equity, arising under this Constitution, the Laws of the United States, and Treaties made, or which shall be made, under their Authority;—to all Cases affecting Ambassadors, other public Ministers and Consuls;—to all Cases of admiralty and maritime Jurisdiction;—to Controversies to which the United States shall be a Party;—to Controversies between two or more States; —between a State and Citizens of another State [altered by the Eleventh Amendment]—between Citizens of different States—between Citizens of the same State claiming Lands under Grants of different States, and between a State, or the Citizens thereof, and foreign States, Citizens or Subjects. In all Cases affecting Ambassadors, other public Ministers and Consuls, and those in which a State shall be Party, the supreme Court shall have original Jurisdiction. In all the other Cases before mentioned, the supreme Court shall have appellate Jurisdiction, both as to Law and Fact, with such Exceptions, and under such Regulations as the Congress shall make. . . .

I

The Federalist No. 78

ALEXANDER HAMILTON

In a now classic essay published anonymously as Publius, *Alexander Hamilton in* The Federalist No. 78 *defended the establishment of a federal judiciary as "the least dangerous to the political rights of the Constitution; because it will be least in a capacity to annoy or injure them . . ." and has "no influence over either the sword or the purse. . . ." He also argued that in interpreting the Constitution, the judiciary had "neither FORCE nor WILL, but merely judgment" and that its decisions depended on the support of the people.*

IN UNFOLDING the defects of the existing Confederation, the utility and necessity of a federal judicature have been clearly pointed out. It is the less necessary to recapitulate the considerations there urged, as the propriety of the institution in the abstract is not disputed; the only questions which have been raised being relative to the manner of constituting it, and to its extent. To these points, therefore, our observations shall be confined. . . .

First. As to the mode of appointing the judges; this is the same with that of appointing the officers of the Union in general, and has been so fully discussed in the two last numbers, that nothing can be said here which would not be useless repetition.

Second. As to the tenure by which the judges are to hold their places; this chiefly concerns their duration in office; the provisions for their support; the precautions for their responsibility.

According to the plan of the convention, all judges who may be appointed by the United States are to hold their offices *during good behavior;* which is conformable to the most approved of the State constitutions and among the rest, to that of this State. Its propriety having been drawn into question by the adversaries of that plan, is no light symptom of the rage for objection, which disorders their imaginations and judgments. The standard of good behavior for the continuance in office of the judicial magistracy, is certainly one of the most valuable of the modern improvements in the practice of government. In a monarchy it is an excellent barrier to the despotism of the prince; in a republic it is a no less excellent barrier to the encroachments and oppressions of the representative body. And it is the best expedient which can be devised in any government, to secure a steady, upright, and impartial administration of the laws.

Whoever attentively considers the different departments of power must perceive, that, in a government in which they are separated from each other, the judiciary, from the nature of its functions, will always be the least dangerous to the political rights of the Constitution; because it will be least in a capacity to annoy or injure them. The Executive not only dispenses the honors, but holds the sword of the community. The legislature not only commands the purse, but prescribes the rules by which the duties and rights of every citizen are to be regulated. The judiciary, on the contrary, has no influence over either the sword or the purse; no direction either of the strength or of the wealth of the society; and can take no active resolution whatever. It may truly be said to have neither FORCE nor WILL, but merely judgment; and must ultimately depend upon the aid of the executive arm even for the efficacy of its judgments.

This simple view of the matter suggests several important conse-quences. It proves incontestably, that the judiciary is beyond comparison the weakest of the three departments of power; that it can never attack with success either of the other two; and that all possible care is requisite to enable it to defend itself against their attacks. It equally proves, that though individual oppression may now and then proceed from the courts of justice, the general liberty of the people can never be endangered from that quarter; I mean so long as the judiciary remains truly distinct from both the legislature and the Executive. For I agree, that "there is no liberty, if the power of judging be not separated from the legislative and executive powers." And it proves, in the last place, that as liberty can have nothing to fear from the judiciary alone, but would have every thing to fear from its union with either of the other departments; that as all the effects of such a union must ensue from a dependence of the former on the latter, notwithstanding a nominal and apparent separation; that as, from the natural feebleness of the judiciary, it is in continual jeopardy of being overpowered, awed, or influenced by its co-ordinate branches; and that as nothing can contribute so much to its firmness and independence as permanency in office, this quality may therefore be justly regarded as an indispensable ingredient in its constitution, and, in a great measure, as the citadel of the public justice and the public security.

The complete independence of the courts of justice is peculiarly essential in a limited Constitution. By a limited Constitution, I understand one which contains certain specified exceptions to the legislative authority;

such, for instance, as that it shall pass no bills of attainder, no *ex post facto* laws, and the like. Limitations of this kind can be preserved in practice no other way than through the medium of courts of justice, whose duty it must be to declare all acts contrary to the manifest tenor of the Constitution void. Without this, all the reservations of particular rights or privileges would amount to nothing.

Some perplexity respecting the rights of the courts to pronounce legislative acts void, because contrary to the Constitution, has arisen from an imagination that the doctrine would imply a superiority of the judiciary to the legislative power. It is urged that the authority which can declare the acts of another void, must necessarily be superior to the one whose acts may be declared void. As this doctrine is of great importance in all the American constitutions, a brief discussion of the ground on which it rests cannot be unacceptable.

There is no position which depends on clearer principles, than that every act of a delegated authority, contrary to the tenor of the commission under which it is exercised, is void. No legislative act, therefore, contrary to the Constitution, can be valid. To deny this, would be to affirm, that the deputy is greater than his principal; that the servant is above his master; that the representatives of the people are superior to the people themselves; that men acting by virtue of powers, may do not only what their powers do not authorize, but what they forbid.

If it be said that the legislative body are themselves the constitutional judges of their own powers, and that the construction they put upon them is conclusive upon the other departments, it may be answered, that this cannot be the natural presumption, where it is not to be collected from any particular provisions in the Constitution. It is not otherwise to be supposed, that the Constitution could intend to enable the representatives of the people to substitute their *will* to that of their constituents. It is far more rational to suppose, that the courts were designed to be an intermediate body between the people and the legislature, in order, among other things, to keep the latter within the limits assigned to their authority. The interpretation of the laws is the proper and peculiar province of the courts. A constitution is, in fact, and must be regarded by the judges, as a fundamental law. It therefore belongs to them to ascertain its meaning, as well as the meaning of any particular act proceeding from the legislative body. If there should happen to be an irreconcilable variance between the two, that which has the superior obligation and validity ought, of course, to be preferred; or, in other words, the Constitution ought to be preferred to the statute, the intention of the people to the intention of their agents.

Nor does this conclusion by any means suppose a superiority of the judicial to the legislative power. It only supposes that the power of the people is superior to both; and that where the will of the legislature, declared in its statutes, stands in opposition to that of the people, declared in the Constitution, the judges ought to be governed by the latter rather than the former. They ought to regulate their decisions by the fundamental laws, rather than by those which are not fundamental. . . .

It can be of no weight to say that the courts, on the pretense of a repugnancy, may substitute their own pleasure to the constitutional intentions of the legislature. This might as well happen in the case of two contradictory statutes; or it might as well happen in every adjudication upon any single statute. The courts must declare the sense of the law; and if they should be disposed to exercise WILL instead of JUDGMENT, the consequence would equally be the substitution of their pleasure to that of the legislative body. The observation, if it prove any thing, would prove that there ought to be no judges distinct from that body.

If, then, the courts of justice are to be considered as the bulwarks of a limited Constitution against legislative encroachments, this consideration will afford a strong argument for the permanent tenure of judicial offices, since nothing will contribute so much as this to that independent spirit in the judges which must be essential to the faithful performance of so arduous a duty.

This independence of the judges is equally requisite to guard the Constitution and the rights of individuals from the effects of those ill humors, which the arts of designing men, or the influence of particular conjunctures, sometimes disseminate among the people themselves, and which, though they speedily give place to better information, and more deliberate reflection, have a tendency, in the meantime, to occasion dangerous innovations in the government, and serious oppressions of the minor party in the community. Though I trust the friends of the proposed Constitution will never concur with its enemies, in questioning that fundamental principle of republican government, which admits the right of the people to alter or abolish the established Constitution, whenever they find it inconsistent with their happiness, yet it is not to be inferred from this principle, that the representatives of the people, whenever a momentary inclination happens to lay hold of a majority of their constituents, incompatible with the provisions in the existing Constitution, would, on that account, be justifiable in a violation of those provisions; or that the courts would be under a greater obligation to connive at infractions in this shape, than when they had proceeded wholly from the cabals of the representative body. Until the people have, by some solemn and authoritative act, annulled or changed the established form, it is binding upon themselves collectively, as well as individually; and no presumption, or even knowledge, of their sentiments, can warrant their representatives in a departure from it, prior to such an act. But it is easy to see, that it would require an uncommon portion of fortitude in the judges to do their duty as faithful guardians of the Constitution, where legislative invasions of it had been instigated by the major voice of the community.

But it is not with a view to infractions of the Constitution only, that the independence of the judges may be an essential safeguard against the effects of occasional ill humors in the society. These sometimes extend no farther than to the injury of the private rights of particular classes of citizens, by unjust and partial laws. Here also the firmness of the judicial magistracy is of vast importance in mitigating the severity and confining the operation of such laws. It not only serves to moderate the immediate mischiefs of those which may have been passed, but it operates as a check upon the legislative body in passing them; who, perceiving that obstacles to the success of iniquitous intention are to be expected from the scruples of the courts, are in a manner compelled, by the very motives of the injustice they meditate, to qualify their attempts. This is a circumstance calculated to have more influence upon the character of our governments, than but few may be aware of. The benefits of the integrity and moderation of the judiciary have already been felt in more States than one; and though they may have displeased those whose sinister expectations they may have disappointed, they must have commanded the esteem and applause of all the virtuous and disinterested. Considerate men, of every description, ought to prize whatever will tend to beget or fortify that temper in the courts; as no man can be sure that he may not be to-morrow the victim of a spirit of injustice, by which he may be a gainer to-day. And every man must now feel, that the inevitable tendency of such a spirit is to sap the foundations of public and private confidence, and to introduce in its stead universal distrust and distress.

That inflexible and uniform adherence to the rights of the Constitution, and of individuals, which we perceive to be indispensable in the courts of justice, can certainly not be expected from judges who hold their offices by a temporary commission. Periodical appointments, however regulated, or by whomsoever made, would, in some way or other, be fatal to their necessary independence. If the power of making them was committed either to the Executive or legislature, there would be danger of an improper complaisance to the branch which possessed it; if to both, there would be an unwillingness to hazard the displeasure of either; if to the people, or to persons chosen by them for the special purpose, there would be too great a disposition to consult popularity, to justify a reliance that nothing would be consulted but the Constitution and the laws.

There is yet a further and a weightier reason for the permanency of the judicial offices, which is deducible from the nature of the qualifications they require. It has been frequently remarked, with great propriety, that a voluminous code of laws is one of the inconveniences necessarily connected with the advantages of a free government. To avoid an arbitrary discretion in the courts, it is indispensable that they should be bound down by strict rules and precedents, which serve to define and point out their duty in every particular case that comes before them; and it will readily be conceived from the variety of controversies which grow out of the folly and wickedness of mankind, that the records of those precedents must unavoidably swell to a very considerable bulk, and must demand long and laborious study to acquire a competent knowledge of them. Hence it is that there can be but few men in the society who will have sufficient skill in the laws to qualify them for the stations of judges. . . .

— PUBLIUS

2

Constitutional Interpretation: A Contemporary Ratification

JUSTICE WILLIAM J. BRENNAN, JR.

Justice William J. Brennan, Jr. was appointed to the Supreme Court in 1956 by Republican President Dwight D. Eisenhower. He served on the Court until 1991 and became known as a leading liberal and one of the most influential justices in the latter half of the twentieth century. In the selection here, excerpted from a 1985 lecture at the Text and Teaching Symposium at Georgetown University, Justice Brennan discusses the dynamics of constitutional interpretation and applying the "majestic generalities" that guarantee the due process and equal protection of the law.

———

THE CONSTITUTION IS fundamentally a public text—the monumental charter of a government and a people—and a Justice of the Supreme Court must apply it to resolve public controversies. For, from our beginnings, a most important consequence of the constitutionally created separation of powers has been the American habit, extraordinary to other democracies, of casting social, economic, philosophical, and political questions in the form of law suits, in an attempt to secure ultimate resolution by the Supreme Court. In this way, important aspects of the most fundamental issues confronting our democracy may finally arrive in the Supreme Court for judicial determination. Not infrequently, these are the issues upon which contemporary society is most deeply divided. . . .

Two other aspects of my relation to this text warrant mention. First, constitutional interpretation for a federal judge is, for the most part, obligatory. When litigants approach the bar of the court to adjudicate a constitutional dispute, they may justifiably demand an answer. Judges cannot avoid a definitive interpretation because they feel unable to, or would prefer not to, penetrate to the full meaning of the Constitution's provisions. Unlike literary critics, judges cannot merely savor the tensions or revel in the ambiguities inhering in the text—judges must resolve them.

Second, consequences flow from a Justice's interpretation in a direct and immediate way. A judicial decision respecting the incompatibility of Jim Crow with a constitutional guarantee of equality is not simply a contemplative exercise in defining the shape of a just society. It is an order — supported by the full coercive power of the State — that the present society change in a fundamental aspect. Under such circumstances the process of deciding can be a lonely, troubling experience for fallible human beings conscious that their best may not be adequate to the challenge. We Justices are certainly aware that we are not final because we are infallible; we know that we are infallible only because we are final. One does not forget how much may depend on the decision. More than the litigants may be affected. The course of vital social, economic, and political currents may be directed.

These three defining characteristics of my relation to the constitutional text — its public nature, obligatory character, and consequentialist aspect — cannot help but influence the way I read that text. When Justices interpret the Constitution, they speak for their community, not for themselves alone. The act of interpretation must be undertaken with full consciousness that it is, in a very real sense, the community's interpretation that is sought. Justices are not platonic guardians appointed to wield authority according to their personal moral predilections. Precisely because coercive force must attend any judicial decision to countermand the will of a contemporary majority, the Justices must render constitutional interpretations that are received as legitimate. The source of legitimacy is, of course, a wellspring of controversy in legal and political circles. At the core of the debate is what the late Yale Law School professor Alexander Bickel labeled "the counter-majoritarian difficulty." Our commitment to self-governance in a representative democracy must be reconciled with vesting in electorally unaccountable Justices the power to invalidate the expressed desires of representative bodies on the ground of inconsistency with higher law. Because judicial power resides in the authority to give meaning to the Constitution, the debate is really a debate about how to read the text, about constraints on what is legitimate interpretation.

There are those who find legitimacy in fidelity to what they call "the intentions of the Framers." In its most doctrinaire incarnation, this view demands that Justices discern exactly what the Framers thought about the question under consideration and simply follow that intention in resolving the case before them. It is a view that feigns self-effacing deference to the specific judgments of those who forged our original social compact. But in truth it is little more than arrogance cloaked as humility. It is arrogant to pretend that from our vantage we can gauge accurately the intent of the Framers on application of principle to specific, contemporary questions. All too often, sources of potential enlightenment such as records of the ratification debates provide sparse or ambiguous evidence of the original intention. Typically, all that can be gleaned is that the Framers themselves did not agree about the application or meaning of particular constitutional provisions, and hid their differences in cloaks of generality. Indeed, it is far from clear whose intention is relevant — that of the drafters, the congressional disputants, or the ratifiers in the states? — or even whether the idea of an original intention is a coherent way of thinking about a jointly drafted document drawing its authority from a general assent of the states. And apart from the problematic nature of the sources, our distance of two centuries cannot but work as a prism refracting all we perceive. One cannot help but speculate that the chorus of lamentations calling for interpretation faithful to "original intention" — and proposing nullification of interpretations that fail this quick litmus test — must inevitably come from persons who have no familiarity with the historical record.

Perhaps most importantly, while proponents of this facile historicism justify it as a depoliticization of the judiciary, the political underpinnings of such a choice should not escape notice. A position that upholds constitutional claims only if they were within the specific contemplation of the Framers in effect establishes a presumption of resolving textual ambiguities against the claim of constitutional right. It is far from clear what justifies such a presumption against claims of right. Nothing intrinsic in the nature of interpretation — if there is such a thing as the "nature" of interpretation — commands such a passive approach to ambiguity. This is a choice no less political than any other; it expresses antipathy to claims of the minority to rights against the majority. Those who would restrict claims of right to the values of 1789 specifically articulated in the Constitution turn a blind eye to social progress and eschew adaptation of overarching principles to changes of social circumstance.

Another, perhaps more sophisticated, response to the potential power of judicial interpretation stresses democratic theory: because ours is a government of the people's elected representatives, substantive value choices should by and large be left to them. This view emphasizes not the transcendent historical authority of the Framers but the predominant contemporary authority of the elected branches of government. Yet it has similar consequences for the nature of proper judicial interpretation. Faith in the majoritarian process counsels restraint. Even under more expansive formulations of this approach, judicial review is appropriate only to the extent of ensuring that our democratic process functions smoothly. Thus, for example, we would protect the freedom of speech merely to ensure that the people are heard by their representatives, rather than as a separate, substantive value. When, by contrast, society tosses up to the Supreme Court a dispute that would require invalidation of a legislature's substantive policy choice, the Court generally would stay its hand because the Constitution was meant as a plan of government and not as an embodiment of fundamental substantive values.

The view that all matters of substantive policy should be resolved through the majoritarian process has appeal under some circumstances, but I think it ultimately will not do. Unabashed enshrinement of majority will would permit the imposition of a social caste system or wholesale confiscation of property so long as a majority of the authorized legislative body, fairly elected, approved. Our Constitution could not abide such a situation. It is the very purpose of a Constitution—and particularly of the Bill of Rights—to declare certain values transcendent, beyond the reach of temporary political majorities. The majoritarian process cannot be expected to rectify claims of minority right that arise as a response to the outcomes of that very majoritarian process. As James Madison put it:

The prescription in favor of liberty ought to be levelled against that quarter where the greatest danger lies, namely, that which possesses the highest prerogative of power. But this is not found in either the Executive or Legislative departments of Government, but in the body of the people, operating by the majority against the minority.[1]

Faith in democracy is one thing, blind faith quite another. Those who drafted our Constitution understood the difference. One cannot read the text without admitting that it embodies substantive value choices; it places certain values beyond the power of any legislature. Obvious are the separation of powers; the privilege of the Writ of *Habeas Corpus*; prohibition of Bills of Attainder and *ex post facto* laws; prohibition of cruel and unusual punishments; the requirement of just compensation for official taking of property; the prohibition of laws tending to establish religion or enjoining the free exercise of religion; and, since the Civil War, the banishment of slavery and official race discrimination. With respect to at least such principles, we simply have not constituted ourselves as strict utilitarians. While the Constitution may be amended, such amendments require an immense effort by the people as a whole.

To remain faithful to the content of the Constitution, therefore, an approach to interpreting the text must account for the existence of these substantive value choices and must accept the ambiguity inherent in the effort to apply them to modern circumstances. The Framers discerned

1. *Annals of Congress: The Debates and Proceedings in the Congress of the United States* 437 (Washington, D.C.: Gales and Seaton, 1834).

fundamental principles through struggles against particular malefactions of the Crown; the struggle shapes the particular contours of the articulated principles. But our acceptance of the fundamental principles has not and should not bind us to those precise, at times anachronistic, contours. Successive generations of Americans have continued to respect these fundamental choices and adopt them as their own guide to evaluating quite different historical practices. Each generation has the choice to overrule or add to the fundamental principles enunciated by the Framers; the Constitution can be amended or it can be ignored. Yet with respect to its fundamental principles, the text has suffered neither fate. Thus, if I may borrow the words of an esteemed predecessor, Justice Robert Jackson, the burden of judicial interpretation is to translate "the majesty generalities of the Bill of Rights, conceived as part of the pattern of liberal government in the eighteenth century, into concrete restraints on officials dealing with the problems of the twentieth century."[2]

We current Justices read the Constitution in the only way that we can: as twentieth-century Americans. We look to the history of the time of framing and to the intervening history of interpretation. But the ultimate question must be: what do the words of the text mean in our time? For the genius of the Constitution rests not in any static meaning it might have had in a world that is dead and gone, but in the adaptability of its great principles to cope with current problems and current needs. What the constitutional fundamentals meant to the wisdom of other times cannot be their measure to the vision of our time. Similarly, what those fundamentals mean for us, our descendants will learn, cannot be the measure to the vision of their time. This realization is not, I assure you, a novel one of my own creation. Permit me to quote from one of the opinions of our Court, *Weems v. United States*, written nearly a century ago:

Time works changes, brings into existence new conditions and purposes. Therefore, a principle to be vital must be capable of wider application than the mischief which gave it birth. This is peculiarly true of constitutions. They are not ephemeral enactments, designed to meet passing occasions. They are, to use the words of Chief Justice John Marshall, "designed to approach immortality as nearly as human institutions can approach it." The future is their care and provision for events of good and bad tendencies of which no prophesy can be made. In the application of a constitution, therefore, our contemplation cannot be only of what has been, but of what may be.[3]

2. *West Virginia State Board of Education v. Barnette*, 319, 624, 639 (1943).
3. *Weems v. United States* 317, 349 (1910).

Interpretation must account for the transformative purposes of the text. Our Constitution was not intended to preserve a preexisting society, but to make a new one, to put in place new principles that the prior community had not sufficiently recognized. Thus, for example, when we interpret the Civil War Amendments to the charter—abolishing slavery, guaranteeing blacks equality under law, and guaranteeing blacks the right to vote—we must remember that those who put them in place had no desire to enshrine the status quo. Their goal was to make over their world, to eliminate all vestige of slave caste. Having discussed at some length how I, as a Supreme Court Justice, interact with this text, I think it is time to turn to the fruits of this discourse. For the Constitution is a sublime oration on the dignity of man, a bold commitment by a people to the ideal of libertarian dignity protected through law. Some reflection is perhaps required before this can be seen.

The Constitution on its face is, in large measure, a structuring text, a blueprint for government. And when the text is not prescribing the form of government, it is limiting the powers of that government. The original document, before addition of any of the amendments, does not speak primarily of the rights of man but of the abilities and disabilities of government. When one reflects on the text's preoccupation with the scope of government as well as its shape, however, one comes to understand that what this text is about is the relationship of the individual and the state. The text marks the metes and bounds of official authority and individual autonomy. When one studies the boundary that the text marks out, one gets a sense of the vision of the individual embodied in the Constitution.

As augmented by the Bill of Rights and the Civil War Amendments, this text is a sparkling vision of the supremacy of the human dignity of every individual. This vision is reflected in the very choice of democratic self-governance: the supreme value of a democracy is the presumed worth of each individual. And this vision manifests itself most dramatically in the specific prohibitions of the Bill of Rights, a term which I henceforth will apply to describe not only the original first eight amendments, but the Civil War Amendments as well. It is a vision that has guided us as a people throughout our history, although the precise rules by which we have protected fundamental human dignity have been transformed over time in response to both transformations of social condition and evolution of our concepts of human dignity.

Until the end of the nineteenth century, freedom and dignity in our country found meaningful protection in the institution of real property. In a society still largely agricultural, a piece of land provided men not just with sustenance but with the means of economic independence, a necessary precondition of political independence and expression. Not surprisingly, property relationships formed the heart of litigation and of legal practice, and lawyers and judges tended to think stable property relationships the highest aim of the law.

But the days when common-law property relationships dominated litigation and legal practice are past. To a growing extent economic existence now depends on less certain relationships with government — licenses, employment, contracts, subsidies, unemployment benefits, tax exemptions, welfare, and the like. Government participation in the economic existence of individuals is pervasive and deep. Administrative matters and other dealings with government are at the epicenter of the exploding law. We turn to government and to the law for controls which would never have been expected or tolerated before this century, when a man's answer to economic oppression or difficulty was to move two hundred miles west. Now hundreds of thousands of Americans live entire lives without any real prospect of the dignity and autonomy that ownership of real property could confer. Protection of the human dignity of such citizens requires a much modified view of the proper relationship of individual and state.

In general, problems of the relationship of the citizen with government have multiplied and thus have engendered some of the most important constitutional issues of the day. As government acts ever more deeply upon those areas of our lives once marked "private," there is an even greater need to see that individual rights are not curtailed or cheapened in the interest of what may temporarily appear to be the "public good." And as government continues in its role of provider for so many of our disadvantaged citizens, there is an even greater need to ensure that government act with integrity and consistency in its dealings with these citizens. To put this another way, the possibilities for collision between government activity and individual rights will increase as the power and authority of government itself expands, and this growth, in turn, heightens the need for constant vigilance at the collision points. If our free society is to endure, those who govern must recognize human dignity and accept the enforcement of constitutional limitations on their power conceived by the Framers to be necessary to preserve that dignity and the air of freedom which is our proudest heritage. Such recognition will not come from a technical understanding of the organs of government, or the new forms of wealth they administer. It requires something different, something deeper — a personal confrontation with the wellsprings of our society. Solutions of constitutional questions from that perspective have become the great challenge of the modern era. All the talk in the last half-decade about shrinking the government does not alter this reality or the challenge it imposes. The modern activist state is a concomitant of the complexity of modern society; it is inevitably with us. We must meet the challenge rather than wish it were not before us.

The challenge is essentially, of course, one to the capacity of our constitutional structure to foster and protect the freedom, the dignity, and the rights of all persons within our borders, which it is the great design of the Constitution to secure. During the time of my public service, this challenge has largely taken shape within the confines of the interpretive question whether the specific guarantees of the Bill of Rights operate as restraints on the power of state government. We recognize the Bill of Rights as the primary source of express information as to what is meant by constitutional liberty. The safeguards enshrined in it are deeply etched in the foundation of America's freedoms. Each is a protection with centuries of history behind it, often dearly bought with the blood and lives of people determined to prevent oppression by their rulers. The first eight amendments, however, were added to the Constitution to operate solely against federal power. It was not until the Thirteenth and Fourteenth Amendments were added, in 1865 and 1868, in response to a demand for national protection against abuses of state power, that the Constitution could be interpreted to require application of the first eight amendments to the states.

It was in particular the Fourteenth Amendment's guarantee that no person be deprived of life, liberty, or property without process of law that led us to apply many of the specific guarantees of the Bill of Rights to the states. In my judgment, Justice Cardozo best captured the reasoning that brought us to such decisions when he described what the Court has done as a process by which the guarantees "have been taken over from the earlier articles of the federal bill of rights and brought within the Fourteenth Amendment by a process of absorption . . . [that] has had its source in the belief that neither liberty nor justice would exist if [those guarantees] . . . were sacrificed."[4] But this process of absorption was neither swift nor steady. As late as 1922 only the Fifth Amendment guarantee of just compensation for official taking of property had been given force against the states. Between then and 1956 only the First Amendment guarantees of speech and conscience and the Fourth Amendment ban of unreasonable searches and seizures had been incorporated — the latter, however, without the exclusionary rule to give it force. As late as 1961,

---

4. *Palko v. Connecticut*, 302 U.S. 319, 326 (1937).

I could stand before a distinguished assemblage of the bar at New York University's James Madison Lecture and list the following as guarantees that had not been thought to be sufficiently fundamental to the protection of human dignity so as to be enforced against the state: the prohibition of cruel and unusual punishments, the right against self-incrimination, the right to assistance of counsel in a criminal trial, the right to confront witnesses, the right to compulsory process, the right not to be placed in jeopardy of life or limb more than once upon accusation of a crime, the right not to have illegally obtained evidence introduced at a criminal trial, and the right to a jury of one's peers.

The history of the quarter century following that James Madison Lecture need not be told in great detail. Suffice it to say that each of the guarantees listed above has been recognized as a fundamental aspect of ordered liberty. Of course, the above catalogue encompasses only the rights of the criminally accused, those caught, rightly or wrongly, in the maw of the criminal justice system. But it has been well said that there is no better test of a society than how it treats those accused of transgressing against it. Indeed, it is because we recognize that incarceration strips a man of his dignity that we demand strict adherence to fair procedure and proof of guilt beyond a reasonable doubt before taking such a drastic step. These requirements are, as Justice Harlan once said, "bottomed on a fundamental value determination of our society that it is far worse to convict an innocent man than to let a guilty man go free."[5] There is no worse injustice than wrongly to strip a man of his dignity. And our adherence to the constitutional vision of human dignity is so strict that even after convicting a person according to these stringent standards, we demand that his dignity be infringed only to the extent appropriate to the crime and never by means of wanton infliction of pain or deprivation. I interpret the Constitution plainly to embody these fundamental values.

Of course the constitutional vision of human dignity has, in this past quarter century, infused far more than our decisions about the criminal process. Recognition of the principle of "one person, one vote" as a constitutional one redeems the promise of self-governance by affirming the essential dignity of every citizen in the right to equal participation in the democratic process. Recognition of so-called "new property" rights in those receiving government entitlements affirms the essential dignity of the least fortunate among us by demanding that government treat with decency, integrity, and consistency those dependent on its benefits for their very survival. After all, a legislative majority initially decides to create

5. *In re Winship*, 397 U.S. 358, 372 (1970).

governmental entitlements; the Constitution's Due Process Clause merely provides protection for entitlements thought necessary by society as a whole. Such due process rights prohibit government from imposing the devil's bargain of bartering away human dignity in exchange for human sustenance. Likewise, recognition of full equality for women — equal protection of the laws — ensures that gender has no bearing on claims to human dignity.

Recognition of broad and deep rights of expression and of conscience reaffirm the vision of human dignity in many ways. They too redeem the promise of self-governance by facilitating — indeed demanding — robust, uninhibited, and wide-open debate on issues of public importance. Such public debate is, of course, vital to the development and dissemination of political ideas. As importantly, robust public discussion is the crucible in which personal political convictions are forged. In our democracy, such discussion is a political duty; it is the essence of self-government. The constitutional vision of human dignity rejects the possibility of political orthodoxy imposed from above; it respects the right of each individual to form and to express political judgments, however far they may deviate from the mainstream and however unsettling they might be to the powerful or the elite. Recognition of these rights of expression and conscience also frees up the private space for both intellectual and spiritual development free of government dominance, either blatant or subtle. Justice Brandeis put it so well sixty years ago when he wrote: "Those who won our independence believed that the final end of the State was to make men free to develop their faculties; and that in its government the deliberative forces should prevail over the arbitrary. They valued liberty both as an end and as a means."[6]

I do not mean to suggest that we have in the last quarter century achieved a comprehensive definition of the constitutional ideal of human dignity. We are still striving toward that goal, and doubtless it will be an eternal quest. For if the interaction of this Justice and the constitutional text over the years confirms any single proposition, it is that the demands of human dignity will never cease to evolve. . . .

You have doubtless observed that this description of my personal encounter with the constitutional text has in large portion been a discussion of public developments in constitutional doctrine over the last quarter century. That, as I suggested at the outset, is inevitable because my interpretive career has demanded a public reading of the text. This public encounter with the text, however, has been a profound source of personal

6. *Whitney v. California*, 274 U.S. 357 (1927).

inspiration. The vision of human dignity embodied there is deeply moving. It is timeless. It has inspired Americans for two centuries, and it will continue to inspire as it continues to evolve. That evolutionary process is inevitable and, indeed, it is the true interpretive genius of the text.

If we are to be as a shining city upon a hill, it will be because of our ceaseless pursuit of the constitutional ideal of human dignity. For the political and legal ideals that form the foundation of much that is best in American institutions — ideals jealously reserved and guarded throughout our history — still form the vital force in creative political thought and activity within the nation today. As we adapt our institutions to the ever-changing conditions of national and international life, those ideals of human dignity — liberty and justice for all individuals — will continue to inspire and guide us because they are entrenched in our Constitution. The Constitution with its Bill of Rights thus has a bright future, as well as a glorious past, for its spirit is inherent in the aspirations of our people.

3

Originalism: The Lesser Evil

JUSTICE ANTONIN SCALIA

Justice Scalia was appointed to the Supreme Court by Republican President Ronald Reagan in 1986. A leading conservative jurist, he has championed an approach to interpreting the Constitution and Bill of Rights based on an "original understanding" of the documents, and challenged the jurisprudence of liberal judges, like Justice Brennan (see Chapter 2). In the excerpt here, Justice Scalia advances his approach, on which he has further elaborated in his book A Matter of Interpretation *(1997) and most recently in a "Foreword" to* Originalism: A Quarter-Century of Debate *(2007), among other off-the-bench publications.*

———

IT MAY SURPRISE the layman, but it will surely not surprise the lawyers here, to learn that originalism is not, and had perhaps never been, the sole method of constitutional exegesis. It would be hard to count on the fingers of both hands and the toes of both feet, yea, even on the hairs of one's youthful head, the opinions that have in fact been rendered not on the basis of what the Constitution originally meant, but on the basis of what the judges currently thought it desirable for it to mean. That is, I suppose, the sort of behavior Chief Justice Hughes was referring to when he said the Constitution is what the judges say it is. But in the past, nonoriginalist opinions have almost always had the decency to lie, or at least to dissemble, about what they were doing—either ignoring strong evidence of original intent that contradicted the minimal recited evidence of an original intent congenial to the court's desires, or else not discussing original intent at all, speaking in terms of broad constitutional generalities with no pretense of historical support. . . . It is only in relatively recent years, however, that nonoriginalist exegesis has, so to speak, come out of the closet, and put itself forward overtly as an intellectually legitimate device. To be sure, in support of its venerability as a legitimate interpretive theory there is often trotted out John Marshall's statement in *McCulloch v. Maryland* that "we must never forget it is a constitution we are expounding"[1]—as though the implication of that state-

---

1. *McCulloch v. Maryland*, 17 U.S. (4 Wheat.) 316, 407 (1819).

ment was that our interpretation must change from age to age. But that is a canard. The real implication was quite the opposite: Marshall was saying that the Constitution had to be interpreted generously because the powers conferred upon Congress under it had to be broad enough to serve not only the needs of the federal government originally discerned but also the needs that might arise in the future. If constitutional interpretation could be adjusted as changing circumstances required, a broad initial interpretation would have been unnecessary.

Those who have not delved into the scholarly writing on constitutional law for several years may be unaware of the explicitness with which many prominent and respected commentators reject the original meaning of the Constitution as an authoritative guide. Harvard Professor Laurence H. Tribe, for example, while generally conducting his constitutional analysis under the rubric of the open-ended textual provisions such as the Ninth Amendment, does not believe that the originally understood content of those provisions has much to do with how they are to be applied today. The Constitution, he has written, "invites us, and our judges, to expand on the . . . freedoms that are uniquely our heritage,"[2] and "invites a collaborative inquiry, involving both the Court and the country, into the contemporary content of freedom, fairness, and fraternity."[3] Stanford Dean Paul Brest, having (in his own words) "abandoned both consent and fidelity to the text and original understanding as the touchstones of constitutional decisionmaking,"[4] concludes that "the practice of constitutional decisionmaking should enforce those, but only those, values that are fundamental to our society."[5] While Brest believes that the "text," "original understanding," "custom," "social practices," "conventional morality," and "precedent" all strongly inform the determination of those values, the conclusions drawn from all these sources are "defeasible in the light of changing public values."[6] Yale Professor Owen Fiss asserts that, whatever the Constitution might originally have meant, the courts should give "concrete meaning and application" to those values that "give our society an identity and inner coherence [and] its distinctive public morality."[7] Oxford Professor (and expatriate American) Ronald Dworkin calls

2. Laurence H. Tribe, *God Save This Honorable Court* 45 (New York: Random House, 1985).
3. Laurence H. Tribe, *American Constitutional Law* 771 (Westbury, N.Y.: The Foundation Press, 2d ed. 1988).
4. Paul Brest, "The Misconceived Quest for the Original University," 60 *Boston University Law Review* 204, 226 (1980).
5. Ibid., at 227.
6. Ibid., at 229.
7. Owen Fiss, "The Supreme Court 1978 Term—Foreword: The Forms of Justice," 93 *Harvard Law Review* 1, 9, 11 (1979).

for "a fusion of constitutional law and moral theory."[8] Harvard Professor
Richard Parker urges, somewhat more specifically, that constitutional law
"take seriously and work from (while no doubt revising) the classical
conception of a republic, including its elements of relative equality, mobili-
zation of citizenry, and civic virtue."[9] More specifically still, New York
University Professor David Richards suggests that it would be desirable
for the courts' constitutional decisions to follow the contractarian moral
theory set forth in Professor John Rawls' treatise, *A Theory of Justice*.[10]
And I could go on.

The principal theoretical defect of nonoriginalism, in my view, is its
incompatibility with the very principle that legitimizes judicial review of
constitutionality. Nothing in the text of the Constitution confers upon
the courts the power to inquire into, rather than passively assume, the
constitutionality of federal statutes. That power is, however, reasonably
implicit because, as Marshall said in *Marbury v. Madison*, (1) "[i]t is emphatically the province and duty of the judicial department to say what the
law is," (2) "[i]f two laws conflict with each other, the courts must decide
on the operation of each," and (3) "the constitution is to be considered,
in court, as a paramount law."[11] Central to that analysis, it seems to me,
is the perception that the Constitution, though it has an effect superior
to other laws, is in its nature the sort of "law" that is the business of the
courts — an enactment that has a fixed meaning ascertainable through the
usual devices familiar to those learned in the law. If the Constitution were
not that sort of a "law," but a novel invitation to apply current societal
values, what reason would there be to believe that the invitation was
addressed to the courts rather than to the legislature? One simply cannot
say, regarding that sort of novel enactment, that "[i]t is emphatically the
province and duty of the judicial department" to determine its content.
Quite to the contrary, the legislature would seem a much more appropriate
expositor of social values, and its determination that a statute is compatible
with the Constitution should, as in England, prevail.

Apart from the frailty of its theoretical underpinning, nonoriginalism
confronts a practical difficulty reminiscent of the truism of elective politics
that "You can't beat somebody with nobody." It is not enough to demonstrate that the other fellow's candidate (originalism) is no good; one must

8. Ronald Dworkin, *Taking Rights Seriously* 149 (Cambridge: Harvard University Press,
1977).
9. Richard Parker, "The Past of Constitutional Theory — And Its Future," 42 *Ohio State
Law Journal* 223, 258 n. 146 (1981).
10. David Richards, "Constitutional Privacy, The Right to Die and the Meaning of Life:
A Moral Analysis," 22 *William & Mary Law Review* 327, 344–47 (1981).
11. *Marbury v. Madison*, 5 U.S. (1 Cranch.) 137, 177 (1803).

also agree upon another candidate to replace him. Just as it is not very meaningful for a voter to vote "non-Reagan," it is not very helpful to tell a judge to be a "non-originalist." If the law is to make any attempt at consistency and predictability, surely there must be general agreement not only that judges reject one exegetical approach (originalism), but that they adopt another. And it is hard to discern any emerging consensus among the nonoriginalists as to what this might be. Are the "fundamental values" that replace original meaning to be derived from the philosophy of Plato, or of Locke, or Mills, or Rawls, or perhaps from the latest Gallup poll? This is not to say that originalists are in entire agreement as to what the nature of their methodology is; as I shall mention shortly, there are some significant differences. But as its name suggests, it by and large represents a coherent approach, or at least an agreed-upon point of departure. As the name "nonoriginalism" suggests (and I know no other, more precise term by which this school of exegesis can be described), it represents agreement on nothing except what is the wrong approach.

Finally, I want to mention what is not a defect of nonoriginalism, but one of its supposed benefits that seems to me illusory. A bit earlier I quoted one of the most prominent nonoriginalists, Professor Tribe, to the effect that the Constitution "invites us, and our judges, to expand on the . . . freedoms that are uniquely our heritage."[12] I think it fair to say that that is a common theme of nonoriginalists in general. But why, one may reasonably ask — once the original import of the Constitution is cast aside to be replaced by the "fundamental values" of the current society — why are we invited only to "expand on" freedoms, and not to contract them as well? [In 1988] we decided a case, *Coy v. Iowa*,[13] in which, at the trial of a man accused of taking indecent liberties with two young girls, the girls were permitted to testify separated from the defendant by a screen which prevented them from seeing him. We held that, at least absent a specific finding that these particular witnesses needed such protection, this procedure violated that provision of the Sixth Amendment that assures a criminal defendant the right "to be confronted with the witnesses against him." Let us hypothesize, however (a hypothesis that may well be true), that modern American society is much more conscious of, and averse to, the effects of "emotional trauma" than was the society of 1791, and that it is, in addition, much more concerned about the emotional frailty of children and the sensitivity of young women regarding sexual abuse. If that is so, and if the nonoriginalists are right, would it not have been

---

12. Laurence H. Tribe, *God Save This Honorable Court*, p. 45.
13. *Coy v. Iowa*, 108 S.Ct. 2798 (1988).

possible for the Court to hold that, even though in 1791 the confrontation clause clearly would not have permitted a blanket exception for such testimony, it does so today? Such a holding, of course, could hardly be characterized as an "expansion upon" preexisting freedoms. Or let me give another example that is already history: I think it highly probable that over the past two hundred years the Supreme Court, though not avowedly under the banner of "nonoriginalist" interpretation, has in fact narrowed the contract clause of the Constitution well short of its original meaning. Perhaps we are all content with that development — but can it possibly be asserted that it represented an expansion, rather than a contraction, of individual liberties? Our modern society is undoubtedly not as enthusiastic about economic liberties as were the men and women of 1789; but we should not fool ourselves into believing that because we like the result the result does not represent a contraction of liberty. Nonoriginalism, in other words, is a two-way street that handles traffic both to and from individual rights.

Let me turn next to originalism, which is also not without its warts. Its greatest defect, in my view, is the difficulty of applying it correctly. Not that I agree with, or even take very seriously, the intricately elaborated scholarly criticisms to the effect that (believe it or not) words have no meaning. They have meaning enough, as the scholarly critics themselves must surely believe when they choose to express their views in text rather than music. But what is true is that it is often exceedingly difficult to plumb the original understanding of an ancient text. Properly done, the task requires the consideration of an enormous mass of material — in the case of the Constitution and its Amendments, for example, to mention only one element, the records of the ratifying debates in all the states. Even beyond that, it requires an evaluation of the reliability of that material — many of the reports of the ratifying debates, for example, are thought to be quite unreliable. And further still, it requires immersing oneself in the political and intellectual atmosphere of the time — somehow placing out of mind knowledge that we have which an earlier age did not, and putting on beliefs, attitudes, philosophies, prejudices and loyalties that are not those of our day. It is, in short, a task sometimes better suited to the historian than the lawyer. . . .

I can be much more brief in describing what seems to me the second most serious objection to originalism: In its undiluted form, at least, it is medicine that seems too strong to swallow. Thus, almost every originalist would adulterate it with the doctrine of *stare decisis* — so that *Marbury v. Madison* would stand even if Professor Raoul Berger should demonstrate unassailably that it got the meaning of the Constitution wrong. (Of course recognizing *stare decisis* is seemingly even more incompatible with nonoriginalist theory: If the most solemnly and democratically adopted text of the Constitution and its Amendments can be ignored on the basis of current values, what possible basis could there be for enforced adherence to a legal decision of the Supreme Court?) But *stare decisis* alone is not enough to prevent originalism from being what many would consider too bitter a pill. What if some state should enact a new law providing public lashing, or branding of the right hand, as punishment for certain criminal offenses? Even if it could be demonstrated unequivocally that these were not cruel and unusual measures in 1791, and even though no prior Supreme Court decision has specifically disapproved them, I doubt whether any federal judge — even among the many who consider themselves originalists — would sustain them against an eighth amendment challenge. It may well be, as Professor Henry Monaghan persuasively argues, that this cannot legitimately be reconciled with originalist philosophy — that it represents the unrealistic view of the Constitution as a document intended to create a perfect society for all ages to come, whereas in fact it was a political compromise that did not pretend to create a perfect society even for its own age (as its toleration of slavery, which a majority of the founding generation recognized as an evil, well enough demonstrates). Even so, I am confident that public flogging and handbranding would not be sustained by our courts, and any espousal of originalism as a practical theory of exegesis must somehow come to terms with that reality.

One way of doing so, of course, would be to say that it was originally intended that the cruel and unusual punishment clause would have an evolving content — that "cruel and unusual" originally meant "cruel and unusual for the age in question" and not "cruel and unusual in 1791." But to be faithful to originalist philosophy, one must not only say this but demonstrate it to be so on the basis of some textual or historical evidence. Perhaps the mere words "cruel and unusual" suggest an evolutionary intent more than other provisions of the Constitution, but that is far from clear; and I know of no historical evidence for that meaning. And if the faint-hearted originalist is willing simply to posit such an intent for the "cruel and unusual punishment" clause, why not for the due process clause, the equal protection clause, the privileges and immunity clause, etc.? When one goes down that road, there is really no difference between the faint-hearted originalist and the moderate nonoriginalist, except that the former finds it comforting to make up (out of whole cloth) an original evolutionary intent, and the latter thinks that superfluous. It is, I think, the fact that most originalists are faint-hearted and most nonoriginalists are moderate (that is, would not ascribe evolving content to such clear provisions as the requirement that the President be no less than thirty-five years of age) which accounts for the fact that the sharp divergence between the two philosophies does not produce an equivalently sharp divergence in judicial opinions.

Having described what I consider the principal difficulties with the originalist and nonoriginalist approaches, I suppose I owe it to the listener to say which of the two evils I prefer. It is originalism. I take the need for theoretical legitimacy seriously, and even if one assumes (as many nonoriginalists do not even bother to do) that the Constitution was originally meant to expound evolving rather than permanent values, as I discussed earlier I see no basis for believing that supervision of the evolution would have been committed to the courts. At an even more general theoretical level, orginalism seems to me more compatible with the nature and purpose of a Constitution in a democratic system. A democratic society does not, by and large, need constitutional guarantees to insure that its laws will reflect "current values." Elections take care of that quite well. The purpose of constitutional guarantees — and in particular those constitutional guarantees of individual rights that are at the center of this controversy — is precisely to prevent the law from reflecting certain changes in original values that the society adopting the Constitution thinks fundamentally undesirable. Or, more precisely, to require the society to devote to the subject the long and hard consideration required for a constitutional amendment before those particular values can be cast aside.

I also think that the central practical defect of nonoriginalism is fundamental and irreparable: the impossibility of achieving any consensus on what, precisely, is to replace original meaning, once that is abandoned. The practical defects of originalism, on the other hand, while genuine enough, seem to me less severe. While it may indeed be unrealistic to have substantial confidence that judges and lawyers will find the correct historical answer to such refined questions of original intent as the precise content of "the executive Power," for the vast majority of questions the answer is clear. The death penalty, for example, was not cruel and unusual punishment because it is referred to in the Constitution itself; and the right of confrontation by its plain language meant, at least, being face-to-face with the person testifying against one at trial. For the non-originalist, even these are open questions. As for the fact that originalism is strong medicine, and that one cannot realistically expect judges (probably myself included) to apply it without a trace of constitutional perfectionism: I suppose I must respond that this is a world in which nothing is flawless, and fall back upon G. K. Chesterton's observation that a thing worth doing is worth doing badly.

It seems to me, moreover, that the practical defects of originalism are defects more appropriate for the task at hand—that is, less likely to aggravate the most significant weakness of the system of judicial review and more likely to produce results acceptable to all. If one is hiring a reference-room librarian, and has two applicants, between whom the only substantial difference is that the one's normal conversational tone tends to be too loud and the other's too soft, it is pretty clear which of the imperfections should be preferred. Now the main danger in judicial interpretation of the Constitution — or, for that matter, in judicial interpretation of any law — is that the judges will mistake their own predilections for the law. Avoiding this error is the hardest part of being a conscientious judge; perhaps no conscientious judge ever succeeds entirely. Nonoriginalism, which under one or another formulation invokes "fundamental values" as the touchstone of constitutionality, plays precisely to this weakness. It is very difficult for a person to discern a difference between those political values that he personally thinks most important, and those political values that are "fundamental to our society." Thus, by the adoption of such a criterion judicial personalization of the law is enormously facilitated. (One might reduce this danger by insisting that the new "fundamental values" invoked to replace original meaning be clearly and objectively manifested in the laws of the society. But among all the varying tests suggested by nonoriginalist theoreticians, I am unaware that that one ever appears. Most if not all nonoriginalists, for example, would strike down the death penalty, though it continues to be widely adopted in both state and federal legislation.)

Originalism does not aggravate the principal weakness of the system, for it establishes a historical criterion that is conceptually quite separate from the preferences of the judge himself. And the principal defect of that approach — that historical research is always difficult and sometimes inconclusive — will, unlike nonoriginalism, lead to a more moderate rather than a more extreme result. The inevitable tendency of judges to think that the law is what they would like it to be will, I have no doubt, cause most errors in judicial historiography to be made in the direction of projecting upon the age of 1789 current, modern values—so that as applied, even as applied in the best of faith, originalism will (as the historical record shows) end up as something of a compromise. Perhaps not a bad characteristic for a constitutional theory. Thus, nonoriginalists can say, concerning the principal defect of originalism, "Oh happy fault." Originalism is, it seems to me, the librarian who talks too softly. Having made that endorsement, I hasten to confess that in a crunch I may prove a faint-hearted originalist. I cannot imagine myself, any more than any other federal judge, upholding a statute that imposes the punishment of flogging. But then I cannot imagine such a case's arising either. In any event, in deciding the cases before me I expect I will rarely be confronted with making the stark choice between giving evolutionary content (not yet required by *stare decisis*) and not giving evolutionary content to particular constitutional provisions. The vast majority of my dissents from nonoriginalist thinking (and I hope at least some of those dissents will be majorities) will, I am sure, be able to be framed in the terms that, even if the provision in question has an evolutionary content, there is inadequate indication that any evolution in social attitudes has occurred. That — to conclude this largely theoretical talk on a note of reality — is the real dispute that appears in the case: not between nonoriginalists on the one hand and pure originalists on the other, concerning the validity of looking at all to current values; but rather between, on the one hand, nonoriginalists, fainthearted originalists and pure-originalists-accepting-for-the-sake-of-argument-evolutionary-content, and, on the other hand, other adherents of the same three approaches, concerning the nature and degree of evidence necessary to demonstrate that constitutional evolution has occurred.

I am left with a sense of dissatisfaction, as I am sure you are, that a discourse concerning what one would suppose to be a rather fundamental — indeed, the most fundamental — aspect of constitutional theory and practice should end so inconclusively. But it should come as no surprise. We do not yet have an agreed-upon theory for interpreting statutes, either. I find it perhaps too laudatory to say that this is the genius of the common law system; but it is at least its nature.

4

Our Democratic Constitution

JUSTICE STEPHEN G. BREYER

Justice Stephen G. Breyer was appointed to the Supreme Court by Democratic President Bill Clinton in 1994. The selection here excerpts his James Madison Lecture at New York University School of Law that advances his pragmatic or consequentialist approach to interpreting the Constitution and the Bill of Rights. In it he takes issue with purely textualist and "originalist" approaches to constitutional interpretation. Justice Breyer subsequently elaborated the themes in his 2005 book Active Liberty: Interpreting Our Democratic Constitution.

———

THE UNITED STATES is a nation built on principles of human liberty — a liberty that embraces concepts of democracy. The French political philosopher Benjamin Constant understood the connection. He distinguished between liberty as practiced by the ancient Greeks and Romans and the "liberty" of the eighteenth- and nineteenth-century "moderns."[1] Writing thirty years after the French Revolution and not long after the adoption of our American Constitution, Constant said that the "liberty of the ancients" consisted of an "active and constant participation in collective power." The ancient world, he added, believed that liberty consisted of "submitting to all the citizens, without exception, the care and assessment of their most sacred interests." . . . Constant distinguished that "liberty of the ancients" from the more "modern liberty" consisting of "individual independence" from governmental restriction. . . .

I shall argue that, when judges interpret the Constitution, they should place greater emphasis upon the "ancient liberty," that is, the people's right to "an active and constant participation in collective power." I believe that increased emphasis upon this active liberty will lead to better constitutional law — law that will promote governmental solutions consistent with individual dignity and community need.

At the same time, my discussion will illustrate an approach to constitu-

---

1. Benjamin Constant, "The Liberty of the Ancients Compared with That of the Moderns," (1819) in *Political Writings* 309, 309–28 (Biancamaria Fontana trans. & ed., 1988).

tional interpretation that places considerable weight upon consequences—consequences valued in terms of basic constitutional purposes. It disavows a contrary constitutional approach, a more "legalistic" approach that places too much weight upon language, history, tradition, and precedent alone while understating the importance of consequences. If the discussion helps to convince you that the more "consequential" approach has virtue, so much the better.

Three basic views underlie my discussion. First, the Constitution, considered as a whole, creates a framework for a certain kind of government. Its general objectives can be described abstractly as including: (1) democratic self-government; (2) dispersion of power (avoiding concentration of too much power in too few hands); (3) individual dignity (through protection of individual liberties); (4) equality before the law (through equal protection of the law); and (5) the rule of law itself. . . .

Second, the Court, while always respecting language, tradition, and precedent, nonetheless has emphasized different general constitutional objectives at different periods in its history. Thus one can characterize the early nineteenth century as a period during which the Court helped to establish the authority of the federal government, including the federal judiciary. During the late nineteenth and early twentieth centuries, the Court underemphasized the Constitution's efforts to secure participation by black citizens in representative government—efforts related to the participatory "active liberty" of the ancients. At the same time, it overemphasized protection of property rights, such as an individual's freedom to contract without government interference, to the point where President Franklin [Delano] Roosevelt commented that the Court's *Lochner*-era decisions had created a legal "no-man's land" that neither state nor federal regulatory authority had the power to enter.[2]

The New Deal Court and the Warren Court reemphasized "active liberty." The former did so by dismantling various *Lochner*-era distinctions, thereby expanding the scope of democratic self-government. The latter did so by interpreting the Civil War Amendments in light of their purposes to mean what they say, thereby helping African-Americans become members of the Nation's community of self-governing citizens—a community that the Court expanded further in its "one person, one vote" decisions.[3]

---

2. See, for example, *Lochner v. New York*, 198 U.S. 45 (1905) striking down workplace health regulations on substantive due process grounds. W.E. Leuchtenburg, *The Supreme Court Reborn* 133 (New York: Oxford University Press, 1995).
3. See, for example, *Baker v. Carr*, 369 U.S. 186 (1962) finding that the Equal Protection Clause justified federal court intervention to review voter apportionment; *Reynolds v. Sims*, 377 U.S. 533 (1964) requiring application of the "one person, one vote" principle to state legislatures; *Gomillion v. Lightfoot*, 383 U.S. 663 (1960) striking down racial gerrymandering on Fifteenth Amendment grounds.

More recently, in my view, the Court has again underemphasized the importance of the citizen's active liberty. I will argue for a contemporary reemphasis that better combines "the liberty of the ancients" with that "freedom of governmental restraint" that Constant called "modern."

Third, the real-world consequences of a particular interpretive decision, valued in terms of basic constitutional purposes, play an important role in constitutional decision making. To that extent, my approach differs from that of judges who would place nearly exclusive interpretive weight upon language, history, tradition, and precedent. In truth, the difference is one of degree. Virtually all judges, when interpreting a constitution or a statute, refer at one time or another to language, to history, to tradition, to precedent, to purpose, and to consequences. Even those who take a more literal approach to constitutional interpretation sometimes find consequences and general purposes relevant. But the more "literalist" judge tends to ask those who cannot find an interpretive answer in language, history, tradition, and precedent alone to rethink the problem several times before making consequences determinative. The more literal judges may hope to find, in language, history, tradition, and precedent, objective interpretive standards; they may seek to avoid an interpretive subjectivity that could confuse a judge's personal idea of what is good for that which the Constitution demands; and they may believe that these "original" sources more readily will yield rules that can guide other institutions, including lower courts. These objectives are desirable, but I do not think the literal approach will achieve them, and, in any event, the constitutional price is too high. . . .

To focus upon that active liberty, to understand it as one of the Constitution's handful of general objectives, will lead judges to consider the constitutionality of statutes with a certain modesty. That modesty embodies an understanding of the judges' own expertise compared, for example, with that of a legislature. It reflects the concern that a judiciary too ready to "correct" legislative error may deprive "the people" of "the political experience, and the moral education and stimulus that come from . . . correcting their own errors."[4] It encompasses that doubt, caution, prudence, and concern — that state of not being "too sure" of oneself — that Learned Hand described as the "spirit of liberty."[5] In a word, it argues for traditional "judicial restraint." . . .

I begin with free speech and campaign finance reform. The campaign finance problem arises out of the recent explosion in campaign costs along

4. James Bradley Thayer, *John Marshall* 107 (1901).
5. Learned Hand, *The Spirit of Liberty* 3rd edition, (New York: Knopf, 1960), p. 190; cf. at p. 109: "If [a judge] is in doubt, he must stop, for he cannot tell that the conflicting interests in the society for which he speaks would have come to a just result."

with a vast disparity among potential givers. . . . A very small number of individuals underwrite a very large share of these enormous costs. . . . The basic constitutional question, as you all know, is not the desirability of reform legislation but whether, how, or to what extent the First Amendment permits the legislature to impose limitations or ceilings on the amounts individuals, organizations, or parties can contribute to a campaign or on the kinds of contributions they can make. The Court has considered this kind of question several times; I have written opinions in several of those cases; and here I shall rephrase (not go beyond) what I already have written.

One cannot (or, at least, I cannot) find an easy answer to the constitutional questions in language, history, or tradition. The First Amendment's language says that Congress shall not abridge "the freedom of speech." But it does not define "the freedom of speech" in any detail. The nation's founders did not speak directly about campaign contributions. . . .

Neither can I find answers in purely conceptual arguments. Some argue, for example, that "money is speech"; others say "money is not speech." But neither contention helps much. Money is not speech, it is money. But the expenditure of money enables speech; and that expenditure is often necessary to communicate a message, particularly in a political context. A law that forbids the expenditure of money to convey a message could effectively suppress that communication.

Nor does it resolve the matter simply to point out that campaign contribution limits inhibit the political "speech opportunities" of those who wish to contribute more. Indeed, that is so. But the question is whether, in context, such a limitation abridges "the freedom of speech." And to announce that this kind of harm could never prove justified in a political context is simply to state an ultimate constitutional conclusion; it is not to explain the underlying reasons.

To refer to the Constitution's general participatory self-government objective, its protection of "active liberty" is far more helpful. That is because that constitutional goal indicates that the First Amendment's constitutional role is not simply one of protecting the individual's "negative" freedom from governmental restraint. The amendment in context also forms a necessary part of a constitutional system designed to sustain that democratic self-government. The amendment helps to sustain the democratic process both by encouraging the exchange of ideas needed to make sound electoral decisions and by encouraging an exchange of views among ordinary citizens necessary to their informed participation in the electoral process. It thereby helps to maintain a form of government open to participation (in Constant's words, by "all the citizens, without exception").

The relevance of this conceptual view lies in the fact that the campaign finance laws also seek to further the latter objective. They hope to democratize the influence that money can bring to bear upon the electoral process, thereby building public confidence in that process, broadening the base of a candidate's meaningful financial support, and encouraging greater public participation. They consequently seek to maintain the integrity of the political process — a process that itself translates political speech into governmental action. Seen in this way, campaign finance laws, despite the limits they impose, help to further the kind of open public political discussion that the First Amendment also seeks to encourage, not simply as an end, but also as a means to achieve a workable democracy.

For this reason, I have argued that a court should approach most campaign finance questions with the understanding that important First Amendment-related interests lie on both sides of the constitutional equation, and that a First Amendment presumption hostile to government regulation, such as "strict scrutiny," is consequently out of place. Rather, the Court considering the matter without the benefit of presumptions must look realistically at the legislation's impact, both its negative impact on the ability of some to engage in as much communication as they wish and the positive impact upon the public's confidence and consequent ability to communicate through (and participate in) the electoral process. . . .

I am not saying that focus upon active liberty will automatically answer the constitutional question in particular campaign finance cases. I argue only that such focus will help courts find a proper route for arriving at an answer. The positive constitutional goal implies a systemic role for the First Amendment, and that role, in turn, suggests a legal framework, that is, a more particular set of questions for the Court to ask. Modesty suggests where, and how, courts should defer to legislatures in doing so. The suggested inquiry is complex. But courts both here and abroad have engaged in similarly complex inquiries where the constitutionality of electoral laws is at issue. That complexity is demanded by a Constitution that provides for judicial review of the constitutionality of electoral rules while granting Congress the effective power to secure a fair electoral system. . . .

I turn next to federalism. My example suggests a need to examine consequences valued in terms of active liberty.

The Court's recent federalism cases fall into three categories. First, the Court has held that Congress may not write laws that "commandeer" a state's legislative or executive officials, say by requiring a state legislature to write a particular kind of law (for example, a nuclear waste storage law)[6] or by requiring a local official to spend time enforcing a federal policy (for example, requiring a local sheriff to see whether a potential gun buyer has a criminal record).[7] Second, the Court has limited Congress's power (under the Commerce Clause or the Fourteenth Amendment) to force a state to waive its Eleventh Amendment immunity from suit by private citizens.[8] Third, the Court has limited the scope of Congress's Commerce Clause powers, finding that gun possession near local schools and violence against women in local communities did not sufficiently "affect" interstate commerce.[9]

Although I dissented in each recent case, I recognize that each holding protects liberty in its negative form — to some degree. Each of them, in one respect or another, makes it more difficult for the federal government to tell state and local governments what they must do. To that extent they free citizens from certain restraints that a more distant central government might otherwise impose. But constitutional principles of federalism involve active as well as negative freedom. They impose limitations upon the distant central government's decision making not simply as an anti-restrictive end but also as a democracy-facilitating means.

My colleague Justice [Sandra Day] O'Connor has set forth many of the basic connections. By guaranteeing state and local governments broad decision making authority, federalist principles facilitate "novel social and economic experiments," secure decisions that rest on knowledge of local circumstances, and help to develop a sense of shared purposes among local citizens. Through increased transparency, they make it easier for citizens to hold government officials accountable. And by bringing government closer to home, they help maintain a sense of local community. In all these ways they facilitate and encourage citizen participation in governmental decision making — Constant's classical ideal. We must evaluate the Court's federalism decisions in terms of both forms of liberty — their necessary combination. When we do so, we shall find that a cooperative federalism, allocating specific problem-related roles among national and state governments, will protect both forms of liberty today, including the active liberty that the Court's decisions overlook.

A concrete example drawn from toxic chemical regulation exemplifies the kind of technologically-based problem modern governments are asked to solve. Important parts of toxic substance regulation must take place at

6. *New York v. United States*, 505 U.S. 144 (1992).
7. *Printz v. United States*, 521 U.S. 898, 921 (1997).
8. E.g., *Board of Trustees of the University of Alabama v. Garrett*, 531 U.S. 356 (2001); *Seminole Tribe of Florida v. Florida*, 517 U.S. 44 (1996).
9. *United States v. Morrison*, 529 U.S. 598 (2000); *United States v. Lopez*, 514 U.S. 549 (1995).

the national level. Chemical substances ignore state boundaries as they travel through air, water, or soil, and consequently they may affect the environment in more than one state. Their regulation demands a high level of scientific and technical expertise, to which the federal government might have ready access, at least initially. A federal regulator might be better able than state regulators to create, for example, a uniform risk discourse designed to help ordinary citizens better understand the nature of risk. And only a federal regulator could set minimum substantive standards designed to avoid a race to the bottom among states hoping to attract industry.

At the same time, certain aspects of the problem seem better suited for decentralized regulation by state or local governments. The same amounts of the same chemical may produce different toxic effects depending upon local air, water, or soil conditions. The same standard will have different economic effects in different communities. And affected citizens in different communities may value the same level of toxic substance cleanup quite differently. To what point should we clean up the local waste dump and at what cost?

Modern efforts to create more efficient regulation recognize the importance of that local involvement. They seek a kind of cooperative federalism that would, for example, have federal officials make expertise available to state and local officials while seeking to separate expert and fact-related matters from more locally-based questions of value. They would also diminish reliance upon classical command-and-control regulation, supplementing that regulation with incentive-based, less-restrictive regulatory methods, such as taxes and marketable rights. Such efforts, by placing greater power to participate and to decide in the hands of individuals and localities, can further both the negative and active liberty interests that underlie federalist principles. But will the Court's recent federalism decisions encourage or discourage those cooperative, or incentive-based, regulatory methods?

In my view, the "commandeering" decisions, such as *United States v. Printz*, might well hinder a cooperative program, for they could prevent Congress from enlisting local officials to check compliance with federal minimum standards. Rather, Congress would have to create a federal enforcement bureaucracy (or, perhaps, create unnecessary federal spending programs). Given ordinary bureaucratic tendencies, that fact, other things being equal, will make it harder, not easier, to shift regulatory power to state and local governments. It will make it more difficult, not easier, to experiment with incentive-based regulatory methods. And while some argue that Congress can bypass the "commandeering" decisions through selective and aggressive exercise of its spending power (at least as that doctrine currently exists), there is little evidence that Congress has taken this path.

I can make this same point with another example underlined by the tragic events of September 11. In a dissenting opinion, Justice [John Paul] Stevens wrote that the "threat of an international terrorist, may require a national response before federal personnel can be made available to respond. . . . Is there anything [in the Constitution] that forbids the enlistment of state officers to make that response effective?"[10] That enlistment, by facilitating the participation of local and state officials, would help both the cause of effective security coordination and the cause of federalism.

The Eleventh Amendment decisions could hinder the adoption of certain kinds of "less restrictive" regulatory methods. Suppose, for example, that Congress, reluctant to expand the federal regulatory bureaucracy, wished to encourage citizen suits as a device for ensuring state-owned (as well as privately-owned) toxic waste dump compliance. Or suppose that Congress, in order to encourage state or local governments to impose environmental taxes, provided for suits by citizens seeking to protest a particular tax assessment or to obtain a tax refund.

Decisions in the third category — the Court's recent Commerce Clause power decisions — would neither prohibit nor facilitate citizen participation in "cooperative" or "incentive-based" regulatory programs. Still, the Court's determination to re-weigh congressional evidence of "interstate effects" creates uncertainty about how much evidence is needed to find the constitutionally requisite effect. And certain portions of the Court's reasoning, such as its refusal to aggregate "non-economic" causes of interstate effects, create considerable doctrinal complexity.[11] Both may leave Congress uncertain about its ability to legislate the details of a cooperative federal, state, local, and regulatory framework. This uncertainty, other things being equal, makes it less likely that Congress will enact those complex laws — laws necessarily of national scope. To that extent, one can see these decisions as unhelpful to the cause of active liberty.

I do not claim that these consequences alone can prove the majority's holding wrong. I suggest only that courts ask certain consequence-related questions and not rely entirely upon logical deduction from text or precedent. I ask why the Court should not at least consider the practical effects on local democratic self-government when it elaborates the Constitution's

---

10. *Printz v. United States,* 940 (Stevens, J., dissenting).
11. See *United States v. Lopez,* 514 U.S. 549, 625–31 (1995) (Breyer, J., dissenting).

principles of federalism — principles that seek to further that kind of government. . . .

I next turn to a different kind of example. It focuses upon current threats to the protection of privacy, defined as "the power to control information about oneself." It seeks to illustrate what active liberty is like in modern America when we seek to arrive democratically at solutions to important technologically based problems. And it suggests a need for judicial caution and humility when certain privacy matters, such as the balance between free speech and privacy, are at issue.

First, I must describe the "privacy" problem. That problem is unusually complex. It clearly has become even more so since the terrorist attacks. For one thing, those who agree that privacy is important disagree about why. Some emphasize the need to be left alone, not bothered by others, or that privacy is important because it prevents people from being judged out of context. Some emphasize the way in which relationships of love and friendship depend upon trust, which implies a sharing of information not available to all. Others find connections between privacy and individualism, in that privacy encourages nonconformity. Still others find connections between privacy and equality, in that limitations upon the availability of individualized information leads private businesses to treat all customers alike. For some, or all, of these reasons, legal rules protecting privacy help to ensure an individual's dignity.

For another thing, the law protects privacy only because of the way in which technology interacts with different laws. Some laws, such as trespass, wiretapping, eavesdropping, and search-and-seizure laws, protect particular places or sites, such as homes or telephones, from searches and monitoring. Other laws protect, not places, but kinds of information, for example laws that forbid the publication of certain personal information even by a person who obtained that information legally. Taken together these laws protect privacy to different degrees depending upon place, individual status, kind of intrusion, and type of information.

Further, technological advances have changed the extent to which present laws can protect privacy. Video cameras now monitor shopping malls, schools, parks, office buildings, city streets, and other places that present law leaves unprotected. Scanners and interceptors can overhear virtually any electronic conversation. Thermal imaging devices detect activities taking place within the home. Computers record and collate information obtained in any of these ways, or others. This technology means an ability to observe, collate, and permanently record a vast amount of information about individuals that the law previously may have made available for collection but which, in practice, could not easily have been recorded and collected. The nature of the current or future privacy threat depends upon how this technological/legal fact will affect differently situated individuals.

These circumstances mean that efforts to revise privacy law to take account of the new technology will involve, in different areas of human activity, the balancing of values in light of predictions about the technological future. . . .

The complex nature of these problems calls for resolution through a form of participatory democracy. Ideally, that participatory process does not involve legislators, administrators, or judges imposing law from above. Rather, it involves law revision that bubbles up from below. Serious complex changes in law are often made in the context of a national conversation involving, among others, scientists, engineers, businessmen and women, and the media, along with legislators, judges, and many ordinary citizens whose lives the new technology will affect. That conversation takes place through many meetings, symposia, and discussions, through journal articles and media reports, through legislative hearings and court cases. Lawyers participate fully in this discussion, translating specialized knowledge into ordinary English, defining issues, creating consensus. Typically, administrators and legislators then make decisions, with courts later resolving any constitutional issues that those decisions raise. This "conversation" is the participatory democratic process itself.

The presence of this kind of problem and this kind of democratic process helps to explain, because it suggests a need for, judicial caution or modesty. That is why, for example, the Court's decisions so far have hesitated to preempt that process. In one recent case the Court considered a cell phone conversation that an unknown private individual had intercepted with a scanner and delivered to a radio station.[12] A statute forbade the broadcast of that conversation, even though the radio station itself had not planned or participated in the intercept. The Court had to determine the scope of the station's First Amendment right to broadcast given the privacy interests that the statute sought to protect. The Court held that the First Amendment trumped the statute, permitting the radio station to broadcast the information. But the holding was narrow. It focused upon the particular circumstances present, explicitly leaving open broadcaster liability in other, less innocent, circumstances.

The narrowness of the holding itself serves a constitutional purpose. The privacy "conversation" is ongoing. Congress could well rewrite the

12. *Bartnicki v. Vopper*, 532 U.S. 514 (2001).

statute, tailoring it more finely to current technological facts, such as the widespread availability of scanners and the possibility of protecting conversations through encryption. A broader constitutional rule might itself limit legislative options in ways now unforeseeable. And doing so is particularly dangerous where statutory protection of an important personal liberty is at issue.

By way of contrast, the Court held unconstitutional police efforts to use, without a warrant, a thermal imaging device placed on a public sidewalk.[13] The device permitted police to identify activities taking place within a private house. The case required the Court simply to ask whether the residents had a reasonable expectation that their activities within the house would not be disclosed to the public in this way — a well-established Fourth Amendment principle. Hence the case asked the Court to pour new technological wine into old bottles; it did not suggest that doing so would significantly interfere with an ongoing democratic policy conversation.

The privacy example suggests more by way of caution. It warns against adopting an overly rigid method of interpreting the Constitution — placing weight upon eighteenth-century details to the point where it becomes difficult for a twenty-first-century court to apply the document's underlying values. At a minimum it suggests that courts, in determining the breadth of a constitutional holding, should look to the effect of a holding on the ongoing policy process, distinguishing, as I have suggested, between the "eavesdropping" and the "thermal heat" types of cases. And it makes clear that judicial caution in such matters does not reflect the fact that judges are mitigating their legal concerns with practical considerations. Rather the Constitution itself is a practical document — a document that authorizes the Court to proceed practically when it examines new laws in light of the Constitution's enduring, underlying values.

My fourth example concerns equal protection and voting rights, an area that has led to considerable constitutional controversy. Some believe that the Constitution prohibits virtually any legislative effort to use race as a basis for drawing electoral district boundaries — unless, for example, the effort seeks to undo earlier invidious race-based discrimination.[14] Others believe that the Constitution does not so severely limit the instances in which a legislature can use race to create majority-minority districts. Without describing in detail the basic argument between the two positions, I wish to point out the relevance to that argument of the Constitution's democratic objective.

13. *Kyllo v. United States*, 533 U.S. 27 (2001).
14. See, for example, *Hunt v. Cromartie*, 526 U.S. 541 (1999).

That objective suggests a simple, but potentially important, constitutional difference in the electoral area between invidious discrimination, penalizing members of a racial minority, and positive discrimination, assisting members of racial minorities. The Constitution's Fifteenth Amendment prohibits the former, not simply because it violates a basic Fourteenth Amendment principle, namely that the government must treat all citizens with equal respect, but also because it denies minority citizens the opportunity to participate in the self-governing democracy that the Constitution creates. By way of contrast, affirmative discrimination ordinarily seeks to enlarge minority participation in that self-governing democracy. To that extent it is consistent with, and indeed furthers, the Constitution's basic democratic objective. That consistency, along with its more benign purposes, helps to mitigate whatever lack of equal respect any such discrimination might show to any disadvantaged member of a majority group. . . .

My last example focuses upon statutory interpretation and a potential relationship between active liberty and statutory drafting. Students of modern government complain that contemporary political circumstances too often lead Congress to ignore its own committees and to draft legislation, through amendments, on the House or Senate floor. This tendency may reflect a membership that is closely divided between the parties, single-interest pressure groups that (along with overly simplified media reporting) discourage compromise, or an election system in which voters tend to hold individuals rather than parties responsible. The consequence is legislation that is often silent, ambiguous, or even contradictory in respect to key interpretive questions. In such cases the true answer as to what Congress intended about such issues as the creation of a private right of action, the time limits governing an action, the judicial deference due an agency's interpretation of the statute, or other technical questions of application may well be that no one in Congress thought about the matter.

How are courts, which must find answers, to interpret these silences? Of course, courts will first look to a statute's language, structure, and history to help determine the statute's purpose, and then use that purpose, along with its determining factors, to help find the answer. But suppose that these factors, while limiting the universe of possible answers, do not themselves prove determinative. What then?

At this point courts are typically pulled in one of two directions. The first is linguistic. The judge may try to tease further meaning from language and structure, followed by application of language-based canons of interpretation designed to limit subjective judicial decision making. The second is purposive. Instead of deriving an artificial meaning through the use of general canons, the judge will ask instead how a (hypothetical) reasonable member of Congress, given the statutory language, structure, history, and purpose, would have answered the question, had it been presented. The second approach has a theoretical advantage. It reminds the judge of the law's democratic source, that is, that it is in Congress, not the courts, where the Constitution places the authority to enact a statute. And it has certain practical advantages sufficient in my view to overcome any risk of subjectivity.

The Court recently considered the matter in an administrative law case. The question was whether a court should defer to a customs inspector's on-the-spot ad hoc interpretation of a customs statute. A well-known administrative law case, *Chevron v. Natural Resources Defense Council*, sets forth an interpretive canon stating that, when an agency-administered statute is ambiguous, courts should defer to a reasonable agency interpretation. But how absolute is *Chevron's* canon? Does it mean that courts should normally defer or always defer? The Court held that *Chevron* was not absolute. It required deference only where Congress would have wanted deference. And the Court suggested criteria for deciding what Congress would have wanted where Congress provided no indication and perhaps did not think about the matter.

Why refer to a hypothetical congressional desire? Why produce the complex and fictional statement, "it seems unlikely Congress would have wanted courts to defer here"? The reason is that the fiction provides guidance of a kind roughly similar to that offered by Professor [Arthur Linton] Corbin's "reasonable contracting party" in contract cases.[15] It focuses the judge's attention on the fact that democratically elected individuals wrote the statute in order to satisfy certain human purposes. And it consequently increases the likelihood that courts will ask what those individuals would have wanted in light of those purposes. In this instance, I believe the approach favored reading exceptions into *Chevron's* canon where necessary to further those statutory purposes.

That flexibility is important. Dozens of different agencies apply thousands of different statutes containing untold numbers of lacunae in untold numbers of different circumstances. In many circumstances, as *Chevron* suggests, deference makes sense; but in some circumstances deference does not make sense. The metaphor — by focusing on what a reasonable person likely would have wanted — helps bring courts to that conclusion. To treat *Chevron's* rule purely as a judicial canon is less likely to do so. . . .

---

15. See John D. Calamari & Joseph M. Perillo, *The Law of Contracts* §§ 3–10 (2d ed. 1977).

The instances I have discussed encompass different areas of law —
speech, federalism, privacy, equal protection, and statutory interpretation.
In each instance, the discussion has focused upon a contemporary social
problem — campaign finance, workplace regulation, environmental regulation, information-based technological change, race-based electoral dis-
tricting, and legislative politics. In each instance, the discussion illustrates
how increased focus upon the Constitution's basic democratic objective
might make a difference — in refining doctrinal rules, in evaluating consequences, in applying practical cautionary principles, in interacting with
other constitutional objectives, and in explicating statutory silences. In
each instance, the discussion suggests how that increased focus might
mean better law. And "better" in this context means both (1) better able
to satisfy the Constitution's purposes, and (2) better able to cope with
contemporary problems. The discussion, while not proving its point purely
through logic or empirical demonstration, uses examples to create a pattern. The pattern suggests a need for increased judicial emphasis upon
the Constitution's democratic objective.

My discussion emphasizes values underlying specific constitutional
phrases, sees the Constitution itself as a single document with certain
basic related objectives, and assumes that the latter can inform a judge's
understanding of the former. Might that discussion persuade those who
prefer to believe that the keys to constitutional interpretation instead
lie in specific language, history, tradition, and precedent and who fear
that a contrary approach would permit judges too often to act too subjec-
tively?

Perhaps so, for several reasons. First, the area of interpretive disagreement is more limited than many believe. Judges can, and should, decide
most cases, including constitutional cases, through the use of language,
history, tradition, and precedent. Judges will often agree as to how these
factors determine a provision's basic purpose and the result in a particular
case. And where they differ, their differences are often differences of
modest degree. Only a handful of constitutional issues — though an important handful — are as open in respect to language, history, and basic purpose
as those that I have described. And even in respect to those issues, judges
must find answers within the limits set by the Constitution's language.
Moreover, history, tradition, and precedent remain helpful, even if not
determinative.

Second, those more literalist judges who emphasize language, history,
tradition, and precedent cannot justify their practices by claiming that is
what the Framers wanted, for the Framers did not say specifically what

factors judges should emphasize when seeking to interpret the Constitution's open language. Nor is it plausible to believe that those who argued about the Bill of Rights, and made clear that it did not contain an exclusive detailed list, had agreed about what school of interpretive thought should prove dominant in the centuries to come. Indeed, the Constitution itself says that the "enumeration" in the Constitution of some rights "shall not be construed to deny or disparage others retained by the people." . . .

Third, judges who reject a literalist approach deny that their decisions are subjective and point to important safeguards of objectivity. A decision that emphasizes values, no less than any other, is open to criticism based upon (1) the decision's relation to the other legal principles (precedents, rules, standards, practices, institutional understandings) that it modifies; and (2) the decision's consequences, that is, the way in which the entire bloc of decision-affected legal principles subsequently affects the world. The relevant values, by limiting interpretive possibilities and guiding interpretation, themselves constrain subjectivity; indeed, the democratic values that I have emphasized themselves suggest the importance of judicial restraint. An individual constitutional judge's need for consistency over time also constrains subjectivity. . . .

Fourth, the literalist does not escape subjectivity, for his tools, language, history, and tradition can provide little objective guidance in the comparatively small set of cases about which I have spoken. In such cases, the Constitution's language is almost always nonspecific. History and tradition are open to competing claims and rival interpretations. Nor does an emphasis upon rules embodied in precedent necessarily produce clarity, particularly in borderline areas or where rules are stated abstractly. Indeed, an emphasis upon language, history, tradition, or prior rules in such cases may simply channel subjectivity into a choice about: which history? Which tradition? Which rules? The literalist approach will then produce a decision that is no less subjective but which is far less transparent than a decision that directly addresses consequences in constitutional terms.

Finally, my examples point to offsetting consequences — at least if "literalism" tends to produce the legal doctrines (related to the First Amendment, to federalism, to statutory interpretation, to equal protection) that I have criticized. Those doctrines lead to consequences at least as harmful, from a constitutional perspective, as any increased risk of subjectivity. In the ways that I have set out, they undermine the Constitution's efforts to create a framework for democratic government — a government that, while protecting basic individual liberties, permits individual citizens to govern themselves. . . .

[T]he Constitution provides a framework for the creation of democratically determined solutions, which protect each individual's basic liberties and assure that individual equal respect by government, while securing a democratic form of government. We judges cannot insist that Americans participate in that government, but we can make clear that our Constitution depends upon their participation. . . .

PART TWO

Due Process in
Historical Perspective

AMENDMENT 5
No person shall . . .
be deprived of life, liberty, or property,
without due process of law. . . .

AMENDMENT 14
Section 1 . . . No State shall make or enforce any law
which shall abridge the privileges or immunities
of citizens of the United States;
nor shall any State deprive any person of life, liberty, or property,
without due process of law;
nor deny to any person within its jurisdiction
the equal protection of the laws.

5

The Path of Due Process of Law

WALTON H. HAMILTON

An acclaimed Yale University historian of the Founding and the New Deal, Walton H. Hamilton published the article excerpted here in Ethics *in 1938. He provides philosophical insight into constitutional history by narrating the story of how in the late nineteenth century the Supreme Court came to embrace a "liberty of contract" as a substantive, unenumerated right protected by the Fourteenth Amendment guarantee that "No state . . . shall deprive a person of life, liberty, or property, without the due process of law." From 1898 to the constitutional crisis of 1937, the Court handed down 401 rulings invalidating state legislation, more than half (212) of which relied on the Fourteenth Amendment. The Court's defense of laissez-faire capitalism and conservative Social Darwinism—that is, the philosophy of the survival of the fittest—put it on a collision course with progressive legislation aimed at regulating child labor and setting standards for minimum wages, maximum hours, and other working conditions. The era, as Hamilton discusses, became identified with* Lochner v. New York *(1905) and ultimately came to a crashing halt in 1937, when the doctrine of economic substantive due process was abandoned. After the Court invalidated much of the early New Deal, Democratic President Franklin D. Roosevelt proposed his "Court-packing" plan to increase the size of the Court from nine to fifteen on the deceitful ground that the justices were too old and too overworked, but actually simply to secure a majority favorable to progressive economic legislation. Following Justice Oliver Wendell Holmes's dissent in* Lochner, *FDR and other New Deal liberals denounced the Court's "judicial activism" in thwarting the will of democratic majorities, called for "judicial self-restraint" and deference to the political process, and blasted the Court for committing the "original sin" of constitutional interpretation—namely, creating an unenumerated right out of whole constitutional cloth—and becoming a "super-legislature." While the Senate debated FDR's Court-packing plan in the spring of 1937, a bare majority of the Court handed down its "switch-in-time-that-saved-nine" rulings, repudiating* Lochner's *liberty of contract doctrine and assuring the Senate's defeat of FDR's plan.*

THE PHRASE "due process of law" is of ancient lineage. For a long time it had been an authoritative term for the established ways of justice. An injunction that "no person" shall "be deprived of life, liberty or property without due process of law" had for decades reposed quietly within the Fifth Amendment. It served a necessary purpose in forestalling arbitrary imprisonments, in preventing seizures of possessions, in compelling resort to ordinary procedures, and in forbidding public officials to act without legal warrant. But in all the years that stretched away from the early days of the Constitution to the close of the Civil War it was not an invitation to those who found acts of Congress distasteful to appeal to the judiciary for relief. Save for an *obiter dictum* here and there—as by Mr. Chief Justice Taney in the *Dred Scott* case—the records of the United States Supreme Court are singularly unconcerned over what later became so mighty a matter. A like provision adorned with procedural concern the constitution of many a state. As the Civil War approached, a New York court declared that due process had to do with the substance of legislation;[1] and in litigious cause or congressional speech state acts which denied to freed men of color the full privileges of citizenship were challenged as against due process of law. But such a demand for a substantive reading was casual and lacked authority. If there was a higher law in whose name legislation might be struck down by a court, it was elsewhere in the Constitution or in the great unchartered domain of natural rights. In reputable opinion due process of law was firmly fixed within the ancient domain of procedure.

It was the Civil War which disturbed the verbal calm. The course of events made the emancipation of the slaves a military and political necessity. The ways of thought again became receptive to the philosophy of Mr. Jefferson and to the self-evident truths of the Declaration of Independence. The rights "to life, liberty and the pursuit of happiness"—already inalienable within an order of nature—were written into the constitutions of several of the conquered southern states. An injunction in perpetuity against slavery and involuntary servitude were made a part of the supreme law of the land, and a correlative amendment undertook to safeguard the rights of the newly enfranchised blacks. It began with the novel declaration that "all persons born or naturalized in the United States, and subject to the jurisdiction thereof, are citizens of the United States and of the state wherein they reside." Then, in words whose revolutionary character could be appreciated only by men of the age who had been steeped in an older political philosophy, it was provided that "no State shall make or enforce any law which shall abridge the privileges or immunities of citizens of the United States; nor shall any State deprive any person of life, liberty,

---

1. *Wynehamer v. People*, 13 N.Y. 378 (1856).

or property without due process of law; nor deny to any person within its jurisdiction the equal protection of the laws." A number of other provisions, all relating to matters growing out of the late rebellion, were followed by a final section which granted, not to the courts but "to the Congress," "power to enforce, by appropriate legislation, the provisions of this article." . . .

If words are in want of definition, the proper appeal is to the law. And it was hardly half a decade after the amendment had been adopted before the meaning of its high-sounding phrases became the concern of the United States Supreme Court. Due process made its judicial entree with the fanfare of trumpets and in the livery of a strange master. The men who had taken part in the late rebellion had been disenfranchised; the reconstruction program of the black Republican Congress was in full swing; and in the states which had made up the Confederacy the legislatures had fallen into the hands of freed men of color and carpetbaggers. A flood of reckless legislation ensued; some marked by social vision, some savoring strongly of privilege and corruption, all anathema to the white aristocracy which before the war had been in the saddle. The Old South had lost in war and at the polls. But someone within its defeated ranks had the vague idea that an appeal to the courts might yet save the situation. Whose it was is lost to history. But an adage was current, "Leave it to God and Mr. Campbell"—and presently Hon. John Archibald Campbell was putting his ex-judicial mind to a difficult problem.

Who chose the particular statute which in single combat was to stand for hundreds of its kind has escaped the record. But whether choice fell to an unknown, to Mr. Campbell, or to a group, a more strategic selection could not have been made. An act of the legislature of Louisiana had granted to a corporation of seventeen persons for a period of twenty-five years an exclusive franchise in respect to the slaughtering of animals for meat in the parish of New Orleans and the two next adjacent. In giving effect to the act, a citizen had been enjoined from the sale of his land for a rival slaughter-house; a like interdict had been laid upon a boatload of cattle headed for market by an unorthodox route; butchers who for years had done their deadly work were no longer free to follow their trade; and the local public was forced to have commerce with a monopoly or turn vegetarian. Here were, ready at hand, causes as perfect as if they had been fashioned for the oncoming judicial ordeal.[2] They offered all the

---

2. The suits were consolidated and in the reports appear as the "*Slaughter House* Cases," 16 Wallace 36 (1873).

raw materials which a popular legal crusade demanded; they gave opportunity to all the symbols by which the emotions are stirred and the judge-within-the-man is moved. American institutions were being flaunted; a monopoly, odious at law and to the people, had been given a legislative blessing; the laborer had been denied his biblical doom and God-given right to work. The enemy was an octopus of a corporation; the cause was the cause of the workingman; the rights at stake were the rights of man. The requisite stuff of persuasion was there; there was need only to chisel it into a compelling legal argument.

The situation clearly invited a challenge of the statute in the name of the higher law. But to Mr. Campbell no ready-made formula was at hand. He had daringly to blaze a new trail; and a number of briefs which are rather successive drafts of the same argument than complementary lines of reasoning attest the arduous progress of his labor. It is impossible for the lawyer of today, with a head full of the things that came later, to appraise the quality of his performance, and even the historian with his art of re-creation can form no certain judgment. In his briefs there is nothing of clean-cut concept, of rule of law chiseled with neatness and precision, of sweep of syllogism to its inevitable therefore. They are clothed in a rhetoric alien to the legal persuasion of today. But history is here— its pages are filled with the conditions of the working classes in America, in England and Scotland, in France and Prussia. Learning is here—there is hardly a page not adorned with its apt quotation from some writer on government, jurisprudence, economics, or philosophy. Authority is here—citation of cases are alternated with statements from Turgot and Guizot; Buckle and De Tocqueville; Hallam, Macaulay, and G. C. Lewis; Mr. Jefferson and Adam Smith; John C. Calhoun, Mr. Justice Curtis, and Cooley on *Constitutional Limitations*. A sentence from the *Wealth of Nations* which makes of a man's right to his trade both a liberty and a property was copied from the brief into a dissenting opinion and to this day goes resounding down the law reports. Even the arts have their dialectical due in an occasional line of poetry or a rhymed couplet of a negro minstrel.

The books were at hand—and a skill in their use—to serve the cause of the butchers. The task was to mold a medley of materials into a legal entity. Mr. Campbell had only foresight—not the hindsight of a later generation. His endeavor is marked not with the delicate articulation of the codifier but by the daring of the adventurer and the fumbling of the pioneer. His strategy had the audacity of an ex-member pleading before his old court, of an ex-rebel confronting his victorious enemies. He abandoned the older parts of the Constitution whose well-litigated clauses did not point his way and took his stand upon an article which as yet had drawn forth no judicial utterance. He decided to add another to the many paradoxes with which the history of legal doctrine is strewn. The Fourteenth Amendment was intended to secure the rights of the recently emancipated blacks against their former masters. The ink upon the fresh constitutional entry was hardly dry; yet he proposed to use the self-same article to guard the rights of the southern whites against the political power of the newly liberated Negroes. . . .

With such a philosophic start it was easy to get down to constitutional concretions. Although the reasons are not neatly tooled, the substance of the argument is repeated again and again with cumulative effect. The Fourteenth Amendment created a national citizenship, fitted it out with "privileges and immunities," and placed this heritage from times of old beyond the power of the state government. These privileges and immunities are nothing other than the natural rights of man. Among these rights— quoting Mr. Jefferson and the new constitution of Louisiana—are "life, liberty and the pursuit of happiness." It is—in an argument helped along by Turgot, Adam Smith, and Mr. Campbell's own common sense— impossible for a man to sustain life, to enjoy liberty, and to pursue happiness if denied the chance to work. Man "has a right to labor for himself and not at the will or under the constraint of another." Moreover, a man's right in his own labor is not only a liberty but a property as well. As "a natural right of person" it is a liberty; in "its results or the expectation of results" it is a property—the only property of substance the workingman possesses. It follows that he has a natural right to dispose of his service— note the quiet appearance of a term which later made a mighty sound— by "freedom of contract." An argument so surely upon its way was not to be halted here; and, with strokes so deft that the transition is unobtrusive, Mr. Campbell converts an abstract right to work into the worker's vested interest in his occupation. Every trade must—in an order of nature to which the Constitution has come into accord—be open to all who choose to take its chances; and "no kind of occupation, employment or trade can be imposed upon" the workingman "or prohibited to him so as to avoid election on his part." Here, then, in tangible and specific terms is a constitutional right, a privilege and an immunity of citizenship, a liberty and a property, a claim to the equal protection of the laws, which the national government must under solemn mandate maintain against a state legislature gone astray.

And, having given concretion to his absolutes, with telling strokes the attorney drove the argument home. He had no quarrel with the state in its exercise of the police power; its right to promote by legislation "salubrity, security and order" is not challenged; but the statute on trial is not a health measure. Instead "the recitals of concern for the general welfare," the "delusive and deceitful promises of public good," the "expression of an unusual benevolence for the domestic comfort or the sanitary care of a neglected community" is sheer pretense. The statute emerges from "no proper legislative procedure"; it serves no motive—note the usage of the time—"of the public utility." On the contrary its one characteristic, its sole import, is to create a private corporation and to grant to a favored group of seventeen the exclusive privilege of an ordinary occupation. The ordinance was a return to the age of feudalism; it had created a banality in favor of a single firm; Louisiana had, in defiance of the federal Constitution, become "enthralled ground." There is at issue not one jot or tittle of regulation by the state which those who are pressing the suits wish to avoid. Instead a monopoly—under the ban of the common law, intolerable in a democracy, forbidden by the Fourteenth Amendment— has been created at the expense of men who have made "an ancient trade the business of their lives." The Louisiana statute abridges the privileges and immunities of citizens of the United States; it denies to persons life, liberty, and property without due process of law; it takes from them the equal protection of the laws. Liberty and property were before there was law. The rights of man, which belong to the order of nature, are above "the chartered rights" of a corporation. The cause is that of the workingman, of the community, and of the Constitution.

It was a powerful—even if not quite successful—appeal. In the decision all the justices who spoke for the court or in dissent addressed themselves to Mr. Campbell's argument. At its judicial debut four out of nine were converted to a novel constitutional doctrine, and the majority of five found it hard going to contrive a dialectical answer. Chance got in its deft stroke and shaped the course of constitutional events by a single vote. As Mr. ex-Justice Campbell, the southerner, argued for national sovereignty, Mr. Justice Miller, the northerner, denied it. As the native of Georgia argued that all citizens were one people in an indivisible union, the unionist from Iowa refused to curb the authority of the states. As the ex-Confederate asserted that whites and blacks were equal before the Constitution, the abolitionist on the bench refused to erase the color line. There was, according to the court, a citizenship of the United States, but Mr. Justice Miller neglected to remove it from the realm of the abstract, to define its terms or to endow it with substantive rights. The Fourteenth was an addendum to the Thirteenth Amendment; it had been designed to make secure the rights of the blacks. But white men, though industrious artisans, were without benefit of its coverage. The legislature had passed the statute as a health measure, and with the act of a sovereign state the court would not interfere.

It was, however, only as a judgment to go at that. Mr. Justice Field boldly spread upon the record a powerful dissent. The court like lost sheep had gone astray; he with three of his colleagues—especially he— were sound in a just-discovered faith. There was a citizenship of the United States, whose privileges and immunities had by the Constitution been put beyond the reach of the state, and that citizenship knew neither race nor color. The rhetoric was the rhetoric of Field, but the ideas were visible imports from the Campbell briefs. A milder echo of the same argument reappeared as the opinion of Mr. Justice Bradley. In the midst of a paragraph toward the end—as if it were a passing thought—he set it down that a possible mandate with which to curb the power of the legislature might be found in "due process of law." So the cause was lost. The "privileges and immunities of citizenship" lost dominance in constitutional law—and we hear little more of it until its ghost returns after sixty-five years to serve a cause of tax avoidance of the vintage of 1935.

But the loss of a cause is not the loss of a doctrine. Fate, attended by coincidence and paradox, was on the job to pull a trick more audacious than a storyteller would dare to invent. The butchers, still intent upon following the ox to the shambles, had lost their case but not their persistence. The good citizens of the state, with suffrage restored, presently reclaimed the legislature. By statute the monopoly was stripped of its franchise, and the butchers were again free to follow their trade. This time it was the Crescent City Company which refused to accept the voice of the people and girded itself for judicial combat. As the situation demanded, the two combatants exchanged positions, legal weapons, and arguments. The monopoly hurled at the court the Campbell brief done up in fresh verbiage. Since privileges and immunities had failed to prevail, under the thin veil of the refutable doctrine of obligation of contract, the familiar arguments were recited as a denial of liberty and property without due process of law. Counsel for the other side, perhaps a little shamefacedly, went to Washington with pleas for the supremacy of the police power, ably buttressed by the judgment of the United States Supreme Court in the *Slaughter-House* cases.

It was with no unity of feeling that the court welcomed the return of the prodigal case. Mr. Justice Miller and his erstwhile colleagues must have felt a trifle embarrassed; and their brethren, Field and Bradley, JJ., could hardly restrain the thought, "O Lord, Thou hath delivered mine

enemy into mine hands." The cause which in the *Slaughter-House* cases
Mr. Justice Miller had sustained and the doctrine he had used in its support
were now in collision. He had to desert the cause of reconstruction and
renounce a legislative grant he had pronounced valid—or he had to recant
a neatly woven constitutional argument. In the emergency he did not
hesitate; he forsook secular cause and political concern and valiantly made
a stand upon his dialectic. In his "the opinion of the court" he took many
pages to say in substance, "The legislature has given and the legislature
has taken away; blessed be the name of the legislature."

Had Field and Bradley, JJ., been ordinary men, a period might then
have been written to "due process" as it had been to "privileges and
immunities." Had they been content to join Miller, J., and the majority
of the court, or to concur without opinion, the attempt to fuse substance
into the Fourteenth Amendment might not have survived this return and
more ignominious defeat. The result was to them admirable; but they
could not allow their joy at the discomfort of Mr. Justice Miller to blind
them to the acuteness of their own plight. As the power of the state was
vaulted aloft, they hit upon a telling—even if outrageous—strategy. As
they viewed with an inward dialectical joy the loss of all its exclusive
privileges by the Crescent City Company, so the call was for a separate
concurring opinion. In this, with superb audacity, they argued, not that
the charter had been rightfully taken away but that it had never been
lawfully granted; not that the second act of the Louisiana legislature was
valid but that the first act had all these years been invalid. Miller, J., had
for the court argued the *Crescent City* case; Field and Bradley, JJ., in
certainty and a dissenting concurrence, reargued and redecided the *Slaughter-House* cases. The unusual occasion was seized; the peculiar turn of
events was capitalized for a little more than it was rightfully worth. And,
under the signatures of two eminent jurists, the doctrine of due process
was set down in the law reports as an alternative reading to the police
power.

After these decisive defeats, the Fourteenth Amendment came quietly
into constitutional law. The pomp and circumstance which had attended
the previous causes was absent. A municipal ordinance in California had
made a pretty verbal display to the effect that laundries carried on in
brick buildings were within the law; but, if housed in wooden structures,
the authorities must be satisfied that the chance of fire was not a hazard
to public safety. In obvious intent and in administration it said that the
trade was open to the whites but that orientals were to be subjected to
the closest scrutiny before admission to so exclusive a club. Yick Wo,
denied the right to work at his chosen trade, essayed judicial combat, had

syllogisms broken in his behalf, and came away with the signal victory of the highest court in the land. His right to his trade was as good as that of any other man.[3] The victory was scored, not by a recently emancipated black, not by a southern white whose pride in race did not forbid the use of the Negro's legal protection, but by a yellow man from China. Against the arbitrary act of the state "equal protection of the laws" came into constitutional law where "privileges and immunities" and "due process" had been denied admission. And the new doctrine had been accepted by the court without a single vote in dissent.

The breath of life had been breathed into the Fourteenth Amendment. The right to work at one's chosen occupation had at last become a part of the supreme law of the land. The substance to which "equal protection" gave a verbal home could pass on by contagion into a liberty and a property fortified by "due process." Eighteen years had passed since the amendment was adopted and fourteen since Mr. Campbell had blazed the path for a novel doctrine. But at last, in 1886, even against the action of the state, the rights of man had been accorded the protection of the Constitution.

Yet long before this decision another course of events was under way. The Campbell arguments were much too useful to be left to butchers, bakers, and laundry workers. At the bar, and at least before the bench, we find them presently clad in the livery of an alien master. In his briefs — with all their concern for the liberties of the workingman — ex-Justice Campbell could not leave the word "property" alone. He made the right to work a property; and somewhat abstractly, on his own and within quotation marks, he declared the idea that property derives from the state to be the most revolutionary of notions; for, "if the state creates, the state can destroy." As with the individual, so with the nation-on-the-make, no clean-cut line was to be drawn; liberty was the liberty to acquire property. To Mr. Justice Field, rounding out his decades on the high judicial bench, liberty and property came to be a single word with a constant shift of accent to the right. In the *Crescent City* case the familiar dialectic contrived as a plea for liberty appeared in the service of corporate privileges. And long before Yick Wo won his legal tilt against Hopkins and California, attorneys for corporations as plaintiffs in error were presenting in brief and oration a round of exquisite variations on a theme of Campbell.

Although lawyers were admonished for pleading reasons that had been rejected, the recitation went on. In the challenge to the regulation of

3. *Yick Wo v. Hopkins*, 118 U.S. 356 (1886).

grain elevators, to the railway legislation of Granger days, to legislative attempts to abate or to subdue the trade in alcoholic beverages, the theme was omnipresent. It was always put forward as a defense of the frontiers of business enterprise against legislative attack. If invariably it fell before the police powers of the state, it acquired momentum and an enhancing repute in the opinions in dissent. As the decade of the eighties moved along, general admissions that legislation must meet the standards of due process were wrung from the court while it was still loath to apply the doctrine in the instant case. It was, however, not until the nineties that the personnel of the bench became radical enough to give effect to novel doctrine. Then, by judicial surgery, the Interstate Commerce Act was stripped of its sting and the Sherman Anti-trust Act limited to an innocuous domain. Although the first real program of national regulation was rendered impotent rather than declared invalid, and the Fourteenth Amendment was not called into service, a judicial opinion had come to prevail in which a due process, fitted out with substance, might by the court be thrown as a buttress about corporate interest.

The first decisive commitments came—if not off stage—at least in the realm of *dicta*. In arguing a case of tax avoidance for a railway company, Mr. Roscoe Conkling attempted to use a humble confession to advance the cause of his client. He hinted that the Fourteenth Amendment was the result of a conspiracy between politicians and industrialists; and admitted that, in congressional committee, the word "person" had been chosen instead of "citizen" to extend the protection of the due process clause to the corporation. His prestige at the bar was at its height; he had refused the high office then held by Mr. Chief Justice Waite and the hardly less honored seat then occupied by Mr. Justice Blatchford. He quoted at some length from the minutes of the congressional committee; and, although the record had not been published and he did not produce it, his remarks made quite an impression. It left no decisive imprint in the reports; for, although the court found it easy to listen to elaborate constitutional argument, it found it difficult to resolve the issue. As the months passed without result, a motion to dismiss was allowed on the ground that the question had become moot, and the issue was left in abeyance.[4] It was long afterward that the minutes of the committee were made available, and it was discovered that Conkling had taken excerpts from their context,

---

4. *San Mateo County v. Southern Pacific R.R.*, 116 U.S. 138. The case was argued December 19, 20, 21, 1882; as the passage of time brought no decision, a motion to dismiss was eventually made on December 17, 1885, and allowed four days later. It is of note that the official record is so barren of the issue in controversy that there is no mention of Conkling's name, and only the attorneys appearing on the motion to dismiss are listed.

tempered entries to his cause, and reshaped quotations to serve his argumentative purpose.

But decades before historical research was to reveal a deliberate indulgence in historical error his confidential knowledge had had its effect. Four years later, in 1886, an attorney for the same railroad, in another case of tax avoidance, proposed to argue the same issue. He was stopped by Mr. Chief Justice Waite, who announced that the court was prepared to admit, without argument, that a corporation was a person within the intendment of the equal protection clause.[5] Again a case, elaborately argued on constitutional grounds, was disposed of without recourse to constitutional doctrine; and the elevation of the corporation to the protective eminence of a person remained a *dictum*. But the *dictum* was set down in the reports; and, oblivious to its lack of authority, it began presently to assert its claim as a holding.

The eighties gave way to the more receptive attitude of the nineties. Courts must await their causes; and from the play of minds upon issues which are potential the law takes its course. A simple case from Minnesota concerned with the regulation of railroad rates touched off a conflict of values and quickened the germs of doctrine into life. A state commission, acting in pursuance of statute, had fixed rates for milk moving within the boundaries of the commonwealth. No notice had been given, no hearing held, no opportunity accorded for the presentation of evidence. A railroad company, denied an opportunity to present witnesses, regarded the act of the commission as "unjust, unreasonable and confiscatory" and appealed to the judiciary. To minds steeped in the requisites of common law process such behavior was most irregular, and the majority of the court chose to find a procedural issue.[6] The act deprived "the Company of its right to a judicial investigation, by due process of law, under the forms and with the machinery provided by the wisdom of successive ages for the investigation judicially of the truth of a matter in controversy." It "substitutes as an absolute finality the action of the Railroad Commission" which "cannot be regarded as clothed with judicial function or possessing the machinery of a court of justice." As a result—with an easy transition from procedure to substance—if "without a judicial investigation" the company "is deprived of the power of charging reasonable rates," it is "deprived of the lawful use of its property and thus, in substance and effect of the property

5. *Santa Clara County v. Southern Pacific R.R. Co.*, 118 U.S. 394 (1886) at p. 396. The point had been voluminously argued in briefs submitted by counsel.
6. *Chicago Milwaukee and St. Paul Ry. Co. v. Minnesota*, 134 U.S. 118 (1890). The opinion of the court was delivered by Mr. Justice Blatchford; but the line of argument bears the craftsmanship of Mr. Justice Brewer.

itself." Thus the ancient right of access to the court, with little bother of what is a proper cause of action, is used to proclaim a judicial overlordship over what had up to the moment been set down as the province of the legislature. . . .

Another six years passed. A number of significant causes came and went stamped with the attitude of the changing bench. But not until 1897—and then only through a reaching-out toward issues that need not have been raised—did an opportunity come for a better fitting of due process to the current temper of the court. A Louisiana statute had prescribed a regulation of insurance companies within the state; the officials had attempted to bring under its penal provisions a firm which had contracted for marine insurance upon shipments of cotton with a New York company. It seems to have been admitted by all concerned that the contracts had been made in New York and that in the instant case the only matter of local concern was the notices sent of shipments upon which the insurance was to take effect. It was easy enough for the court to waive so incidental a part of the transaction out from under the act. That done, the decision of the case demanded no more than the simple comment that an act of Louisiana had no application to a matter beyond the jurisdiction of the state. It might even have been declared null and void as an interference with commerce among the several states. But so obvious a disposition was not for the new blood within the court. Mr. Justice Peckham, a fresh recruit, had the zeal of the reformer and a faith in the enlightened opinion of his own day untroubled by doubt. The holding depends upon the way the question is put; and he chose—with the consent of his brethren—to view the act as a "real" interference with "the liberty of the defendants to place insurance on property of their own" where they pleased. Thus the issue became larger, more general, and more significant than the unresolved query in the litigation. As thus stated no question of the right of the court to review the matter was raised by any of the nine justices. That hurdle had been gotten over by a succession of rhetorical yieldings in a number of important cases— helped along by the high vault in the Minnesota milk rate case. As formulated by the spokesman for the court, business privilege was squarely opposed to state regulation with "due process of law" as the arbiter.[7]

It is idle to argue that he went out of his way to do it; for, to the individualistic mind of Mr. Justice Peckham, his was the only way. It was a superb opportunity to bring the orthodoxy of classical economics into the higher law, and he was not going to allow it to pass. In a rhetoric

7. *Allgeyer v. Louisiana*, 165 U.S. 578 (1897).

which is strangely familiar, the dissent of yesterday becomes the opinion of the court. He quotes Mr. Justice Bradley in the *Crescent City* case as if he had been the spokesman for the court; and the familiar arguments, even the illustrations of the Campbell brief, are repeated. The "inalienable rights" of the Declaration of Independence; the pursuit of happiness; the right of the butcher, the baker, and the candlestick-maker are all there. As Peckham quotes Bradley, who paraphrases Campbell—thus piling a superfluous Ossa upon a Pelion of *dicta*—"I hold that the liberty of pursuit—the right to follow any of the ordinary callings of life—is one of the privileges of a citizen of the United States." Although the path of his argument is beset with questions, his faith in the efficacy of free contract to take care of all the affairs of business rises above all bother over relevance. The privileges and immunities of citizenship may be outmoded, but there is a constitutional successor. A nimble sentence may be made to travel a long doctrinal way; its hurried words may overcome formidable obstacles where the argument at a leisurely pace would break down. Thus, "it is true that these remarks are made in regard to questions of monopoly, but they well describe the rights which are covered by the word 'liberty,' as contained in the Fourteenth Amendment." The "privilege" quoted is that of "pursuing an ordinary calling or trade"; but—without setting down a period or evoking a therefore—smoothly he glides along through "the acquiring, holding, and selling" of "property" to "the right to make all proper contracts in relation thereto." Thus, in the name of due process of law, freedom of contract is thrown up as a fence about the domain of business enterprise against the incursions of the state. And no one on the high bench said to the contrary.

In the *Allgeyer* case "the police power" remained in the background. The cause had little concern with human rights; a trio of judicial bows acknowledged an abstract authority to regulate; and judicial silence prevented a conflict between an upstart due process and the more venerable doctrine. Again the next year a head-on collision was avoided when—with Brewer and Peckham, JJ., in dissent—a statute of Utah establishing an eight-hour day in smelters and underground mines won the imprimatur of the court;[8] and it was only in 1905 that due process first won in a clean-cut combat with the police power. A statute of New York had limited the hours of employees in bakeshops to ten in any one day or sixty in any one week; and, because of his lack of workaday respect for the act, the People of New York were at odds with a certain Mr. Lochner. The judgment of the Supreme Court—one of the habitual five to four

---

8. *Holden v. Hardy*, 169 U.S. 366 (1898).

variety—was again delivered by the learned jurist and sound economist, Mr. Justice Peckham.[9] He had only to elaborate his former argument, now fortified by the official citation of *Allegeyer v. Louisiana.* Freedom of contract, in respect to trade or employment, was an aspect of the liberty and property which a state might not abridge without due process of law. The challenge of the police power was met by a formidable parade of personal and common-sense opinion that the hours of bakers had little or no relation to the public health.

Again the distinguished jurist made the question before the court far broader than the issue which the case presented. If such an act were allowed to stand, "a printer, a tinsmith, a locksmith, a carpenter, a cabinet maker, a dry goods clerk, a bank's, a lawyer's, or a physician's clerk"— in inelegant verbal parade—would "all come under the power of the legislature." In fact "no trade, no occupation, no mode of earning one's living, could escape this all pervading power." Since "there is no contention that bakers as a class are not equal in intelligence and capacity to men in other trades" or are "not able to assert their rights and care for themselves," the real question is the general use of "the protecting arm of the state" to interfere with "the independence of judgment and of action" among men of every occupation. "Statutes of the nature of that under review limiting the hours in which grown and intelligent men may labor to earn their living, are meddlesome interference with the rights of the individual." And, since such "interference on the part of the legislatures of the several states with the ordinary trades and occupations of the people" seemed "to be on the increase," it was time to call a halt. The opinion of the court was intended to be an apostolic letter to the many legislatures in the land appointing limits to their police power and laying a ban upon social legislation.

So it might have become but for the dissent. Mr. Justice Harlan objected that the question of the relation of hours to health was one of fact; that as reasonable men members of the legislature were entitled to their opinion; and that "there are few, if any, questions in political economy about which entire certainty may be predicated." With him White and Day, JJ., concurred. A youngster of sixty-four, newly come to the court, seized his chance and scribbled the most famous dissent in all legal history. Mr. Justice Holmes insisted that "general propositions do not decide concrete cases." He accused the court of interpolating economic doctrine, insisted that "a constitution is not intended to embody a particular economic theory, whether of paternalism and the organic relation of the

9. *Lochner v. New York,* 198 U.S. 45 (1905).

citizen to the state or of laissez faire"; and protested against freezing the
law into "Mr. Herbert Spencer's *Social Statics*." It is common for latter-
day liberals to set this down as the first blast of the trumpet in behalf of
a social oversight of human rights; but the historian is more likely to view
it as a lance worthily broken in behalf of an ancient cause now in retreat.
But the four dissenters saw as clearly as the five, who, by the virtue of
being one more, were the court, that the challenged act might be "the
first installment of a general regulation of the hours of work"; and they
wished to keep the way open. It was probably too late for Harlan, J., or
even for Holmes, J., to argue that in such matters the legislature was the
sole and exclusive judge and that the court had no rightful power of
review; at least such an argument was not attempted. The all but equal
vote led to an even balance of doctrines. Neither the police power nor due
process was to be preferred; in an even-handed formula liberty and property
are to be set against public policy; as case follows case these concepts are
to be filled with the values of life, a balance is to be struck and a judgment
rendered. An engaging number of rules for the game of review have come
and gone; the decisions of the court have with the circumstances, its personnel, and the temper of the times swung now toward one side, now toward
the other. But the balance of values recorded in *Lochner v. People of New
York* has endured as the judicial formula for the ultimate judgment upon
legislation designed to promote the public interest.

Thus a collusion of occasions and persons, causes and ideas, shaped the
course of doctrinal events. It was quite untouched by conspiracy, unless it
be of the gods or of that Providence which is said to preside over American
institutions. A constitutional doctrine contrived to protect the natural rights
of men against corporate monopoly was little by little commuted into a
formula for safeguarding the domain of business against the regulatory
power of the state. The chartered privileges of the corporation became
rights which could be pleaded in equity and at law against the government
which created them. In a litigious procedure in which private right was
balanced against the general good the ultimate word was given to the
judiciary. A last ironic note attends the closing story; the words of the
doctrine of due process remain true to their democratic origin; it is only
the substance which has come to serve a strange master. But such an
antithesis of language and content is "of the nature of things." . . .

All of this has to do with the rhetoric of the coming of due process.
The account has as its narrow concern a sequence of judicial events; it
is drawn from the official records of a single court; in all its detail it can
be supported by the sanctions of exact documentation. But the larger

story of the making of the doctrine lies elsewhere; in the development of industrialism, in the changing state of opinion, in the assembly of ideas from far and near into a principle of law, in urges within an economic order that could not be judicially denied. A part of that history has been written; distinguished scholars have garnered from legal literature the germs of the doctrine and have shown how the catholic concept of due process offered a home to notions of natural rights. But if the raw material has been exhibited and the verbal history of the doctrine written, the impulses within the social order—in particular, economic interest and legal persuasion—have not been accorded their part in the drama. Here off stage are the forces which gave life to abstractions. The records of the court reflect only in a series of passing shadows their tumultuous vitality. And the history of due process is far more than the judicial record it has left.

A shift from rhetoric to logic, from recorded doctrine to compelling impulse, is an engaging hazard. It is an inquiry into a series of "if's," many of which escaped actuality by the narrowest of margins. If in the *Slaughter-House* cases the Campbell argument had commanded just one vote more, what difference would it have made? We would doubtless by now possess an august corpus on the privileges and immunities of citizenship, and the entries under due process would be correspondingly thin. But would the hypothetical domain be a great and humane code concerned with the rights of man? Or would the corporation, which became a person, just as easily have passed into the protected position of a citizen of the United States? And, in such an event, would the only change be that all that is now written down as liberty and property would be entered as the privileges of citizenship?

Or was the logic of the commitment inevitable—and the specific legal doctrine by which business enterprise sought immunity from regulation a mere rhetorical device? Due process was fashioned from the most respectable ideological stuff of the later nineteenth century. The ideas out of which it was shaped were in full accord with the dominant thought of the age. They were an aspect of common sense, a standard of economic orthodoxy, a test of straight thinking and sound opinion. In the domain of thought their general attitude was omnipresent. In philosophy it was individualism; in government, laissez faire; in economics, the natural law of supply and demand; in law, the freedom of contract. The system of thought had possessed every other discipline; it had in many a domain reshaped the law to its teachings. A respect for the obligations of contract had been set down in the Constitution in 1787; the "ancient maxim," *caveat emptor*, had become dominant in the law of sales by the forties; an individual responsibility for industrial accidents was definitely established in torts shortly after the middle of the century. An impact that had been irresistible elsewhere should surely have won its way into constitutional law. Its coming seemed inevitable; the constitutional concept which it made its domicile was a mere matter of doctrinal accident. Words on parchment could not be adamant before so powerful a thrust; privileges and immunities, due process, equal protection, were all available; and, had there been no Fourteenth Amendment, "the obligations" might have been made to encompass "the freedom" of contract; or, as a last resort, a vague natural right as a higher law might have been found to permeate the whole Constitution. . . .

Freedom of contract took up its abode within "due process of law" too late for easy and secure lodgment. Its legal insecurity may rest upon personnel; a change of a justice here and there would have affected mightily the course of judicial events. It seems strange that so many jurists stood steadfast against the seductions of laissez faire; history, political science, and economics can boast no such record. Or it may be due to the older and established doctrine that the state might intervene with regulation to promote public safety, public health, public morals, and public welfare—against which the cause of the independence of the business system could achieve only a partial success. Or does the whole story, in irony, paradox, and compromise, derive from the innate conservatism of the law—a rock of ages which even the untamed strength of laissez faire could move but could not blast?

6

Economic Due Process and the Supreme Court:
An Exhumation and Reburial

ROBERT G. McCLOSKEY

Robert G. McCloskey was a political scientist and constitutional scholar who taught for many years at Harvard College. The excerpt here is from a highly regarded article published in the 1962 Supreme Court Review. *In it, McCloskey provocatively questions the Supreme Court's so-called post-1937 "double standard" in assuming the reasonableness of economic legislation, while giving greater scrutiny to other civil rights and liberties, in stark contrast to the Court's pre-1937 embrace of the doctrine of economic substantive due process and enforcement of the "liberty of contract." McCloskey makes a strong case against the Court's double standard and complete abandonment of the protection of economic liberty under the Fourteenth Amendment due process clause, in spite of ultimately concluding that the Court should not revive the doctrine of "liberty of contract."*

━━━━◆━━━━

AMERICAN POLITICAL LIFE has often been marked by a tendency to adopt policies today and to think about them in some remote tomorrow, if at all. This national habit of mind is presumably rooted in our famous pragmatic temperament. Much can be—and has been—said for it. But the attribute, like most attributes, has the defects of its merits. If Jack builds a house without thinking the plan through in advance, he may then justly congratulate himself that he is at least sheltered from the elements while his more deliberative neighbor still shivers. But he should not be surprised if it turns out that the corners are a little awry or that the second bedroom impinges on what he hoped would be an ample living room. He must accommodate himself to the fact that the *ad hoc* decisions of the past may set unforeseen limits on his way of life in the future.

These general reflections about American propensities and their consequences are also applicable to the modern history of America's peculiar institution, the Supreme Court of the United States. Since about 1937, the Court has been rebuilding its constitutional dwelling place, knocking down a wall here, constructing a new corridor there, in response to a bewildering succession of conflicting impulses. If these impulses are united by some commonly shared understanding about the form and extent of the ultimate structure, the Justices have been remarkably taciturn about revealing it. Vast new areas of constitutional supervision have been opened in such decisions as *Palko v. Connecticut, Burstyn v. Wilson,* and *Brown v. Board of Education,* to name only three among many. Other regions, once significant, have been closed off to judicial intervention: the fields of the national commerce power and of economic due process are the standard examples. . . .

The purpose of this paper is to trace one such development in the disorderly constitutional flux of the past twenty-five years: the decline and virtual demise of "economic due process." . . .

The judicial reaction against economic due process after 1937 is unique in the history of the Supreme Court. There have been gradual shifts from negativism to permissiveness, as in the anti-trust field during the decades after *E. C. Knight;* there have been abrupt departures from salient negative doctrines as in *Nebbia* or in *Graves v. New York.* But it is hard to think of another instance when the Court so thoroughly and quickly demolished a constitutional doctrine of such far-reaching significance. . . .

Yet that is what happened. There is no need to retell the familiar story in detail, but a few high points are worth repeating. *West Coast Hotel v. Parrish* is commonly and rightly thought of as the watershed case. We know that it was because of what occurred thereafter. But the actual words of Chief Justice Hughes in that case did not suggest very plainly that the whole doctrine of substantive due process was scheduled for destruction. He spoke of the wage regulation as "reasonable," citing a 1911 decision, and he even invoked in defense of the present law the distinction made in 1908 between men and women as parties to a labor contract. It was still possible to believe, then, that the Court was merely overruling *Adkins,* but maintaining its power to strike down other economic legislation that might fail the reasonableness test. . . .

But by 1941, in *Olsen v. Nebraska,* the Court was ready to take another long stride away from the pre-1937 doctrine. The subject matter of this case evoked fond memories of those bygone days, for it concerned regulation of employment-agency rates, and such regulation had been roundly condemned by the old Court in *Ribnik v. McBride.* But now Mr. Justice Douglas, for a unanimous Court, not only repudiated *Ribnik* and its famous doctrine of "business affected with a public interest," but came close to announcing that the issue of economic regulation was no longer of judicial concern. There is no requirement, he said, that the State make out a case for the needfulness or appropriateness of the law. "Differences of opinion on that score suggest a choice which 'should be left where . . . it was left by the Constitution—to the states and to Congress.'" There was no suggestion here, as there was in *West Coast Hotel* and *Carolene Products*, that the State must point to facts which might reasonably justify the regulation. The presumption of constitutionality was no longer debatable. *Olsen* suggested, as a contemporary comment put it, that there was then "a complete lack of constitutional foundation for the assertion of private right under the due process clause where contractual or proprietary interests are involved." . . .

This was the result. But it is of some interest to note how the result had been achieved. Obviously two paths lay open. One was that which seemed to be suggested by Mr. Justice Black's dissent in *Connecticut General Life Insurance Co. v. Johnson*, i.e., to repudiate in explicit and unmistakable terms the very bases for the Court's jurisdiction over economic questions. Such a course was at least imaginable. The Justices might have reconsidered not only the corporation-as-person doctrine, as Black proposed, but the very idea of substantive due process in the economic field. They might, that is, have held in so many words that economic legislation was no longer subject to judicial review on the question whether it had a "rational basis." . . .

The other possibility was to retain the rhetoric of the rational basis standard, but to apply it so tolerantly that no law was ever likely to violate it. This was the course ultimately chosen, one more consonant with Stone's view that such issues were better dealt with "gradually and by intimation." Even Douglas seems to have accepted the rational basis concept for these rhetorical purposes.

This was perhaps the "judicial" way to bring the result about. It preserved some shreds of the idea of continuity, and that idea, myth or not, is important to the constitutional tradition. It enabled the Justices to feel their way along toward a policy whose contours were probably not yet clear in their own minds. It may have helped to maintain unanimity: it is hard enough to understand how Justice Roberts could have accepted the *Olsen* opinion; it is even harder to envision him concurring in an explicit renunciation of all judicial authority to protect property holders.

So much at least can be said for the approach chosen, leaving aside for the moment the question whether the result itself was desirable. But the matter has another aspect. When policies are established "gradually and by intimation," when the question of their existence is partially obscured by preservation of the old rhetoric, there is always a chance that the destruction of those policies will not be recognized. A flat decision to discard substantive due process root-and-branch would have compelled the Justices to explain themselves, to examine the basis for their abnegation. In the actual event they have never fully done so, at least in public, and this leaves, to say the least, a large gap in the rationale that underlies the structure of modern constitutional law. . . .

What then was the explanation of this extraordinary shift in judicial values? It must be emphasized that this is not merely the question why the Court took leave of the unyielding negativism represented by such judgments as *Adair v. United States* or *Coppage v. Kansas* or by the anti–New Deal dogmatics of 1934–1936. That question may not be an easy one, for historical questions seldom are, but its mysteries are not unfathomable. An answer would have to begin with the specific enigma of Justice Roberts; after that the road is comparatively clear. His shift in 1937 created a majority opposed to the extreme version of constitutional laissez faire, and it was to be expected that that majority would be strengthened as new appointments were made in the following years. The shift from *Morehead v. New York ex rel. Tipaldo* to *West Coast Hotel*, startling though it was as a specific event, was not beyond prediction: the basis for it had been well laid in the recent past by both judges and scholars.

The harder question is: Why did the Court move all the way from the inflexible negativism of the old majority to the all-out tolerance of the new? Why did it not establish a halfway house between the extremes, retaining a measure of control over economic legislation but exercising that control with discrimination and self-restraint?

Precisely such a halfway house had frequently been described in judicial opinions of the past, so there is little chance that the post-1937 Justices had overlooked its conceptual existence. Justice Brandeis in *New State Ice Co. v. Liebmann* had admonished the Court against erecting its prejudices into legal principles but had still conceded that "the reasonableness of every regulation is dependent on the relevant facts." Indeed, he conducted an exhaustive examination of those facts in his opinion. Justice Stone had himself carefully adumbrated such a position, saying in *Ribnik* that price regulation is within the States' power when "any combination of circumstances seriously curtails the regulative force of competition, so that buyers or sellers are placed at such a disadvantage in the bargaining struggle that a legislature might reasonably anticipate serious consequences to the community as a whole." To be sure, Justice Holmes had, in *Tyson & Brother v. Banton,* laid down a standard comparable in its permissiveness to the

Olsen doctrine: "The truth seems to me to be that, subject to compensation when compensation is due, the legislature may forbid or restrict any business when it has a sufficient force of public opinion behind it." This is the *de facto* policy of the modern Court. But Stone, as has been said, filed a separate dissent in *Tyson*, and even Holmes in other opinions had conceded that the supposed rational basis of economic statutes is subject to judicial scrutiny. As a result of such scrutiny, the Court would not strike down an arguably rational law, but it would require some showing by the State that there was a basis for believing it to be rational and would consider evidence to the contrary presented by the affected business. Laws like those involved in the *Lee Optical* case and in *Daniel v. Family Security Life Ins. Co.* might be invalidated, or at any rate more sharply queried.

Assuming then that this standard—this modest residue of the old economic supervision—was consciously and purposefully rejected, what explains the rejection? And, to make the difficulty a little more acute, what accounts for the fact that such survivors of the old Court as Stone and Roberts concurred in the choice, that the *Olsen* opinion was unanimous? A couple of "behavioral" or psychological explanations come to mind as possibilities. They are put forward diffidently, for motive is hard to ascertain with respect to only one man; when a group of nine highly sophisticated individuals is involved, the complexities become awesome.

For one thing, it may be that Stone and Roberts joined in the movement so as to preserve the rhetoric of supervision and thus some faint shadow of doctrinal continuity. Black, as his biographer says, wanted to "reject utterly and completely the doctrine . . . that the due-process clause gives to courts the power to determine the reasonableness of regulations." . . .

A second possible explanation may be more fruitful, since it relates, not only to the question why the veterans were willing to retreat so far, but also why the newer Justices seemed resolved to do so. It is that extremism had bred extremism in thinking about the role of the Supreme Court. Between 1923 and 1937, a conservative majority had, from time to time, embraced a policy of adamant resistance to economic experiment, and this obstructionist spirit had reached its zenith in the judicial reaction against the New Deal. What the Chief Justice himself had said in the *Railroad Retirement* case was true of the conservative majority in most of the great anti-New Deal decisions. That majority had raised a barrier, not only against particular features of the law, but "against all legislative action of this nature by declaring that the subject matter itself lies beyond the reach" of governmental authority. This intransigence had tended to discredit the whole concept of judicial supervision in the minds of those who felt that government must have reasonable leeway to experiment with the economic order. The result was that the two wings of the Court (and of the country) had almost ceased to communicate with each other. . . .

Factors like these may help to explain the impulse to discard the old due process doctrine, bag and baggage. Yet one would like to think that a more thoughtful process was going on somewhere below the surface, that the policy of virtual abdication was not merely a reflex against the excesses of the past but a considered and justified decision about the proper scope of judicial review. The written record to support such a supposition is not, alas, very convincing. Scattered remarks in decisions cited above, and in others, assailed the dead horse of "the Allgeyer-Lochner-Adair-Coppage" doctrine, i.e., the Justices argued against "social dogma" and for "increased deference to the legislative judgment" in the economic field. But they did not explain why the abuses of power in those earlier decisions justified abandonment of the power itself, nor why the deference to the legislature should be carried to the point of complete submission. The nearest thing to an explanation is perhaps to be found in Mr. Justice Frankfurter's concurrence in *American Federation of Labor v. American Sash & Door Co.*, where he argued that "the judiciary is prone to misconceive the public good" and that matters of policy, depending as they do on imponderable value issues, are best left to the people and their representatives. This is a coherent and not unconvincing viewpoint, but the trouble with it has always been that it implied similar judicial withdrawal, not only from the economic field, but from other areas that pose questions of policy, such as freedom of expression. Well aware of this difficulty, Frankfurter tried to meet it in this opinion by declaring that matters like press censorship and separation of church and state are different, because "history, through the Constitution, speaks so decisively as to forbid legislative experimentation" with them. Scholarship has since provided reason to doubt that history speaks so plainly after all, even on these subjects, and without a strong historical rationale the argument falters badly, for the arguments against judicial intervention in economic affairs become arguments against intervention in the policy sphere generally. Learned Hand of course was ready to accept this implication and Frankfurter himself has come very near to it. But it is certainly not the dominant doctrine of the modern Court, which has fairly consistently held to the "dual standard" enunciated by Stone in the *Carolene Products* case. So we are left with a judicial policy which rejects supervision over economic matters and asserts supervision over "personal rights"; and with a rationale, so far as the written opinions go, that might support withdrawal from both fields but does not adequately justify the discrimination between them.

The Doubtful Distinction between Economic and Civil Rights

Although no such rationale can be detected in the written opinions, however, the possibility of its existence cannot be entirely dismissed. The Supreme Court has sometimes preferred to leave ultimate arguments unexpressed, to let justification for a course of conduct, as well as the course itself, emerge "gradually and by intimation." And this may be the case with the great retreat from economic supervision. Perhaps there is a coherent apologia for that retreat; perhaps this apologia was in the Justices' minds when they shaped the modern constitutional policy. The second "perhaps" can never be transmuted into certainty unless the art of judicial psychoanalysis reaches unforeseen heights. But its plausibility may increase if it appears that there is a rationale which *might* have formed the basis of the policy.

The arguments for demoting economic rights to their modern lowly constitutional status—lowly when compared with "personal rights"—fall into two categories. First, there is a group of arguments based on judgments about the nature and relative importance of the rights concerned. For example, it is sometimes argued that laws limiting freedom of expression impinge on the human personality more grievously than do laws curbing mere economic liberty, and that the Court is therefore justified in protecting the former more zealously than the latter. The individual has, *qua* individual, "the right to be let alone." The right to free choice in the intellectual and spiritual realm is particularly precious to him. A major difficulty with this formulation is that there is the smell of the lamp about it: it may reflect the tastes of the judges and dons who advance it, rather than the real preferences of the commonality of mortals. Judges and professors are talkers both by profession and avocation. It is not surprising that they would view freedom of expression as primary to the free play of their personalities. But most men would probably feel that an economic right, such as freedom of occupation, was at least as vital to them as the right to speak their minds. Mark Twain would surely have felt constrained in the most fundamental sense, if his youthful aspiration to be a riverboat pilot had been frustrated by a State-ordained system of nepotism. Needless to say, no disparagement of freedom of expression is here intended. But its inarguable importance to the human spirit, on the one hand, does not furnish an adequate ground for downgrading all economic rights, on the other.

So much for a purely individual-centered justification for the disparity between economic rights and other civil liberties. Another suggested rationale looks toward the community rather than the separate individuals within it. Progress, it is said, "is to a considerable extent the displacement of error which once held sway as official truth by beliefs which in turn have yielded to other beliefs." To encourage societal progress, it is important then to protect "those liberties of the individual which history has attested as the indispensable conditions of an open as against a closed society," e.g., freedom of expression.

Presumably this "open society" argument would be relevant no matter how the political system was organized—even a benevolent autocracy must tolerate freedom of expression or risk stagnation. But Alexander Meiklejohn has contended that the point takes on an extra dimension when applied to popular government, to democracy as the West understands that term. In any political system, so the argument runs, the ruler must be fully informed if he is to govern well, and he cannot be fully informed when someone else is deciding what ideas he shall be allowed to hear. In a democracy the people are sovereign, and it follows that they and no one else must decide what and whom they will listen to. And it further follows that the Constitution must protect any freedoms that help the people to acquire "the intelligence, integrity, sensitivity, and generous devotion to the general welfare that, in theory, casting a ballot is assumed to express. In short, the special importance of certain civil rights derives from their special relationship to the process of self-government. Other rights, including the economic, can be abridged when the legislature deems abridgment desirable. . . .

The whole "open society" line of argument in its various forms is convincing enough as a justification for protecting the free trade in ideas. If one feels the need to explain why the free speech guarantees are important, these explanations will do pretty well for a start. But they are rather less satisfactory as the basis for a policy of *not* protecting economic freedom, of regarding it as unimportant in a democratic system. For one thing, it is not entirely clear why liberty of economic choice is less indispensable to the "openness" of a society than freedom of expression. Few historians would deny that the growth of entrepreneurial and occupational freedom helped to promote material progress in England in the eighteenth and nineteenth centuries and in America after the Civil War (although they might of course argue that the price paid for this progress was unconscionably high). It is one thing to argue that economic liberty must be subject to rational control in the "public interest"; it is quite another to say in effect that it is not liberty at all and that the proponent of the "open society" can therefore regard it as irrelevant to progress. . . .

Judicial Capacity in the Realm of Economic Regulation

For one reason or another then, none of these justifications of the Court's modern hands-off policy in the economic field quite stands up. The distinctions they rely on, between economic rights on the one hand and personal rights on the other, tend to blur when we examine them. And, even if it were thought that the distinctions were tenable, the case would remain incomplete. It might, squeezing it hard, justify a difference in the kind and degree of protection afforded economic rights; but it would not warrant a policy of no protection at all.

Although the policy of abdication cannot be justified in terms of an analysis of the nature and relative unimportance of the rights concerned, there is a second line of thought that merits consideration. Perhaps the decision to leave economic rights to the tender mercy of the legislative power is based on the idea that the Supreme Court is peculiarly ill-equipped to deal with this subject. No one would argue that the right enshrined in Article IV, the guarantee of a republican form of government, is unimportant. Yet the Court has refused to protect it, because of well-founded doubts about judicial competence to make effective judgments in this field. It may be that similar doubts underlie the policy of abdication in the area of economic affairs.

At first blush, this argument seems highly persuasive, at least in broad terms. Anyone familiar with the entanglements resulting from *Smyth v. Ames* will be alive to its merits. Probably no court was really equipped to make the intricate and imponderable economic judgments that the doctrine of that case entailed. And those who remember the Court's crusades against the rise of the welfare state may be dubious about judicial competence on somewhat different grounds. They may feel that economic policy is not only beyond the reach of the Court's expertise, but beyond the reach of its practical power. Whether the nation shall have a minimum-wage law; whether the government shall control prices; whether social security shall be publicly guaranteed—these are questions so "high" and so basic that no court could determine them even if it should. They involve in a word the momentous issue of the welfare state itself, and that issue will be determined by "dominant opinion" with or without judicial approval.

There are, of course, economic subjects so recondite that judicial surveillance of them would be anomalous. The choice between "historical cost" and "replacement cost" as a basis for rate making must be made by the legislature, not because it will always choose well, but because the judiciary lacks the knowledge and expertise for distinguishing good from bad in this area. But this point will carry only as far as its logic will bring it, and there are fields of economic regulation less intricate than the problem of public utility rates. To be sure, even the problems raised in these fields may not be simple. A fair evaluation of Oklahoma's need for its anti-optician law would require the Court to make judgments about a complex matter. But this can be said about most questions that reach the Supreme Court in any field. Our problem is not to identify the issues that present difficulties and then to discard them as improper subjects for judicial review. That would be to abandon judicial review in most of the fields where it is now exercised. Our problem is to determine whether economic statutes always or usually involve such extraordinary difficulties that a modest judiciary must eschew them, even though that same judiciary does claim the competence to judge other, more difficult, issues.

Is it easier for example for the Court to appraise a law empowering a board of censors to ban an "immoral" movie than a law empowering a real estate licensing board to deny a license unless the applicant is of "good moral character"? The two standards would seem to be equally vague and the possibility of arbitrary administrative action would seem to be as menacing in one situation as in the other. Is it plainly easier to balance New Hampshire's need to get information against Paul Sweezy's right to withhold it, than it is to balance South Carolina's need to stamp out the funeral insurance business against the right of an agent of the Family Security Life Insurance Company to make a living selling such insurance? The "public need" in both cases was all but invisible. Is it easier to see that the State corporate registration law in *N.A.A.C.P. v. Alabama* was being used to facilitate private reprisals against Association members than it is to see that State boards of plumbers, barbers, and morticians sometimes use their publicly granted powers to protect the private financial interests of present guild members to the disadvantage of non-members?

The point is not that the cited cases should necessarily have been decided differently, but rather that the issues they present stand on a common level of difficulty and that judicial scrutiny seems as feasible (or unfeasible) for one issue as for the other. And the further, related, point is that there are kinds and kinds of economic subjects and that it is difficult to fashion a generalization that applies to all. Some subjects may be so inscrutable that judicial review cannot fruitfully cope with them; but this is not a justification for avoiding other economic subjects which are no more opaque than the "personal rights" issues that are the standard coinage of judicial discourse these days. . . .

. . . In short, while doubts about judicial expertise and power may warrant withdrawal from some economic questions, they cannot justify withdrawal from all such questions, unless the doubter is willing to go the full distance with Learned Hand and give up most of the residue of modern judicial review. . . .

Nevertheless it is legitimate, and perhaps timely, for an observer of the Court's work to ask whether constitutional law *should* move down that road again, whether the Court should reassert its claim to examine the reasonableness of economic legislation. . . . The Court could not reestablish "laissez faire" even if it wanted to; some economic matters are too big for the Court to handle and some are too intricate. The question is simply whether the Court should begin to apply a modest but real version of the rational-basis standard in economic fields that are not intrinsically inaccessible to the judicial power.

As has been argued earlier, none of the usual justifications for saying "no" to this question will quite do. Some of the rights involved, such as occupational freedom, are not unimportant, nor are they necessarily any more beyond the reach of judicial capacity than other rights which the Justices have chosen to protect. If this were 1937, if the Court were poised on the brink of the modern constitutional era, the case for retaining some constitutional limits in the economic field might be strong. Those who planned the course of future events might well feel that the objective of a just society would be best served by a judicial policy in which economic rights held a respected place. But the year is not 1937 . . . and modern constitutional policy has developed, not by plan but by impulse, not as a coherent body of doctrine but as a congeries of *ad hoc* responses. These circumstances raise a point that takes us back to the opening paragraphs of this essay. They may constitute in themselves a compelling reason for leaving economic due process in repose.

The reason has to do with what might be called judicial economy. The Court's personal-rights decisions in the past twenty-five years have involved constitutional law in some of the most difficult and emotion-charged issues that modern American government faces. The problem of defining and defending the legal rights of Negroes, in a society that has long shamefully neglected their rights, is alone formidable enough to tax the intellectual and power resources of a single tribunal. Yet this is only the beginning of the lofty assignments the Justices have set for themselves. They have undertaken to evaluate governmental encroachments on political and artistic expression, to supervise, in increasing degree, State administration of criminal law. And each of these major personal-rights categories is replete with subcategories, each of which poses ample problems of its own. . . .

Even if there were no practical, political limitations on the range of Court power, this multitude of self-imposed tasks would be intimidating. The lines between liberty and authority, between justice and injustice, between the necessary and the intolerable, are not easy to draw in a single field: to lay them down in such a variety of fields requires a whole series of painstaking evaluations in which not only intuition, but hard, searching analysis must play its part. It is a common and just complaint that the modern Court has so far failed to develop reasoned formulations for many of its judgments in the personal-rights area. This means that important work is left undone each time the Court gathers to itself a new subject for review. Having spent the last twenty-five years assuming new tasks, the Justices could easily spend the next twenty-five working out the problem of how those tasks should be done. These considerations in themselves might argue against taking on any further assignments for the time being, leaving the question of practical power out of account.

In the long run, however, that issue cannot be left out of account. The Supreme Court is an agency of government and, like other agencies of government, must work within the limits of political possibility. It has been suggested above that a revival of economic due process in connection with a subject like occupational freedom would not by itself overstrain the Court's power. But when the prospect of such a development is considered against the background of other recent assumptions of authority, the calculus may be very different. Various personal-rights decisions during that period have taxed not only the "time-chart" and the reasoning power of the Justices but their effective prestige as well. . . .

All things considered, then, it seems best that the cause of economic rights be left by the Supreme Court to lie in its uneasy grave. This need not mean that the legislatures of the nation are warranted in ignoring them, nor that the State courts, applying their own constitutions, should be indifferent to plausible due-process claims. These rights, or some of them, do have a bearing on the justness of a society and on the happiness and well-being of the people who live in it. If the Supreme Court of today had a free hand in choosing the subjects of judicial review, there might well be an argument for choosing the right to work over some of the other subjects that engage Court attention. But it does not have a free hand; its liberty of choice has been considerably foreclosed by the episodic course of constitutional law since 1937. The Supreme Court, like the American political system of which it is a part, proceeds by impulse rather than by design, pragmatically rather than foresightedly. Like the United States, the Court derives advantages from this approach; but like the United States, the Court, too, is bound by its limitations.

7

The Nationalization of the
Bill of Rights in Perspective

RICHARD C. CORTNER

Richard C. Cortner is professor emeritus at the University of Arizona Political Science Department and an author of numerous books on the Supreme Court and civil rights and civil liberties. The selection here comes from his book The Supreme Court and the Second Bill of Rights: The Fourteenth Amendment and the Nationalization of the Bill of Rights *(1981). In it, Cortner reviews the controversies over the Supreme Court's nationalization of guarantees of the Bill of Rights by selectively incorporating them into the due process clause of the Fourteenth Amendment and making them applicable to the states, no less than the federal government. In the excerpt here, Cortner concludes by considering the consequences for federalism, claims to civil rights and liberties, and the role of the Supreme Court in American politics.*

———

THE NATIONALIZATION of the Bill of Rights under the Due Process Clause of the Fourteenth Amendment came to an end with the Supreme Court's decision in *Benton v. Maryland.* This was understandably so, since by 1969 only the Second and Third Amendments, the Grand Jury Clause of the Fifth Amendment, the Seventh Amendment and the Excessive Fines and Bail Clause of the Eighth Amendment remained as parts of the Bill of Rights that had not been made applicable to the states in the decisions of the Court. And only the Excessive Fines and Bail Clause appeared to be a likely candidate for future nationalization. The *Benton* case thus marked the end of a remarkable era of constitutional development that had transformed the structure of constitutional protection for political and civil liberties in the United States and had profoundly altered the nature of the federal system.

The Process of Nationalization: An Overview

Viewing the creation of the second bill of rights in perspective, the nationalization process may be viewed as falling into four stages: (1) the period from the decision of the *Slaughter House Cases* in 1873 to the decision in *Twining* v. *New Jersey* in 1908, during which the Court at first seemed to deny the possibility of the nationalization of the Bill of Rights but finally opened the door to that development; (2) the stage of the nationalization of the First Amendment, beginning with *Gitlow v. New York* in 1925 and ending with the decision of *Everson* v. *Board of Education* in 1947; (3) the period from the 1930s to 1961 during which the Court approached problems of criminal procedure in state cases under the fair trial rule; and finally, (4) the period of selective incorporationism from 1961 to 1969, during which most of the criminal-procedure provisions of the Bill of Rights were applied to the states.

The first stage of the nationalization process, of course, began with the decisions in the *Slaughter House Cases* (1873) and *Hurtado v. California* (1884) in which the Court enunciated the doctrines of dual citizenship and nonsuperfluousness and thus appeared to doom any prospect that either the Privileges and Immunities Clause or the Due Process Clause of the Fourteenth Amendment might serve as vehicles for the nationalization of the Bill of Rights. It is usual to associate the influential roles of interest groups with constitutional litigation in the twentieth century, but the role played by the railroads in constitutional litigation during the period between the Civil War and the turn of the century may be viewed as rather similar to the roles played by the National Association for the Advancement of Colored People, the American Civil Liberties Union, and other groups familiar to students of more recent constitutional developments. As the nation's first great, modern interstate industry, the railroads were the first nationally organized interest to attempt to use the Fourteenth Amendment as a federal constitutional shield against hostile state policies, and in the process the litigation efforts of the railroads led the Court to at least implicitly repudiate the doctrine of the *Hurtado* case.

In order to successfully convert the Fourteenth Amendment into such a shield for railroad interests, their lawyers had to convince the Court to change the meaning of due process so that it encompassed both substantive rights and corporate interests. The railroad lawyers were eminently successful on both counts: the Court's formal acceptance of substantive due process came in an 1890 railroad case, *Chicago, Milwaukee & St. Paul Railroad v. Minnesota*, and the Court had also accepted corporations as "persons" protected by the Due Process Clause in another railroad case, *Santa Clara County v. Southern Pacific Railroad*.

The Court's acceptance in these earlier cases of the idea that the Due Process Clause imposed substantive as well as procedural limitations upon exercises of state power paved the way for the Court's 1897 decision in *Chicago, Burlington & Quincy Railroad Co. v. Chicago* that just compensation for private property taken for public purposes was required by the Due Process Clause. The railroad lawyers' earlier success in convincing the Supreme Court to accept the concept of substantive due process was of even greater importance to the future of the nationalization of the Bill of Rights, however, than the first nationalization breakthrough in the *Chicago, Burlington & Quincy Railroad Co.* case, for the Court's acceptance of substantive due process laid the necessary groundwork in due process theory for the nationalization of the substantive rights in the Bill of Rights—primarily the rights guaranteed in the First Amendment.

The Court's decision in the *Chicago, Burlington & Quincy Railroad* case, on the other hand, considerably muddled the theory by which the Court was determining the relationship between the Bill of Rights and the Due Process Clause. The Court again relied upon the *Hurtado* case in its *Maxwell v. Dow* decision in 1900 that the Due Process Clause did not require jury trials in state criminal proceedings, yet the *Hurtado* doctrine of nonsuperfluousness was logically irreconcilable with the *Chicago, Burlington & Quincy Railroad Co.* holding that the Due Process Clause imposed a just-compensation requirement upon the states.

The Court's rather puzzling reluctance to openly acknowledge that the doctrine of nonsuperfluousness was incompatible with the nationalization of any right in the Bill of Rights continued in the decision of *Twining v. New Jersey* in 1908. In *Twining* the Court emphasized the permanence of the doctrine of dual citizenship as a bar to any possible use of the Privileges and Immunities Clause as a vehicle of nationalization, but the Court's interpretation of the Due Process Clause in *Twining* again involved an implicit repudiation of the doctrine of nonsuperfluousness without an open acknowledgment that this was so. For only by holding that the Due Process Clause of the Fifth Amendment protected some rights similar to rights protected by other parts of the Bill of Rights could the Court's concession in *Twining*, that the Due Process Clause of the Fourteenth Amendment might protect certain rights similar to those in the Bill of Rights, be reconciled with the assumption in the doctrine of nonsuperfluousness, that the Due Process Clauses of the Constitution were identical in meaning. Not only would such a holding have been exceedingly peculiar, but it would have contradicted the other assumption in the doctrine of nonsuperfluousness, that there was nothing repetitive or superfluous in the Bill of Rights. Yet the Court did not reverse the *Hurtado* doctrine in the *Twining* case, and the doctrine's official burial did not come until Chief Justice Hughes's cryptic remark in *DeJonge v. Oregon* in 1937 that "explicit mention [of a right in the Bill of Rights] does not argue exclusion elsewhere."

During the first phase of the nationalization process, therefore, the Court had laid the theoretical basis for the nationalization of the substantive rights in the Bill of Rights by its acceptance of the concept of substantive due process. In its handling of the relationship of the Due Process Clause to the Bill of Rights, on the other hand, the Court had embraced fundamentally incompatible theories and had made no systematic attempt to untangle the theoretical problems that had resulted. Despite the Court's failure to satisfactorily deal with these problems in *Twining*, however, its statement in that case that the Due Process Clause might guarantee rights similar to some of those in the Bill of Rights did open the door to the nationalization process—a door that had appeared to be firmly shut by the *Slaughter House Cases* and *Hurtado v. California.*

The next phase of the nationalization process, of course, involved the nationalization of the First Amendment freedoms, a process that began with the Court's statement of the famous "assumption" in *Gitlow v. New York* in 1925 and ended with the nationalization of the Establishment Clause in *Everson v. Board of Education* in 1947. One of the most remarkable aspects of the nationalization of First Amendment freedoms was the fact that each of the leading cases involved in that process reached the Court under the sponsorship of an interest group. The American Civil Liberties Union was the most ubiquitous interest-group participant in the nationalization of First Amendment freedoms, having sponsored the *Gitlow* case while also jointly sponsoring with the International Labor Defense (ILD) the litigation in *Stromberg v. California* and *DeJonge v. Oregon.* The litigation resulting in the nationalization of freedom of the press in *Near v. Minnesota* was sponsored by the American Newspaper Publishers' Association (ANPA), with financing from the Chicago *Tribune*, while the nationalization of the Free Exercise Clause resulted from the Jehovah's Witnesses' sponsorship of *Cantwell v. Connecticut.* And, finally, *Everson v. Board of Education* came to the Court through the efforts of the Junior Order of United American Mechanics (JOUAM) of New Jersey.

Given this diversity of sponsors, the pattern of interest-group participation in the nationalization of First Amendment freedoms was therefore much less stable and orderly than the pattern noted in other areas of constitutional policy. . . .

Analysts of constitutional litigation have noted in recent years the frequent use of "test case" tactics by interest groups participating in such litigation—tactics that include careful selection of issues to be litigated, recruitment of plaintiffs, deliberate selection of the judicial forums in which to litigate, attempts to control the timing and sequence of litigation, etc. With the exception of the *Everson* case, however, the litigation resulting in the nationalization of First Amendment freedoms did not arise as a result of the use of classic test-case tactics by the interest groups that sponsored the cases, nor were the results achieved in those cases a consequence of any overall, coordinated interest-group strategy.

Instead, the litigation in the *Gitlow, Stromberg, DeJonge,* and *Cantwell* cases was initiated by criminal prosecutions brought by governmental authorities, and there is no evidence that the litigation in these cases was deliberately provoked by the participating interest groups for the purposes of creating test cases. Although it is possible to argue that any case involving the Jehovah's Witnesses during the 1930s and 1940s was a test case because of their policy of appealing all adverse rulings, there is nonetheless no evidence that the *Cantwell* case was deliberately planned by the Witnesses as a vehicle for establishing freedom of religion as a guarantee of the Due Process Clause of the Fourteenth Amendment. . . .

Thus, although interest-group sponsorship of the First Amendment cases was of crucial importance, the very diversity of the groups participating in the nationalization process involving the First Amendment precluded any centrally orchestrated strategy of litigation that might have resulted in a coordinated theoretical justification of nationalization in the arguments before the Court. Indeed, after Walter Pollak, on behalf of the ACLU and Benjamin Gitlow, persuaded the Court to state its "assumption" in the *Gitlow* case, the attorneys for the appellants in the subsequent First Amendment cases simply took the *Gitlow* assumption as a reality and did not discuss in any systematic way the theoretical question of how, and under what theoretical premises, the freedoms of the First Amendment had become applicable to the states. The group sponsorship of the cases nationalizing the First Amendment therefore did not result in any group formulation of a consistent constitutional theory of nationalization—a circumstance that may occur when only one or a few groups participate in the litigation of more narrow constitutional-policy issues.

If there was to be a theoretical justification of the application of the First Amendment to the states, therefore, such a justification had to come from the Supreme Court itself. During the process of the nationalization of the First Amendment, however, the Court continued the same disregard for the theoretical problems of nationalization that it had evidenced during the first phase of the nationalization process. Since the last major statement by the Court regarding the relationship between the Bill of Rights and the Due Process Clause had been in the *Twining* case, the Court presumably was operating upon the basis of the *Twining* theory at the outset of the nationalization of the First Amendment. But the *Twining* theory—that the Due Process Clause might guarantee certain rights similar but not identical to rights in the Bill of Rights—had clearly been abandoned by the Court as its theory of nationalization by 1940, when the Court began announcing that the First Amendment applied to the states in the identical way that it applied to the federal government.

Typically, the Court did not explain why or when the *Twining* theory had been jettisoned as the theory of nationalization, or, indeed, that the *Twining* theory had ever been the basis of the nationalization process, even at the outset. From the Court's various expressions, during the 1940s, of the view that the First Amendment applied to the states, it would appear that the Court had come to this conclusion for two reasons. First, the post-1937 Court apparently was convinced, at least for a time, that defining the meaning of the Due Process Clause by the specifics of the First Amendment would reduce the judicial discretion in interpreting the clause that had led to the due process mischief of the pre-1937 Court. Second, it appears that the Court's application of the First Amendment to the states was also influenced by the support of a majority on the Court for the concept of "preferred freedoms"—a concept presaged by Chief Justice Hughes's opinions for the Court in the *Stromberg* and *DeJonges* cases, implicit in Justice Cardozo's opinion in the *Palko* case, and finally formalized, at least by a footnote, in Justice Stone's *Carolene Products* (1938) opinion.

These justifications for the nationalization of the First Amendment, however, were never stated by the Court in any systematic theoretical formulation justifying nationalization, but must instead be gleaned from a variety of its opinions. A process that had begun (in the words of Klaus Heberle) as a process of "absent-minded incrementalism" therefore ended essentially as it had begun. The result was clear—by 1947 the First Amendment was considered to be fully applicable to the states—but the Court remained rather uninformative regarding how and upon what theoretical premises that result had been reached.

When the First Amendment had been applied to the states, the nationalization process entered its third phase, which was to last until the incorporation breakthrough of the early 1960s. The central problem of this period was the tension between the Court's application of the First Amendment to the states in the identical way in which it applied to the federal government and the Court's *Twining*–fair trial approach to issues of criminal procedure in state trials. Its resistance to the application of the criminal-procedure provisions of the Bill of Rights to the states in the identical way the First Amendment applied to them appears to have rested upon two foundations.

The first was the view of a majority of the Court—as Justice Cardozo had indicated in the *Palko* case (1937)—that the criminal-procedure provisions of the Bill of Rights were not, at least as they applied in federal proceedings, "of the very essence of a scheme of ordered liberty." On the other hand, the right to a fair trial in state proceedings was considered by the Court to be a fundamental right, and insofar as rights similar but not identical to the procedural protections of the Bill of Rights were essential to a fair trial, the Court was willing to enforce those similar rights in state criminal trials.

The second foundation of the Court's fair trial approach to matters of criminal procedure reflected a respect on its part for the fact that the enforcement of the criminal law was, and remains, a primary responsibility of the states within the federal system; and the Court was therefore reluctant to unduly interfere in this area that had traditionally been the province of the states. Ironically, however, this deference to federalism had not been deemed by the Court to be a sufficient reason not to apply the substantive limitations of the First Amendment to the states.

The dominant episode of this third phase of the nationalization process was undoubtedly the *Adamson* decision (1947), and the impassioned debate between Justices Frankfurter and Black on the relative merits of the fair-trial approach and of Black's total-incorporation position. Although he won the battle with Black in the *Adamson* case, Frankfurter's defense of the fair-trial approach nonetheless added some confusion to the theory of nationalization, which was already hardly a model of clarity. One of his reasons for not applying the Self-Incrimination Clause to the states was that the Due Process Clauses of the Constitution were identical in meaning, but this assertion was simply not true by 1947, when the First Amendment had been fully applied to the states—and indeed had not been true since the *Chicago, Burlington & Quincy Railroad Co.* case in 1897. And Frankfurter's view that the Due Process Clause imposed upon state proceedings the "canons of decency and fairness which express the notions of justice of English-speaking peoples even toward those charged with the most heinous offenses" proved to be an almost unfathomable guide to the meaning of due process—as the Court's subsequent decisions indicated.

The phase of nationalization during the dominance of the fair-trial rule nonetheless produced significant interpretations of the Due Process Clause by the Court. The "core" of the Fourth Amendment was held to be applicable to the states in the *Wolf* case (1949), and the requirement of public trials was held to be a due process requirement in the *Oliver* case (1948), at least as retroactively interpreted by the Court. Perhaps as important, however, was the fact that the due process standards imposed by the Court upon state proceedings were progressively tightened during the regime of the fair-trial rule. . . .

The progressive stringency of the due process standards the Court applied to the states under the fair-trial rule thus made the final, incorporationist stage of the nationalization process less of a drastic departure from the established course of constitutional development than it otherwise might have been. Indeed, the incorporationist and fair-trial approaches to the interpretation of the Due Process Clause coalesced in the *Gideon* case in 1963, with the adherents of both approaches agreeing that appointed counsel was required for indigent defendants in all serious state criminal cases. And both the incorporationists and the adherents of the fair trial approach agreed that the Due Process Clause imposed confrontation and compulsory-process requirements upon the states in the *Pointer* (1965) and *Washington* (1967) cases.

As the most staunch defender of the *Twining*–fair trial approach, Justice Harlan of course insisted that the crucial point was that the requirements for counsel, confrontation, and compulsory process that were being recognized by the Court had as their source the Due Process Clause and not the Bill of Rights, and were thus similar, and not identical, to their counterparts in the Bill of Rights. Even if Harlan's views had prevailed in the 1960s, however, it appears that the restrictions imposed by the Due Process Clause upon state criminal trials would have increased, and that those restrictions would have been quite similar to many of the criminal-procedure provisions of the Bill of Rights.

For the selective incorporationists who dominated the last stage of the nationalization process, of course, most but not all of the rights in the Bill of Rights applied to the states via the Due Process Clause, and those rights that did apply were identical to the same rights in the Bill of Rights. Selective incorporationism thus rejected Justice Black's view that all of the Bill of Rights applied to the states, while accepting his view that any right applicable to the states was identical to its counterpart in the Bill of Rights. The selective incorporationists also accepted the view, advanced by Black in the *Adamson* case, that defining the meaning of the Due Process Clause by most of the rights in the Bill of Rights would reduce the discretionary power of the Court in interpreting the Due Process Clause and thus diminish the potential for the sort of judicial abuse of due process that had occurred in the past.

The Due Process Clause has not, however, been confined to serving only as a vehicle for applying most of the Bill of Rights to the states. The

Court has held without reference to the specifics of the Bill of Rights, for example, that procedural due process is violated if the state obtains a conviction on the basis of testimony known to be perjured or if the state suppresses evidence favorable to the accused. Due process is also violated, it has been held, if a defendant is convicted and punished without any evidence of guilt.

When the Court faced the question of whether the Due Process Clause protected substantive rights not listed in the Bill of Rights in *Griswold v. Connecticut* in 1965, the selective incorporationists also abandoned Justice Black's position that the meaning of the Due Process Clause was supplied by the Bill of Rights and by it alone. Over Black's vigorous protest, the Court thus held that substantive rights beyond those in the Bill of Rights were indeed protected by the Due Process Clause, thus contradicting not only one of Black's justifications for total incorporation but also one of the justifications advanced for selective incorporation. Although Black could ultimately applaud the fact that the process of selective incorporation had resulted in the application of most of the Bill of Rights to the states, he nonetheless failed to ever win a majority on the Court for total incorporation, and he also lost the battle over the future of the Due Process Clause in the *Griswold* case. Neither substantively nor procedurally, therefore, has the meaning of the Due Process Clause been confined to the specifics of the Bill of Rights.

Also inherent in the position of the selective incorporationists was the rejection of the argument, championed by the adherents of the *Twining*–fair-trial approach, that the imposition of the criminal-procedure specifics of the Bill of Rights upon the states would violate the principles of federalism. The selective incorporationists argued, to the contrary, that nebulous due-process standards formulated by the Court under the fair trial rule had led to unpredictable and arbitrary intrusions of federal judicial power in state proceedings, and that the imposition of the specifics of the Bill of Rights would thus, in fact, improve federal-state relations. On this point, the incorporationists had a powerful argument derived from the fair trial approach to the right to counsel in state proceedings. After over thirty years of following the fair trial rule in counsel cases, the Court was requested by the attorneys general of twenty-three states to reverse itself in the *Gideon* case (1963) and to apply the full Sixth Amendment Assistance of Counsel Clause in state proceedings. The *Gideon* case thus represented a major blow to the federalism premises of the fair-trial approach—from which it never recovered—while also supplying the incorporationists with a powerful argument against contentions that selective incorporation violated the premises of federalism.

Although the basic premises of selective incorporationism may be gleaned from the incorporationist decisions of the 1960s, the selective-incorporationist majority never formulated a systematic statement of the theory and justification of its position. The selective incorporationists thus never indicated whether they accepted the overall validity of Black's views as to the intentions of the framers of the Fourteenth Amendment and rejected only the proposition that the framers intended to apply all of the Bill of Rights to the states. Nor did the selective incorporationists ever formulate any precise criteria by which they would determine which rights were worthy of incorporation and which were not. For this inattention to overall theoretical problems, the selective incorporationists, of course, had precedent aplenty from the behavior of the Court throughout the nationalization process. But there was considerable justification for Justice Harlan's charge that the majority of the Court during the 1960s had "compromised on the ease of [Justice Black's] incorporationist position, without its internal logic."

Whatever their theoretical shortcomings may have been, once they had achieved a majority on the Court in the early 1960s the selective incorporationists pursued their objective with determination and what at times appeared to be unseemly haste. The nationalization of the First Amendment had occurred over a period of twenty-two years, but in contrast the nationalization of the criminal-procedure provisions occurred during the relatively short span of eight years, between 1961 and 1969. And although it may be argued that the interest groups that sponsored the First Amendment cases played a considerable part in setting the agenda of nationalization, it was clear during the 1960s that the selective-incorporationist majority of the Court was setting its own agenda for the national-ization of the criminal-procedure provisions. In contrast to the First Amendment cases, the cases nationalizing the criminal-procedure provisions of the Bill of Rights during the 1960s were not sponsored by interest groups — with the lone exception of the Lawyers Constitutional Defense Committee's (LCDC) sponsorship of *Duncan v. Louisiana*. The Court's agenda thus was not orchestrated by outside forces during the nationaliza-tion of the criminal procedure provisions, but rather the Court itself pushed the nationalization process by reaching out in some cases to nation-alize criminal-procedure rights or by directing in other cases that argu-ments of counsel focus upon the issue of nationalization.

In three of the criminal-procedure cases, for example — *Mapp v. Ohio* (1961), *Robinson v. California* (1962), and *Pointer v. Texas* (1965) — the Court nationalized the Fourth Amendment and the exclusionary rule, the Cruel and Unusual Punishment Clause, and the Confrontation Clause even though those rights had not been the focus of the arguments of counsel involved in those cases. And it could be argued that a Court less intent upon nationalization would have found that the Connecticut courts had applied federal standards of self-incrimination in the *Malloy* case, or that it was unnecessary to reach the double jeopardy claim in the *Benton* case because a reversal of Benton's larceny conviction would not affect his ultimate sentence.

In addition to reaching out for rights to nationalize, the Court also focused the attention of counsel upon nationalization issues by specifically ordering arguments on those issues in its grants of certiorari. The Court thus directed in *Gideon v. Wainwright, Washington v. Texas,* and *Benton v. Maryland* that counsel focus their arguments on the question of nationalizing the Assistance of Counsel Clause, the Compulsory Process Clause, and the Double Jeopardy Clause. In the cases nationalizing the criminal-procedure provisions during the 1960s, therefore, the incorporationists on the Court demonstrated that they had not only a policy goal clearly in mind but also a will to pursue that goal with vigor. The result was the completion of the nationalization process upon the basis of incorporationist premises as well as the "revolution in criminal procedure" of the 1960s.

Perhaps the dominant feeling one is left with after an overview of the nationalization process is disappointment that this crucial constitutional development was not more satisfactorily justified by the Court in terms of constitutional theory. Of course this constitutional development occurred in an incremental manner over a span of many years and overlapping the terms of a large number of the members of the Court, and therefore a single, uniformly followed constitutional theory should perhaps not be expected. Eugene Rostow has said, on the other hand, that the "discussion of problems and the declaration of broad principles by the courts is a vital element in the community experience through which American policy is made. The Supreme Court is, among other things, an educational body, and the Justices are inevitably teachers in a vital national seminar." To the extent that rational justification and explanation by the Court is important to the legitimization of constitutional change, it can fairly be said that the Court neglected one of its important functions in regard to the nationalization of the Bill of Rights.

The Nationalization Process and the Federal System

In the course of drastically changing the structure of protection for political and civil liberties in the United States, the nationalization of the

Bill of Rights necessarily also altered fundamentally the nature of the federal system. At the time of the Civil War, the Bill of Rights was applied only to exercises of federal power and as such was the subject of almost no litigation in the Supreme Court. For the protection of their basic substantive rights, such as freedom of speech and of religion, as well as for criminal-procedure protections, citizens had to depend upon the provisions of the laws and constitutions of their respective states. And with the exception of the Commerce Clause, the Contract Clause, and the Supremacy Clause, the hand of the federal Constitution lay very lightly upon the states in terms of restricting the exercise of their powers. It was this pre-Civil War federal system that the Supreme Court sought to preserve in its decisions in the *Slaughter House Cases* and the *Hurtado* case—despite the ratification of the Fourteenth Amendment—and it was this federal system that the nationalization process altered so fundamentally.

Although the nationalization process thus involved a basic change in the relationship between the federal and state governments within the federal system, it is one of the more remarkable aspects of the nationalization of the First Amendment that counsel representing state interests in that litigation did not more vigorously resist the nationalization process. . . .

By the time of the incorporation breakthrough of the 1960s, legal representatives of the states had created national organizations such as the National Association of State Attorneys General (NASAG) and the National District Attorneys Association (NDAA), through which a defense of state interests could be articulated. It is ironic, however, that the most significant intervention in the nationalization litigation by such organizations came with the intervention of the attorneys general of twenty-three states in the *Gideon* case, supporting the reversal of *Betts v. Brady* (1942) and the application of the Assistance of Counsel Clause to the states. Only the attorneys general of Alabama and North Carolina, on the other hand, supported the retention of the *Betts* regime. The National District Attorneys Association also filed an *amicus* brief in *Malloy v. Hogan* (1964), but that brief focused upon the need to retain the validity of state grants of immunity from prosecution and was not directed to an argument against the applicability of the Self-Incrimination Clause to the states. In the remaining cases nationalizing the criminal-procedure provisions, there were only sporadic *amicus* interventions by representatives of state interests, such as the *amicus* intervention by the New York attorney general in the *Duncan* case and by the California attorney general in the *Malloy* case.

It is possible that there was not more opposition to the nationalization of the criminal-procedure provisions by the organized legal representatives of state interests because in at least some of the nationalizing cases, the Court unexpectedly reached out to decide cases on issues that had not appeared to be the primary issues in those cases. This was notably true of *Mapp v. Ohio*, in which the central issue appeared to be a First Amendment issue but which resulted in the Court's application of the Fourth Amendment and the exclusionary rule to the states. It is highly likely that if the search-and-seizure issue had appeared to be the central issue in the *Mapp* case, the National District Attorneys Association almost certainly would have intervened as *amicus curiae* in opposition to the nationalization of the Fourth Amendment and the exclusionary rule, since after the Court's decision in the *Mapp* case was announced, the NDAA joined the state of Ohio in a rather angry petition for rehearing. . . .

Of course, avenues of protest against or resistance to the decisions of the Supreme Court exist outside the process of litigation that produces decisions by the Court, and there were protests against the course of the Court's decisions by state interests outside the litigation process. Interestingly enough, however, the most dramatic protest against the Court for allegedly undermining the federal system came in the 1950s, before the Court began the process of selective incorporation of the criminal-procedure provisions of the Bill of Rights. This protest occurred in 1958, when the Conference of State Chief Justices voted overwhelmingly in favor of a resolution criticizing the Supreme Court for promoting "an accelerating trend towards increasing power of the national government and correspondingly contracted power of the state governments." The principles of federalism were endangered, the state chief justices asserted, by "the extent of the control over the actions of the states which the Supreme Court exercises under its views of the Fourteenth Amendment." . . .

The nationalization process therefore met with a variety of forms of resistance from representatives of state interests. At no time, however, did the opposition to the process of nationalization seriously threaten to mount a direct attack upon the Court itself, such as withdrawing appellate jurisdiction from the Court or reversing the Court via constitutional amendment. Since the nationalization of the Bill of Rights entailed a fundamental alteration of the federal system and of the status of the states within that system, it is not surprising that there was criticism and some resistance by state interests and officials to that process. What is surprising in retrospect is that there was not more criticism and resistance than there appears to have been.

The Second Bill of Rights and the Constitutional System

The creation of a second bill of rights through the Due Process Clause of the Fourteenth Amendment established a new system of constitutional protection for basic individual rights in the United States. Whereas, prior to the adoption of the Fourteenth Amendment and the nationalization process that followed, the basic rights of the individual were almost exclusively dependent upon state law for their protection, the nationalization process has resulted in a dual system of constitutional protection for those rights. The nationalization process, of course, insured that basic individual rights would henceforth be protected by the federal Constitution from invasion by either the national or the state governments. But the rights thus protected are also protected by bills of rights in the constitutions of the states, which guarantee rights either identical or parallel to those guaranteed in the federal Bill of Rights and the Fourteenth Amendment.

The nationalization of the Bill of Rights has not, therefore, reduced the state courts to the status of being mere transmitters of Supreme Court decisions interpreting federal constitutional rights; instead, the state courts retain considerable leeway for creativity regarding the interpretation of their own state bills of rights. The state courts thus retain the power to interpret state bills of rights more broadly than the Supreme Court may interpret the rights guaranteed by the Fourteenth Amendment, and indeed this has occurred on numerous occasions. . . .

The state courts thus retain a residual power of creativity in constitutional interpretation through the construction of their own state constitutions, and interests that perceive themselves as disadvantaged by the Supreme Court's interpretation of the federal Constitution may find refuge in state-court interpretations of state constitutions. Following the Supreme Court's renunciation of its role as censor of socioeconomic policy after 1937, for example, conservative economic interests found themselves stripped of the federal constitutional protections they had previously enjoyed. Conservative spokesmen, particularly members of the bar, therefore argued that the best litigation strategy for seeking protection of economic rights was to invoke the provisions of state constitutions without reference to the federal Constitution.

It is one of the ironies of American constitutional development that when in the 1970s the Burger Court began to construe more conservatively the rights guaranteed by the Fourteenth Amendment—especially criminal-procedure protections—liberals adopted the same tactic that conservative spokesmen had previously urged after 1937. There was thus a liberal rediscovery of the state courts and state constitutions in the 1970s, led in part by Justice Brennan, a leading architect of the selective incorporationism of the 1960s, who pointedly noted both in his opinions on the Court and in a law-review article that the state courts were free to interpret their state constitutions more liberally than the Court was interpreting the Fourteenth Amendment. And some state supreme courts did indeed construe the criminal-procedure provisions of their state constitutions as prohibiting practices that would have been upheld by the Supreme Court under the Fourteenth Amendment. While the nationalization of the Bill of Rights imposed significant new restrictions upon the state judiciaries and increased federal judicial power, the state judiciaries were nonetheless not reduced to impotence by that process, but rather retained considerable power to play an independent role in the protection of political and civil liberties.

In addition to its impact upon the federal system and the state judiciaries, the nationalization of the Bill of Rights also changed the agenda of litigation encountered by the Supreme Court. Prior to the adoption of the Fourteenth Amendment, litigation requiring the interpretation of the Bill of Rights by the Supreme Court had to involve challenges to exercises of federal power. Such challenges based upon the provisions of the Bill of Rights had been almost nonexistent prior to the Civil War, and indeed throughout the nineteenth century, with the result that the Court was not a significant source of civil and political liberties policy until the twentieth century. There were also only a very limited number of important criminal-procedure decisions rendered by the Supreme Court during the nineteenth century, primarily because of the limited criminal jurisdiction then being exercised by the federal government and because appeals to the Supreme Court in federal criminal cases was highly restricted until almost the turn of the century.

As a consequence, modern constitutional law governing political and civil liberties has largely been the product of Supreme Court decisions rendered in the twentieth century, and the nationalization of the Bill of Rights was a leading reason why that has been the case. Rather than being confined to litigation raising issues under the Bill of Rights involving the federal government, as a result of the nationalization process the docket of the Court was opened to litigation challenging an almost unlimited array of state and local policies that had previously been insulated from attack on the basis of the Bill of Rights. The result was that the Court was called upon to render more significant interpretations of political and civil liberties than ever before, and in almost every field from freedom of speech to criminal procedure, a majority of the cases in which the Court rendered decisions on civil and political liberties were cases challenging state policies under the Fourteenth Amendment.

In his speech introducing the constitutional amendments that were to become the Bill of Rights, James Madison took special note of his proposal that the states also be prohibited from invading the rights of conscience, freedom of the press, and trial by jury in criminal cases. This proposed amendment, he said, was "of equal, if not greater importance" than the other proposed amendments restricting the powers of the national government. Despite his belief that "the State Governments are as liable to attack these invaluable privileges as the General Government is, and therefore ought to be as cautiously guarded against," Madison failed in his attempt to include a restriction on the powers of the states in the Bill of Rights.

Through the nationalization of the Bill of Rights via the Due Process Clause of the Fourteenth Amendment, the Supreme Court more than made up for Madison's failure on this score, and while most Americans undoubtedly believe that the Bill of Rights is the most important source of their liberties, the fact is that when fundamental liberties are tested in Supreme Court litigation, the Constitution is most often interpreted on the basis of the Due Process Clause of the Fourteenth Amendment as it applies most of the Bill of Rights to the states. It is therefore no exaggeration to say that the process of nationalization has transformed the Due Process Clause of the Fourteenth Amendment into our second bill of rights, a bill of rights more salient to the liberty of the average American than the original document authored by Madison and ratified by the states in 1791.

8

Due Process, Government Inaction, and Private Wrongs

DAVID A. STRAUSS

David A. Strauss is a law professor at the University of Chicago Law School. The excerpt here is from his 1989 article in the Supreme Court Review *critically analyzing the Supreme Court's ruling in* DeShaney v. Winnebago County Department of Social Services *(1989). In* DeShaney, *the Court rejected a substantive due process claim that social workers should be held liable for their inaction in leaving four-year-old Joshua DeShaney in the custody of his father, even though they had evidence of child abuse, and subsequent beatings by his father left Joshua permanently brain damaged. In the excerpt here, Strauss further discusses the case and illuminates the current Court's reluctance to expand the substantive and procedural protection of the Fourteenth Amendment due process clause.*

———

WHATEVER ELSE the government is supposed to do, it is supposed to protect citizens against violence by other citizens. Whatever else the social contract requires, it at least requires this much. [In 1989], *DeShaney v. Winnebago County Department of Social Services*, the Supreme Court appeared to rule that this most basic duty of government is not enforceable as a matter of constitutional law. "As a general matter," the Court said, "a State's failure to protect an individual against private violence simply does not constitute a violation of the Due Process Clause." . . .

The Court's approach is mistaken on at least three levels. First, even assuming that there is such a thing as government inaction, it is wrong to say that a failure to act cannot constitute a violation of the Due Process Clause. There are core violations of the Due Process Clause that consist of inaction indistinguishable from the official conduct in *DeShaney*. Second, private wrongdoing is never simply the product of government inaction. Government action—in the sense in which the Court itself used the term in *DeShaney*—exists every time an individual is the victim of private violence. Third, and most fundamental, the distinction between action and inaction can be coherently defined only by importing common law notions into constitutional law, specifically by making constitutional litigation a species of common law litigation. There is no legitimate basis for assigning such a role to the common law. . . .

Joshua DeShaney, a four-year-old boy, was the victim of the particularly barbarous private acts of violence that led to the *DeShaney* litigation. The perpetrator was Joshua's father, Randy DeShaney, who was awarded custody of Joshua following a divorce. Between January 1982 and March 1984, various employees of Winnebago County, Wisconsin, where the DeShaneys lived, received information suggesting that Joshua was the victim of child abuse. For example, on several occasions Joshua was treated at county hospitals for injuries that hospital employees thought might be the product of child abuse; on her visits to the DeShaney home, a social services agency caseworker noticed a number of suspicious injuries; and on her last two visits before March 1984, the caseworker was not allowed to see Joshua. The caseworker meticulously recorded the information but the county did not seek to have Joshua removed from his father's home. The caseworker also made notes in her files, and comments to others, suggesting that she believed that Joshua was the victim of child abuse.

In March 1984, after Joshua was beaten so severely that he fell into a coma, doctors who operated on him discovered evidence of repeated blows to the head over a long period of time. The result of the beatings was that Joshua is severely brain damaged and will spend the rest of his life in an institution for the profoundly retarded. Randy DeShaney was convicted of child abuse and sentenced to prison.

Joshua and his mother sued Winnebago County, its Department of Social Services, and several county employees and officials. They alleged that the county's failure to protect Joshua from his father violated Joshua's constitutional rights. They based their claim on 42 U.S.C. §1983 and the Due Process Clause of the Fourteenth Amendment.

The Supreme Court upheld a grant of summary judgment for the defendants. The Court concluded, on the basis of text and precedent, that the Due Process Clause does not, in general, require the government to protect individuals against private wrongs. The Court acknowledged one exception to this rule: "when the State takes a person into its custody and holds him there against his will, the Constitution imposes upon it a corresponding duty to assume some responsibility for his safety." Accordingly, the Court said, the government would be responsible for providing protection against private violence to state prisoners and involuntary patients in state hospitals. The Court left open the possibility that the state would have a similar obligation to children in state-operated foster homes.

But since Joshua was injured while in his father's custody, not the State's, the Court ruled that this exception was inapplicable.

Notwithstanding this categorical language, the holding of *DeShaney* is in fact limited. The Court characterized the plaintiffs' claim as "one invoking the substantive rather than the procedural component of the Due Process Clause." The Court left open the possibility that persons in Joshua's position might recover under the procedural component if they could show that state law created "an 'entitlement' to receive protective services in accordance with the terms of [a] statute." The plaintiffs did not raise, and the Court did not consider, any arguments under the Equal Protection Clause. . . .

While the holding of *DeShaney*, properly understood, is therefore narrow, the reasoning that the Court used has broad implications and reflects a distinct theoretical orientation toward constitutional litigation. The same reasoning has persuaded many lower court judges as well. The idea has a simple allure: the Due Process Clause only forbids the government from actively injuring people. It does not require the government to protect people from private wrongs. So long as the government is not acting, it cannot violate the Due Process Clause. The Constitution is a charter of "negative rather than positive liberties" designed to protect people from the government rather than from each other.

This reasoning is wrong in several respects, and the theoretical approach it reflects is utterly inadequate. First, there are forms of government "inaction," indistinguishable from the conduct of the defendants in *DeShaney* (at least as the Court viewed that conduct), that unquestionably violate the Due Process Clause. Second, *DeShaney* presented a form of undoubted state action that arguably caused the injury to Joshua; the Court did not explain why that state action was not sufficient to establish a claim under the Due Process Clause. Third, the Court's exception for "custodial" arrangements such as prisons and state hospitals is not really an exception at all. The principle underlying that exception implies that the government has "affirmative" duties not only to persons in custody but to someone in Joshua DeShaney's situation and, in fact, to every person in society. Finally, the distinction between action and inaction cannot be defined at all unless one borrows common law notions: the implicit definition of government "action" used by the Court is that government action occurs when the government invades common law interests. This definition cannot be justified.

Even assuming that separate categories of government action and inaction can be identified, the principle that the government is liable only for the former and not for the latter produces implausible results.

Suppose that police officers learn that a murder is about to occur that they can prevent with minimal cost. Ordinarily they would intervene without hesitation. But in this case they decide not to do so because the targeted victim is someone whom they believe is guilty of another crime. The officers would rather see him killed by private persons than brought to trial where, they fear, he might escape with an acquittal or a light sentence.

This must be a case of government inaction, assuming there is such a thing. The police officers did not instigate or facilitate the murder in any way, except to refrain from intervening. They did not make the victim worse off than he would have been if the officers had never become aware of his predicament.

But it seems clear that this kind of government failure to act violates the Due Process Clause. A summary execution of a suspect by the authorities would be the clearest possible violation of the Due Process Clause. The hypothetical example is no different except for the fortuity that there were private persons who planned to do the murder. The *DeShaney* approach would allow the existence of that fortuity to make the difference between a flagrant violation of the Due Process Clause and an action that is not a constitutional violation at all. There is no reason to attach such significance to a fortuity.

This hypothetical case is indistinguishable from *DeShaney*, at least as the Supreme Court viewed that case. In *DeShaney* social services workers, instead of police officers, failed to intervene to prevent private violence; that difference is immaterial. Of course, in *DeShaney* the state of mind of the government officials was different. There was no allegation that they acted out of a desire to see Joshua injured. Had the Supreme Court decided *DeShaney* on the ground that the state officials lacked the necessary state of mind to violate the Constitution, the holding would be less vulnerable to criticism, and much less significant.

But the Court explicitly declined to decide the case on that ground. It followed the court of appeals in assuming that the defendants' state of mind was sufficiently culpable to violate the Constitution. It ruled in favor of the officials on the ground that they had only engaged in inaction, not action. That does not distinguish *DeShaney* from the hypothetical police inaction case. To put the point another way, under *DeShaney*, child protective services employees would not violate the Due Process Clause even if they deliberately refused to intervene because they wanted to see a child harmed (because of a grudge against a family or out of a bizarre belief that child abuse constitutes proper discipline, for example).

The Due Process Clause requires that a judge be impartial. That requirement applies to suits between private parties, as well as suits against the government. Plaintiffs, as well as defendants, are protected by this requirement. None of these propositions has ever been seriously disputed.

But the plaintiff in a private action is, by definition, seeking to have the government act against alleged private wrongdoing. A plaintiff who loses a private suit is the victim of private harm and government inaction—the government failure to stop or correct the harm—just like the victim in *DeShaney*.

Suppose a plaintiff seeking, say, to enjoin a trespass by a private party, loses his or her case because the judge is biased. (Suppose the judge has a financial interest aligned with the defendant.) That is a clear violation of the Due Process Clause. In what sense, however, is this an instance of government action, as opposed to inaction? The case is just like *DeShaney* (again leaving state of mind aside), except that the official who refused to intervene against the private wrongdoing is a judge instead of a social worker. Thus the *DeShaney* approach leads to a wholly implausible conclusion in connection with an issue that goes to the core of the Due Process Clause, the right to trial before an impartial judge. . . .

In his dissent in *DeShaney*, Justice Brennan urged that this government action contributed to Joshua's injuries. His argument was that by establishing such a program, the government discouraged others—private persons and other government agencies—from intervening to protect Joshua. This argument reflects the tort rule that an individual has no obligation to attempt the rescue of a person endangered by another's conduct, but can be held liable if the rescue attempt is carried out negligently. The theory is that the rescue attempt may have worsened the victim's situation by causing the victim to forgo other sources of aid or by discouraging other potential rescuers from coming to the victim's aid.

It is difficult—for many reasons—to know whether as an empirical matter, Justice Brennan's argument is correct. Certainly the existence of some government services discourages private rescue. For example, if the government establishes an emergency telephone service for people to call when they need medical care, people are discouraged from calling on private sources for help. If the emergency service then gives bad advice, the government's action has unquestionably caused any resulting injury. *DeShaney* is a more difficult case, because it is less obvious that private rescuers would have appeared if there were no state protective services.

In *DeShaney*, it is not implausible to say, as the court of appeals did, that it is too "conjectural" to argue that others would have rescued Joshua had they not relied on the social service agencies to do so. But the court of appeals' solution does not justify the Supreme Court's sweeping statement that the government generally cannot be held liable in cases of "inaction." In some such cases, for example that involving the emergency telephone service, the causal connection will not be conjectural at all. . . .

To its general rule that "inaction" does not violate the Due Process Clause, the *DeShaney* Court established an exception, for instances in which "the State takes a person into custody and holds him there against his will." For example, *Youngberg v. Romeo* held that the Due Process Clause guarantees mental patients who are involuntarily committed to a state hospital a right to the services that are needed to ensure their "reasonable safety" from attacks by others. *Estelle v. Gamble* held that prisoners' constitutional rights are violated when prison authorities show deliberate indifference toward their serious medical needs. The Court in *DeShaney* explicitly left open the possibility that the state might have "an affirmative duty to protect" a child in Joshua DeShaney's situation if the child were in a "foster home operated by [state] agents."

The basis for this exception is unclear. The Court seemed to say that the government's duty to act arises in these cases because the government has taken an individual into custody against his or her will. The courts of appeals have generally held that a state has a duty to provide some degree of protection against private wrongdoing only when the state has either "put a [person] in a position of danger from private persons" or has "cut off sources of private aid." For example, the Court of Appeals for the Seventh Circuit has held that state employees may be liable for arresting the driver of a car containing small children and leaving the children alone on a major highway.

Whatever the basis for this exception, it cannot be confined to exceptional cases such as prisons. Joshua DeShaney's situation did not differ in any relevant respect from the situation of the persons to whom this exception applies. And what is true of Joshua DeShaney in this respect is equally true of every person. . . .

The underlying logic of the Court's ruling in *DeShaney*—and its fundamental inadequacy—can be better understood if one sees the Court's reasoning as implicitly based on a particular approach to constitutional litigation. This approach is coherent, and it has venerable roots. But it has now been thoroughly, and correctly, rejected. Indeed, it is flatly inconsistent with Section 1983.

This underlying view is that a plaintiff may not bring an action alleging a violation of the Constitution unless he or she can also show that a common law interest was invaded. The Court did not consider what the defendants in *DeShaney* did to be "action" because the defendants did not infringe any common law interests of Joshua DeShaney. The Court said at one point: "it is well to remember . . . that the harm was inflicted not by the State of Wisconsin, but by Joshua's father." This sentence (which the Court thought obvious) is true only if the terms are given common law meanings: if "inflicted" means an actual touching and the only "harm" is the battery. But if causation is expanded beyond physical invasion, or "harm" includes the deprivation of a fair opportunity for state protection, the statement is not obviously true.

Similarly, the Court established a separate category for "custodial" institutions, because the individuals inhabiting them have suffered an infringement of a common law interest at the hands of the state. That is why the Court saw state action when the state placed an individual in a prison, state hospital, or (perhaps) foster home. In those cases, the state did something that, if done by a private person, would constitute an invasion of a common law interests. But the Court does not see state action when the state helps establish and maintain conventional family relations, and it certainly does not see state action when the state maintains property, contract, and other rules that effectively confine people in certain economic and social positions. That is because in those cases there is no infringement of common law interests.

Thus the Court explained its treatment of "custodial" institutions by saying that "it is the State's affirmative act of restraining the individual's freedom to act on his own behalf—through incarceration, institutionalization, or other similar restraint of personal liberty which is the 'deprivation of liberty' triggering the protections of the Due Process Clause. . . . " As the dissent pointed out, this assertion is incorrect on its face. The prisoner or involuntary patient who sues because he was injured while institutionalized is complaining about the injury, not about the decision to institutionalize him; that initial decision conformed to the Due Process Clause. But one can make sense of the Court's statement if one views it as reflecting an implicit assimilation of constitutional to common law wrongs. At common law, taking custody of a person creates an obligation to exercise due care in protecting that person's safety.

It appears, therefore, that the Court in *DeShaney* is implicitly requiring plaintiffs raising constitutional claims to establish that the state has invaded some common law interest. The roots of this approach are in what Justice Harlan called (in the course of rejecting it in his opinion in *Bivens v.*

Six Unknown Named Agents) the "'state-created right—federal defense'
model" of constitutional litigation. Under this model, the Constitution
creates no implied rights of action. A constitutional right therefore cannot
be the basis for a plaintiff's claim. Constitutional rights can still be enforced
in a variety of ways, notably as defenses in actions brought by the government. But a plaintiff cannot bring suit on the basis of a constitutional
right alone. . . .

But the problem with the "state right–federal defense" approach—
that is, with the notion that a plaintiff complaining of a constitutional
violation must also show an invasion of a common law interest—is that
it has been thoroughly and deservedly repudiated. Section 1983 explicitly
authorizes actions based on the Constitution alone against state officials.
Bivens removed any doubt that constitutional rights can ground actions
against federal officials, even in the absence of a common law wrong.
Many clear constitutional violations—ranging from racial discrimination
to illegal mail openings—do not always involve the invasion of common
law interests and commonly will go unremedied unless the victim can
bring suit directly under the Constitution. To the extent that the *DeShaney*
Court's distinction between action and inaction implicitly required a
common law invasion as a prerequisite for a suit to enforce constitutional
rights—and that seems to be a reasonable account of what the Court
was doing—the Court's action reflects an outmoded and inappropriately
restrictive view of constitutional litigation.

How should the problem of government obligations to protect against
private wrongs be addressed? The broad language of the *DeShaney* opinion
blurs two distinct issues. The first is whether the government must provide
some absolute minimum level of protection against private wrongdoing.
The second is whether, assuming that the government has established a
program designed to protect citizens against private wrongs, a government
official's improper conduct in administering the program can violate the
Due Process Clause even when that conduct takes the form of inaction
rather than action. These issues are analytically independent: the resolution
of one does not depend on the answer to the other.

The question whether the government owes its citizens some absolute
level of protection against private wrongdoing is one of substantive, rather
than procedural, due process. That is because the claim is that there exists
a minimum level of protection against private wrongs that the government
must provide, irrespective of the procedures the government affords. As
I explained earlier, *DeShaney* did not present the question whether the

government may withhold all protection against private wrongs. There was no allegation in *DeShaney* that the state denied all protection to Joshua. In fact the state enforced the criminal law against his father, and there is no reason to doubt that it stood ready to enforce a damages remedy in tort.

Nonetheless, the opinion contains sweeping language suggesting that the Due Process Clause does not require a state to provide even "minimal levels of safety and security." The "purpose" of the Due Process Clause, the Court said, "was to protect the people from the State, not to ensure that the State protected them from each other." The Court also relied on the language of the Clause—the word "deprive," it asserted, referred to government action, not to the government's failure to protect against private action—and on cases that asserted that the Due Process Clause creates "no affirmative right to governmental aid."

None of the arguments I have made so far draws this aspect of *DeShaney* into question. In fact, there is no basis for criticizing the Court's holding (as opposed to its language) on this aspect of *DeShaney*. But the Court's broad language is incorrect. The best interpretation of the Due Process Clause is that it requires the states to provide some level of protection against private violence.

This conclusion should not be surprising. In fact, the view suggested by the language of *DeShaney*—that the government has no duty at all to protect citizens against private wrongs—is novel. It has generally been assumed that the states have some obligation to maintain common law remedies, or their equivalent, to some degree. Apparently no state has ever sought to deny all protection against private wrongs. And when the states have rescinded particular common law remedies, the Supreme Court, in upholding the action, has relied on the fact that the state provided an adequate alternative remedy. . . .

My argument so far establishes only that the Due Process Clause requires the government to provide some level of protection against private batteries. Nothing I have said suggests what level of protection is sufficient. Nor are the cases helpful; since the end of the *Lochner* era, the Court has not invalidated a state measure on the ground that it abrogated common law rights.

As a matter of first principles, it is possible to argue that the government has a duty, enforceable in damages (but not by specific relief), to protect its citizens against every tort. The effect of this rule would be that any victim of a tort could recover damages from the government. Since the government would be free to proceed against the tortfeasor, the effect would be that the government would provide compensation when the tortfeasor was judgment proof. This regime would be practicable; many governments have voluntarily established compensation programs for the victims of crimes.

This regime would raise several complex policy issues. Forcing the government to internalize all the costs of its law enforcement decisions in this way would have some advantages; the government would be less able to save on enforcement costs by permitting politically powerless groups to be victimized by private violence at an especially high rate. The moral hazard problem would be mitigated because of administrative costs and because standard measures of compensation substantially under-compensate for many torts. On the other hand, so long as the government can define the conduct that constitutes a tort, this regime would create an incentive for the government to make more conduct lawful. For that reason, it might be better to confine the requirement of compensation to certain categories of torts. In general, while the policy implications of such a regime would have to be worked out, it is not unthinkable as a matter of first principles. It was, however, rejected by the Supreme Court even before *DeShaney*, and its rejection in *DeShaney* cannot be viewed as dictum.

The alternative is to require some level of protection short of complete protection. . . . Under this approach, the government is not responsible (even in damages) for all private wrongs, or even all private violence, but it cannot withdraw all remedies. Obviously it is difficult to specify a position between those two poles. But this difficulty is not a reason to reject the conclusion that the government has some obligation to provide a minimum level of protection against private wrongs.

The problem is analogous to that of determining whether Congress has provided adequate remedies for constitutional violations. Congress has broad latitude to prescribe remedies for constitutional violations. For example, Congress need not provide a compensatory remedy for every constitutional wrong. But there must be some limit on Congress's power to deny remedies for constitutional wrongs. Otherwise, Congress could effectively nullify the substantive constitutional provision.

The Supreme Court has never specified where this limit might be. In general, the Court seems concerned with whether a remedial scheme reflects a rational, comprehensive effort to remedy the relevant category of constitutional violations. This suggests that, by analogy, it might be sensible to require that governments satisfy a standard akin to the arbitrary and capricious rule in their decisions about the level and allocation of resources devoted to combatting private wrongdoing.

In practice, such a standard would require little more than what well-established equal protection standards would require, if they were seriously enforced. Every government provides law enforcement services to some degree, and political pressures ensure that they will continue to do so. The controversies arise not over the total abrogation of all systems of law enforcement but over selective failures to enforce the law. There are claims, for example, that local governments, without adequate reasons, do not vigorously enforce laws against certain crimes (such as domestic violence) or in certain geographical areas (such as low-income areas inhabited by minorities). . . .

The second issue, squarely raised by the facts of *DeShaney*, is: assuming that there exists a government program to provide some protection against private wrongdoing, under what circumstances do errors in the administration of the program violate the Due Process Clause? The Court's broad language in *DeShaney* suggests that maladministration cannot violate the Due Process Clause when it takes the form of government inaction. . . .

. . . The Court has said on many occasions, including *DeShaney* itself, that the Due Process Clause "was intended to prevent government 'from abusing [its] power.'" As the hypothetical examples show, government officials can abuse their power by wrongfully withholding government services or protection, as well as by wrongfully inflicting harm on citizens. Indeed, the Supreme Court traces the "abuse of power" notion to the origins of the Due Process Clause in Magna Carta, which forbade deprivations of liberty and property "other than by the law of the land." This suggests that an abuse of power consists of a failure to administer the law. It suggests no reason to exclude failures that consist of a refusal to extend protection.

The Court should, therefore, have ruled in *DeShaney* that an official abuse of power (a term that obviously must be defined) violates the Due Process Clause, irrespective of whether it takes the form of "action" or "inaction." Such a rule would produce no obviously implausible results and would avert the wholly implausible results of the police inaction and judicial bias hypotheticals. . . .

Two questions remain. First, when a government official abusively withholds affirmative government protection, what is the liberty or property interest that is infringed? This question is significant because, as I will explain, the answer requires that current understandings of "liberty" and "property" under the Due Process Clause be modified. Second, how should "abuse of power" be defined?

At first glance it might appear that when the government wrongfully fails to protect a citizen against battery (as in the police inaction case and allegedly in *DeShaney*) or trespass (as in the judicial bias hypothetical), the government has invaded a common law interest. On further examination, however, this appears to be incorrect. Judicial bias violates the Due Process Clause even if the plaintiff seeks vindication of an interest not protected by the common law. Official abuses of power can occur in connection with any regulatory or benefit program, not just government programs designed to protect common law interests. . . .

If, in the judicial bias hypothetical, the plaintiff is not deprived of a common law interest in property, of what interest is he or she deprived? Under current understandings, the general rule is that apart from common law interests, a property interest exists only when state law prescribes an entitlement in terms that limit the discretion of the officials administering the program. But a plaintiff seeking to enforce a statutory interest is entitled to an impartial judge even if the statute does not limit the judge's discretion. Suppose, for example, that a statute provides for an award of attorney's fees in the sole discretion of the judge. A claimant under the statute who was denied fees by a blatantly biased judge would surely have been deprived of property without due process. But neither a common law interest nor a nondiscretionary statutory entitlement would have been at stake.

Perhaps the best way to understand this situation is that the statutes creating a government program—even a highly discretionary government program—always implicitly create one property interest: an entitlement to a fair decision. That is, roughly speaking, even a fully discretionary program creates an interest, protected by the Due Process Clause, in a decision based on the government's agenda rather than the private agenda of the responsible official. This is certainly a reasonable inference from the establishment of a government program; when the legislature creates a program, it intends that the program be administered in a way that furthers governmental interests, not the personal interests of the administrators. . . .

The final question is how to define an abuse of power for purposes of this branch of the analysis. The current state of the law is as follows. A state official does not violate the Due Process Clause by simply erring in the interpretation of state law or "negligently" administering state law, even if the effect of the negligent action is to invade a liberty or property interest. On the other hand, it has never been disputed that an "intentional" infringement of such an interest violates the Clause. The Court has held that "deliberate indifference" can be sufficient to show a violation of the Cruel and Unusual Punishment Clause of the Eighth Amendment, and in *DeShaney* the Court suggested that the Due Process Clause should be interpreted in a parallel fashion, at least when applied to "custodial" institutions. The Court has left open the question whether "gross negligence" or "recklessness" is sufficient to constitute a "depriv[ation]" under the Due Process Clause. The courts of appeals are divided over where to draw the line in this theoretically narrow, but practically quite significant, space.

This framework might simply be extended to cases of so-called inaction. Indeed, the notion of "deliberate indifference" suggests inaction. Sometimes, of course, it will be difficult to decide whether a refusal to provide protection against private wrongs was reckless or merely negligent (assuming that is the point where the line is to be drawn). But such difficult judgments are necessary even in cases of government "actions"—that is, government invasions of common law interests. The common problem of determining whether police have used excessive force in arresting a suspect is an example.

Courts reviewing government "inaction" may have to consider an additional category of concerns, because often a failure to protect against private violence will be justified on the ground that scarce government resources were better used in other ways. But not all cases of "inaction" depend on difficult decisions about resource allocation. In addition, courts already assess government decisions defended on this ground—both in the cases involving "custodial" institutions in which the Court acknowledges that inaction can violate the Due Process Clause and in reviewing federal agencies' failures to act under the federal Administrative Procedure Act and other statutes. There will often be reason for courts to give substantial deference to government decisions about resource allocation. But there is no need to define an arbitrary and essentially indefensible category of "inaction" that is entirely off-limits.

There is an ancient antinomy between justice, viewed as the unyielding, logical application of settled rules, and mercy, viewed as making exceptions to those rules for cases where they produce heartless results. But it is a mistake—perhaps an increasingly common one—to think that any argument for results that immediately appeal to one's sympathy must be based on sentiment or emotion rather than reason. The Court in *DeShaney*, making this mistake, insisted that the logic of the law compelled it to rule against the sympathetic plaintiffs. The errors in the Court's analysis make its insistence especially ironic.

PART THREE

Freedom of Expression

AMENDMENT *I*
Congress shall make no law
. . . abridging the freedom of speech,
or of the press . . .

9

The System of Freedom of Expression

THOMAS I. EMERSON

*Thomas I. Emerson began his legal career working for a number of govern-
ment agencies during the New Deal, then, in 1946, he joined the faculty
of Yale University's School of Law, where he taught for over four decades.
In 1966, he published a very influential book,* Toward a General Theory
of the First Amendment, *laying out broad principles that came to define
liberal legalism's view of the scope of the First Amendment's protection for
freedom of speech and press. The excerpt here is from his subsequent statement
of the basic normative principles and values underlying an expansive interpretation of freedom of speech and press in his now classic book,* The System
of Freedom of Expression *(1970).*

THE SYSTEM OF freedom of expression in a democratic society
rests upon four main premises. These may be stated, in capsule form, as
follows:

First, freedom of expression is essential as a means of assuring individual
self-fulfillment. The proper end of man is the realization of his character
and potentialities as a human being. For the achievement of this self-
realization the mind must be free. Hence suppression of belief, opinion,
or other expression is an affront to the dignity of man, a negation of
man's essential nature. Moreover, man in his capacity as a member of
society has a right to share in the common decisions that affect him. To
cut off his search for truth, or his expression of it, is to elevate society
and the state to a despotic command over him and to place him under
the arbitrary control of others.

Second, freedom of expression is an essential process for advancing
knowledge and discovering truth. An individual who seeks knowledge
and truth must hear all sides of the question, consider all alternatives, test
his judgment by exposing it to opposition, and make full use of different
minds. Discussion must be kept open no matter how certainly true an
accepted opinion may seem to be; many of the most widely acknowledged
truths have turned out to be erroneous. Conversely, the same principle
applies no matter how false or pernicious the new opinion appears to be;
for the unaccepted opinion may be true or partially true and, even if

wholly false, its presentation and open discussion compel a rethinking and retesting of the accepted opinion. The reasons which make open discussion essential for an intelligent individual judgment likewise make it imperative for rational social judgment.

Third, freedom of expression is essential to provide for participation in decision making by all members of society. This is particularly significant for political decisions. Once one accepts the premise of the Declaration of Independence—that governments "derive their just powers from the consent of the governed"—it follows that the governed must, in order to exercise their right of consent, have full freedom of expression both in forming individual judgments and in forming the common judgment. The principle also carries beyond the political realm. It embraces the right to participate in the building of the whole culture, and includes freedom of expression in religion, literature, art, science, and all areas of human learning and knowledge.

Finally, freedom of expression is a method of achieving a more adaptable and hence a more stable community, of maintaining the precarious balance between healthy cleavage and necessary consensus. This follows because suppression of discussion makes a rational judgment impossible, substituting force for reason; because suppression promotes inflexibility and stultification, preventing society from adjusting to changing circumstances or developing new ideas; and because suppression conceals the real problems confronting a society, diverting public attention from the critical issues. At the same time the process of open discussion promotes greater cohesion in a society because people are more ready to accept decisions that go against them if they have a part in the decision-making process. Moreover, the state at all times retains adequate powers to promote unity and to suppress resort to force. Freedom of expression thus provides a framework in which the conflict necessary to the progress of a society can take place without destroying the society. It is an essential mechanism for maintaining the balance between stability and change.

The validity of the foregoing premises has never been proved or disproved, and probably could not be. Nevertheless our society is based upon the faith that they hold true and, in maintaining a system of freedom of expression, we act upon that faith. The considerations just outlined thus represent the values we seek in a system of freedom of expression and the functions that system is intended to perform. It should be added that, while our current system of freedom of expression is a product of constitutional liberalism, the values and functions which underlie it are essential to any open society regardless of the particular form its political, economic and social institutions may take.

Two basic implications of the theory underlying our system of freedom of expression need to be emphasized. The first is that it is not a general measure of the individual's right to freedom of expression that any particular exercise of that right may be thought to promote or retard other goals of the society. The theory asserts that freedom of expression, while not the sole or sufficient end of society, is a good in itself, or at least an essential element in a good society. The society may seek to achieve other or more inclusive ends—such as virtue, justice, equality, or the maximum realization of the potentialities of its members. These are not necessarily gained by accepting the rules for freedom of expression. But, as a general proposition, the society may not seek them by suppressing the beliefs or opinions of individual members. To achieve these other goals it must rely upon other methods: the use of counter-expression and the regulation or control of conduct which is not expression. Hence the right to control individual expression, on the ground that it is judged to promote good or evil, justice or injustice, equality or inequality, is not, speaking generally, within the competence of the good society.

The second implication, in a sense a corollary of the first, is that the theory rests upon a fundamental distinction between belief, opinion, and communication of ideas on the one hand, and different forms of conduct on the other. For shorthand purposes we refer to this distinction hereafter as one between "expression" and "action." As just observed, in order to achieve its desired goals, a society or the state is entitled to exercise control over action—whether by prohibiting or compelling it—on an entirely different and vastly more extensive basis. But expression occupies an especially protected position. In this sector of human conduct, the social right of suppression or compulsion is at its lowest point, in most respects nonexistent. A majority of one has the right to control action, but a minority of one has the right to talk.

This marking off of the special status of expression is a crucial ingredient of the basic theory for several reasons. In the first place, thought and communication are the fountainhead of all expression of the individual personality. To cut off the flow at the source is to dry up the whole stream. Freedom at this point is essential to all other freedoms. Hence society must withhold its right of suppression until the stage of action is reached. Secondly, expression is normally conceived as doing less injury to other social goals than action. It generally has less immediate consequences, is less irremediable in its impact. Thirdly, the power of society and the state over the individual is so pervasive, and construction of doctrines, institutions, and administrative practices to limit this power so difficult, that only by drawing such a protective line between expression and action is it possible to strike a safe balance between authority and freedom.

In constructing and maintaining a system of freedom of expression the major controversies have arisen not over acceptance of the basic theory, but in attempting to fit its values and functions into a more comprehensive scheme of social goals. These issues have revolved around the question of what limitations, if any, ought to be imposed upon freedom of expression in order to reconcile that interest with other individual and social interests sought by the good society. Most of our efforts in the past to formulate rules for limiting freedom of expression have been seriously defective through failure to take into consideration the realistic context in which such limitations are administered. The crux of the problem is that the limitations, whatever they may be, must be applied by one group of human beings to other human beings.

First of all, it is necessary to recognize the powerful forces that impel men towards the elimination of unorthodox expression. Most men have a strong inclination, for rational or irrational reasons, to suppress opposition. On the other hand, persons who stand up against society and challenge the traditional view usually have similarly strong feelings about the issues they raise. Thus dissent often is not pitched in conventional terms, nor does it follow customary standards of polite expression. Moreover, the forces of inertia within a society ordinarily resist the expression of new ideas or the pressures of the underprivileged who seek a change. And the longer-run logic of the traditional theory may not be immediately apparent to untutored participants in the conflict. Suppression of opinion may thus seem an entirely plausible course of action; tolerance a weakness or a foolish risk.

Thus it is clear that the problem of maintaining a system of freedom of expression in a society is one of the most complex any society has to face. Self-restraint, self-discipline, and maturity are required. The theory is essentially a highly sophisticated one. The members of the society must be willing to sacrifice individual and short-term advantage for social and long-range goals. And the process must operate in a context that is charged with emotion and subject to powerful conflicting forces of self-interest.

These considerations must be weighed in attempting to construct a theory of limitations. A system of free expression can be successful only when it rests upon the strongest possible commitment to the positive right and the narrowest possible basis for exceptions. And any such exceptions must be clear-cut, precise, and readily controlled. Otherwise the forces that press toward restriction will break through the openings, and freedom of expression will become the exception and suppression the rule.

A second major consideration in imposing restrictions upon expression is the difficulty of framing precise limitations. The object of the limitation is usually not the expression itself but its feared consequences. Repression of expression is thus purely a preventive measure and, like all preventive measures, cuts far more widely and deeply than is necessary to control the ensuing conduct. Moreover, the infinite varieties and subtleties of language, and other forms of communication, make it impossible to construct a limitation upon expression in definite terms. Thus a wide area of expression is brought within reach of the limitation and enormous discretionary power placed in the hands of those who administer it.

Again, the apparatus of government required for enforcement of limitations on expression, by its very nature, tends towards administrative extremes. Officials charged with the duties of suppression already have or tend to develop excessive zeal in the performance of their task. The accompanying techniques of enforcement—the investigations, surveillance, searches and seizures, secret informers, voluminous files on the suspect—all tend to exert a repressive influence on freedom of expression. In addition, the restrictive measures are readily subject to distortion and to use for ulterior purposes.

Finally we must take into account the whole impact of restriction upon the healthy functioning of a free society. Limitations are seldom applied except in an atmosphere of public fear and hysteria. This may be deliberately aroused or may simply be the inevitable accompaniment of repression. Under such circumstances the doctrines and institutions for enforcing the limitations are subjected to intense pressures. Moreover, while some of the more hardy may be willing to defy the opposition and suffer the consequences, the more numerous are likely to be unwilling to run the risks. Similarly, persons whose cooperation is needed to permit the full flow of open discussion—those who own the means of publication or the facilities for communication—are likely to be frightened into withholding their patronage and assistance.

The lesson of experience, in short, is that the limitations imposed on discussion, as they operate in practice, tend readily and quickly to destroy the whole structure of free expression. They are very difficult to keep in hand; the exceptions are likely to swallow up the principle. Maintenance of a system of free expression, therefore, is not an easy task. This is especially true as we confront the conditions of today. We have tended over the years to refine and delineate more carefully the restrictions we seek to impose. But the new problems arising out of modern industrial society make the issues more delicate and troublesome than at any other time in our history.

10

Arguing the "Pentagon Papers" Case

ERWIN N. GRISWOLD

Erwin N. Griswold taught for many years at Harvard Law School, where he served as dean from 1945 to 1967. In 1967, Democratic President Lyndon B. Johnson appointed him solicitor general and he continued in that position under Republican President Richard M. Nixon until June 1973, when he went into private legal practice. During his professional career, Griswold argued 117 cases before the Supreme Court—a record surpassed in the twentieth century by only two others. One of the landmark cases he argued was the so-called Pentagon Papers case, New York Times, Co. v. United States *(1971), in which the government sought a permanent injunction against the* New York Times *and the* Washington Post *from publishing leaked portions of a top secret history of America's involvement in the controversial war in Viet Nam. The excerpt here is from his 1992 autobiography,* Ould Fields, New Corne: The Personal Memoirs of a Twentieth Century Lawyer. *In it, Griswold reflects on the law and the behind-the-scenes politics of the Supreme Court's landmark ruling on the First Amendment doctrine of no prior restraint.*

WHEN I FIRST HEARD about the Pentagon Papers, on Sunday, June 13, 1971, I was in Florida with my wife, where I had gone to speak at a meeting of the Florida Bar Association. The first installment of the Pentagon Papers was printed by the *New York Times* on that day. When I saw this, I said to my wife that this case would almost surely go to the Supreme Court. But I shrugged my shoulders, because I thought that it could not possibly get there for some time. It could not get to my office until the fall, I felt, so I need not be concerned about it now.

We returned to Washington that afternoon, and I found a message that I should report to the Attorney General's office at once. When I arrived there, a number of Department lawyers were assembled, including the Attorney General, and Robert Mardian, the Assistant Attorney General for the National Security Division. I did not realize how far matters had proceeded, and I asked whether it was desirable to take any action with respect to the publication. If there was "any dirt" in the papers, it had all occurred in previous administrations, since the forty-seven volumes of the papers closed with the end of the Johnson Administration. I raised the question why the Nixon Administration should be concerned about this. In addition, I wondered, in a preliminary way, whether the Government had "any ground to stand on." The general thrust of the First Amendment was against the Government's position, and there was no statute which undertook to give the Government authority to prevent publication of classified material even in national security cases. I pointed out that the system of security classification was based on an Executive Order, and that no penalty had ever been provided by Congress for failure to comply with a classification under that order. Moreover, as far as I could see, the restraints established by the Order applied only to government employees, and thus were not applicable to the newspapers.

Actually, the whole imbroglio of the Pentagon Papers case was largely due to a broad misunderstanding, which could have been avoided if the courts had been willing to take the time to ascertain what was actually before them. This was not an unreasonable thing to do in view of the fact that the *Times* had held the papers for nearly three months before bringing them to publication. The Government had the Pentagon Papers, which contained some material which was important to the security of the United States. The Government had no reason to think that what the newspapers had was in any way different from "The Pentagon Papers," which the Government had compiled.

Over the years, it has slowly become apparent that, with relatively small exceptions, the newspapers did not have any of the material with which the Government was primarily concerned. If this had been known at the time, there might well have been no Pentagon Papers case. The case actually before the Court did not in fact present the security problems which the Government, with reason, feared it did. But the only way the Government lawyers could find this out was through the allowance of a reasonable period of time to examine what the newspapers actually had. With the benefit of hindsight, it now seems clear that it would have been wise for the Court to do what the Second Circuit Court of Appeals did, namely, to allow time to determine what risks the case actually involved.

The *New York Times* case was filed in the Federal District Court in New York on Tuesday, June 15th. I had no role in the trial since the Supreme Court was not yet involved. The responsible officers in New York were Assistant Attorney General Mardian, and the United States Attorney for the Southern District of New York, Whitney North Seymour, Jr. The district court refused to grant an injunction solely for the purpose of providing time in which to determine whether there was anything in the papers which, if published, would imperil national security. That case went on appeal to the Second Circuit, where the court, on Monday, June 21, 1971, by a 5–3 vote, directed the issuance of a stay, and remanded the case to the District Court to ascertain what was in the papers held by the *Times*.

While these proceedings were being held in New York, copies of the materials were given to the *Washington Post*. I was told that "it had been determined" that we should do everything we could to prevent publication of the papers. I assumed that this meant the White House, and very likely the President, but no definite information was given about this. At that time, I knew nothing about the President's intense concern about "leaks." Nor did I know that Henry Kissinger was then about to go to China on a very secret mission, and that there might be legitimate fears that the Chinese would be very cautious in their dealings with the United States if they felt that the United States could not "keep secrets."

The *Washington Post* case was tried before Judge Gesell in the District Court in the District of Columbia on Monday and Tuesday, June 21 and 22. At the conclusion of the trial the court declined to enter an injunction against the publication of the papers by the *Washington Post*. An appeal to the United States Court of Appeals for the District of Columbia Circuit was immediately authorized, and the court set it down for hearing on Wednesday, June 23. I had assumed that Robert Mardian, the Assistant Attorney General for the National Security Division of the Department would argue the case in the Court of Appeals.

While the case was being tried, I felt more and more that it was a very unfortunate situation and that perhaps some way could be found to bring about an adjustment. I had met Mrs. Graham, publisher of the *Post*, since she was the widow of Philip Graham, a member of the Harvard Law School Class of 1939, who had been a student of mine. After the case had gone to the Court of Appeals, on Wednesday, June 23, 1971, I called her on the telephone, and said that I thought that the case was regrettable and that it seemed to me that it ought to be possible to come to some sort of an agreement, or, at least, to minimize the controversy. She was very pleasant, but intimated that she was not informed as to details.

Mrs. Graham referred me to Benjamin Bradlee, the Executive Editor of the *Post*. Shortly thereafter, I talked with Mr. Bradlee, by telephone. I told him that there were certain items which caused the Government great concern, and I added that I did not think that the *Post* really wanted to publish those items, or needed to do so. He asked me what items I had in mind, and I referred him to several. In this conversation I relied on information given me by Mr. Mardian, and members of his staff, and by Whitney North Seymour, Jr., the United States Attorney who was in charge of the *New York Times* case before the Second Circuit in New York.

After a while, Mr. Bradlee called me back and said: "We don't have any of those items." This took me by surprise, and the only explanation I could think of was that only a portion of the papers had been delivered to the *Post*, and the papers they received did not include these items. I then said: "Well, please tell me what you do have, and I will tell you which ones give us concern." He responded: "Oh, no. We could not do that. That would disclose our source." This put me in a rather frustrating spot, since I already knew the source. I had seen J. Edgar Hoover at a meeting, and he told me that they knew that the source was Daniel Ellsberg. But he asked me not to disclose this to anyone, since they thought there were others who participated, and they did not want any disclosure while they were looking for these others. So, I could not tell Mr. Bradlee that I knew the source.

From this and other matters, a fact has slowly become apparent to me which has not been made clear in previous discussions of the Pentagon Papers case. The papers which Ellsberg had, and which he gave to the *New York Times*, the *Washington Post*, the *Boston Globe*, and other newspapers, were not the same as the forty-seven volumes of Pentagon Papers of which a few sets were made, one of which was kept in the safe of the Secretary of Defense. This resulted from two factors. In the *first* place, Ellsberg, while he was an employee in the process of compiling and editing the Pentagon Papers, did not have access to all of the papers in their exact final form. And, *second*, we now know that Ellsberg deliberately withheld important items in the material he did have.

Thus there was no clear way to raise precise issues. The newspapers had a set of copies which bore an appreciable resemblance to the Pentagon Papers, but were different in many ways. On the other hand, the Government had the Pentagon Papers, but had no way of knowing what the newspapers had. In this situation, any effort to come to an agreement was bound to fail, without disclosure by the newspapers which they did not feel was feasible.

On the Wednesday morning after Judge Gesell's decision, the Attorney General called me to his office, and said that he would like to have me argue the case in the Court of Appeals. I replied "Mr. Attorney General, I have never seen even the outside of the Pentagon Papers. I do not know what is in them, and I have given no real study to the applicable law." His response was: "Well, Dean, if you don't want to argue the case, I suppose I can get someone else." I then stood up straight and said: "Mr. Attorney General, if you want me to argue the case, I will do it."

On returning to my office, I called my wife on the telephone. I asked her to bring me a pair of black shoes, to replace the brown ones that I was wearing. I also asked her to bring a "quiet" tie which I could wear instead of the somewhat gaudy one I had on. And, finally, I asked her to put a little lunch in a paper bag, and bring these things to the Department of Justice. In due course, they arrived, while I worked feverishly on learning what I could about the facts and the law of the case, with the great assistance of my First Deputy, Daniel M. Friedman.

The case was heard by the full bench of the Court of Appeals on Wednesday afternoon. About a half hour before the argument, I left the department to walk to the Court of Appeals. I felt that the fresh air and the mild exercise of the walk might clear my thinking somewhat. When I got to the Court of Appeals, it was almost impossible to enter, since the corridors and the courtroom were thronged with reporters, with many photographers outside the door.

It is quite unusual for a Solicitor General to appear in one of the lower courts. When I finally got into the courtroom, one of the deputy clerks asked me: "Who is going to move your admission?" I replied that I had been admitted to practice before the Court of Appeals in about 1932. His response was that their records did not go back that far, and that he would act on my statement that I had been admitted.

I argued the case, in a rather feckless way, since I did not know much about it, and still had never seen even the outside of the Pentagon Papers. We now know (though I knew nothing about it at the time) that the *Washington Post* (presumably through their counsel) communicated with the court of appeals during its closed session following the argument. They agreed "not to publish 'very limited quotations from two documents which the *Post* did not deem to be of reportorial significance.'"

One of the difficulties in reconstructing the events in connection with the Pentagon Papers is the fact that things happened so fast, and under such pressure, that it is very hard to know who in the government knew what, and when he knew it. While the *New York Times* case was in the District Court of New York, and in the Court of Appeals for the Second Circuit, the responsible officer of the Government was the United States Attorney Whitney North Seymour, Jr. Similarly, Assistant Attorney General Robert Mardian was the responsible officer in the *Washington Post* case while it was in the lower courts, even though I was assigned to argue it in the Court of Appeals. In the ordinary case, which is usually pending in the Department of Justice for months, there is adequate opportunity for exchange of information. This opportunity was not available in the Pentagon Papers case simply because of the pell mell way in which the courts proceeded.

For example, there is a rumor, said to originate from a Supreme Court Law Clerk, that, after the case went to the Supreme Court, "an army general" delivered some papers to Chief Justice Burger, or (in another version) to the Clerk's office. I can only say that I never heard anything about such an event, and I feel fairly sure that, if I had known about it, I would have been concerned about it, and would not forget about it. It may be that Assistant Attorney General Mardian knew about this (if it occurred) and simply did not have an opportunity to pass the word to me.

On Thursday, June 24th, we received word from the Clerk of the Court of Appeals that the court had affirmed Judge Gesell's decision, thus denying an injunction in the *Washington Post* case. My deputy, Daniel Friedman, and I discussed the situation. We felt that it was not decent for the *New York Times*, which had first published the papers, to be subject to an injunction, while the *Washington Post* was free to publish. Accordingly, we prepared an application to the Supreme Court for an order staying publication by the *Washington Post* until the *Post* case and the *Times* case could be heard together. While this application was being typed, I said to Friedman, "Let's add the following to the application." So, these two lines were put in: "If the Court wishes to treat this application as a petition for certiorari, we have no objection." This must be the shortest petition for certiorari in the history of the United States. It was filed in the early evening of Thursday, June 24th. The *New York Times* had filed a petition for certiorari about noon of the same day.

The next day, Friday, June 25th, at noon, Chief Justice Burger called me on the telephone. He said: "The Court has granted both petitions for certiorari. The case will be heard at 11:00 a.m. tomorrow, and briefs will be exchanged by both sides in the courtroom."

At this point, I arranged to have a set of the Pentagon Papers brought into my office. They were accompanied by an Army Staff Sergeant, with many decorations, who sat beside them. Shortly thereafter, my secretary came into the office. The sergeant pointed to her and said: "Who's she?" I replied, "She is my secretary." His response was "Is she cleared?" I replied that I did not know, but that she was my secretary, and I had to have her assistance. The Sergeant then said: "If she is not cleared, she cannot come in here."

I then confronted the United States Army, and said: "In this office, I am in charge. I am responsible for this case, and I cannot do my work without the aid of my secretary. Will you please leave, at once, and report to your superior whatever you feel that you should report." To my surprise, and relief, he did leave, and I had no further problem in that area.

In the meantime, I had made arrangements through Assistant Attorney General Mardian for three persons to come to my office that afternoon, each for a half-hour meeting. One was Vice Admiral Noel Naylor, director of the National Security Agency. Another was William B. Macomber, Jr., Deputy Under Secretary of State for Administration (a graduate of the Harvard Law School), and the third was Lieutenant General Melvin Zais, director of operations for the Joint Chiefs of Staff. I asked each of these gentlemen to tell me what was really dangerous in the Pentagon Papers, and would cause appreciable harm to the interests or the security of the United States. I had a yellow pad in my hand, and I noted down the page references for their responses. I had in the back of my mind the thought that the publication of the plain text of any coded telegram would be serious, since it would provide information for breaking the code. Admiral Naylor laughed at this, and said: "That has not been true since about 1935." At that point, I felt that about half of my case, as I had analyzed it so far, went out the window. Admiral Naylor went on to say that there was a separate code for each message, that printing a plain text of a telegram would help to break the code for that message, and that, of course, was of no importance, since the plain text of the message was already available.

From these discussions, I picked out forty-one specific items and then undertook to study each of them as carefully as I could in the limited time available.

By this time, Daniel Friedman and I had agreed that he would write the "open brief" for the Government, while I would write the "secret brief." Mr. Friedman, as would be expected, produced a fine brief, showing a number of instances where prior restraint on publication had been granted. These included such matters as forbidding the use of wording like "Whites Only" in advertising for houses or employment, similar illustrations in labor law (where an employer cannot threaten to fire his employees if they join a labor union), and the whole area of copyright law. Knowing that the "open brief" would be well done, I was able to devote all of my time and thought to the "secret brief."

After examining the items which had been brought to my attention by my three visitors, I felt that there were only a few that had any chance of finding favor before the Supreme Court. I finally reduced these to eleven items, which I summarized in the closed brief. One of these items, on which I particularly relied, consisted of four volumes of the Papers, known as the "Negotiating Track." I devoted a full page to these materials in my closed or secret brief, with the conclusion that "The publication of this material is likely to close up channels of communication which might otherwise have some opportunity of facilitating the closing of the Vietnam War." In my oral argument, I laid particular emphasis on this material.

After finishing the dictation of the closed brief, at about three o'clock in the morning, I decided to go home. I felt that I should get at least some sleep before the argument was scheduled the following morning. My secretary stayed and completed the typing of the brief. Just before leaving, I recalled that the forty-seven volumes of the Pentagon Papers were in my office, and that the office was not secure. It quickly occurred to me, though, that the F.B.I. headquarters was just down the corridor from my office, and that I could get somebody from there to take charge of the papers. I reached for the Department of Justice telephone book, and was surprised to find that the F.B.I. telephone numbers were not included in the book. Eventually, a number was found, and very quickly an F.B.I. agent came and took charge of the papers. I arranged with him that the papers would be delivered to the Supreme Court at 10:30 the next morning, where I had them put on the counsel's table so that they might be available in case any question arose with respect to some particular item.

The next morning, I returned to the office at about eight o'clock. It was Saturday morning, and there is no general help available in the Department of Justice on Saturday. My secretary and I ran off copies of the thirteen legal sized pages of the brief on the new Xerox machine. In those days, they had no facility for collating, so we arranged chairs around the perimeter of my office. We then put the pile of copies, one page to a chair, and walked around the room assembling the copies, hoping that we got them in the proper order. We made about twenty copies altogether, and I assembled thirteen copies to take to the Court, ten to be filed with the Clerk's office, one for me, one for Alex Bickel, counsel for the *New York Times*, and one for William Glendon, counsel for the *Washington Post*. We had found a rubber stamp reading "Top Secret," and put its mark on the outside cover of each copy.

By this time, it was about nine-thirty on Saturday morning. Over the night, I had ruminated about the eleven items, and had finally come to the conclusion that our only chance of success was to waive objection to the printing of the great bulk of the material, but to seek an injunction as to the eleven items on which I had specifically relied. I realized that this was a great change in the position of the Government, and I came to the conclusion that I should inform Attorney General Mitchell. I knew that he had gone to Alabama to make a speech on Friday evening, and that he would not be returning to Washington until the wee hours of Saturday morning.

I thought that I ought to give him a decent time for rest. At about nine-thirty, however, I called him and said: "Mr. Attorney General, we have this Pentagon Papers case this morning." He said, "Yes, I know. It is a very important case. I wish you good luck." I then said: "There is something on which I think I should have your approval. I am taking the position that we waive objection to the publication of everything in the papers except eleven items. I have reviewed the papers as carefully as I can, and it is my view that the only ground we have to stand on where there is a chance of success is with respect to these eleven items." I can still hear his response: "Well, Dean, I do not see how I can approve that." At this point, I nearly collapsed. Here I was with the case scheduled for argument in a little more than an hour, and the brief I had prepared did not meet the approval of my superior. After a few seconds, though, Mr. Mitchell said: "I have never read the papers, and do not know what is in them. But you are in charge of the case, and if it is your view that that is the proper way to handle it, I am behind you." Of course, he was right. I should not have asked him to approve my action, since I knew that he was not familiar with the content of the papers. He was very generous in giving me his backing and support, and I appreciated the position he took.

I then proceeded to the Supreme Court with the thirteen copies of both briefs, the open brief and the secret brief, in my briefcase. When I got there, I found the Pentagon Papers already installed on counsel's table, and a different sergeant, with decorations, sitting beside them. I first put out ten copies of the brief, and the sergeant said: "What are you going to do with those?" I said: "I am going to file them with the Clerk of the Court, one for each Justice, and one for the Clerk's file." The response was: "Is the Clerk cleared?" I said that I did not know whether the Clerk was cleared or not, but that I did know my responsibility as counsel for the Government in the case, and that the only chance we had to get our views before the Court was to file the briefs with the Clerk. I then took the briefs to the Clerk's office where they were filed, in accordance with the rules of the Court. When I returned to the courtroom, I picked out two more copies. The sergeant said "What are you going to do with them?" I said: "I am going to give one to Mr. Bickel, counsel for the *New York Times*, and one to Mr. Glendon, counsel for the *Post*." The response to this was: "That's treason, that is giving them to the enemy." However, I was not intimidated, and I handed the briefs to the two counsel, knowing that our only chance to communicate to the two newspapers the matters with respect to which we had real concern was through the material in these briefs.

At precisely eleven o'clock, the Court came in, and the Justices took their seats. I had filed a motion that a portion of the argument be held *in camera*, without the public present. The purpose of this was to give me the opportunity to discuss the details of at least some of the eleven items on which the brief relied. I was not surprised when this motion was denied, though it did restrict my presentation. I then addressed the Court.

The argument was recorded, as all Supreme Court arguments are. Eventually, these recordings go to the National Archives, where they are available for scholarly and historical proposes. A friend of mine, Professor Paul R. Baier of the Law School of Louisiana State University, obtained a copy of this recording, and made it available to me. Every four or five years or so, I get this tape out and play it. It brings back interesting memories. Considering the difficulty of the case I had, and the inadequate knowledge I had of the actual facts, I feel that I did all right.

Justices Black, Brennan and Douglas were especially hostile. Justice Black, interrupting Justice Marshall, said "Does not the First Amendment say 'no law' and do you not think that 'no law' means no law?" Justice Black included my response in his opinion, as showing how wrong I was. I must say, though, that it still seems to me that there was something to my answer. I said:

> Now, Mr. Justice [Black], your construction of * * * [the First Amendment] is well known, and I certainly respect it. You say that no law means no law, and that should be obvious. I can only say, Mr. Justice, that to me it is equally obvious "no law" does not mean "no law," and I would seek to persuade the Court that that is true. * * * [T]here are other parts of the Constitution that grant powers and responsibilities to the Executive, and * * * the First Amendment was not intended to make it impossible for the Executive to function or to protect the security of the United States.

My only criticism of myself about this is that I should have said: "Yes, Mr. Justice, and the Constitution says 'Congress shall make no law * * * ' And *Congress* has made no law in this case."

As is well known, the Supreme Court held that the publication by the two newspapers could not be enjoined. Three members of the Court (Black, Douglas, and Brennan, JJ.) held that there could be no prior restraint in any case. Three Justices of the Court (Marshall, Stewart, and White, JJ.) held that there could be a prior restraint in some cases, but that there was not sufficient ground for such an order in this case. And three members of the Court (Burger, C.J., and Harlan and Blackmun, JJ.) held that an injunction should be allowed in order to enable the Court to have time to find out whether items presenting a serious threat to security were involved.

The Monday following the argument, I went to my office, and found Mr. Glendon, counsel for the *Washington Post*, standing outside my door. I said: "Mr. Glendon, what brings you here?" He said: "I have never seen a copy of your secret brief." I replied: "Why, Mr. Glendon, I personally handed you a copy of that brief in the courtroom last Saturday morning." His response was: "Yes, and as soon as the argument was over, that security guard came up and took the brief away from me."

I then gave a copy of the secret brief to Mr. Glendon. He said that it did not mean much to him unless he could see the Pentagon Papers, and find out just which items we were concerned about. I then called J. Fred Buzhardt, Jr., General Counsel of the Defense Department. He was very courteous, and said that he would be glad to make the Pentagon Papers available to Mr. Glendon if he would come to the Pentagon. He added, though, that since the material was classified, Mr. Glendon could not make copies of any of the items, and could not take notes about them. I communicated this to Mr. Glendon, and he then went to the Defense Department. How much he was able to remember about what he saw, I do not know.

Although the Court's decision went against us, I sometimes say, for my own amusement, that we won the Pentagon Papers case. I think that the Court reached a useful decision. As things have worked out, we now know that there was probably not adequate ground for an injunction in that case, in part because the newspapers did not have all of the Papers. A majority of the Court did not say that there can *never* be a prior restraint on publication. This means that the media have a great deal of freedom, as they should have. On the other hand, it means that there can be items where publication can be enjoined, like, to use an old example, the sailing dates of troop ships. Thus, the net result is that the media have great freedom. On the other hand, as a result of this decision, they also have great responsibility, and are clearly reminded that they must act responsibly. The admonition that there are some times when publication can be subject to restraint is a useful reminder to the press that it has responsibility in the area as well as privileges.

II

Defending Pornography

NADINE STROSSEN

Nadine Strossen is a professor at New York Law School. From 1991 through 2008 she was president of the American Civil Liberties Union (ACLU). The ACLU was founded in 1920 by Roger Baldwin in order to defend labor and other liberal causes. As a result of the ACLU's championing of test cases, the Supreme Court gradually expanded the scope of the First Amendment's guarantees for freedom of speech and religion. The ACLU has more than 375,000 members and affiliates in all fifty states. In the excerpt here from her book Defending Pornography: Free Speech, Sex, and the Fight for Women's Rights *(1995), Strossen counters feminists like Catharine MacKinnon and uncompromisingly defends pornography.*

———

"PORNOGRAPHY" is a vague term, which *Webster's International Dictionary* defines as "a depiction (as in writing or painting) . . . of erotic behavior designed to cause sexual excitement." In short, it is sexual expression that is meant to, or does, provoke sexual arousal or desire.

The term has no legal definition or significance. The category of sexually oriented expression that the Supreme Court has held to be subject to restriction is labeled "obscenity." In recent times, the word "pornography" has assumed such negative connotations that it tends to be used as an epithet to describe—and condemn—whatever sexually oriented expression the person using it dislikes. As one wit put it, "What turns *me* on is 'erotic,' but what turns *you* on is 'pornography'"! Likewise, Walter Kendrick's comprehensive 1987 study of the subject, *The Secret Museum: Pornography in Modern Culture*, makes clear that the term "pornography" consistently has been applied to whatever sexual representations a particular dominant class or group does not want in the hands of another, less dominant class or group.

Indeed, the dread *P* word has been used still more loosely and pejoratively, to tar *any* disfavored idea or expression. A striking—and ironic— example of this phenomenon is contained on the jacket of Catharine MacKinnon's 1993 book *Only Words*. Reinforcing fears about the vague, expansive bounds of the "pornography" that MacKinnon and her allies seek to suppress, the book jacket blurb by law professor Patricia Williams castigates criticism of MacKinnon's ideas as "intellectual pornography."

Even the so-called Meese Pornography Commission, which issued its controversial report in 1986, did not attempt to define the term. In contrast, the procensorship feminists use this stigmatized word to underscore that they seek to suppress a category of sexual expression that is, in theory, distinguishable from the category banned under traditional "obscenity" laws. Essentially, "obscene" speech is sexual speech that the community deems "immoral," whereas in model legislation drafted by MacKinnon and Dworkin, "pornography" is defined as the "sexually explicit subordination of women through pictures and/or words." . . .

. . . I use the term "pornography" to refer to the sexually oriented expression that MacKinnon, Dworkin, and their supporters have targeted for suppression. As I show, though, this definition is so amorphous that it can well encompass any and all sexual speech. . . .

We are in the midst of a full-fledged "sex panic," in which seemingly all descriptions and depictions of human sexuality are becoming embattled. Right-wing senators have attacked National Endowment for the Arts grants for art whose sexual themes—such as homoeroticism or feminism—are allegedly inconsistent with "traditional family values." At the opposite end of the political spectrum, students and faculty have attacked myriad words and images on campus as purportedly constituting sexual harassment. Any expression about sex is now seen as especially dangerous, and hence is especially endangered. The pornophobic feminists have played a very significant role in fomenting this sex panic, especially among liberals and on campuses across the country. . . .

Moving even beyond nudity or partial nudity, the sex panic has engulfed certain forms of clothing that some observers might deem provocative. In a 1994 *Ms.* magazine discussion on pornography, writer Ntozake Shange described one such situation that she said was "very heavy on my heart":

I was on the cover of *Poets & Writers* and I wore a pretty lace top. In the next two issues, there were letters asking if *Poets & Writers* is now a flesh magazine—why was I appearing in my underwear? Bare shoulders are exploitation now?

In response, Andrea Dworkin, another participant in the *Ms.* discussion, confirmed that she would indeed see Shange's photograph as exploitation: "It's very hard to look at a picture of a woman's body and not see it with the perception that her body is being exploited." . . .

But this should not be an either-or choice, should it? Are women not—along with men—sexual beings, as well as students or employees? Is women's sexuality really incompatible with their professional roles? Is it really increasing women's autonomy, options, and full-fledged societal participation to posit such an incompatibility? Have we not learned from history, and from other cultures, that the suppression of women's sexuality tends to coincide with the suppression of women's equality? And that when women's sexuality has been banished from the public sphere, women themselves are also banished from key roles in that sphere?

Far from advancing women's equality, this growing tendency to equate any sexual expression with gender discrimination undermines women's equality. Women are, in effect, told that we have to choose between sexuality and equality, between sexual liberation and other aspects of "women's liberation," between sexual freedom and economic, social, and political freedom. This dangerous equation of sexual expression with gender discrimination, which is at the heart of the feminist antipornography movement, is a central reason that movement is so threatening to the women's rights cause.

The misguided zeal to strip all sexual expression from workplaces and campuses, in an alleged effort to strip those places of gender-based discrimination, now has reached even to subtle interpersonal expressions, prone to subjective perceptions and interpretations, such as looks and glances. A growing number of campus policies . . . extend the concept of harassment to "sexually suggestive looks." Likewise, a survey about the sexual harassment of female doctors by their patients, published in the prestigious *New England Journal of Medicine* in December 1993, included "suggestive looks" among the "offenses" reported. In fact, though newspaper headlines trumpeted the dramatic conclusion that 75 percent of the female doctors surveyed said that they had been sexually harassed by patients, further reading revealed that "most of the offenses involved suggestive looks and sexual remarks."

Are women doctors, faculty, and students to be relegated to a figurative equivalent of the purdah of traditional Hindus and Muslims, or the clothing and segregation requirements of orthodox Jews—designed to prevent men from looking at women, and to "protect" women from men's looks? While these traditional religious practices shield women from the eyes of anyone outside their domestic circles, they also imprison women within those domestic circles. The outside world cannot see women, and women cannot see the outside world. . . .

All censorship measures throughout history have been used disporportionately to silence those who are relatively disempowered and who seek to challenge the status quo. Since women and feminists are in that category, it is predictable that any censorship scheme—even one purportedly designed to further their interests—would in fact be used to suppress expression that is especially important to their interests.

That prediction has proven accurate in our neighboring country of Canada, which in 1992 adopted the definition of pornography advocated by MacKinnon, Dworkin, and other procensorship feminists: sexually explicit expression that is "dehumanizing" or "degrading" to women. The Canadian authorities have seized upon this powerful tool to suppress lesbian and gay publications and feminist works, and to harass lesbian and gay bookstores and women's bookstores. . . .

At the heart of the Supreme Court's extensive free speech jurisprudence are two cardinal principles. The first specifies what is *not* a sufficient justification for restricting speech, and the second prescribes what *is* a sufficient justification. A Dworkin-MacKinnon–style antipornography law violates both of these core principles. Accordingly, for such a law to be upheld, the very foundations of our free speech structure would have to be torn up.

The first of these basic principles requires "content neutrality" or "viewpoint neutrality." It holds that government may never limit speech just because any listener—or even, indeed, the majority of the community—disagrees with or is offended by its content or the viewpoint it conveys. The Supreme Court has called this the "bedrock principle" of our proud free speech tradition under American law. In recent years, the Court has steadfastly enforced this fundamental principle to protect speech that conveys ideas that are deeply unpopular with or offensive to many, if not most, Americans: for example, burning an American flag in a political demonstration against national policies, and burning a cross near the home of an African-American family that had recently moved into a previously all-white neighborhood.

The viewpoint-neutrality principle reflects the philosophy that, as first stated in pathbreaking opinions by former Supreme Court justices Oliver Wendell Holmes and Louis Brandeis, the appropriate response to speech with which one disagrees in a free society is not censorship but counter-speech—*more* speech, not *less*. Persuasion, not coercion, is the solution.

Rejecting this philosophy, the feminist procensorship position targets for suppression a category of sexual expression precisely because of its viewpoint—specifically, a gender-discriminatory viewpoint. Because of this fatal constitutional flaw, all Dworkin-MacKinnon–style antipornography laws will continue to be ruled unconstitutional, as were the two such laws that courts have reviewed to date, as long as our courts continue to enforce the viewpoint-neutrality principle.

The feminist antipornography laws also violate the second cardinal principle that is central to free speech law—that a restriction on speech can be justified only when necessary to prevent actual or imminent harm to an interest of "compelling" importance, such as violence or injury to others. This is often summarized as the "clear and present danger" requirement. As Justice Oliver Wendell Holmes observed in a much-quoted opinion, the First Amendment would not protect someone who falsely shouted "Fire!" in a theater and caused a panic.

This second core free speech principle entails two essential prerequisites for justifying any speech restriction: that the expression will cause direct, imminent harm to a very important interest, and that only by suppressing it can we avert such harm. Each of these requirements is crucial for preserving free expression, and neither is satisfied by advocates of suppressing pornography. . . .

It has become fashionable among some law professors, of whom Catharine MacKinnon is a prominent example, to question the ongoing relevance of classic First Amendment principles, and I certainly endorse and engage in the constant critical reexamination of all established legal principles. Reexamining the landmark Holmes and Brandeis free speech opinions that I have cited has left me more impressed than ever with their universal, timeless force. They remain relevant and persuasive, specifically in the context of the current pornography debate. Further, the majority rulings that these dissents so powerfully criticize stand as sobering reminders of how much freedom we would lose should we accept the procensorship feminists' call to revive the now discredited "bad tendency" approach that these rulings reflect. . . .

Pornography is, again, "designed to cause sexual excitement." Yet the fact that expression arouses feelings and passions does not justify giving it less First Amendment protection than expression that is likely to arouse a more intellectual response. If that were the case, then much literature and art would surely have to join sexually oriented speech as second-class citizens under the First Amendment. But the Supreme Court long has held that the First Amendment extends to all forms of art and entertainment, and has rejected attempts to construe it more narrowly as applying only to ideas or information. Indeed, if all emotion-provoking discourse were relegated to a less protected status, then much political speech—which is at the apex of First Amendment protection—would have to be similarly demoted.

12

Communication and the Capitalist Culture

RONALD K. L. COLLINS
DAVID M. SKOVER

Ronald K. L. Collins is a scholar at the Washington, D.C. office of the First Amendment Center and David M. Skover is a professor at the Seattle University School of Law. Both clerked for appellate court judges and together in the 1990s published a series of provocative law review articles that challenged the broad protection afforded mass commercial communications by the Supreme Court and conventional First Amendment theory. The excerpt here comes from their 1996 book, The Death of Discourse, *and calls into question First Amendment principles for protecting freedom of expression by highlighting the disjunction between First Amendment theory and contemporary trends in mass commercial communications and popular culture.*

ONE NEED NOT master *The Wealth of Nations* or *Das Kapital* to discern that the character of communication in America is largely determined by its capitalistic economic system. The question relevant for an Adam Smith or a Karl Marx—whether the impact of commerce upon communication produces a better or worse society—need not be addressed now. What is more immediately relevant to our inquiry is the question of how the commercial culture of mass advertising affects the key free speech values identified by the Court and commentators.

One thing is absent from most of the learned legal treatments of commercial speech—reality. Few in the law see the need to understand the advertisers' world as the advertisers do. And few see the implications of the *actual* workings of advertising on their visions of free speech. Once seen, the connection of commerce to communication radically alters the views of both the defenders and critics of commercial speech.

Those who champion the role of reason in the marketplace either do not understand the functioning of today's marketplace or do not understand the function of yesterday's reason. The reality of the mass-advertising marketplace is simply

IMAGE IS ALL

Image, not information, is the touchstone of much of our commercial communication. The next time you think of reason-why advertising, look at any popular magazine:

- Liqueur ad with suggestive beach scene: "All over the country, people are enjoying Sex on the Beach."
- Women's blue-jeans ad with Matisse-influenced drawings and Picasso-esque sketches of women: "Woman Combing Hair" and "Woman With Gold Hoops."
- Four-page clothing ad with scenes of a couple hugging and kissing with an American flag waving in the background: "A kiss is still a kiss/The Spirit of Today's Generation."

The flood of such examples from the print and electronic media alike suggests that "the information model has never had much relevance for national consumer product advertising. The explicit function of spectacular image-based . . . advertising is not so much to inform as it is to persuade." . . .

Entire categories of commercial communication are essentially bereft of any real informational content. For cosmetics, fragrances, alcohol, tobacco, clothes, and other products, billions of advertising dollars say much about image and little about information. The mass advertiser all too often strives to create a lifestyle environment with "minimal 'logical' connection with the product." These efforts give new meaning to the Latin root for advertisement: *advertere*—to direct one's mind toward. Indeed, studies indicate that "the depiction of consumers as rational, problem-solving beings is actually a highly limited description of buyer behaviour."

Mass advertisers and their mass consumers have embraced the reality of commercial communication: There is no place for the mind in the marketplace.

Those who rely on the criteria of false and deceptive speech to confine the constitutional boundaries of commercial communication either do not understand the appeal of mass advertising or do not understand its relationship to truth. The reality of the mass-advertising marketplace is simply

TRUTH IS IRRELEVANT

Trained to scrutinize advertisements for accurate informational claims, the public watchdogs (such as the Federal Trade Commission) and their industry counterparts (such as the National Advertising Review Council) have less and less to do in today's imagistic ad world. For example, how would such oversight groups determine the truth or falsity of the following commercial messages?

• Soft-drink commercial depicting a rock singer performing in front of, and mingling with, a teenage audience at a drive-in movie theater: "Don't care about movie stars who live in Hollywood. Don't like their attitude; don't think I ever could. Don't want the good taste, I know what tastes good. Why is the best thing always misunderstood? Just give me what the doctor ordered. Just what the doctor ordered. Hey, give me a [brand named soda]."
• Cigarette ad with a man and two women frolicking in a swimming pool: "Alive with pleasure!"
• Designer-jeans ad with a woman unzipping a man's trousers; opposite page photograph of man raising middle finger of right hand in obscene gesture: [Brand name of product].
• Cologne ad supposedly picturing a father holding his young son: "[Brand name] for Men."

For this and much advertising that is not deliberately and explicitly informational, the dichotomies of truth versus falsity and deceptive versus accurate are purposeless. The hyperbole created by image, personality, and lifestyle advertising cannot be evaluated along the same matrix as empirical claims generally found in product-information advertising. This is what Jules Henry labeled "pecuniary truth," a philosophy contained in three postulates: "Truth is what sells. Truth is what you want people to believe. Truth is that which is not legally false."

In the regime of pecuniary truth, successful advertising techniques use words and images to push expectations beyond their reasonable orbit so that the consumer may yield uncritically to an ad's persuasive force. For example, does anyone really believe that smoking a particular brand of cigarettes will make him or her alive with pleasure? Does anyone really believe that splashing on a specific cologne will more endear a father to his son? Of course we do not literally believe these messages but only act as if they could be true. Developing Henry's argument, Judith Williamson drove home the pointlessness of legal regulation of pecuniary truth: Advertisements are "so uncontrollable, because whatever restrictions are made in terms of their verbal content or 'false claims', there is no way of getting at their use of images and symbols. . . . [I]t is images and not words which ultimately provide the currency in ads."

The honorable Justice Holmes notwithstanding, mass advertisers and their mass consumers are well aware of yet another reality of commercial communication: There is no test of truth in the marketplace.

Those who laud the public's "right" to know either do not understand what it would really mean for the public to *know* or what it would really mean to impose such a right on America's commercial media. The reality of the mass-advertising marketplace is simply

THERE IS NO RIGHT TO KNOW

The right to know is a notion of the public's constitutional guaranty to a full and unfettered measure of information—quantitatively and qualitatively sufficient to promote rational decisionmaking in all matters, political, economic, and otherwise. This right is inextricably tied to both the rationality model of the marketplace of ideas and the political model of participatory governance. In fact, such a right was collaterally touted as a justification for First Amendment freedom in the *Virginia Pharmacy* case, which championed the informational function of commercial expression. For these reasons, the right cannot be honored in a highly commercial culture where image is all, where truth is irrelevant, and where citizen democracy is eclipsed by consumer democracy. This is but another way of saying that the right to know cannot coexist easily with commercial mass advertising.

Those who defend the traditional First Amendment faith in individual autonomy and who therefore oppose the rise of the corporate self and the consumer self either do not understand the relationship between commerce and communication or do not understand the futility of attempts to divorce the two in our capitalistic system. The reality of the mass-advertising marketplace is simply

WE ARE AS WE CONSUME

"The business of America is business," said "Silent Cal" Coolidge. This axiom holds as true in our culture generally as it does in our economy. That is, America's highly advanced capitalism thrives on the union of the economic marketplace with the marketplace of ideas. Our identity as Americans is a combination of *citizen self* and *consumer self*. This identity is molded by communication filled with the symbols of commerce. In today's America, it is ever more difficult to detect any form of public expression, including religious speech, that can remain altogether free of commercial taint. Even "noncommercial" public television and radio are becoming increasingly sponsor-dependent. Ultimately, it is impossible to disentangle commerce from communication and preserve America as we know it. . . .

From a First Amendment definitional standpoint, it is increasingly difficult to demarcate the realms of the commercial from those of the political and cultural, to distinguish commercial expression from the most preferred forms of democratic speech. For example, is a cigarette company's campaign to celebrate the Bill of Rights a commercial or political venture? Is an alcohol company's campaign to publicize the dangers of drinking and driving a commercial or humanistic measure? Is a shopping mall association's campaign to "honor" our soldiers in the Gulf War a commercial or a patriotic gesture? Is a clothing company's campaign to "end racism and the killing of people in the streets" a commercial or a social message? Is such advertising a mercenary form of the "fighting faith" of the First Amendment? . . .

Those who equate commercial speech with political dissent either underestimate or overestimate the subversive force of dissent. The reality of the mass-advertising marketplace is simply

THERE IS NO ABSOLUT®
RIGHT TO DISSENT

In our consumerist popular culture, virtually no form of dissent is forbidden. In fact, dissent is typically encouraged. Young and old alike are invited to reveal their rebel stripes by donning a James Dean, John Wesley Harding, or Axl Rose T-shirt. For the more radical, Malcolm X baseball caps are commercially available. Rappers, punks, and Mapplethorpe types all may, to paraphrase Shakespeare, strut and fret their hour upon the stage of pop life and then be seen and heard no more. Skinheads and Manson-family members, too, are in demand on the tabloid and TV talk-show circuit. And the big tent certainly has room enough for the opposite—the likes of the National Federation of Decency, Morality in Media, and the American Family Association—so long as they do not lock arms with Senator Jesse Helms (R.–N.C.) to legislate morality. All messages are created equal, since almost all can be adapted to suit the commercial culture, where truth and untruth, morality and immorality, tumble together. What cannot be tolerated by the gatekeepers of commerce, however, is dissent that poses a clear and present danger to the capitalist culture and its economy. Of course, far-reaching expression on the fringe—for example, Andres Serrano's *Piss Christ*—may temporarily be sacrificed in order to appease lawmakers. *Culture-jamming*, by contrast, is one form of dissent that the captains of commerce are not likely to countenance. But what kind of dissent is this?

- An advertising photo of a riderless horse grazing in a snow-covered graveyard, with the caption "Marlboro Country."
- An advertising photo of a bedraggled, middle-aged woman sitting at the breakfast table, holding a cigarette and a glass of vodka, with the caption "Every morning's a Smirnoff morning."
- A television commercial showing an innocent-looking youngster with a fixed stare, as the voice-over announces: "Kathy is eight, and she's addicted . . . it changes the way she talks . . . the way she acts . . . the way she thinks. She is addicted . . . to television."

Culture-jamming, the method common to these examples, is a subversive practice designed to expropriate and sabotage the meaning of commercial messages. Typically, culture-jamming aims for autocannibalization: Commercials or advertisements devour themselves. Just as the entertainment-consumption complex filched America's most cherished images, language, and values, so the culture jammers now use the same tactics to obstruct that complex. These pop culture dissidents "draw upon the given facts of our society, this cacophony of fragmentary media images, to describe things as they are." . . .

The same Justice Holmes who laid the foundation for the marketplace-of-ideas metaphor in the era of the syndicalists was also the one who warned laissez-faire capitalists that "a constitution is not intended to embody a particular economic theory." Holmes did not foresee, however, a world where the metaphor would override the warning. He did not imagine a nation where the symbol of the marketplace of ideas would itself become the handmaiden of commerce. Just as "[l]ate nineteenth- and twentieth-century financial and industrial moguls went to sleep at night secure in the knowledge that their world turned on the principles of economic laissez-faire," so late twentieth-century advertisers sleep soundly believing that commercial communication is generally safe in the free speech marketplace.

If commercial communication is safe, it is not because it *actually* furthers the First Amendment's traditional values of rational decisionmaking and self-realization. Rather, it is because it has effectively co-opted the marketplace metaphor. Meanwhile, the defenders of commercial speech both on and off the Court have ignored the difference between today's commercial expression and the noble purposes of the First Amendment. If they were to be frank, they would concede that the real reason for constitutional protection of modern mass advertising is less ennobling: It is speech in the service of selling.

PART FOUR

Freedom of Religion

AMENDMENT *1*
Congress shall make no law
respecting an establishment of religion,
or prohibiting the free exercise thereof . . .

13

Habits of the Heart

ROBERT N. BELLAH AND OTHERS

Borrowing Alexis de Tocqueville's phrase "habits of the heart," Robert N. Bellah, a sociologist at the University of California, Berkeley, and his associates — Richard Madsen, William M. Sullivan, Ann Swidler, and Steven M. Tipton — studied individualism and commitment in American life and produced a highly acclaimed book, Habits of the Heart *(1985). In the excerpt here, Bellah and his colleagues concede the importance of individualism and religious pluralism, but contend that throughout history, Americans have found fulfillment in religious communities that unify, rather than divide.*

———

RELIGION IS ONE of the most important of the many ways in which Americans "get involved" in the life of their community and society. Americans give more money and donate more time to religious bodies and religiously associated organizations than to all other voluntary associations put together. . . . Though Americans overwhelmingly accept the doctrine of the separation of church and state, most of them believe, as they always have, that religion has an important role to play in the public realm. But as with every other major institution, the place of religion in our society has changed dramatically over time.

Religion in American History

America itself had religious meaning to the colonists from the very beginning. The conjunction of the Protestant Reformation and the discovery and settlement of a new world made a profound impression on the early colonists. They saw their task of settlement as God-given: an "errand into the wilderness," an experiment in Christian living, the founding of a "city upon the hill." Many early settlers were refugees from persecution in England. They sought religious freedom, not as we would conceive of it today, but rather to escape from a religious establishment with which they disagreed in order to found a new established church. They were seeking religious uniformity, not religious diversity. Of course there were some, even in the seventeenth century, who had ideas of

religious freedom that we would more readily recognize, and down
through the centuries, America has been a "promised land" to immigrants
in part because it has allowed them to practice their religion in their own
way. But religion had been part of the public order for too long in the
history of the West for the colonists quickly or easily to give up the idea
of an established church.

Indeed, a pattern of establishment characterized most of the American
colonies throughout their history. There was one publicly supported
church even when others were tolerated. In some states, establishment
continued even after the Revolution (the First Amendment only forbade
establishment at the federal level), and it was not until 1833 that Massachusetts gave up the last vestiges of establishment. Once religion is disestab-
lished, it tends to become part of the "private sphere," and privatization
is part of the story of American religion. Yet religion, and certainly biblical
religion, is concerned with the whole of life — with social, economic,
and political matters as well as with private and personal ones. Not only
has biblical language continued to be part of American public and political
discourse, the churches have continuously exerted influence on public
life right up to the present time.

In colonial New England, the roles of Christian and citizen, though
not fused, were very closely linked. The minister was a public officer,
chosen by the town and not only by church members. Even when dissent
gradually came to be tolerated, the established Congregational church
was the focus of community life and its unifying institution. Sermons
were preached annually on election day. What has been called New
England "communalism" valued order, harmony, and obedience to authority, and these values centered on the figure of the "settled minister." Such
a minister was "both the keeper and purveyor of the public culture, the
body of fundamental precepts and values that defined the social community,
and an enforcer of the personal values and decorum that sustained it."

Today religion in America is as private and diverse as New England
colonial religion was public and unified. One person we interviewed has
actually named her religion (she calls it her "faith") after herself. . . .

It was undoubtedly pressure from the dissenting sects, with their large
popular following, on the one hand, and from that significant portion of
the educated and politically effective elite influenced by Enlightenment
thought on the other, that finally led to the disestablishment of religion
in the United States. Yet the full implications of disestablishment were
not felt immediately. In the early decades of the republic, American society,
particularly in small towns, remained stable and hierarchical, and religion
continued to play its unifying public role. George Washington, whatever

his private beliefs, was a pillar of the Episcopal church. He was a frequent
attender and long served as a vestryman, though he was never observed
to receive communion. It was religion as part of the public order that he
was thinking of when, in his Farewell Address, he called "religion and
morality" the "indispensable supports [of] political prosperity." He
doubted that "morality can be maintained without religion" and suggested
that these two are the "great pillars of public happiness" and the "firmest
props of the duties of men and citizens."

By the early decades of the nineteenth century, the older communal
and hierarchical society was rapidly giving way in the face of increasing
economic and political competition, and religious change accompanied
social change. Even in the longer-settled areas, ministers could no longer
count on the deference due to them as part of a natural elite, while in
the newer and rapidly growing western states no such hierarchical society
had ever existed. With rapid increase in the numbers of Baptists and
Methodists, religious diversity became more pronounced than ever. By
the 1850s, a new pattern of religious life had emerged, significantly
privatized relative to the colonial period, but still with important public
functions.

. . . The mid-nineteenth-century town, though considerably more
consensual than the suburban town today, was nonetheless very different
from the colonial township. No longer unified religiously and politically
around a natural elite of "the wise and the good," it was much more
publicly egalitarian. For religion to have emphasized the public order in
the old sense of deference and obedience to external authorities would
no longer have made sense. Religion did not cease to be concerned with
moral order, but it operated with a new emphasis on the individual and
the voluntary association. Moral teaching came to emphasize self-control
rather than deference. It prepared the individual to maintain self-respect
and establish ethical commitments in a dangerous and competitive world,
not to fit into the stable harmony of an organic community. Religious
membership was no longer unified. Even in the smaller communities, it
had become highly segmented.

The unity that the old township had sought was now seen as a
property of the segmented church community, and so in important respects
privatized. Together with segmentation came a sharper distinction between spheres. The religious and secular realms that had appeared so closely
intertwined in colonial America were now more sharply distinguished.
Churches, no longer made up of the whole community but only of the
like-minded, became not so much pillars of public order as "protected
and withdrawn islands of piety." Sermons turned more "to Christ's love

than to God's command." They became less doctrinal and more emotional and sentimental. By the middle of the nineteenth century the "feminization" of American religion that Ann Douglas has described was fully evident. Religion, like the family, was a place of love and acceptance in an otherwise harsh and competitive society.

It was largely this new, segmented and privatized religion that Tocqueville observed in the 1830s. If Washington's analysis of religion was nostalgic for the old hierarchical society, Tocqueville's analysis recognized its value in the new individualistic one. Tocqueville saw religion primarily as a powerful influence on individual character and action. He suggested that the economic and political flux and volatility of American society was counterbalanced by the fact that "everything in the moral field is certain and fixed" because "Christianity reigns without obstacles, by universal consent." Tocqueville was fully aware of and applauded the separation of church and state, and yet, while recognizing that religion "never intervenes directly in the government of American society," he nevertheless considered it "the first of their political institutions." Its political function was not direct intervention but support of the mores that make democracy possible. In particular, it had the role of placing limits on utilitarian individualism, hedging in self-interest with a proper concern for others. The "main business" of religion, Tocqueville said, "is to purify, control, and restrain that excessive and exclusive taste for well-being" so common among Americans.

Tocqueville saw religion as reinforcing self-control and maintaining moral standards but also as an expression of the benevolence and self-sacrifice that are antithetical to competitive individualism. He said that Christianity teaches "that we must do good to our fellows for love of God. That is a sublime utterance: man's mind filled with understanding of God's thought; he sees that order is God's plan, in freedom labors for this great design, ever sacrificing his private interests for this wondrous ordering of all that is, and expecting no other reward than the joy of contemplating it." Here Tocqueville expressed the hope that the destructiveness of utilitarian individualism could be countered with a generalized benevolence, rooted in sublime emotions "embedded in nature," that is, in an expressive individualism. His generalized analysis of religion kept him from noticing within some of the religious traditions those "second languages" that we have argued provide better alternatives to utilitarian individualism than expressive individualism alone can do. But with respect to second languages, Tocqueville offers us little guidance. He is better at posing the problem of individualism and showing us where to look for alternatives than at close analysis of the alternatives themselves.

American religion has always had a rich treasury of second languages in the Bible itself and the lived traditions descending from it. Yet the relegation of religion to the private sphere after disestablishment tended to replace the specificity of those second languages with a vague and generalized benevolence. Privatization placed religion, together with the family, in a compartmentalized sphere that provided loving support but could no longer challenge the dominance of utilitarian values in the society at large. Indeed, to the extent that privatization succeeded, religion was in danger of becoming, like the family, "a haven in a heartless world," but one that did more to reinforce that world, by caring for its casualties, than to challenge its assumptions. In this respect, religion was a precursor of therapy in a utilitarian managerial society.

Yet therapeutic privatization, the shift from casuistry to counseling, was not the whole story. In the very period in which the local church was becoming a "protected and withdrawn island," evangelical Protestantism was spawning an array of institutions and organizations that would have a major impact on public life. The early nineteenth century saw a great expansion in the numbers of the Protestant clergy as many new functions besides the parish ministry opened up. New educational institutions, both colleges and divinity schools, were central to this wave of expansive influence. The clergyman as professor exerted influence not only in the classroom but on the lecture circuit and in periodicals and books. Numerous societies were established to distribute bibles and tracts, carry on missionary activities at home and abroad, work for temperance and Sabbath observance, and combat slavery. All of these raised money, hired functionaries, issued publications, and spoke to a national audience about the public meaning of Christian ideals. After bitter dissension over the issues of temperance and slavery early in the nineteenth century, most local congregations opted for unity and harmony, either excluding those who differed or suppressing controversial issues. But this was not just privatization; it also involved a division of labor. Through societies and voluntary associations, the Christian clergy and laity could bring their concerns about temperance and slavery, or whatever, to the attention of their fellow citizens without disturbing the warm intimacy and loving harmony of the local congregation.

Nor did the churches have a monopoly over religious language in the nineteenth century any more than in the eighteenth. Abraham Lincoln was known to be skeptical of church religion, yet he found in biblical language a way to express the most profound moral vision in nineteenth-century America. He articulated both the moral justification for emancipation and the grounds for reconciliation with unrivaled profundity in prose that drew not only from biblical symbols but from the rhythms of the Authorized Version. In his writings, we can see that biblical language is both insistently public and politically demanding in its implications.

Religious Pluralism

The American pattern of privatizing religion while at the same time allowing it some public functions has proven highly compatible with the religious pluralism that has characterized America from the colonial period and grown more and more pronounced. If the primary contribution of religion to society is through the character and conduct of citizens, any religion, large or small, familiar or strange, can be of equal value to any other. The fact that most American religions have been biblical and that most, though of course not all, Americans can agree on the term "God" has certainly been helpful in diminishing religious antagonism. But diversity of practice has been seen as legitimate because religion is perceived as a matter of individual choice, with the implicit qualification that the practices themselves accord with public decorum and the adherents abide by the moral standards of the community.

Under American conditions, religious pluralism has not produced a purely random assortment of religious bodies. Certain fairly determinate principles of differentiation — ethnic, regional, class — have operated to produce an intelligible pattern of social differentiation among religious groups, even though there remains much fluidity. Most American communities contain a variety of churches, and the larger the community the greater the variety. In smaller towns and older suburbs, church buildings draw significant public attention. They cluster around the town square or impressively punctuate the main streets. Local residents know very well who belongs where: the Irish and Italians go to the Catholic church and the small businessman to the Methodist church, whereas the local elite belong to the Presbyterian and, even more likely, Episcopal churches. . . .

The Local Congregation

We may begin a closer examination of how religion operates in the lives of those to whom we talked by looking at the local congregation, which traditionally has a certain priority. The local church is a community of worship that contains within itself, in small, so to speak, the features of the larger church, and in some Protestant traditions can exist autonomously. The church as a community of worship is an adaptation of the Jewish synagogue. Both Jews and Christians view their communities as existing in a covenant relationship with God, and the Sabbath worship around which religious life centers is a celebration of that covenant. Worship calls to mind the story of the relationship of the community with God: how God brought his chosen people out of Egypt or gave his only begotten son for the salvation of mankind. Worship also reiterates the obligations that the community has undertaken, including the biblical insistence on justice and righteousness, and on love of God and neighbor, as well as the promises God has made that make it possible for the community to hope for the future. Though worship has its special times and places, especially on the Sabbath in the house of the Lord, it functions as a model or pattern for the whole of life. Through reminding the people of their relationship to God, it establishes patterns of character and virtue that should operate in economic and political life as well as in the context of worship. The community maintains itself as a community of memory, and the various religious traditions have somewhat different memories.

The very freedom, openness, and pluralism of American religious life makes this traditional pattern hard for Americans to understand. For one thing, the traditional pattern assumes a certain priority of the religious community over the individual. The community exists before the individual is born and will continue after his or her death. The relationship of the individual to God is ultimately personal, but it is mediated by the whole pattern of community life. There is a givenness about the community and the tradition. They are not normally a matter of individual choice. . . .

The Religious Center

For a long time what have been called the "mainline" Protestant churches have tried to do more than this. They have offered a conception of God as neither wholly other nor a higher self, but rather as involved in time and history. These churches have tried to develop a larger picture of what it might mean to live a biblical life in America. They have sought to be communities of memory, to keep in touch with biblical sources and historical traditions not with literalist obedience but through an intelligent reappropriation illuminated by historical and theological reflection. They have tried to relate biblical faith and practice to the whole of contemporary life — cultural, social, political, economic — not just to personal and family morality. They have tried to steer a middle course between mystical fusion with the world and sectarian withdrawal from it.

Through the nineteenth century and well into the twentieth, the mainline churches were close to the center of American culture. The religious intellectuals who spoke for these churches often articulated issues in ways widely influential in the society as a whole. But for a generation or more, the religious intellectuals deriving from the mainline Protestant churches have become more isolated from the general culture. This is in part because they, like other scholars, have become specialists in fields where only specialists speak to one another. Their isolation also derives in part from the long pressure to segregate our knowledge of what is, gained through science, from our knowledge of what ought to be, gained through religion, morality and art. Finally, the religious intellectuals have themselves lost self-confidence and become vulnerable to short-lived fads. For some years now, they have failed to produce a [Paul] Tillich or [Reinhold] Niebuhr who might become the center of fruitful controversy and discussion. Without the leavening of a creative intellectual focus, the quasi-therapeutic blandness that has afflicted much of mainline Protestant religion at the parish level for over a century cannot effectively withstand the competition of the more vigorous forms of radical religious individualism, with their claims of dramatic self-realization, or the resurgent religious conservatism that spells out clear, if simple, answers in an increasingly bewildering world.

But just when the mainline Protestant hold on American culture seemed decisively weakened, the Roman Catholic church after Vatican II entered a much more active phase of national participation. Though never without influence in American society, the Catholic church had long been more concerned with the welfare of its own members, many of them immigrants, than with moulding the national society. The period 1930–60 was a kind of culmination of a long process of institution building and self-help. The church, still a minority, but long the largest single denomination, grew in confidence as the majority of its constituents attained middle-class respectability. An educated and thoughtful laity was thus ready to respond to the new challenges the Second Vatican Council opened up in the early 1960s. The unprecedented ecumenical cooperation that brought Catholics together with Protestants and Jews in a number of joint endeavors from the period of the Civil Rights movement to the present has created a new atmosphere in American religious life. With the American Catholic bishops' pastoral letter of May 3, 1983, on nuclear warfare, the promise of Vatican II began to be fulfilled. The Catholic church moved toward the center of American public life, invigorating the major Protestant denominations as it did so.

Recently Martin Marty, in the light of this new situation, has attempted to describe the religious center as what he calls "the public church." The public church, in Marty's sense, includes the old mainline Protestant churches, the Catholic church, and significant sectors of the evangelical churches. It is not a homogeneous entity but rather a "communion of communions" in which each church maintains the integrity of its own traditions and practices even while recognizing common ground with the others. Without dissolving its Christian particularity, the public church welcomes the opportunity for conversation, and on occasion joint action, with its Jewish, other non-Christian, and secular counterparts, particularly where matters of the common good are concerned. The public church is not triumphalist—indeed it emerges in a situation where Christians feel less in control of their culture than ever before—but it wishes to respond to the new situation with public responsibility rather than with individual or group withdrawal. The public church and its counterparts in the non-Christian religions offer the major alternative in our culture to radical religious individualism on the one hand and what Marty calls "religious tribalism" on the other.

. . . Time and again in our history, spiritually motivated individuals and groups have felt called to show forth in their lives the faith that was in them by taking a stand on the great ethical and political issues of the day. During the Revolution, the parish clergy gave ideological support and moral encouragement to the republican cause. Christian clergy and laity were among the most fervent supporters of the antislavery cause, just as Christians involved in the Social Gospel movement and its many ramifications did much to ameliorate the worst excesses of early industrial capitalism. Of course, the churches produced opponents of all these movements—the American religious community has never spoken with one voice. On occasion, a significant part of the religious community has mounted a successful crusade that the nation as a whole later came to feel was unwise—for example, the Temperance movement that led to a constitutional amendment prohibiting the sale of alcoholic beverages in the United States. But without the intervention of the churches, many significant issues would have been ignored and needed changes would have come about much more slowly.

To remind us of what is possible, we may call to mind one of the most significant social movements of recent times, a movement overwhelmingly religious in its leadership that changed the nature of American society. Under the leadership of Martin Luther King, Jr., the Civil Rights movement called upon Americans to transform their social and economic institutions with the goal of building a just national community that would respect both the differences and the interdependence of its members. It did this by combining biblical and republican themes in a way that included, but transformed, the culture of individualism.

Consider King's "I Have a Dream" speech. Juxtaposing the poetry of the scriptural prophets — "I have a dream that every valley shall be exalted, every hill and mountain shall be made low" — with the lyrics of patriotic anthems — "This will be the day when all of God's children will be able to sing with new meaning, 'My country 'tis of thee, sweet land of liberty, of thee I sing'" — King's oration reappropriated that classic strand of the American tradition that understands the true meaning of freedom to lie in the affirmation of responsibility for uniting all of the diverse members of society into a just social order. "When we let freedom ring, when we let it ring from every village and hamlet, from every state and every city, we will be able to speed up the day when all of God's children, black men and white men, Jews and Gentiles, Protestants and Catholics, will be able to join hands and sing the words of that old Negro spiritual. 'Free at last! Free at last! Thank God almighty, we are free at last!'" For King, the struggle for freedom became a practice of commitment within a vision of America as a community of memory. We now need to look at that national community, our changing conceptions of it, and what its prospects are.

14

Culture Wars: The Struggle to Define America

JAMES DAVIDSON HUNTER

James Davidson Hunter is a Professor of Sociological and Religious Studies at the University of Virginia and author of Evangelicalism: The Coming Generation *(1987). The excerpt here is from his 1991 book* Culture Wars: The Struggle to Define America, *in which Hunter argues that there is a growing cultural war in the United States. New alliances among old and new religious organizations, according to Hunter, are producing increasing political battles over the family, art, education, and the law.*

———

[A] "CULTURE WAR" in America? The very thought or possibility of a deeply rooted and historically pivotal cultural conflict in America strains our imagination.

Our difficulty in coming to terms with the idea of such a conflict in contemporary America arises largely from the absence of conceptual categories or analytical tools for understanding cultural conflict. We simply lack ways of thinking about the subject. The predominant images of contemporary cultural conflict focus on religious and cultural hostilities played out in other parts of the world: the suppression of the Kurds in Iraq; the struggle of Sikh nationalists to establish their own homeland in northwest India; the political offensive of Gush Emunim, the political organ of Jewish fundamentalism in Israel, in its efforts to maintain the purity of orthodoxy in a pluralistic society; and the continuing hostilities between the Hindu Tamil minority and the Sinhalese Buddhist majority in northern Sri Lanka. As vivid and arresting as these images may be, they are foreign to the everyday experience of most Americans, distant from us both spatially and culturally. Thus, few Americans can relate personally, much less passionately, to the interests and concerns these images represent.

These images should not be seen as so remote, however, for they can provide metaphors for our thinking about religious and cultural conflict in our country. Of course, the particular cast of cultural players on the American scene is different from those found in other countries. Likewise, the character of the actual cultural conflict played out in the United States is very distinctive. Nevertheless, the story underlying cultural conflict in numerous places throughout the world—a story about the struggle for power—resonates with narratives found in America's not-so-distant past. An understanding of that past is essential for coming to terms with the unfolding conflict of the present.

Cultural Conflict: The American Story

The memory need only be prodded lightly to recall that Protestant hostility toward Catholicism (and, to a far lesser extent, Catholic resentment of Protestantism) provides one of the dominant motifs of early modern American history. Understanding the American experience even as late as the nineteenth century requires an understanding of the critical role played by anti-Catholicism in shaping the character of politics, public education, the media, and social reform.

Of course, the mutual hostility of Protestants and Catholics had been implacable since the time of the Reformation and Counter-Reformation in the sixteenth century. For their rejection of church tradition and ecclesiastical authority, Protestants were regarded by Catholics as infidels who had abandoned the true faith; for their elevation of "arcane rituals" to the status of scriptural truth and for their elevation of papal authority to the status of the authority of Christ, Catholics were regarded by Protestants as heretics who had perverted the true faith.

Needless to say, these tensions were not only religious or theological in nature. Indeed, the split between Catholics and Protestants during the Reformation generated one of the most enduring and consequential *political* divisions in Western experience. More than a century (between 1559 and 1689) of religious warfare within and among the nations of Western Europe can be attributed to these interreligious hostilities. And even after the age of religious wars had formally come to an end, the political tensions between these religious and cultural traditions continued to affect the institutional fabric of Western life. Prejudice, discrimination, and even physical violence were commonplace for the Protestant minorities in southern Europe (France, Spain, Italy, and Portugal) and the Catholic minorities in the north (Britain, Germany, Holland, and Scandinavia).

America, of course, was colonized primarily by emigrating European Protestants of one stripe or another. It is not surprising, then, that anti-Catholic sentiment emigrated to American shores as well, and became woven into the unofficial political and cultural traditions of the colonists.

In fact, anti-Catholicism in America reached something of an apex in the nineteenth century. For one, many of the major urban daily newspapers displayed a prominent anti-Catholic prejudice: the *Chicago Tribune*, for example, played a significant role in inciting anti-Catholic agitation through the 1840s and 1850s. There was also an enormous literature exclusively devoted to discrediting the Catholic presence. Between 1800 and 1860, American editors published at least 25 daily, weekly, or bi-monthly newspapers and 13 monthly or quarterly magazines opposing Catholicism, while American publishing houses published more than 200 anti-Catholic books. The most titillating and popular of this literature presented accounts of priests and nuns who had abandoned their faith because of their experiences of torture, mental brutality, and even sexual offense. One of the first and certainly the most famous of these accounts, Maria Monk's *Awful Disclosures of the Hotel Dieu Convent: The Secrets of Black Nunnery Revealed* (1836), sold over 300,000 copies. . . .

Anti-Catholicism also ignited the great school wars of the mid–nine-teenth century, visible in Philadelphia and Boston but particularly in New York, due to the outspoken views of John Hughes, an Irishman and the presiding bishop in that city. Because skills, values, and habits of life are passed on to children in school, it was inevitable that the schools would be an arena of cultural conflict, where the majority would assert its power and minority cultures would struggle to maintain a voice. Despite advocates' claims that the common schools of New York were nonsectarian, the Public School Society of New York retained textbooks that contained numerous overt anti-Irish and anti-Catholic statements. They also maintained the practice of a daily reading and recitation of the (Protestant) King James version of the Bible. When the Public School Society refused to accommodate Catholic interests either by allowing Catholic religious instruction after hours or by providing public funds to be used for the establishment of public schools of a Catholic nature, the Catholic community suffered.

Yet perhaps the most vociferous expressions of anti-Catholicism came from anti-Catholic societies (such as the American Protestant Association, the Christian Alliance, the American and Foreign Christian Union, the American Protective Association, and American Alliance) and anti-Catholic political parties (such as the Native American parties of the 1840s, the Know-Nothing party of the 1850s, and the Republican party of the 1850s and 1860s). Importantly, these organizations were most successful in precisely the states where Catholics were most numerous Thus, they became significant not only for organizing and voicing both popular and elite resentment against Catholics but for mobilizing electoral opinion against the interests of a rapidly expanding Catholic community that remained both severely disadvantaged and largely powerless.

But Catholics are not the only religious minority that has endured hardship in America. The memory only needs to be prodded a bit further to recall the ways in which interreligious hostility has extended to Judaism. Christianity has long held Jews in the ambivalent status of being both God's chosen people, who had been miraculously sustained throughout the generations, and an unfaithful people who suffered deservedly for their betrayal of the Messiah. This was no less true for the Evangelical pietism that prevailed through the nineteenth century. In America, the remnants of Puritan culture retained a deep sympathy with the "People of the Book" and an identification with the Old Testament imagery of a people "in covenant with God." Still, in their view, the sufferings of the diaspora were the just punishments of a vengeful God for a people who had rebelled against His purposes.

Yet while the religious component was never absent, the secular and specifically economic behavior of Jews received the most vicious exploitation in stereotypes. Jews were portrayed as crude, aggressively greedy Shylocks whose conduct in business was always opportunistic and very often unscrupulous. Jews were the pawnbrokers, petty white-collar criminals, and merchants of the big cities, perennially in pursuit of the bargain and conspicuous in their display of new wealth. Such was the imagery presented in popular dramas featuring Jews (like Melter Moss in *The Ticket-of-Leave Man* [1864], Mo Davis in *Flying Scud* [1867], Dicey Morris in *After Dark* [1868], and Mordie Solomons in *The Lottery of Life* [1867]). Popular novels of the period echoed the theme; at least three of Horatio Alger's stories, for example, contain Jews of this cast as minor characters. The portrait was reinforced throughout dozens of inexpensive and sensationalized dime novels written at the end of the century. Herman Stoll, the unscrupulous German-Jewish Wall Street broker in Albert Aiken's *The White Witch* (1871) and the shady operator Aaron Mosenstein in Aiken's *Dick Talbot and the Ranch King* (1892) are just two examples. Jews were similarly stereotyped in the works of Gilbert Jerome, Prentiss Ingraham, H. P. Halsy, and J. R. Coryell, the author of the popular Nick Carter stories.

Despite the vulgar stereotyping and the popular concern about the "Hebrew conquest of the financial centers of New York," anti-Semitism was never greatly politicized in the way that anti-Catholicism had been. Jews never appeared to present a cultural or demographic threat equivalent to that posed by the Catholics. Nevertheless, various forms of anti-Jewish discrimination did characterize the last two decades of the nineteenth century and the first three decades of the twentieth in particular. For one, quotas limited the admission of Jews to private schools, colleges, and medical schools as late as the 1920s. As an upwardly mobile Jewish population began to migrate out of its ethnic and religious enclaves, restrictive covenants were placed in the deeds of homes, allowing real estate agents to refuse to rent apartments to Jews, and landlords to hang "To Let" signs with the addendum "No Jews." These practices extended to membership in social clubs and to the enjoyment of summer and weekend resorts. At Saratoga, Manhattan Beach, and Coney Island, in the Catskills and other resorts throughout New York and New Jersey, placards were raised that stated, "No Jews or Dogs Admitted Here." In retaliation, Jews purchased several prestigious hotels in most of the resort towns and formed their own elite clubs in New York, Baltimore, Rochester, Detroit, and other major cities. In sum, the discrimination faced by Jews in the last decades of the nineteenth century and the first decades of the twentieth, while in many ways different from that experienced by the mainly Irish Catholics, was no less hostile. The net effect was to exclude and control.

Less visible motifs of cultural conflict in American history include hostility toward Mormons. From the founding of the Mormon Church in 1830, Mormons were subject to harassment and persecution. The governor of Missouri stated in 1838, "The Mormons must be treated as enemies and must be exterminated or driven from the state, if necessary, for the public good." And in several states, mainly in the South, they were. Joseph Smith and his brother were jailed and then killed by a mob in Illinois in 1844; four Mormon missionaries were killed by a mob in Cane Creek, Tennessee, in 1884: and numerous others became victims of murder, beatings, tar-and-featherings, and other acts of violence.

In all of these instances cultural tension arose not simply from academic disagreement over the proper form of ecclesiastical structures or a theoretical argument over doctrinal truths. Rather, America's uneasy pluralism implied a confrontation of a deeper nature—a competition to define social reality. Through the nineteenth and early twentieth century cultural discord was kindled, in general, by two competing tendencies. On one hand, there was the quest on the part of various minority cultures to carve out a space in American life where they could each live according to the imperatives of conscience and the obligations of community without harassment or reprisal. Such a space would provide the base from which to expand their own legitimate interests as a distinct moral community. On the other hand, there was the endeavor of Protestants and a largely Protestant-based populism to ward off any challenges—to retain their advantage in defining the habits and meaning of American culture.

The End of an Age?

The conflicts involving Protestants, Catholics, Jews, and Mormons are indeed a prominent part of the American heritage, and yet even these experiences are largely removed from contemporary American experience. The reason for this is that all signs would seem to point to a growing sense of tolerance among Protestants, Catholics, and Jews (as well as Mormons and others too).

One series of national surveys conducted between 1966 and 1984, for example, showed that strong prejudicial feeling both for and against different religious faiths declined. Neutrality (or what may actually be mutual indifference) among Catholics, Protestants, and Jews generally increased while antipathy toward various groups declined. Another general indication of growing interreligious tolerance is found in the answers to questions about the suitability of presidential candidates who personally identify with one or another religious tradition. In 1958 one of every four Americans (25 percent) claimed to be opposed to a nominee who was Catholic, but by 1987 that number had decreased to only 8 percent. Likewise, in 1958, 28 percent said that they would not vote for a candidate who was Jewish. By 1987, this figure had dropped to only 10 percent.

The research on anti-Semitism in post-World War II America points in the same direction. Once again, the trends point to a rapid *decrease* in the proportion of the population holding negative perceptions of Jews. For example, non-Jews are now far less likely to believe that Jews "have a lot of irritating faults," or are "unscrupulous," or "more willing than others to use shady practices to get what they want," that they "always like to be at the head of things," or that they are "objectionable neighbors." Non-Jews are also now far less likely to believe that Jews "have too much power," that they "don't care what happens to anyone but their own kind," and that they "are more loyal to Israel than to America."

Even among white Evangelical Protestants, the sector of the population that has historically been most hostile to Jews, anti-Semitic feeling is quite low. According to one survey conducted in 1986 for the Anti-Defamation League of B'nai B'rith, there is no longer any "strong direct evidence" to suggest that "most Evangelical Christians consciously use their deeply held Christian faith and convictions as justification for anti-Semitic views of Jews." Indeed, 90 percent of the Evangelicals disagreed with the statement that "Christians are justified in holding negative attitudes toward Jews since the Jews killed Christ," and less than one in ten agreed that "God doesn't hear the prayer of a Jew." . . .

The expansion of cultural tolerance, it is important to point out, is not an isolated event. It coincides with the slow but steady expansion of political and ideological tolerance (such as tolerance of communists and atheists), racial tolerance (of blacks and Hispanics), and sexual tolerance (of homosexuals and those cohabitating outside of marriage). . . .

The evidence just reviewed provides still another compelling explanation of why the very idea of cultural conflict in contemporary America is so implausible to most Americans. When we look all around the social and political landscape, we see a general harmony among the traditional faiths of the United States; by and large, Protestants get along well with Catholics, Christians get along better with Jews, and even the small number of religious cults are more of a curiosity than a source of widespread resentment and antagonism. If one can argue anything on the basis of scholarly study, it is that the predictions of the Enlightenment age are coming true after all.

But are they? Is the age of cultural and, in particular, religious conflict in America coming to a close?

The answer must be no. The reason is that cultural conflict is taking shape along new and in many ways unfamiliar lines.

New Lines of Conflict: The Argument in Brief

Let me begin to make sense of the new lines of cultural warfare by first defining what I mean by "cultural conflict." I define cultural conflict very simply as political and social hostility rooted in different systems of moral understanding. The end to which these hostilities tend is the domination of one cultural and moral ethos over all others. Let it be clear, the principles and ideals that mark these competing systems of moral understanding are by no means trifling but always have a character of ultimacy to them. They are not merely attitudes that can change on a whim but basic commitments and beliefs that provide a source of identity, purpose, and togetherness for the people who live by them. It is for precisely this reason that political action rooted in these principles and ideals tends to be so passionate.

So what is new about the contemporary cultural conflict? As we have seen, the cultural hostilities dominant over the better part of American history have taken place *within* the boundaries of a larger biblical culture — among numerous Protestant groups, and Catholics and Jews — over such issues as doctrine, ritual observance, and religious organization. Underlying their disagreements, therefore, were basic agreements about the order of life in community and nation — agreements forged by biblical symbols and imagery. But the old arrangements have been transformed. . . . The older agreements have unraveled. The divisions of political consequence today are not theological and ecclesiastical in character but the result of differing worldviews. That is to say, they no longer revolve around specific doctrinal issues or styles of religious practice and organization but around our most fundamental and cherished assumptions about how to order our lives—our own lives and our lives together in this society. Our most fundamental ideas about who we are as Americans are now at odds.

Because this is a culture war, the nub of political disagreement today on the range of issues debated—whether abortion, child care, funding for the arts, affirmative action and quotas, gay rights, values in public education, or multiculturalism—can be traced ultimately and finally to the matter of moral authority. By moral authority I mean the basis by which people determine whether something is good or bad, right or wrong, acceptable or unacceptable, and so on. Of course, people often have very different ideas about what criteria to use in making moral judgments, but this is just the point. It is the commitment to different and opposing bases of moral authority and the world views that derive from them that creates the deep cleavages between antagonists in the contemporary culture war. As we will see, this cleavage is so deep that it cuts *across* the old lines of conflict, making the distinctions that long divided Americans—those between Protestants, Catholics, and Jews— virtually irrelevant.

At this point let me introduce a critical word of qualification. Though competing moral visions are at the heart of today's culture war, these do not always take form in coherent, clearly articulated, sharply differentiated world views. Rather, these moral visions take expression as *polarizing impulses* or *tendencies* in American culture. It is important, in this light, to make a distinction between how these moral visions are institutionalized in different organizations and in public rhetoric, and how ordinary Americans relate to them. In truth, most Americans occupy a vast middle ground between the polarizing impulses of American culture. Many will obviously lean toward one side while many others will tilt toward the other. Some Americans may seem altogether oblivious to either. The point is that most Americans, despite their predispositions, would not embrace a particular moral vision wholly or uncritically. Where the polarizing tendencies in American culture tend to be sharpest is in the organizations and spokes- people who have an interest in promoting a particular position on a social issue. It is they who, perhaps unwittingly, give voice to the competing moral visions. (Even then, I might add, the world views articulated are often less than coherent!) These institutions possess tremendous power in the realm of public discourse. They almost seem to have a life of their own: an existence, power, and agenda independent of the people for whom they presumably speak.

Polarizing Impulses: The Orthodox and the Progressive

To come right to the point, the cleavages at the heart of the contemporary culture war are created by what I would like to call *the impulse toward orthodoxy* and *the impulse toward progressivism*. The terms are imperfect, but each aspires to describe in shorthand a particular locus and source of moral truth, the fundamental (though perhaps subconscious) moral allegiances of the actors involved in the culture war as well as their cultural and political dispositions. Though the terms "orthodox" and "progressive" may be familiar to many, they have a particular meaning here that requires some elaboration.

Let me acknowledge, first off, that the words, orthodox and progressive, can describe specific doctrinal creeds or particular religious practices. Take orthodoxy. Within Judaism, orthodoxy is defined mainly by commitment to Torah and the community that upholds it; within Catholicism, orthodoxy is defined largely by loyalty to church teaching—the Roman Magisterium; and within Protestantism, orthodoxy principally means devotion to the complete and final authority of Scripture. Substantively, then, these labels can mean vastly different things within different religious traditions.

But I prefer to use the terms orthodox and progressive as *formal properties* of a belief system or world view. What is common to all three approaches to *orthodoxy*, for example (and what makes orthodoxy more of a formal property), is *the commitment on the part of adherents to an external, definable, and transcendent authority.* Such objective and transcendent authority defines, at least in the abstract, a consistent, unchangeable measure of value, purpose, goodness, and identity, both personal and collective. It tells us what is good, what is true, how we should live, and who we are. It is an authority that is sufficient for all time. . . .

Within cultural progressivism, by contrast, moral authority tends to be defined by the spirit of the modern age, a spirit of rationalism and subjectivism. Progressivist moral ideals tend, that is, to derive from and embody (though rarely exhaust) that spirit. From this standpoint, truth tends to be viewed as a process, as a reality that is ever unfolding. There are many distinctions that need to be made here. For example, what about those progressivists who still identify with a particular religious heritage? For them, one may note a strong tendency to translate the moral ideals of a religious tradition so that they conform to and legitimate the contemporary *zeitgeist*. In other words, what all *progressivist* world views share in common *is the tendency to resymbolize historic faiths according to the prevailing assumptions of contemporary life.* . . .

I have been talking about the contemporary cultural divide in the context of religious communities in order to highlight the historical novelty of the contemporary situation. But what about the growing number of "secularists"? These people range from the vaguely religious to the openly agnostic or atheistic. While they would probably claim no affiliation with a church or religious denomination, they nevertheless hold deep humanistic concerns about the welfare of community and nation. . . .

Like the representatives of religious communities, they too are divided. Yet public opinion surveys show that a decided majority of secularists are drawn toward the progressivist impulse in American culture. For these people religious tradition has no binding address, no opinion-shaping influence. Some secularists, however, (particularly many secular conservative and neo-conservative intellectuals) are drawn toward the orthodox impulse. For them, a commitment to natural law or to a high view of nature serves as the functional equivalent of the external and transcendent moral authority revered by their religiously orthodox counterparts.

In sum, the contemporary cultural conflict turns upside down (or perhaps inside out) the way cultural conflict has long been waged. Thus, we see those with apparently similar religious or cultural affiliations battling with one another. The culture war encompasses all Americans, religious and "non-religious," in very novel ways.

The orthodox and progressivist impulses in American culture, as I have described them, contrast sources of moral truth and also the allegiances by which people, drawn toward one or the other, live and interpret the world. They also express, somewhat imperfectly, the opposing social and political dispositions to which Americans on opposing sides of the cultural divide are drawn. Here, though, a word of elaboration.

It nearly goes without saying that those who embrace the orthodox impulse are almost always cultural conservatives, while those who embrace progressivist moral assumptions tend toward a liberal or libertarian social agenda. Certainly, the associations between foundational moral commitments and social and political agendas is far from absolute; some people and organizations will cross over the lines, taking conservative positions on some issues and liberal views on others. Yet the relationship between foundational moral commitments and social and political agendas is too strong and consistent to be viewed as coincidental. This is true for most Americans (as seen in public opinion surveys), but it is especially true for the organizations engaged in the range of contemporary disputes. For the practical purposes of naming the antagonists in the culture war, then, we can label those on one side cultural conservatives or moral traditionalists, and those on the other side liberals or cultural progressives. These are, after all, the terms that the actors in the culture war use to describe themselves. The danger of using these "political" labels, however, is that one can easily forget that they trace back to prior moral commitments and more basic moral visions: We subtly slip into thinking of the controversies debated as political rather than cultural in nature. On political matters one can compromise; on matters of ultimate moral truth, one cannot. This is why the full range of issues today seems interminable.

The real novelty of the contemporary situation emerges out of the fact that the orthodox and progressivist communities are not fighting isolated battles. Evangelical Protestants, for example, are not locked in an isolated conflict with liberal Protestants. Nor are theologically progressive Catholics struggling in isolation with their theologically conservative counterparts in the Roman hierarchy. The contemporary culture war is much larger and more complicated. *At the heart of the new cultural realignment are the pragmatic alliances being formed across faith traditions.* Because of common points of vision and concern, the orthodox wings of Protestantism, Catholicism, and Judaism are forming associations with each other, as are the progressive wings of each faith community and each set of alliances takes form in opposition to the influence the other seeks to exert in public culture.

These institutional alliances, it should be noted, are not always influential in terms of the joint power they hold. Some of the groups, after all, are quite small and have few resources. But these institutional alliances are *culturally* significant, for the simple reason that ideological and organizational associations are being generated among groups that have historically been antagonistic toward one another. Had the disagreements in each religious tradition remained simply theological or ecclesiastical in nature, these alliances would have probably never developed. But since the divisions have extended into the broader realm of public morality, the alliances have become the expedient outcome of common concerns. In other words, although these alliances are historically "unnatural," they have become pragmatically necessary. Traditional religio-cultural divisions are

superseded—replaced by the overriding differences taking form out of
orthodox and progressive moral commitments. . . .

The Struggle to Define America

Randall Terry (spokesman for the pro-life organization Operation Rescue): The bottom line is that killing children is not what America is
all about. We are not here to destroy our offspring.

Faye Wattleton (president of Planned Parenthood): Well, we are also not
here to have the government use women's bodies as the instrument
of the state, to force women into involuntary servitude—

Randall Terry (*laughing*): Oh come on, Faye.

Faye Wattleton: —I think that as Americans celebrate the Fourth of July,
our independence, and when we reflect on our personal liberties, this
is a very, very somber time, in which the courts have said that the
most private aspects of our lives are now . . . not protected by the Bill
of Rights and the Constitution. And I believe that that is a time for
Americans to reflect on the need to return to the fundamentals, and
the fundamentals of personal privacy are really the cornerstones upon
which our democracy is built.

Randall Terry: I think that to assume or even suggest that the founding
fathers of this country risked their lives and many of them died so
that we can kill our offspring is pathetic.

Although Randall Terry and Faye Wattleton were debating the morality and legality of abortion, what they said goes far beyond the abortion
controversy. First, the contemporary culture war is not just an expression
of different "opinions" or "attitudes" on this or that issue, like abortion.
If this were all there was to it, the conflict I refer to would be, as someone
once suggested, the "politics of distraction"—a trivial pursuit that keeps
Americans from settling more important matters. No, the conflict is deeper
than mere "differences of opinion" and bigger than abortion, and in fact,
bigger than the culmination of all the battles being waged. As suggested
earlier, the culture war emerges over fundamentally different conceptions
of moral authority, over different ideas and beliefs about truth, the good,
obligation to one another, the nature of community, and so on. It is,
therefore, cultural conflict at its deepest level. . . .

Though the conflict derives from differences in assumptions that are
philosophical and even theological in nature, the conflict does not end
as a philosophical dispute. This is a conflict over how we are to order
our lives together. This means that the conflict is inevitably expressed as

a clash over national life itself. Both Randall Terry and Faye Wattleton acknowledge this in their exchange. Hearing them invoke the Bill of Rights, the "founding fathers," "what America is really all about," and so on, we come to see that the contemporary culture war is ultimately a struggle over national identity — *over the meaning of America*, who we have been in the past, who we are now, and perhaps most important, who we, as a nation, will aspire to become in the new millennium.

15

Blasphemy

LEONARD W. LEVY

*Leonard W. Levy was a Pulitzer Prize–winning author who taught at
Brandeis University and, for over three decades, at Claremont Graduate
School. A prolific author, Levy wrote and edited numerous books on constitutional history and the Supreme Court that have been cited as authoritative
by the Court itself. The excerpt here is from his book* Blasphemy *(1993),
in which he argues that blasphemy of religious figures, symbols, and sacred
texts should (and largely does) receive full protection under the First Amendment's guarantees for freedom of speech and religion.*

———

MOST OF HISTORY, being a register of inhumanities, is not fit
to repeat. It includes prosecutions for blasphemy and its variant misnomer,
heresy. Believing that their religion required intolerance to sustain it,
Christians praised dead saints and persecuted living ones, making martyr-
dom sublime, grief ordinary. Example is always more efficacious than
precept, terrifying examples the most efficacious of all. Because the rewards
of religion were distant, Christians thought that punishment of irreligion
or mistaken religion reinforced the faith.

The verdicts of time mock judgments and alter sensibilities. Socrates,
Aristotle, Jesus, Michael Servetus, Giordano Bruno, George Fox, William
Penn, and Tom Paine were condemned for blasphemy. In the sixteenth
century, Protestantism seemed blasphemous to the Roman Catholic
church; in the next century, Protestant countries punished Unitarians,
Baptists, and Quakers as blasphemers. Beliefs that once staggered society
achieved respectability as fighting faiths.

Historically, the word "blasphemy" has functioned as an epithet to
aggravate or blacken an opinion on sacred matters that is objectionable
to those in authority. They may genuinely feel that their religion has been
assaulted, yet the "blasphemy" may exist only in their minds and not in
the mind of the offender. In one respect, blasphemy, like any form of
criminal libel, is a unique crime. In contrast to embezzlement, murder,
or larceny, whose existence has objective reality, no one knows whether
the crime of blasphemy has occurred until a jury returns a verdict of

guilty. Even then the culprit is guilty of the crime as a matter of law, though he may never have intended to commit it and after his conviction may still believe that he has not done so. He is incapable of understanding that the orthodox, especially biblical literalists, cannot be placated or appeased unless they feel revenged for the abuse of their faith. Blasphemy is a horror to them, for, as an English lawyer of the seventeenth century said, it is "speaking Treason against the Heavenly Majesty, the belching out of execrable words against God, whereby the Deity is reproached." Similarly, a Scottish jurist in the same year, 1678, referred tersely to the crime of "divine laese majesty or treason," and he joined blasphemy to witchcraft and heresy as "treasons against God." Prosecutions for blasphemy, however, have often been "treason" against intellectual liberty and freedom of religion. Over the centuries, the sanctions against blasphemy have inhibited not only religious but artistic, political, scientific, and literary expression.

Blasphemy appears to be in a persistent vegetative state in America, and in a state of suspended animation in Great Britain. Perhaps we no longer live in a time that tries men's souls. In some ways, we have become a numb society. Today almost anything seems endurable, inevitable, or unscotchable. Yet what appears to be a debasing permissiveness may well be worth the freedom it affords in the various forms of human expression. Freedom is often a condition of enlightenment. Elders of today can recall when adolescents furtively read Joyce's *Ulysses* and Farrell's *Studs Lonigan* as dirty books. Unashamed and exploitive hard-core pornography has replaced movies that were censored as "blue" — now a quaint term. By 1971, the Supreme Court of the United States, when reversing a conviction for offensive conduct, quipped that "one man's vulgarity is another's lyric." The case concerned a young man who had worn in public a jacket stenciled with the words "Fuck the Draft" to proclaim his contempt for our involvement in the war in Vietnam. The court understood that the First Amendment protects the emotive as well as the cognitive force of words. It did not, however, understand that some who were exposed involuntarily to the offensive words might have felt repulsion, shock, and even injury.

Nothing seems offensive any longer in a constitutional sense. One may now openly say, without fear of prosecution, that Jesus was a bastard who entertained no notion that he was divine, or that the doctrine of the Trinity is unscriptural and breaches the unity of God. Celebrated theologians and New Testament scholars commonly profess beliefs that once provoked not only coercion of dissent but execution for the dissenters. Men were once hanged for saying something like Thomas Jefferson's remark about "the incomprehensible jargon of the Trinitarian arithmetic, that three are one, and one is three." Lincoln blasphemed by old standards when he supposedly spoke of "the unsoundness of the Christian scheme of salvation and the human origin of the scriptures." People were once imprisoned for scourging Christianity as George Santayana did when he wrote that "Christianity persecuted, tortured, and burned. . . . It kindled wars, and nursed furious hatreds and . . . sanctified . . . extermination and tyranny." Alfred North Whitehead committed what was once a capital blasphemy when he declared that he considered "Christian theology to be one of the great disasters of the human race." Remarks of this nature now are commonplace and, as far as the law and culture are concerned, not the least offensive. . . .

. . . In England, the law still penalizes blasphemy, though it is hardly enforced. In America, the constitutional law of the First Amendment renders blasphemy laws inoperative for practical purposes, yet never has the Supreme Court actually held unconstitutional a blasphemy law. The unthinkable is theoretically possible but realistically unlikely in the extreme, although the contemporary Supreme Court has been packed with conservatives. Not even they would sustain a blasphemy conviction. A criminal law, however, even if only a vestigial relic, is never stone-cold dead until it is repealed or directly held unconstitutional. . . .

American citizens have an obligation to prevent the government from falling into error; no longer is it the business of the government to decide whether citizens have fallen into errors of opinion, taste, or religion. Most Americans probably do not accept the view of Justice Oliver Wendell Holmes that the principle of the Constitution that most imperatively calls for our attachment is "not free thought for those who agree with us but freedom for the thought that we hate." Most, however, would agree with Justice Robert Jackson's declaration: "If there is any fixed star in our constitutional constellation, it is that no official, high or petty, can prescribe what shall be orthodox in politics, nationalism, religion, or other matters of opinion or force citizens to confess by word or act their faith therein." Blasphemy is surely the expression of thought that we hate, and government, in seeking its suppression, enforces orthodoxy and forces citizens to stifle the expression of their beliefs about religion.

Blasphemy can, of course, be painfully offensive to the religious, just as desecration of the flag is offensive to our civil religion of patriotism. The offensiveness of antireligious language is the foremost reason for criminalizing blasphemy. But offensiveness is an insufficient basis for sustaining blasphemy laws. Religion is not entitled to a special protection against offensiveness that is not enjoyed by other matters of public concern.

People are free to express themselves about such matters in ways that offend others, short of personally libeling them or engaging in provocative epithets addressed to specific individuals. Gritty, nasty language in any matter of public concern has constitutional protection. As the Supreme Court declared, in a case dealing with language of racial hatred, a "function of free speech under our system of government is to invite dispute. It may indeed best serve its high purpose when it produces a condition of unrest, creates dissatisfaction with conditions as they are, or even stirs people to anger. It may strike at prejudices and preconceptions and have profound unsettling effects as it presses for acceptance of an idea." If one has a right to try to persuade others to abandon or change their religious beliefs, that right should include ridicule, raillery, and reproach, as it does with respect to other kinds of beliefs. The subject of religion is not entitled to unique immunity. Moreover, incisive rational argument, which the law protects, can be as offensive and subversive of religion as vituperation, sarcasm, and burlesque. . . .

Another conflict between blasphemy laws and the First Amendment derives from the fact that prosecutions implicitly strike at heretical expression. Heresy died as secular crime in the seventeenth century, yet no language can be found blasphemous without a prior understanding of what must not be blasphemed. In effect, blasphemy cannot be prosecuted unless some implicit standard of heresy exists, thus aggravating the abridgment of freedom of speech and religious liberty. . . .

The primary purpose of a blasphemy law is to further religious ends, not secular ones. Discrimination in favor of Christianity denies the equal protection of the laws to other religions. The argument that the law protects against offensiveness is without merit, given the fact that non-Christians can be offended with impunity as far as blasphemy laws are concerned; moreover, religionists can savage agnostics and atheists without having the law be the least bit concerned for their feelings.

Blasphemy prosecutions also tend to violate the equal-protection clause, because they tend to reflect class discrimination. The prosecutions of Edward Moxon, the wealthy bookman, and of *Gay News* were exceptional; defendants have almost always been people of the lower class. Judges and prosecutors in dozens of cases had declared that irreverence and ridicule when addressed to the poor are blasphemous, although the same language in Voltaire or G. B. Shaw, generally read by the more educated classes, enjoyed immunity from prosecution. Different rules governed the couth and the uncouth. In effect, one law existed for the prosperous and well educated, another for the masses. What sold for a pound was acceptable satire; what sold for a penny was blasphemous reviling. Shakespeare had it right in *Measure for Measure* when Isabella says, "That in the captain's but a choleric word, which in the soldier is flat blasphemy." Equal protection of the laws requires the same standards of justice, which blasphemy prosecutions have violated.

Blasphemy laws are also so vague that the very issue in any prosecution is whether the crime has been committed. The jury, which reflects public prejudice, determines that issue. But if a person cannot know whether he has committed a crime until a jury returns a verdict, the law governing that crime should be held void for vagueness. If people of common intelligence must necessarily guess at the meaning of a criminal law and differ about its application, it is unconstitutional as a denial of due process of law. That is an old principle.

Recent decisions of the Supreme Court reveal further evidence of the unconstitutionality of blasphemy prosecutions under the First Amendment. In the flag-burning cases of 1989 and 1990 and in the St. Paul cross-burning case of 1992, the court upheld the right to engage in so-called expressive conduct or symbolic speech that communicates messages of hatred and contempt—for the country, its government, or its officials in the flag-burning cases, and for black Americans or anyone categorized by race, religion, creed, or gender in the cross-burning case. One has a constitutional right to hate American foreign policy, blacks, or Jews. Whatever messages or opinions are communicated by flag burning or cross burning—that is, however expressive such conduct may be—it is a form of conduct, and not literally speech. If the First Amendment protects such conduct, it surely protects mere verbal expressions against religion, no matter how abusive or offensive such speech may be. If a statement is merely obnoxious and not threatening in the sense of inciting or advocating immediate violence, it constitutes free speech. . . .

Freedom of expression has never been freer than now, but it is not limitless. In matters of religion, atheists have the same rights as theists, but not everyone may worship as he pleases, let alone put his beliefs into practice. He might conceivably engage in the murderous rites of the goddess Kali, or unroll his prayer rug in the middle of highway traffic. Cultists who fondle venomous snakes to demonstrate the faith of the true believer (Mark 16:18, Luke 10:19, Acts 28:3–6) can be arrested, because public safety in this instance is a greater value than freedom of faith. One may not exercise one's religion at the expense of the public health, order, or welfare, nor plead conscientious objection to evade civic obligation. Caesar's conscription laws, for example, encompass all with such exceptions as only Congress may make. No one, however sincere, will prevail in alleging that his duty to God makes him decline the importunities of the Internal Revenue Service. Some who have claimed the immunity of their religious beliefs have been convicted of fortune-telling, breach of the peace, polygamy, draft evasion, nudity, the practice of medicine without a license, and blasphemy.

Blasphemy is still a crime in many states of this country, although prosecutions, like Lenin's state, have withered and died away. . . .

Before me is a four-page pamphlet entitled *The Bethlehem Bastard*, written by "K.J." and published by The Kill Club in Boulder, Colorado. The pamphlet expresses its author's psychotic hatreds and rage. The mother of Jesus is "Mary the Whore," "a wanton slut," and Joseph angrily demands, "Which of you fuckers is this 'Holy Ghost'?" It concludes, "There is no God, and Jesus is a fraud. Kill Jesus before Jesus kills you!" The conviction of the author of this tract for hard-core blasphemy, however ill-advised the prosecution, would not have jeopardized the religious freedom of people who argue that God does not exist or that Jesus was not God. Nor would the suppression of the tract threaten the artistic or intellectual freedom of an Andrés Serrano. Serrano's work of "art" entitled *Piss Christ* depicts Christ on the cross submerged in and surrounded by Serrano's urine. Conceivably, Serrano might have been making a comment about the degradation of religion in modern society. *Piss Christ* was subsidized by the National Endowment for the Arts (NEA), which also granted an award assisting the creation of a collage that depicts Christ as an intravenous drug user. The artist of that piece, David Wojnarowicz, did another picture with public tax dollars showing a madonna with the baby Jesus holding a revolver. Another NEA grant sponsored a worthless musing, ostensibly by Lazarus, about his homosexual experience with Jesus. The story is accompanied by a sketch showing Jesus fondling Lazarus's penis.

Prosecution of such "art" or poisonous tracts like *The Bethlehem Bastard* is unconstitutional and, even if not so, would be extremely inadvisable, if only because it would give the works a notoriety that would spread their scum and enhance their financial value; if ignored, they would likely stay unknown or be dismissed as trashy exhibitionism. But the prosecution of such works would not mean that avant-garde art has been thrust under a falling sky. Patrick Buchanan and Jesse Helms protest government funding of anti-Christian art and would probably welcome blasphemy prosecutions. As a result, defenders of freedom of expression reflexively feel obligated to champion it against the forces of darkness and censorship. Assuming that the First Amendment entitles any person to express herself as an artist in any way she pleases, no one has a right to have her art subsidized by the government.

Moreover, when the government underwrites a collage of Christ as a drug addict or the homosexual-Lazarus sketch, it employs its authority on the side of insult against the religious beliefs of most Christians, and non-Christians may feel the outrage too. The First Amendment ensures government neutrality in the arena of religion and irreligion, not government sponsorship of one side against the other. But, of course, government has always utilized tax dollars for religious art. Whether art is religious or antireligious, the First Amendment means also that it is free to circulate, even if it is scum.

The temptation to prosecute must be stilled, not only because revenge is an unworthy objective and exacts a high cost, but also because the fundamental law, as construed by the Supreme Court, commands toleration even of the repugnant. More important, human experience has shown that, even if distinctions can be made between garbage and art, once the garbage gets thrown into the maw of the disposal, distinctions lose force, and more than just garbage gets chewed up. To give an absurd example, the House Un-American Activities Committee once associated little Shirley Temple with those who served the purposes of the Communist Party. McCarthyism is a phenomenon that has been repeated intermittently throughout our history, from the time of the Sedition Act of 1798. The Federal Bureau of Investigation maintained files on scores of poets, novelists, playwrights, columnists, journalists, and other writers deemed subversive, including H. L. Mencken, Pearl Buck, Dale Carnegie, Gertrude Stein, Rex Stout, Tennessee Williams, Damon Runyon, E. B. White, F. Scott Fitzgerald, and William Inge. We should also bear in mind that special interests perennially seek the censorship of *The Merchant of Venice* and *Huckleberry Finn*. The other fellow is always the one who can't maintain the distinction. Whom can we trust to do so? . . .

Whether convictions and judicial rulings that sustain them are enlightened or benighted depends on whether one believes that the downfall of society, the subversion of government, or the dissolution of Christianity or of morality is at stake because of some disgusting literary gaucherie or a hateful publication. Reasonable people should have learned by now that morality can and does exist without religion, and that Christianity is capable of surviving without penal sanctions. The use of the criminal law to assuage affronted religious feelings imperils liberty—not greatly, to be sure, because blasphemy laws have become legal relics in the Anglo-American world. But they are reminders that a special legal preference for religion in general, or for Christianity in particular, violates the Constitution. They are reminders too that the feculent odor of persecution for the cause of conscience, which is the basic principle upon which blasphemy laws rest, has not yet dissipated.

PART FIVE

The Rights of the Accused and Criminal Justice

AMENDMENT 4
The right of the people to be secure
in their persons, houses, papers, and effects,
against unreasonable searches and seizures,
shall not be violated . . .

AMENDMENT 5
No person shall be held to answer for a capital,
or otherwise infamous crime,
unless on a presentment or indictment of a Grand Jury . . . ;
nor shall any person be subject for the same offense
to be twice put in jeopardy of life or limb;
nor shall be compelled in any criminal case
to be a witness against himself,
nor be deprived of life, liberty, or property,
without due process of law . . .

AMENDMENT 6
In all criminal prosecutions, the accused shall enjoy
the right to a speedy and public trial,
by an impartial jury of the State . . .
and to have the assistance of counsel for his defense.

16

Security Versus Civil Liberties

JUDGE RICHARD A. POSNER

One of the founders of the "law and economics movement" at the University of Chicago School of Law, where he continues to teach, Judge Richard A. Posner was appointed to the U.S. Court of Appeals for the Seventh Circuit by Republican President Ronald Reagan. A prolific author, who had served as a law clerk to Justice William J. Brennan, Jr., he is widely recognized as a leading and often provocative jurist. In this selection Judge Posner puts the tradeoffs between security and liberty in "the war against international terrorism," following the September 11, 2001, attacks on the World Trade Center and the Pentagon, in historical and legal perspective. He contributed this essay to The Atlantic Monthly *in December, 2001. Judge Posner further developed the arguments here in a series of books, including* Not a Suicide Pact: The Constitution in a Time of National Emergency *(2006), and* Countering Terrorism: Blurred Focus, Halting Steps *(2007).*

———

IN THE WAKE OF the September 11 terrorist attacks have come many proposals for tightening security; some measures to that end have already been taken. Civil libertarians are troubled. They fear that concerns about national security will lead to an erosion of civil liberties. They offer historical examples of supposed overreactions to threats to national security. They treat our existing civil liberties—freedom of the press, protections of privacy and of the rights of criminal suspects, and the rest—as sacrosanct, insisting that the battle against international terrorism accommodate itself to them.

I consider this a profoundly mistaken approach to the question of balancing liberty and security. The basic mistake is the prioritizing of liberty. It is a mistake about law and a mistake about history. Let me begin with law. What we take to be our civil liberties—for example, immunity from arrest except upon probable cause to believe we've committed a crime, and from prosecution for violating a criminal statute enacted after we committed the act that violates it—were made legal rights by the Constitution and other enactments. The other enactments can be changed relatively easily, by amendatory legislation. Amending the Constitution is much more difficult. In recognition of this the Framers left most of the constitutional provisions that confer rights pretty vague. The courts have made them definite.

Concretely, the scope of these rights has been determined, through an interaction of constitutional text and subsequent judicial interpretation, by a weighing of competing interests. I'll call them the public-safety interest and the liberty interest. Neither, in my view, has priority. They are both important, and their relative importance changes from time to time and from situation to situation. The safer the nation feels, the more weight judges will be willing to give to the liberty interest. The greater the threat that an activity poses to the nation's safety, the stronger will the grounds seem for seeking to repress that activity, even at some cost to liberty. This fluid approach is only common sense. Supreme Court Justice Robert Jackson gave it vivid expression many years ago when he said, in dissenting from a free-speech decision he thought doctrinaire, that the Bill of Rights should not be made into a suicide pact. It was not intended to be such, and the present contours of the rights that it confers, having been shaped far more by judicial interpretation than by the literal text (which doesn't define such critical terms as "due process of law" and "unreasonable" arrests and searches), are alterable in response to changing threats to national security.

If it is true, therefore, as it appears to be at this writing, that the events of September 11 have revealed the United States to be in much greater jeopardy from international terrorism than had previously been believed—have revealed it to be threatened by a diffuse, shadowy enemy that must be fought with police measures as well as military force—it stands to reason that our civil liberties will be curtailed. They should be curtailed, to the extent that the benefits in greater security outweigh the costs in reduced liberty. All that can reasonably be asked of the responsible legislative and judicial officials is that they weigh the costs as carefully as the benefits.

It will be argued that the lesson of history is that officials habitually exaggerate dangers to the nation's security. But the lesson of history is the opposite. It is because officials have repeatedly and disastrously underestimated these dangers that our history is as violent as it is. Consider such underestimated dangers as that of secession, which led to the Civil War; of a Japanese attack on the United States, which led to the disaster at Pearl Harbor; of Soviet espionage in the 1940s, which accelerated the Soviet Union's acquisition of nuclear weapons and emboldened Stalin to encourage North Korea's invasion of South Korea; of the installation of Soviet missiles in Cuba, which precipitated the Cuban missile crisis; of political assassinations and outbreaks of urban violence in the 1960s; of the Tet Offensive of 1968; of the Iranian revolution of 1979 and the subsequent taking of American diplomats as hostages; and, for that matter, of the events of September 11.

It is true that when we are surprised and hurt, we tend to overreact — but only with the benefit of hindsight can a reaction be separated into its proper and excess layers. In hindsight we know that interning Japanese-Americans did not shorten World War II. But was this known at the time? If not, shouldn't the Army have erred on the side of caution, as it did? Even today we cannot say with any assurance that Abraham Lincoln was wrong to suspend *habeas corpus* during the Civil War, as he did on several occasions, even though the Constitution is clear that only Congress can suspend this right. (Another of Lincoln's wartime measures, the Emancipation Proclamation, may also have been unconstitutional.) But Lincoln would have been wrong to cancel the 1864 presidential election, as some urged: by November of 1864 the North was close to victory, and canceling the election would have created a more dangerous precedent than the wartime suspension of *habeas corpus*. This last example shows that civil liberties remain part of the balance even in the most dangerous of times, and even though their relative weight must then be less.

Lincoln's unconstitutional acts during the Civil War show that even legality must sometimes be sacrificed for other values. We are a nation under law, but first we are a nation. I want to emphasize something else, however: the malleability of law, its pragmatic rather than dogmatic character. The law is not absolute, and the slogan *"Fiat iustitia ruat caelum"* ("Let justice be done though the heavens fall") is dangerous nonsense. The law is a human creation rather than a divine gift, a tool of government rather than a mandarin mystery. It is an instrument for promoting social welfare, and as the conditions essential to that welfare change, so must it change.

Civil libertarians today are missing something else — the opportunity to challenge other public-safety concerns that impair civil liberties. I have particularly in mind the war on drugs. The sale of illegal drugs is a "victimless" crime in the special but important sense that it is a consensual activity. Usually there is no complaining witness, so in order to bring the criminals to justice the police have to rely heavily on paid informants (often highly paid and often highly unsavory), undercover agents, wiretaps and other forms of electronic surveillance, elaborate sting operations, the infiltration of suspect organizations, random searches, the monitoring of airports and highways, the "profiling" of likely suspects on the basis of ethnic or racial identity or national origin, compulsory drug tests, and other intrusive methods that put pressure on civil liberties. The war on drugs has been a big flop; moreover, in light of what September 11 has taught us about the gravity of the terrorist threat to the United States, it becomes hard to take entirely seriously the threat to the nation that drug use is said to pose. Perhaps it is time to redirect law-enforcement resources from the investigation and apprehension of drug dealers to the investigation and apprehension of international terrorists. By doing so we may be able to minimize the net decrease in our civil liberties that the events of September 11 have made inevitable.

17

Terrorism and the Constitution:
Sacrificing Civil Liberties in the Name of National Security

DAVID COLE
JAMES X. DEMPSEY

In contrast to Judge Posner (see Chapter 16), David Cole and James X. Dempsey argue for a defense of civil rights and civil liberties against claims of national security in times of national emergency. The excerpt here is from their book Terrorism and the Constitution: Sacrificing Civil Liberties in the Name of National Security *(2006). Professor Cole teaches at Georgetown University Law Center and is a frequent litigator. James X. Dempsey is the vice president for public policy at the Center for Democracy and Technology.*

As SEPTEMBER 11 dramatically demonstrated, the United States faces a real terrorist threat from abroad. At the same time, however, the United States itself has not been a fertile breeding ground for home-grown terrorism. This may well be because values central to our system of democratic governance make it difficult to nurture within this country the ideological, ethnic, or religious hatred that fuels much terrorism. These values include appreciation of diversity and religious and ethnic tolerance, reflected in our repeated absorption of large influxes of immigrants. They also include constitutional limits on government powers, checks and balances, access to government information, accountability of public officials, and due process accorded in judicial proceedings open to public scrutiny, all of which increase public confidence in government. Perhaps most important is our strong protection for political freedoms of speech and association, with a nearly unlimited right to criticize government and government officials, and a nearly insurmountable presumption against prior censorship, assuring the disaffected that their concerns can be heard without violence.

Unfortunately, much of our official response to the threat of terrorism is incompatible with these core civil liberties values. The 1996 Antiterrorism Act, for example, deems people guilty not on the basis of what they have done, but on the basis of the groups with which they are associated.

It denies one of the most fundamental elements of due process—the right to confront one's accusers in open court. And measures taken after September 11 have similarly threatened basic values—criminalizing speech, imposing guilt by association, conducting trials in secret, engaging in ethnic profiling, and intruding on the privacy of innocent persons. The question is whether we can respond effectively to the new threat of terrorism without jeopardizing the very freedoms that have contributed to our security at home.

The False Trade-Off—Curtailing Liberty Will Not Necessarily Enhance Security

In the ongoing debate over responding to terrorism, many argue that civil liberties must be sacrificed in order to ensure the safety of our democratic way of life. Something unique about the threat of terrorism, it is argued, requires us to alter the constitutional balance we have long struck between government power and personal freedoms. The premise of this argument—so unquestioningly accepted that it often goes unstated—is that antiterrorism measures infringing civil liberties will work. While there are often difficult trade-offs to be made between liberty and security, it does not follow that sacrificing liberties will always, or even generally, promote security.

Efficacy, of course, does not determine the outcome of the constitutional debate. Even if a police state were efficient, it would not reflect our fundamental values. But many of the rights . . . actually promote governmental efficacy in defending the common good. We guarantee the right to confront one's accusers, for example, not only as an element of human dignity but also because we know that cross-examination is an effective engine of truth. Relying on untested evidence not only risks convicting the innocent, but it also means that the search for the truly guilty party may be called off prematurely. We subject executive decisions to judicial review not only because the judicial system gives a voice to individuals but also because we know that the adversarial process can produce a fuller factual record, exposing faulty assumptions, and because deliberative review by life-tenured judges can protect against the rash decisions resulting from the pressures felt by elected officials. We reject guilt by association not only to protect political freedom, but also because a system that holds individuals responsible for their own actions is more closely tailored to deterring crime. We protect freedom of speech not only because it allows room for personal self-expression, but also because the availability of channels for peaceful change promotes stability. We have more to fear from the pressure cooker of repressed dissatisfaction than from the cacophony of dissent. For these reasons, many of the counterterrorism measures that we have criticized are not only unconstitutional, but are also likely to be counterproductive.

Curtailing civil liberties does not necessarily promote national security. In COINTELPRO, the FBI experimented with the massive monitoring of political dissent. It failed to produce any substantial evidence of violent conduct, suggesting that politics is a poor guide and extensive monitoring an ineffective strategy for counterterrorism investigations. Other more recent examples here and abroad have shown that racial and ethnic stereotyping is also a poor basis for security policy. The assassin of Yitzhak Rabin escaped detection because the prime minister's bodyguards were on the lookout for Arab assailants. If police had listened only to those who claimed that the Oklahoma City bombing bore the trademarks of Muslim fundamentalists, they might not have captured Timothy McVeigh as he fled from the crime.

Violations of civil liberties often "work" only in a narrow sense: random or door-to-door searches will uncover contraband in some houses, and torture of arrestees will induce some to provide truthful evidence of wrongdoing, including evidence that may allow the prevention of violent attacks. But these "successes" must be balanced against the wasted resources consumed by fruitless random searches and generalized monitoring of groups or movements, the mistakes caused by reliance on faulty coerced confessions, and, most importantly, the tremendous loss of trust in government (and the consequent shutting off of voluntary cooperation) generated by unfocused investigations and the harassment of communities on the basis of stereotypes. On balance, even measured only in terms of effectiveness, there is little evidence that curtailing civil liberties will do more good than harm.

Implications of a New, More Dangerous Terrorism

In every age, dangers can be cited that make limitations on intelligence operations seem imprudent — threats of such an urgent and unique nature that it seems necessary to expand government powers, at least long enough to turn back the new threat. Today's proponents of expanding government power to fight terrorism argue that the terrorist threat now is qualitatively different than in the past. September 11 certainly gave these arguments added weight.

But the heightened risk of terrorism simply means that the consequences of failing to adopt a sound antiterrorism policy are more serious than ever before. It does not tell us what policy to adopt.

Indeed, aspects of the new threat of terrorism point in quite different directions. Before adopting measures that curtail personal freedom, it might be more effective to address the highly destructive products that pose such serious risk to life. The United States and its allies have not done nearly enough to gain control of the nuclear materials of the former Soviet Union, a project that probably would mean far more to national security than curtailing civil liberties. Lethal biological and chemical materials are widely produced and are subject to inadequate controls. A program of stringent federal regulation of anthrax would have no civil liberties implications, but could meaningfully restrict access to such products by both the malevolent and the merely careless.

It is also clear that not nearly enough was done with investigative and protective authorities that existed before the 1996 and 2001 Acts and that had little to do with intrusions on political freedoms. For example, prior to September 11 there were repeated warnings about poor airport security. Documents disclosed by the *New York Times* in January 1999 showed that explosives and guns avoided detection in government tests of airline security, due largely to lax practices on the part of screening personnel. Similarly, it became clear following the embassy bombings in Africa that Washington officials were largely unresponsive to the intense, well-founded, and forcefully expressed concerns of the American ambassador to Kenya, who warned repeatedly that the embassy was insufficiently protected against terrorist attack. Indeed, the CIA repeatedly told the State Department that there was an active terrorist group in Kenya connected to Osama bin Laden, since accused of masterminding the bombings there and in Tanzania.

Despite the wartime rhetoric of stamping out terrorism everywhere, the terrorist threat will never be eliminated. We must develop sound responses. But in doing so, we should be careful not to sacrifice the fundamental principles that characterize our democratic identity. The better course is to adhere to our liberal principles, to use the criminal laws to punish those who plan or carry out violent acts, and to invite critics of our government into the practice of democracy and tolerance.

Reforming FBI Counterterrorism Activities

The principles guiding FBI counterterrorism activities were laid down more than fifty years ago, before World War II, and were codified more than twenty-five years ago, while the Cold War was still under way. At that time, the main national security threat was the Soviet Union, which was understood to be conducting a worldwide campaign against the United States through clandestine means and covert proxies.

At the beginning of the Cold War, the criminal law was thought to be of little relevance to this struggle. The foreign agents conducting or directing hostile actions against the United States were often operating under diplomatic immunity. It was assumed that criminal prosecution would reveal too much classified information, compromising continued counterintelligence efforts. Even with respect to United States citizens suspected of spying in the United States, the presumption was against criminal prosecution. Clandestine disruptive actions and double agent operations were justified as the best means of preventing damage to U.S. interests, on the ground that the criminal law was not available.

Major changes over the last two decades have upset many of the assumptions on which FBI national security activities were founded. The Soviet Union has disintegrated. Human rights protection has emerged as a leading principle of U.S. foreign policy (at least in theory). International law has undergone revolutionary change, to the point where the United States now has at its disposal a range of international sanctions to punish state sponsors of terrorism.

Most importantly, criminal law has assumed a primacy in national security policy. It is now routine to arrest and prosecute suspected spies, through trials in which all of the government's evidence is presented publicly and subject to cross-examination. The Classified Information Procedures Act makes such public prosecutions less risky to ongoing operations, while preserving defendants' rights to confront the evidence against them. U.S. criminal law has been given wide extraterritorial effect, reaching almost any attack anywhere in the world against an American citizen, U.S. government property, or property owned by U.S. corporations. International cooperation in the field of criminal law makes it more likely than ever that terrorism can be dealt with through arrest and prosecution in U.S. courts.

A revised view of intelligence is also demanded by another change: The United States, always a diverse society, has become even more so. Consider just religious diversity. There are 3,000 religious denominations and sects in the United States today. Not only are there more Muslims than Episcopalians in the United States, but there is a diversity within this diversity that defies common assumptions. For example, contrary to popular perception, most Muslims in the United States are not of Arab origin and most persons of Arab descent in the United States are not Muslims.

In the face of such diversity, principles of pluralism, tolerance of dissent, and individual rather than group culpability should guide the development of national security, intelligence, and counterterrorism policy. The alternative is a stereotyping that can ossify or mislead the investigative focus. While the FBI was conducting an intensive investigation of the PLO-affiliated PFLP in the 1980s and 1990s, the U.S. government was promoting the signing of an Israeli-PLO peace accord, and the focus of terrorism concern in the Middle East shifted to anti-PLO Muslim fundamentalists. As soon as the FBI launched a massive campaign against Muslim fundamentalists in the wake of the World Trade Center bombing, the Murrah building in Oklahoma City was blown up by white, native-born ex-GIs. And while the FBI and the INS pursued innocent Arab and Muslim political activists, terrorists careful to avoid any showing of religious or political orientation planned and carried out the September 11 attacks. . . .

[A reasonable] counterterrorism program would, in many respects, be the exact opposite of what was reflected in the Antiterrorism Act of 1996 and the Patriot Act of 2001. Where those Acts empowered the FBI to investigate a new, broadly defined offense of "support for terrorism," we would propose express legislative limits on the government's discretion to investigate and prosecute First Amendment activities. Where those Acts expanded the concept of support for terrorism to include support for the political and humanitarian activities of groups that also engage in violence, we advocate limiting the crime of support for terrorism, like any crime of aiding and abetting, to support for activities that are themselves crimes. Where those Acts endorsed guilt by association, we would require the FBI to focus its investigations on collecting evidence of individual culpability. Where those Acts allowed the use of secret evidence, we maintain that the government should subject its evidence to the test of cross-examination. And where those Acts adopted a political approach to terrorism, we insist that the FBI must get out of the business of monitoring political activity and associations, foreign and domestic, and instead dedicate itself to the urgent task of identifying those planning violent activities. Only such a transformation can successfully meet the threat of terrorism without sacrificing our political freedoms.

18

Mapp v. Ohio *and the Fourth Amendment*

PRISCILLA H. MACHADO ZOTTI

Based on interviews and research in the justices' private papers, this selection tells the story behind the Supreme Court's landmark ruling in Mapp v. Ohio, 367 U.S. 643 (1961), *which overturned the decision in* Wolf v. Colorado, 338 U.S. 25 (1949), *and extended the Fourth Amendment's exclusionary rule — excluding evidence obtained by an illegal search and seizure from admission at trial — to state as well as federal courts. A political scientist, Priscilla H. Machado Zotti teaches at the United States Naval Academy. The excerpt here is from her book* Injustice for All: Mapp v. Ohio and the Fourth Amendment *(2005).*

———

ASSIGNED TO THE POWERFUL Bureau of Special Investigation, Sergeant [Carl I.] Delau was acquainted with Cleveland's vice activities. Horse racing and baseball belonged to the whites. Blacks controlled policy and gambling, although this was changing. Pornography was not a large problem, at least not yet. In May of 1957 Delau focused his attention on policy, or numbers wagering. The activities were located primarily in the Sixth and Eighth districts of Cleveland, and Delau was familiar with the principal players. Policy, or clearinghouse, was becoming big business in Cleveland. An illegal game of chance, policy appealed to those of all economic means. Even those with more modest resources could place a wager regularly. They did so often, so much so that the police department of the city of Cleveland formed the Bureau of Special Investigation headed by Lieutenant Martin Cooney, Sergeant Delau's direct superior. The importance of the bureau could not be overstated. Cooney reported directly to the chief of police, Frank W. Story. Delau's chain of command indicated the importance the Cleveland Police Department placed on curtailing vice activities: Delau to Cooney to the chief. The chief of police was very determined to keep Cleveland from being a haven for criminals. He gave Cooney and his Bureau of Special Investigation citywide jurisdiction.

About 3:00 A.M. on May 20, 1957, Sergeant Delau received a telephone call from a resident in the Sixth district. He recognized the voice of twenty-five-year-old Donald King, a young but well-known clearing-house operator who would later become nationally known as the boxing promoter with "that hair." King sounded desperate and bewildered. "Sergeant, they bombed my house."

"Donald, are you sure?" Delau asked King.

King replied, "I don't have a front porch. I can look out and it's gone. I don't have a front door."

Delau knew that King lived on East 151st Street, not far from the Mount Pleasant Police Station. "Did you call the police?"

"No," King said, "I called you first. You are the only one I can trust." He may have called Delau first, but he had a suspicion who bombed his home. King placed a number of calls to others involved in clearinghouse and policy—others that he suspected were involved. He told them he was not scared and would talk to the police.

Within minutes Delau called in the report and was told to go to King's residence at 3713 E. 151st Street to investigate. There he found a clearly rattled Don King amid the rubble that comprised the street-side portion of his home. By daybreak, fifteen officers were on-site. King's residence, what was left of it, was a crime scene. What happened appeared to be a turf war for control of the policy business in Cleveland. Someone using "muscle" was sending King a powerful message, likely another clearinghouse operator competing with King for business and power. Little did Carl Delau know, this was to begin the long chain of events that would forever change the way police conduct investigations in the United States. . . .

Numbers running was labor intensive. It required hiring people to make drop-offs and pickups, as well as bookkeepers, tabulators, look outs, collectors, and strongmen. The army of workers grew as clearinghouses became more and more profitable. Dollree (Doll-ray) Mapp worked occasionally for both Donald King and Shondor Birns, making drops, pickups, and sometimes keeping books. The police knew that she was involved in policy. When staking out known clearinghouses, they would regularly record license plates and later run them through the Department of Motor Vehicles' computer to obtain the name of the owners. Dollree Mapp's name had come up regularly. The police also knew her for her striking appearance. Dolly was a beautiful woman who Delau described as "foxy." . . .

Dollree Mapp's home was a two-story brick house in the Shaker Heights section of Cleveland. Most of the homes along Milverton Road were modest structures with a similarity among them that indicated the entire neighborhood had been built from more or less the same blueprint.

The home, which appeared to be a single-family dwelling, was actually split into two apartments, one upstairs and one downstairs, with a driveway on the left side leading to a garage. Dollree occupied the upstairs with her teenage daughter Barbara Bivens, the child she once shared with her former husband, boxer Jimmy Bivens. The downstairs apartment was rented to Minerva Tate.

Delau and [officer Michael] Haney parked and walked up the drive while [patrolman Michael] Dever went to the front of the home. Delau rang the doorbell located near the side-door nameplate "Mapp." Instead of coming to the door, Dollree Mapp coyly opened the upper window near the driveway and inquired what the officers wanted. Recounting this event in separate discussions over thirty years later, both Haney and Delau said, "I can remember her calling down from the window as if it were yesterday."

"What do you want?" she asked them.

"Hello Dolly. We just wanted to come in and take a quick look around," Delau replied casually.

"Why do you want to come inside? What are you looking for?" she inquired.

Delau didn't exactly know. He certainly wanted to question [Virgil] Ogletree [about running numbers], but beyond that he wasn't sure. These officers knew Dolly Mapp participated in numbers, at least on the fringe. Her car was regularly seen at gaming houses. There was a possibility, as the anonymous caller had insinuated, that they would find evidence of illegal gambling. In fact the police believed that the Mapp house was the location for the California Gold policyhouse. Delau wasn't sure how to respond to Dollree Mapp.

Mapp continued to inquire, now more sarcastically, what Delau wanted in her home. Delau told her nothing concrete. After several more minutes of conversation she said: "I'll call my attorney and see if he thinks I should let you in." Mapp in fact did call the office of her lawyer, A. L. Kearns. She had recently retained Kearns to file a civil suit against her former boyfriend, boxer Archie Moore. The lawsuit appeared to be an attempt to extract money. Mapp charged Moore with breach of promise for refusing to marry her. Mapp eventually dropped the charges and whether Mapp profited financially from the legal maneuver is unclear. Kearns was not available to speak to Mapp so Dolly was put through to one of his partners, Walter Green. Green was a relatively young lawyer whose specialty was not criminal matters and her request was not something with which he was readily familiar.

"Do the police have a search warrant?" he asked.

"I don't know. I didn't ask," she replied.

"Well, don't let them in unless they show you a search warrant, but if they do, you will have to admit them," counseled Green.

It turns out that Green's advice was not correct, at least not in the practice of American criminal law in 1957. While the constitutional principle of search warrant usage existed, the common practice under Ohio law was that search warrants were rarely used. Only when raids were planned well in advance were warrants considered. Most lawful searches occurred without search warrants. . . .

Very few police officers were familiar with the procedures for obtaining a search warrant. The process was used so infrequently that most officers had never secured one as a predicate to a search. . . .

This procedure was not done regularly for many reasons. Occasionally a suspect was "tipped off" by someone that a warrant was being processed. The police would then show up to conduct a search only to find the criminals well prepared for their arrival, the element of surprise taken away. Some of the tipoffs were a result of corruption within city hall. Big-city criminals were savvy and knew that clerks and administrative staffs had information vital to them. Salaries of police officers and other civic workers were low enough that bribes were tempting. In addition, most police felt the procedure of obtaining warrants was cumbersome and a hindrance to law enforcement. Why follow such arduous rules if not absolutely required to? Most of all, the extra step of securing a search warrant seemed to tip the scales of justice in favor of the criminal. An officer's belief of wrongdoing was not enough: a judge would have to concur and grant permission to search.

What existed in Cleveland at the time was a culture of avoiding such steps, classifying them as an unfair advantage to the criminal. Thus few in the police department knew how to obtain search warrants. When warrants were sought, Cooney typically asked Officer John Ungarvy to obtain them. On this particular day he was apparently unavailable and the job fell to Lieutenant White.

After telephoning Cooney, Delau and Haney returned to Mapp's home, believing the search warrant was en route. The three officers waited in their patrolcar for the warrant to be delivered. Mapp, still perched in her upstairs window, could see the police down the street. She called her lawyer again, telling him what she saw from her window. Delau and Haney advised headquarters of events and waited. Dollree advised her attorney and did the same.

By about four o'clock in the afternoon "Lieutenant White arrived on the scene with a search warrant." There were now at least seven police officers outside the Mapp house on Milverton Road. The officers on the scene proceeded accordingly. Again they sought admittance.

The fact that all parties had knowledge of a search warrant is undisputed. At the time the search was conducted all the police officers involved believed that a search warrant was obtained; Mapp's attorney, and initially even Mapp herself, believed that the police were operating with a search warrant. Ironically, no one thought to look to see if the piece of paper so commented on, so significant to future events and American constitutional law, was indeed a warrant to search 14705 Milverton Road, the home of Dollree Mapp. This act of omission is, without a doubt, significant. The very piece of paper at the heart of what would become *Dollree Mapp v. The State of Ohio* wasn't even scrutinized by any of the principal players. All took it for granted that the paper brought to the scene by Lieutenant White was an official search warrant to conduct a search of Dollree Mapp's home for a material witness in the King bombing and for potential possession of gambling paraphernalia. The trifoliate document remained folded, unopened.

Dollree Mapp did not immediately answer the door, and the record reflects that at least one of the several doors to the house was forcibly opened. Carl Delau testified in court that "we did pry the screen door to gain entrance." Walter Green, Mapp's attorney, testified that a policeman "tried to kick in the door" and then "broke the glass in the door and somebody reached in and opened the door and let them in." Mapp testified that "the back door was broken." According to Justice [William O.] Douglas's concurrence in the Supreme Court decision in 1961, "For the next two and a half hours, the police laid siege to the house." . . .

At the time of their entry, Mapp was halfway down the stairs coming toward the front door. She demanded to see the search warrant, noting that the police had had none on their earlier attempt at admittance. One of the officers, Lieutenant White, waived a piece of paper in Mapp's face, indicating that it was the search warrant, which legalized their search. Mapp grabbed the paper and placed it down the front of her dress. The police then restrained her and recovered the so-called warrant. . . . What is important to note is that *at the time* all believed the paper was indeed a search warrant. Only later was the existence of a warrant doubted. On May 23, 1957, everyone, including Dollree Mapp and Carl Delau, believed that a search warrant was the basis for the search of Mapp's home. . . .

Because she "was belligerent in resisting the official rescue of the 'warrant' from her person," the officers handcuffed Mapp to another officer. She was then taken to her bedroom and forced to sit on the bed. Carl Delau later said that the reason for this was to negate any claim that the police stole items from her.

The police made a complete and thorough search of the four-room flat as well as the basement. They searched a dresser, chest of drawers, a closet, and suitcases. They searched the child's bedroom, the living room, the kitchen, and even photo albums and personal papers. The entire second floor was searched.

The police then searched the basement. From a trunk, materials deemed to be obscene were seized. This material was considered lewd and lascivious, and when confronted, Mapp claimed she found the items while cleaning. She asserted that the material belonged to a former boarder, a Morris Jones. She had agreed to store his belongings until his return and had no knowledge of the contents of the trunk. The obscene material included four pamphlets, several photographs, and a pencil doodle. In addition, Officer Haney found in her bedroom dresser *The Affairs of the Troubadour, Little Darlings, London Stage Affairs,* and *Memories of a Hotel Man.* Upon seizure of these items, Mapp replied: "Better not look at those; they might excite you." In a suitcase by the bed, Officer Haney found a hand drawn penciled picture. Sergeant Delau found four groups of obscene photographs. . . .

Here is where the versions of events diverge. By some accounts, the search of Mapp's home is brutal and frightening. A window is broken, the occupant handcuffed, and the search seemingly endless. Other reports indicate that the police broke one pane of a glass door, since the occupant would not provide access, and conducted a thorough yet reasonable search. History, too, has embellished the search of Dollree Mapp, making it extraordinary. Upon review, it is doubtful that it was. She was a notable Cleveland figure and a personality. A beautiful woman, she was linked to two well-known local celebrities (Jimmy Bivens and Archie Moore) as well as members of Cleveland's crime community (Donald King, Shondor Birns, and Virgil Ogletree). The bombing of King's home was sensational because it involved infighting in Cleveland's underworld. Yet looking back the search was no different than many others. That is not to suggest that it did not cross the line between legal and nonlegal, but to make clear that the line did not lie where it does today. The search of Mapp's home was standard procedure in 1957. What is different is not the actions of Delau and Haney but *the reaction* of the Supreme Court of the United States. Whether or not one agrees with the eventual outcome of the Mapp decision of 1961, the events of May 23, 1957, are routine for the day. But times were changing, and "routine" would take on quite a different meaning in the future. . . .

Seven months after the decision of the Supreme Court of Ohio, the Supreme Court of the United States noted probable jurisdiction in the case of *Mapp v. Ohio.* The date was October 24, 1960. With little fanfare it was evaluated by the law clerks within each of the justices' chambers. Justice Clark's clerk, Carl Estes II, drafted a three-page note setting forth the grounds for jurisdictional control of *Mapp v. Ohio.* Most of his memorandum focused on the obscenity statute. His only mention of the search and seizure indicated that despite Mapp's claim of an illegal search, the Ohio law did not appear to breach the *Rochin* standard. Warren's clerk also recommended taking the case, claiming the grounds of which were solely based on the First Amendment. The argument that Mapp was a victim of an illegal search was irrelevant, since Ohio law was applied correctly and consistently with *Wolf v. Colorado.* The issue seemed clear. . . .

However, not everyone saw the First Amendment issues as paramount. In February 1961, Bernard Berkman of the Cleveland branch of the American Civil Liberties Union filed an *amicus curiae,* or friend of the court brief, in docket number 236. In it he argued that the central issue in the case was not what Dolly Mapp possessed but how the police came to seize those possessions. Berkman argued in simple and direct language that Mapp's Fourth Amendment rights were violated. He stated clearly, with an eye on the Fourth Amendment, that she was a victim of an illegal search and seizure. The ACLU *amicus* brief was only two paragraphs long. Berkman did not advocate or present a rationale for his conclusions. He stated what he saw as obvious: the search of Dollree Mapp's home was unreasonable and therefore violated the Fourth Amendment of the United States Constitution.

Timing mattered. Although the case of *Mapp v. Ohio* was accepted for review by the Supreme Court of the United States in the fall of 1960, this might not have been so if it had come at a different time in the doctrinal development of the Constitution. Perhaps the Court would have still taken the case. I doubt it. Even if the justices did decide to address the issues raised in *Mapp v. Ohio,* it is likely the outcome would have been quite different from the status quo. But decades of indecisions that led up to *Mapp v. Ohio* made the legal questions raised by this case even more relevant to a Court that now seemed inclined to change the law. The issues raised were salient. The Fourth Amendment quandary came before the right nine justices at a particular point in their legal development. Clearly questions surrounding searches and seizures were more important for resolution for some of the justices, as we shall see. Remember, too, that for all intents, *Mapp v. Ohio* was taken for review on First Amendment grounds, not Fourth. So a ripe constitutional claim came to the Court under the guise of a freedom of expression issue, the more salient Fourth Amendment question merely a subtext. . . .

When docket number 236 was presented [at the justices' private conference], "The discussion continued to be devoted almost entirely to the constitutionality of the Ohio obscenity statute." It was not difficult for the Brethren to come to an agreement on the state law. Justice Harlan's docket book reflects this consensus. While there was widespread agreement on the state obscenity statute, there was considerable debate about the search and seizure question and the fate of *Wolf v. Colorado.* Justice Douglas indicated to the others that although there was no majority willing to rule on Fourth Amendment grounds, he found the facts in *Mapp* violated both the First and Fourteenth Amendments. Chief Justice Warren and Justice Brennan were in agreement. Still the tie that bound the majority coalition hinged on the First Amendment. Clark too had indicated his interest in seeing *Wolf* overturned. . . . However, there was no consensus. The only majority that existed in *Mapp v. Ohio* at the first conference was on the fate of the Ohio obscenity law. Clark was selected to write the majority opinion.

Clark swiftly realized the opportunity *Mapp* provided. "On the elevator after leaving the conference room, the Texan turned to Black and Brennan and asked, "Wouldn't this be a good case to apply the exclusionary rule and do what *Wolf* didn't do?" The focus of Bernard Berkman's brief resonated. If indeed the search of Mapp's home was illegal, should the evidence be excluded? Was this the opportunity to change *Wolf*? Was this the case that would incorporate the remedy that corresponded with *Wolf's* Fourth Amendment right? Clark was intrigued enough to consider the possibility. No doubt he found support in Brennan, but the author of *Wolf*, Frankfurter, was horrified. On the question of search and seizure Clark could rely on Warren, Brennan, and Douglas. He was one vote shy of a majority opinion that would adjudicate *Mapp* as a Fourth Amendment case. Still, the two-prong approach to Fourth Amendment violations could and would be revisited by the Court. Despite the lack of oral arguments on the matter, or briefs that fully explored the implications for the Fourth Amendment, *Mapp v. Ohio* was in the process of being transformed from a First Amendment case to a Fourth Amendment one.

Clark's drafting of *Mapp* was thorough. . . . Clark circulated his first draft on April 28, 1961. Attached to the draft sent to Hugo Black was the following note. "Hugo — At your convenience I would appreciate your criticisms. This is the first draft and will need some 'polishing.' On the reference to Chicago and N.Y. we have some statistics that refute the assumption that private remedy (damages, prosecution of the officers, etc) afford any relief. Thanks — TCC." Clark argued in this first draft that "Of the 37 states passing on the Weeks exclusionary rule since the *Wolf* decision, 21 have either adopted or adhered to the rule. While in 1949 almost two thirds of the states were opposed to the rule, now 57% of those passing upon it approve. Thus, while 66% admitted the evidence in 1949, only 48% presently adhere to that rule." . . .

Clark pointed out the inconsistency of a federal exclusionary rule but no corresponding state remedy. Under the federal system, some arrests were undoubtedly lost. Quoting [Justice Benjamin] Cardozo, Clark conceded that at times the "criminal is to go free because the constable has blundered." But "The Amendment's protection [can be] made effective for everyone only by upholding it when invoked by the worst of men." Clark took the position that society as a whole benefits despite the windfall that comes to the few. . . .

The core of Clark's opinion would not be altered much by his colleagues, but Clark was wise in attempting to build consensus for his draft. His request to Black was genuine. Indeed Clark's private papers reveal correspondence with Black and Douglas *even before* Clark released his first draft on April 28th. On April 25th Clark sent a note to Black: "Dear Hugo: I hope this is better. I have re-arranged and inserted new material. Thanks for the suggestions. TCC." Clark's early drafts indicate substantial revisions and additions due to Black's input. A note of April 29, 1961: "Dear Tom: That is a mighty fine opinion you have written in No. 236 – *Mapp v. Ohio.* Please join me in it. William O. Douglas." Other justices too felt compelled to express their views. By early May, Clark had heard from Brennan saying that he would join. "May 1, 1961 RE: No. 236 – *Mapp v. Ohio* Dear Tom: Of course you know I think this is just magnificent and wonderful. I have not joined anything since I came with greater pleasure. Sincerely, Bill" The Chief Justice joined as well. In a letter dated May 2nd the Chief writes simply, "Dear Tom: RE: NO. 236 – *Mapp v. Ohio* I agree. E.W."

However, both Potter Stewart and John Marshall Harlan indicated their reservations of Clark's early draft. Stewart responded on May 1st that "As I am sure you anticipated, your proposed opinion in this case came as quite a surprise." Stewart then laid out his concerns succinctly and forcefully. His writings indicate strong reservations. It would seem that Stewart was a clear dissent. . . .

Harlan's response to Clark's first draft was more acerbic. His three and a half pages ended with the by-then obvious conclusion, "Perhaps you will have gathered from the foregoing that I would not be about to join you in your present opinion!" He, like Stewart, believed a consensus was reached on the constitutionality of the Ohio statute and that *Mapp* was an unwise vehicle to alter the ruling in *Wolf*. . . .

At the heart of Harlan's memorandum was the thorny problem of the exclusionary rule's origin. If it was judicially created, as some had argued in *Wolf v. Colorado*, then its constitutional status was less secure than rules that emanated from the text of the Constitution itself. This quibble over the origin of the exclusionary rule was not trivial. Indeed the rule's future would hinge on the debate of its origin. Some of the jurists believed that the legality of a search could be separated from criminal proceedings. The result of a Fourth Amendment violation was a separate question, one subject to the decision of a judge separate from the trial outcome. However, other court members felt the exclusionary rule required judges to protect constitutional violations, Fourth Amendment violations, and that this was integral to what the framers of the Constitution had in mind. Harlan felt that the exclusionary rule was not embedded in the Constitution as Clark argued in his draft. *Wolf* made that clear and the facts of *Mapp* did little to change the status quo. . . .

Justice Clark began working on a response to Harlan almost immediately. By May 3rd he had drafted a memo aimed more at defending his position than attempting to convert Harlan. Like any good lawyer or politician, Clark began by pointing out to Harlan their areas of agreement.

You are quite right with regard to the mere possession of obscene material as a possible First Amendment violation, but, of course, as was pointed out in the Conference, it clearly raises the *Wolf* question to which was made direct reference in the opinion of the Ohio Supreme Court.

Clark even noted that during conference, three justices indicated that the Fourth Amendment problem was an "alternative ground for reversal." While Clark admitted that all controversial cases were grounds for disagreement, "I have a court and therefore my theory has support." Clark again reiterated the growing popularity of the exclusionary rule in state law and his belief, along with those of others, that *Weeks* is a constitutionally based rule. . . .

The die was cast, and Clark's opinion would prevail. . . .

Mapp was the first of this criminal procedure revolution. By the time Earl Warren left the high bench in 1969, little of the Bill of Rights' criminal procedure provisions remained differentiated in state and federal courts.

Neither the Vinson Court before him nor the Burger Court after him would have the impact the Warren Court justices did on criminal procedure. In terms of rights of the accused, *Mapp* was the beginning of the due process revolution. The five-to-four ruling caught law enforcement off guard. What had been acceptable practice prior to the Mapp search in 1957 was no more. The legal community too was stunned by the Court's reach. *Wolf* had indicated that states must set standards for meeting the threshold of Fourth Amendment due process. *Mapp* altered the tone. Criminal procedure safeguards were in the hands of the Supreme Court. Furthermore, replaying the *Mapp* decision throughout the decade in terms of Fifth, Sixth, and Eighth Amendment rights left police reeling, state legislatures gasping, and the legal community uncertain about the role of courts in instituting rapid and complete change in what had been a traditional state function, criminal law. . . .

Even though the Supreme Court of the United States was through with the legal trial of Dollree Mapp, it was far from finished with interpreting the Fourth Amendment. On average the Court docket contained at least ten cases per term turning on Fourth Amendment grounds. Clearly *Mapp* had not laid down a bright-line rule. . . .

[Subsequent rulings, recognizing a "good faith" exception to the exclusionary rule, when police believe they have a valid warrant, have rendered] the rule of exclusion both a blessing and a curse. It is a blessing because it curtails the actions of poorly trained, inexperienced, and negligent police officers. It yields no fruit for the brutal and harassing officer. Few of these exist (although of course, some do), with the majority of law enforcers being public servants who deserve the respect and trust of the citizens they protect. Herein lies the curse. The circuitous and litigious exclusionary rule has virtually created a non-rule. So fact-bound is the Fourth Amendment remedy that the predictive value of the exclusionary rule is almost nil. . . .

19

Fourth Amendment First Principles

AKHIL REED AMAR

Akhil Reed Amar is a professor at Yale Law School and a recognized authority on constitutional law and criminal procedure. This selection comes from his 1994 Harvard Law Review article, which reappears in his 1997 book, The Constitution and Criminal Procedure, *in which he provocatively critiques the Supreme Court's rulings on the rights of the accused under the Fourth, Fifth, and Sixth Amendments. In the excerpt here, Amar criticizes the Supreme Court's rulings on "unreasonable searches and seizures" for making a "mess" of the Fourth Amendment. In re-examining the history and structure of the Fourth Amendment, he challenges conventional wisdom and constitutional doctrines in a number of ways. The "reasonableness" of searches and seizures, for instance, should be determined by juries according to Amar, and the exclusion of illegally obtained (but reliable) evidence in criminal trials is wrong in principle and in practice. Amar concludes by proposing that illegal searches and seizures by police and other governmental misconduct should be deterred through civil damage suits and administrative sanctions, instead of through the Fourth Amendment's "exclusionary rule."*

———————

THE FOURTH AMENDMENT today is an embarrassment. Much of what the Supreme Court has said in the last half-century—that the amendment generally calls for warrants and probable cause for all searches and seizures, and exclusion of illegally obtained evidence—is initially plausible but ultimately misguided. As a matter of text, history, and plain old common sense, these three pillars of modern Fourth Amendment case law are hard to support; in fact, today's Supreme Court does not really support them. Except when it does. Warrants are not required— unless they are. All searches and seizures must be grounded in probable cause—but not on Tuesdays. And unlawfully seized evidence must be excluded whenever five votes say so. Meanwhile, sensible rules that the amendment clearly does lay down or presuppose—that all searches and seizures must be reasonable, that warrants (and only warrants) always require probable cause, and that the officialdom should he held liable for unreasonable searches and seizures—are ignored by the Justices. Sometimes. The result is a vast jumble of judicial pronouncements that is not merely complex and contradictory, but often perverse. Criminals go free while honest citizens are intruded upon in outrageous ways with little or no real remedy. If there are good reasons for these and countless other odd results, the Court has not provided them. . . .

In what follows, I shall first critique the current doctrinal mess and then attempt to sketch out a better way—a package that, taken as a whole, strikes me as far superior to the status quo along any number of dimensions. It is more faithful to constitutional text and history. It is more coherent and sensible. It is less destructive of the basic trial value of truth seeking— sorting the innocent from the guilty. It is more conducive to the basic appellate value of truth speaking; it will help courts to think straight and write true, openly identifying criteria of reasonableness rather than mouthing unreasonable principles that are blindly followed, and then blandly betrayed. Finally, my package, taken as a whole, can be understood by, and draws on the participation and wisdom of, ordinary citizens— We the People, who in the end must truly comprehend and respect the constitutional rights enforced in Our name. . . .

The Mess: A Critique

The words of the Fourth Amendment really do mean what they say. They do not require warrants, even presumptively, for searches and seizures. They do not require probable cause for all searches and seizures without warrants. They do not require—or even invite—exclusions of evidence, contraband, or stolen goods. All this is relatively obvious if only we read the amendment's words carefully and take them seriously.

Warrant Requirement?

The modern Supreme Court has claimed on countless occasions that there is a warrant requirement in the Fourth Amendment. There are two variants of the warrant requirement argument—a strict (per se) variant that insists that searches and seizures always require warrants, and a looser (modified) variant that concedes the need to craft various common-sense exceptions to a strict warrant rule. Both variants fail.

The Per Se Approach. The first (per se) variant interpolates but nevertheless purports to stay true to the text. The amendment contains two discrete commands—first, all searches and seizures must be reasonable; second, warrants authorizing various searches and seizures must be limited (by probable cause, particular description, and so on). What is the relation between these two commands? The per se approach reasons as follows: Obviously, the first and second commands are yoked by an implicit third that no search or seizure may take place except pursuant to a warrant. Although not expressing the point in so many words, the amendment plainly presumes that warrantless searches and seizures are per se unreasonable. Surely executive officials should not be allowed to intrude on citizens in a judicially unauthorized manner. And the mode of proper judicial authorization is the warrant. Why else would the warrant clause exist?

Standing alone, this line of argument is initially plausible. But when all the evidence is in, we shall see that it is plainly wrong. Begin by noting that the per se interpolation is only one of several possible ways of understanding the relationship between the amendment's two commands. Perhaps, for example, there is no logical relation between the two: the first speaks globally to all searches and seizures, whereas the second addresses the narrower issue of warrants. Or, if this reading seems insufficiently holistic, the same result obtains under a more aesthetic reformulation: warrants are not required, but any warrant that does issue is per se unreasonable if not supported by probable cause, particular description, and the rest. As we shall see, this reading ultimately squares more snugly with the amendment's specific words, harmonizes better with its historic context, and makes considerably more common sense. . . .

Arrests without warrants. At common law, arrests—seizures of persons— could take place without warrants in a variety of circumstances. So said the major founding-era commentators. In 1792—one year after ratification of the Fourth Amendment—the Second Congress explicitly conferred this common law arrest power on federal marshals. Relying on this and other broad historical evidence, the modern Supreme Court in *United States v. Watson* carved out an "arrest exception" to its so-called "warrant requirement." But all this raises an obvious logical problem with the "requirement" itself. If an arrest—one of the most intrusive kinds of seizures imaginable—does not require a warrant, why do less intrusive searches and seizures?

Searches pursuant to arrests. . . . [T]he modern Supreme Court has carved out an "incident to arrest exception" to its so-called "warrant requirement" for all searches. But once again, this exception seems to *dis*prove the rule: why should various less intrusive, nonarrest searches be subject to requirements that arrest searches are not?

Not only were warrants unnecessary for "mere evidence" arrest searches; but also warrants could not, historically speaking, support a search for certain types of "mere evidence." The common law search warrants referred to in the warrant clause were solely for stolen goods; various early American statutes extended warrants to searches for smuggled or dangerous goods (gunpowder, diseased and infected items, and the like), contraband, and criminal instrumentalities. If there was probable cause to believe that a place contained these items, an ex parse warrant could issue, without notice to the owner of the place, lest he be tipped off and spirit away the goods, or lest the items cause imminent harm. Even if ultimately innocent, mere possession of these items was suspicious or dangerous enough to justify summary process, and the standard for this process was probable cause. But once searches for mere evidence are allowed, wholly innocent and unthreatening citizens are much more likely to be implicated. With modern forensic techniques, virtually any place could yield "evidence" of some offense, civil or criminal—fingerprints of a next-door neighbor suspected of a traffic offense, carpet fibers relevant to products liability issues, and so on. Under these circumstances, the summary and ex parse procedures underlying warrants become quite problematic on due process grounds. Strictly read, the warrant clause applies only to search warrants akin to traditional search warrants—warrants for contraband, stolen goods, and the like. Once uprooted from this soil, the amendment's "probable cause" formulation becomes awkward and oppressive. (There is always probable cause to believe the government will find *something* in a house—walls, for example—yet surely *that* kind of probable cause cannot always suffice to support an ex parse warrant.) The upshot is not that government may never conduct reasonable searches for "mere evidence" like a murderer's bloodstained shirt, believed to be stashed in the car of an unsuspecting neighbor—that would be silly— but that the *warrant clause* cannot always be stretched to reach these searches. And this straightforward result is yet another signal that many of the most important searches and seizures can and must take place without warrants. . . .

Successful searches and seizures. At common law, it seems that nothing succeeded like success. Even if a constable had no warrant and only weak or subjective grounds for believing someone to be a felon or some item to be contraband or stolen goods, the constable could seize the suspected person or thing. The constable acted at his peril. If wrong, he could be held liable in a damage action. But if he merely played a hunch and proved right—if the suspect *was* a felon, or the goods *were* stolen or contraband— this *ex post* success apparently was a complete defense. . . . We shall return to this point later, but for now it is yet another historical example casting doubt on the so-called warrant requirement. . . .

Exigent circumstances. In a wide range of fast-breaking situations—hot pursuits, crimes in progress, and the like—a warrant requirement would be foolish. Recognizing this, the modern Supreme Court has carved out an "exigent circumstances exception" to its so-called warrant requirement.

Consent searches. If government officials obtain the uncoerced authorization of the owner or apparent owner, surely they should be allowed to search a place, even without a warrant. And the modern Supreme Court has so held. . . .

Plain view searches. When a Secret Service agent at a presidential event stands next to her boss, wearing sunglasses and scanning the crowd in search of any small sign that something might be amiss, she is searching without a warrant. Yet surely this must be constitutional, and the Supreme Court has so suggested. At times, however, the Court has played word games, insisting that sunglass or naked-eye searches are not really searches. But if high-tech binoculars or X-ray glasses are used, then maybe . . .

These word games are unconvincing and unworthy. A search is a search, whether with Raybans or X rays. The difference between these two searches is that one may be much more reasonable than another. In our initial hypothetical, the search is public—the agent is out in the open for all to see; nondiscriminatory—everyone is scanned, not just, say, blacks; unintrusive—no X-ray glasses or binoculars here; consented to—when one ventures out in public, one does assume a certain risk of being seen; and justified—the President's life is on the line. But change these facts, and the outcome changes—not because a nonsearch suddenly becomes a search, but because a search at some point becomes *unreasonable.* . . .

Real life. Finally, consider the vast number of real-life, unintrusive, nondiscriminatory searches and seizures to which modern-day Americans are routinely subjected: metal detectors at airports, annual auto emissions tests, inspections of closely regulated industries, public school regimens, border searches, and on and on. All of these occur without warrants. Are they all unconstitutional? Surely not, the Supreme Court has told us, in a variety of cases. What the Court has not clearly explained, however, is how all these warrantless searches are consistent with its so-called warrant requirement. . . .

The Modified Per Se Approach. At this point, a supporter of the so-called warrant requirement is probably tempted to concede some exceptions and modify the per se claim: warrantless searches and seizures are per se unreasonable, save for a limited number of well-defined historical and commonsensical exceptions.

This modification is clever, but the concessions give up the game. The per se argument is no longer the textual argument it claimed to be; it no longer merely specifies an implicit logical relation between the reasonableness command and the warrant clause. To read in a warrant requirement that is not in the text—and then to read in various nontextual exceptions to that so-called requirement—is not to read the Fourth Amendment at all. It is to rewrite it. What's more, in conceding that, above and beyond historical exceptions, common sense dictates various additional exceptions to the so-called warrant requirement, the modification seems to concede that the ultimate touchstone of the amendment is not the warrant but reasonableness.

According to the modified approach, the Framers did not say what they meant, and what they meant—warrants, always—cannot quite be taken seriously, so today we must make reasonable exceptions. On my reading, the Framers did say what they meant, and what they said makes eminent good sense: all searches and seizures must be reasonable. Precisely because these searches and seizures can occur in all shapes and sizes under a wide variety of circumstances, the Framers chose a suitably general command.

The Per Se Unreasonableness of Broad Warrants. If all this is so, why has the Court continued to pay lip service to the so-called warrant requirement? What is the purpose of the warrant clause, and how does it relate to the more general command of reasonableness? And what is wrong with the logic that drives the warrant requirement—namely, that executive officials should be prohibited from searching and seizing without judicial approval, and that the warrant clause specifies the proper mode of this approval?

To anticipate my answers to these related questions: Perhaps the Justices have been slow to see the light because they do not understand that juries, as well as judges, are the heroes of the Founders' Fourth Amendment story. Indeed, at times, the Founders viewed judges and certain judicial proceedings with suspicion; this unflattering truth may not immediately suggest itself to modern-day judges. The amendment's warrant clause does not require, presuppose, or even prefer warrants—it *limits* them. Unless warrants meet certain strict standards, they are per se unreasonable. . . .

Begin with the doubly flawed logic driving the warrant requirement. Consider the person who issues the warrant. In England, certain Crown *executive* officials regularly exercised this warrant power. We need only recall the fans of the 1763 English case, *Wilkes v. Wood*, whose plot and cast of characters were familiar to every schoolboy in America, and whose lessons the Fourth Amendment was undeniably designed to embody. *Wilkes*—and not the 1761 Boston writs of assistance controversy, which went almost unnoticed in debates over the federal Constitution and Bill of Rights—was *the* paradigm search and seizure case for Americans. Indeed, it was probably the most famous case in late eighteenth-century America, period. In *Wilkes*, a sweeping warrant had been issued by a Crown officer, Secretary of State Lord Halifax. In colonial America, Crown executive officials, including royal governors, also claimed authority to issue warrants. Well into the twentieth century, states vested warrant-issuing authority in justices of the peace — even when such justices also served as prosecutors — and today states confer warrant authority on clerks and "magistrates" who are neither lawyers nor judges and who at times look rather like police chiefs.

Even when a judge issued a warrant, revolutionary Americans greeted the event with foreboding. Before the American Revolution, colonial judges lacked the independence from the Crown that their British brothers had won after the Glorious Revolution. Sitting at the pleasure of the monarch, the King's judicial magistrates in America were at times hard to distinguish from his executive magistrates — especially when a single Crown lackey wore several hats, as often occurred. Nor did the foreboding disappear after the American Revolution, when judges won a measure of institutional independence from the executive branch. Even an Article III judge, after all, had been appointed by the President, looked to the President for possible promotion to a higher court, and drew his salary from the government payroll. What's more, such a judge was an official of the central government — perhaps not so imperial as his Crown-directed colonial predecessors, but suspicious nonetheless. Would the handful of elite federal judges truly be able to empathize with the concerns of ordinary folk? And a single bad apple could spoil the bunch; if even one federal judge was a lord or a lackey, executive officials shopping for easy warrants would know where to go. Far more trustworthy were twelve men, good and true, on a local jury, independent of the government, sympathetic to the legitimate concerns of fellow citizens, too numerous to be corrupted, and whose vigilance could not easily be evaded by governmental judge-shopping. . . .

What would happen if no warrant issued? Here we come to the second big error in the doubly flawed logic driving the warrant requirement. Warrantless intrusions were hardly immune from judicial review in the early years of the Republic. Rather, any official who searched or seized could be sued by the citizen target in an ordinary trespass suit — with both parties represented at trial and a jury helping to decide between the government and the citizen. If the jury deemed the search or seizure unreasonable — and reasonableness was a classic jury question — the citizen plaintiff would win and the official would be obliged to pay (often heavy) damages. Any federal defense that the official might try to claim would collapse, trumped by the finding that the federal action was unreasonable, and thus unconstitutional under the Fourth Amendment, and thus no defense at all. . . .

Now we can see why the Fourth Amendment text most emphatically did not require warrants—why, indeed, its reference to warrants is so plainly negative: "*no* Warrants shall issue, but . . . " The warrant clause says only when warrants may not issue, not when they may, or must. Even if all the minimum prerequisites spelled out in the warrant clause are met, a warrant is still unlawful, and may not issue, if the underlying search or seizure it would authorize would be unreasonable. . . .

At a minimum, of course, a lawful warrant can issue only from one duly authorized, and only if it meets the explicit textual requirements of probable cause, oath, particular description, and so forth. By analogy to the traditional eighteenth-century search warrant, and in order to avoid serious due process concerns, an ex parse search warrant arguably should be allowed only for items akin to contraband and stolen goods, for the probable cause test and the *ex parte* process both presuppose this limited context; if extended to warrants for "mere evidence," the warrant clause at a minimum should require "probable cause" to believe that the custodian would defy a subpoena or—stricter still—would destroy the evidence. It also seems clear that no warrant should issue if the underlying search or seizure would be unreasonable, even if the minimal elements of the warrant clause are met. (Consider, for example, a strip search of high school girls to be conducted by an individual policeman with a 55 percent probability of finding tobacco cigarettes.)

But who should decide what is unreasonable, or whether probable cause is truly met? In the first instance, the issuing magistrate. But what if the citizen target disagrees, and tries to (re)litigate the matter by bringing it before a trial judge and jury for full adversarial adjudication?

If an executive (or only quasi-judicial) magistrate issued the warrant, the verdict of *Wilkes v. Wood* and of Blackstone seems clear. Just as in England, where a general warrant issued by Lord Halifax was, in Blackstone's phrase, "no warrant at all," so too, in America, an unreasonable executive warrant or one without probable cause (from the perspective of the civil jury) is no warrant at all and should therefore support a cause of action against the executive issuer himself. (In England, Wilkes recovered the princely sum of 4,000 pounds from Lord Halifax.) Because the defect of "unreasonableness" or "improbable cause" typically does not appear on the face of the warrant—unlike the defect in the *Wilkes* warrant—inferior officers who merely execute the warrant ministerially might escape liability altogether; if held liable, they should probably be able to implead the executive issuer for indemnification.

When an unreasonable or improbable warrant (from the jury's perspective) issues from a judge—a member of a court of general jurisdiction—things take on a different hue. For unlike an executive official, the judge can claim that, in issuing the warrant, he made the requisite findings of reasonableness and probability and that these findings are res judicata and thus cannot be questioned by a jury but can be overturned only by a higher court. Surely the officials who executed this judicial warrant must be held immune—this immunity is of course why they sought the judicial warrant in the first place—for even if the search was *substantively* incorrect (from the jury's perspective), it was *jurisdictionally* authorized. The usual remedy for an incorrect judicial act is an appeal to a higher court, but this remedy rings hollow in certain contexts, like search warrants and ex parse temporary restraining orders; much of the damage is done before the target has had any real day in court.

This last result should trouble us. From the perspective of the later civil jury, an unreasonable search *has* occurred, or a warrant *has* issued without probable cause. Arguably, the Fourth Amendment was designed to privilege the perspective of the civil jury. If so, perhaps the fairest solution—though one not provided by the common law—would be for the government itself to make amends. After all, its officials sought and executed the warrant, and its judges approved it. An analogy to modern-day inverse condemnation law under the just-compensation clause suggests itself—an analogy perhaps strengthened by the textual parallels between the Fourth Amendment's ban on "seizures" of "papers, houses, and effects" and the Fifth Amendment's rules regarding "tak[ings]" of "private property."

Probable Cause Requirement?

In recognizing various exceptions to its so-called warrant requirement, the modern Court has routinely said that even warrantless searches and seizures ordinarily must be backed by "probable cause." But like its kindred warrant requirement, the probable cause requirement stands the Fourth Amendment on its head.

Begin with the text. The "probable cause" standard applies only to "warrants," not to all "searches" and "seizures." None of the other warrant rules—oath or affirmation, particular description, and so forth—sensibly applies to all searches and seizures: and the Court, bowing to the text and common sense, has never so applied them.

Why, then, has the Court tried to wrench the words "probable cause" from one clause and force them into another? Because of the "fundamental and obvious" notion that "less stringent standards for reviewing the officer's discretion in effecting a warrantless arrest and search would discourage resort to the procedures for obtaining a warrant." In the words of a leading commentator, "the concept of probable cause lies at the heart of the fourth amendment," and it would be "incongruous" if police officers have "greater power to make seizures than magistrates have to authorize them."

But this is simply our old friend, the doubly flawed logic driving the warrant requirement, now dragging along its yoked mate, the probable cause requirement. Contrary to this flawed logic, the Framers did not mind "discourag[ing] resort to . . . a warrant." They wanted to *limit* this imperial and *ex parte* device, so they insisted on a substantial standard of proof—and even that standard, understood in context, justified searches only for items akin to contraband or stolen goods, not "mere evidence." Precisely because officers carrying out warrantless searches and seizures would be accountable to judges and juries in civil damage actions after the fact, no fixed constitutional requirement of probable cause was imposed on all these searches and seizures; they simply had to be reasonable.

Of course, certain intrusive subcategories of warrantless action—arrests, for example—might generally require probable cause at common law, but this is a far cry from the idea that *all* searches and seizures must meet this standard to be reasonable. Supporters of a global probable cause requirement have yet to identify even a single early case, treatise, or state constitution that explicitly proclaims probable cause as the prerequisite for all searches and seizures. On the other side of the ledger, the First Congress clearly authorized various suspicionless searches of ships and liquor storehouses. And let us recall once again the apparent common law rule that a warrantless intrusion could be justified after the fact, even in the absence of objective probable cause *ex ante*, if it succeeded in turning up an actual felon.

So much for text and history. Now consult common sense. If "probable cause" is taken seriously—a good probability of finding items akin to contraband or stolen goods—surely it cannot provide the standard for all searches and seizures. What happens when the government wants to search or seize other items? Here the probable cause test is unilluminating and we need to revert instead to the real "heart of the fourth amendment": reasonableness. In other situations, a probable cause test is not merely unilluminating but downright silly. Must a search that has been consented to by the apparent owner be backed by probable cause? How about a search of items in plain, public view, as when our Secret Service agent scans the crowd, searching for anything unusual? What about metal detector and X-ray searches at airports? Or building code inspections? Or weapons pat-downs by police officers who legitimately fear for their personal safety? Or prison searches? What if a grand jury subpoenas a person precisely to determine whether there may be probable cause to believe a crime has occurred?

Justices and other supporters of the so-called probable cause requirement have only two responses. The first is to claim that all these things are not really "searches" or "seizures." But a search is a search even if consented to, or of an item in plain view, or if conducted via modern magnetic or X-ray technology, or if part of noncriminal law enforcement, or if no more intrusive than a frisk, or if done in prison. . . .

The second response also involves a possible watering down of the text—here, the *probable cause* idea itself. At first blush, the phrase seems to connote a standard akin to more than 50 percent, or at least something higher than, say, 1 percent: a warrant should issue only if it is probable— more likely than not, or at least not highly *un*likely—that the search will turn up the goods. And if limited to the context that gave it birth—the common law search warrant—these words could probably (1) be taken at face value. The words would, no doubt, strictly limit the number of ex parse warrants that could issue; but of course, that was just the point of the warrant clause. However, once wrenched from the warrant clause and (wrongly) proclaimed the heart of the Fourth Amendment, these words must be defined differently.

To begin with, probable cause cannot be a *fixed* standard. It would make little sense to insist on the same amount of probability regardless of the imminence of the harm, the intrusiveness of the search, the reason for the search, and so on. Also, probable cause cannot be a *high* standard. It would make no sense to say that I may not be searched via metal detectors and X-ray machines at JFK unless there is a high likelihood— more than 50 percent, or at least more than 1 percent—that I am toting a gun.

In effect, this approach reads "probable cause" as "reasonable cause." Is it not easier to read the words as written, and say that warrantless searches must simply be reasonable? For unlike the seemingly fixed and high standard of probable cause, reasonableness obviously does require different levels of cause in different contexts, and not always a high probability of success—if, say, we are searching for bombs on planes.

More than intellectual honesty and interpretive aesthetics are at stake, for once "probable cause" is watered down for warrantless searches, how can it be strictly preserved in the warrant clause itself? If 0.1 percent is good enough for airports, why not for warrants? The watering down of "probable cause" necessarily authorizes ex parse warrants on loose terms that would have shocked the Founders. Indeed, the modern Court has explicitly upheld "newfangled warrants" on less than probable cause in explicit violation of the core textual command of the warrant clause. History has been turned on its head, and loose, *ex parte* warrants—general warrants, really—now issue from central officialdom. Once again, apparent textual expansion leads to contraction elsewhere in an inversion of the original amendment's first principles.

Exclusionary Rule?

The modern Court not only has misunderstood the nature of Fourth Amendment rights but also has distorted Fourth Amendment remedies. This distortion has pushed in many directions at once. The Court has failed to nurture and at times has affirmatively undermined the tort remedies underlying the amendment, has concocted the awkward and embarrassing remedy of excluding reliable evidence of criminal guilt, and has then tried to water down this awkward and embarrassing remedy in ad hoc ways.

Let us return once again to the text of the Fourth Amendment. Its global command that all searches and seizures be reasonable applies equally to civil and criminal searches. And its reference to Americans' right to be "secure in their persons, houses, papers, and effects" should remind us of background common law principles protecting these interests of personhood, property, and privacy—in a word, the law of tort.

Typically, if one's person or house or papers or effects are unreasonably trespassed upon, one can bring a civil action against the trespasser. And this is exactly what happened in pre Revolutionary England and America. In a series of landmark English cases—most famously, *Wilkes v. Wood*— oppressive general warrants were struck down in civil jury trespass actions brought against the officials who committed or authorized the unreasonable searches and seizures. In America, both before and after the Revolution, the civil trespass action tried to a jury flourished as the obvious remedy against haughty customs officers, tax collectors, constables, marshals, and the like.

Tort law remedies were thus clearly the ones presupposed by the Framers of the Fourth Amendment and counterpart state constitutional provisions. Supporters of the exclusionary rule cannot point to a single major statement from the Founding—or even the antebellum or Reconstruction eras—supporting Fourth Amendment exclusion of evidence in a criminal trial. Indeed, the idea of exclusion was so implausible that it seems almost never to have been urged by criminal defendants, despite the large incentive that they had to do so, in the vast number of criminal cases litigated in the century after Independence. And in the rare case in which the argument for exclusion was made, it received the back of the judicial hand. . . .

Lochner's Legacy. How then, did exclusion creep into American law? By a series of missteps and mishaps. Because the detailed story has been well told by others, I shall only summarize.

The confusion began with the Supreme Court's landmark 1886 case, *Boyd v. United States.* Collapsing the Fourth Amendment rule against unreasonable seizures into the Fifth Amendment ban on compelled self-incrimination, the *Boyd* Court excluded various papers that the government had in effect subpoenaed and sought to use in a quasicriminal case against the target of the subpoena. The Fourth Amendment's reasonableness clause and the Fifth Amendment's incrimination clause, said the Court, "run almost into each other" and "throw great light on each other." Continuing this conflation of clauses, later cases expanded exclusion to searches and seizures in which the compelled self-incrimination of subpoenas was wholly absent.

Boyd and its immediate progeny involved corporate and regulatory offenses rather than violent crime. These cases took root in a judicial era that we now know by the name *Lochner,* and the spirit inspiring *Boyd* and its progeny was indeed akin to *Lochner's* spirit: a person has a right to his property, and it is unreasonable to use his property against him in a criminal proceeding.

Several things can be said about this intriguing claim. For starters, it surely cannot explain excluding contraband or stolen goods, which were never one's property to begin with—and the Court's eventual expansion of exclusion, four decades after *Boyd,* to cover these categories occurred without cogent explanation. Next, this claim has a certain initial plausibility in the context in which it arose, involving personal papers. To introduce a man's diary as evidence against him is perhaps perilously close to forcing him to take the stand himself. In both cases he is being done in against his will by his own words, words that he has never chosen to share with anyone else. Through a diary, a defendant arguably becomes an involuntary "witness"—one whose words testify against himself at trial. But whatever one thinks of a diary or personal papers, where Fourth and Fifth Amendment concerns may overlap and reinforce, a bloodstained shirt is something else entirely. Diaries and personal papers arguably testify—in the defendant's words, as might the defendant himself as an actual "witness" at trial—but a bloody shirt does not. Only the most peculiar property fetishist could say that everything one owns, bloody shirts and all, is simply an extension of the "person" protected by the Fifth Amendment, in the same way that a diary or a personal paper arguably is. . . .

Boyd's effort to fuse the Fourth and Fifth Amendments has not stood the test of time and has been plainly rejected by the modern Court. *Boyd's* mistake was not in its focus on the concept of Fourth Amendment reasonableness, nor in its laudable effort to read the Fourth Amendment reasonableness clause in light of other constitutional provisions. (Indeed, I shall later call for just such an approach.) Rather, *Boyd's* mistake was to misread both the reasonableness clause and the incrimination clause by trying to fuse them together. At heart, the two provisions are motivated by very different ideas; they do not "run almost into each other" as a general matter. The Fourth, unlike the Fifth, applies equally to civil searches, and the Fifth, unlike the Fourth, is strictly limited to compelled testimony. Even with compelled testimony, it is hard for some to see what transcendent constitutional norm is served by the incrimination clause outside the context in which it arose—political and religious thought crime and speech crime. When it comes to murders and rapes, the intuitive appeal of an expansive reading of the incrimination clause drops dramatically. In ordinary morality, people are encouraged and often obliged to admit their misdeeds, and the law requires a person to testify truthfully even against her dearest childhood friend (when her reluctance to testify is supported by more worthy motives than the urge of thugs to save their skins). To expand the Fifth beyond compelled testimony by fusing it with the Fourth does not serve any overarching constitutional value, apart from now-discredited property fetishism. . . .

The Better Way: A Proposal

As announced at the outset, my aim here is to provide a way out of the mess that is the current Fourth Amendment. Implicit in my critique are the basic elements of an attractive alternative approach. In developing this approach, we need not abandon all that the modern Court has said and done. To be sure, we should reject the extravagant textual and historical claims that the Court has at times made—that the amendment's words implicitly require warrants; that all warrantless searches require probable cause, lest warrants be discouraged; that the incrimination and reasonableness clauses "run almost into each other" as a general matter; and that Founding history supports all this. But beneath this sloppy textual and historical analysis lay genuine concerns to which the Justices were probably responding. As government power became increasingly bureaucratic, and

as highly organized paramilitary police departments emerged, perhaps the
Justices sensed a need to go beyond the common law jury system of
policing the police—and so they latched onto the warrant, and modified
the notion of probable cause. . . .

As it turns out, however, there is a better way to adapt to changes in
the structure of government, and to bring the Fourth Amendment into
the center of constitutional discourse today. And this better way does not
require us to twist the text or to manhandle the historical evidence. Let
us now assemble the elements of this better model, by considering in
turn Fourth Amendment rights, remedies, and regimes of enforcement.

Rights

Rights first. The core of the Fourth Amendment, as we have seen,
is neither a warrant nor probable cause, but reasonableness. Because of
the Court's preoccupation with warrants and probable cause—ordaining
these with one hand while chiseling out exception after exception with
the other—the Justices have spent surprisingly little time self-consciously
reflecting on what, exactly, makes for a substantively unreasonable search
or seizure.

Common-Sense (Tort) Reasonableness. Consider ordinary common-sense
reasonableness. Probability—"probable cause" or something more or
less—is obviously only one variable in a complex equation. To focus on
probability alone as the sine qua non of reasonableness would be a mistake.
Sometimes 0.1 percent is more than enough—consider bombs on planes—
and other times 100 percent may still be unreasonable. (Even if the
government knows with certainty that honest Abe's business log is in his
bedroom and contains a notation relevant to a civil suit between Betty
and Carol, a surprise nighttime search—as opposed to a subpoena—
would typically be unreasonable.) Common sense tells us to look beyond
probability to the importance of finding what the government is looking
for, the intrusiveness of the search, the identity of the search target, the
availability of other means of achieving the purpose of the search, and
so on.

As obvious as all this seems, the Court's obsession with warrants,
probable cause, and criminal exclusion has often made it difficult for the
Justices to admit what common sense requires. At times, the Court has
suggested that, because the core of the amendment involves criminal
investigation, exceptions to strict probable cause should be specially disfavored here. If taken seriously, this upside-down idea would mean that, as
between two equally unintrusive but low-probability searches, the search

justified by a *more* compelling purpose—criminal enforcement to protect person and property—is *less* constitutionally proper. . . .

For another example of how common-sense reasonableness could straighten out Fourth Amendment thinking and writing, consider electronic surveillance. In love with the warrant, the Court has blessed hidden audio and video bugs—even ones that must be installed by secret physical trespass—so long as these bugs are approved in advance by judicial warrant. The problem here is not in considering audio bugs Fourth Amendment "searches"—by ears rather than eyes—of the target's home, and "seizures" of some of her most valuable "effects," namely, her private conversations. The problem is trying to stretch the warrant clause to cover these things. It is not simply that, as Justice Black pointed out in *Katz*, the words of the warrant clause don't seem to fit, contemplating as they do physical things already in existence that can be "particularly described," rather than intangible conversations that don't yet exist. Rather, the problem is that these words, as we have seen, presuppose a search for items akin to contraband or stolen goods, not "mere evidence," such as where the target was and when she was there, which video surveillance could establish. . . .

. . . Simply put, are secret searches and seizures reasonable? Regardless of one's answer, at least one will be asking the right question—talking sense rather than nonsense.

Once we see that secrecy is a key issue raised by electronic surveillance, we also see that the issue arises in many other contexts, too. Consider the undercover cop who poses as someone she is not. From one perspective, whether she carries a bug or not, she is acting openly, not secretly. The target who speaks with our agent and lets her into his confidence knows that his eyes are being "searched" and his words "seized" by his conversation partner. What he does not know, however, is that she is a government official. So here, too, we have an element of secrecy and deception.

When is such deception permissible? Is winning a suspected hit man's confidence by posing as a mobster different from winning entrance into someone's home or car by posing as a stranded motorist? If so, what are the factors that distinguish among deceptions? Once again, the issues here must be organized not around warrants or probable cause but around reasonableness.

Just as a more secret search may be more unreasonable, so too with a more intrusive search. Today's Court recognizes that intrusiveness can make a difference, but the language of warrants and probable cause does not easily accommodate this insight. As we have seen, intrusiveness at times sneaks *sub rosa* into the judicial definition of what counts as a "search" or "seizure." But once we focus on reasonableness, we can more easily admit the truth: metal detection is often more acceptable than a strip search, not because the former is not a search but because it is less intrusive and thus more reasonable. All other things being equal, a compulsory urine test is more problematic if government officials insist on monitoring the production of the specimen. Greater intrusiveness requires greater justification. Only by keeping our eyes fixed on reasonableness as the polestar of the Fourth Amendment can we steer our way to a world where serious, sustained, and sensible Fourth Amendment discourse can occur.

Constitutional Reasonableness. Fourth Amendment reasonableness is not simply a matter of common sense: it is also an issue of constitutional law. For the Fourth Amendment is not merely tort law (in which issues of common-sense reasonableness loom large); it is also emphatically constitutional law. Of course, many obvious intuitions may resonate in both common sense and constitutional law. For example, the common-sense intuition about the special intrusiveness of monitored urine tests can easily be packaged in the language of constitutional privacy.

With this caveat in mind, let us recall a standard technique of constitutional interpretation: parsing one provision—especially if somewhat open-ended—in light of other constitutional provisions. In thinking about the broad command of the Fourth Amendment, we must examine other parts of the Bill of Rights to identify constitutional values that are elements of *constitutional* reasonableness. These other clauses at all times stand as independent hurdles, above and beyond composite reasonableness, that every search or seizure must clear, but the clauses can also serve other functions. They can furnish benchmarks against which to measure reasonableness and components of reasonableness itself. A government policy that comes close to the limit set by one of these independent clauses can, if conjoined with a search or seizure, cross over into constitutional unreasonableness.

For example, . . . [to] justify a search or seizure that lands with disproportionate impact on poor persons or persons of color, the government may at times claim that the poor or the nonwhite are also disproportionate *beneficiaries* of the scheme, because the government search is designed to reduce the risk that they will be victimized by violent crime, or drugs, or what have you. The interests of victims are hard to squeeze into the language of probable cause and warrants but comfortably fit under the canopy of reasonableness. Make no mistake, the issues of race and class— of the police officer, the target of the search or seizure, and the victim of the crime—will not be easy to sort out, but once again we will be asking the right questions, honestly and openly.

As with race and class, so too with sex. Searches and seizures that create opportunities for sexual oppression, harassment, or embarrassment are unreasonable both as a matter of common sense and constitutional morality, whether one uses the language of privacy or equality or both. Throughout my exposition, I have intentionally traded on these intuitions, purposely using gendered hypotheticals to illustrate quintessentially unreasonable searches. These intuitions are neither merely personal nor of recent vintage. Recall, for example, the striking language used by a Pennsylvania Anti-Federalist to conjure up a nightmarish search: an obviously male federal constable might invade the bedroom and the bed of a "woman," "pull[ ] down the clothes of [her] bed" and "search[ ] under her shift." These remarks appeared in 1787.

As the equal protection clause should remind us, constitutional reasonableness encompasses procedural regularity as well as substantive fairness, and the two are often tightly intertwined. Rule-of-law values affirmed in various constitutional ways—the due process, equal protection, and attainder clauses, and the more general separation of powers—teach us to be especially wary of searches and seizures that allow too much arbitrariness and ad hoc-ery, unbounded by public, visible rules promulgated in advance by legislatures and executive agencies. Recall here Justice Jackson's confession, in which he described searches of "every outgoing car," if "executed fairly and in good faith," as possibly "reasonable" even if "undiscriminating." I would say that such a search might well be constitutionally reasonable *precisely because* it is undiscriminating. A broader search is sometimes better—fairer, more regular, more constitutionally reasonable—if it reduces the opportunities for official arbitrariness, discretion, and discrimination. If we focus only on probabilities and probable cause, we will get it backwards. The broader, more evenhanded search is sometimes more constitutionally reasonable even if the probabilities are lower for each citizen searched. . . .

The above examples show just how broad and powerful constitutional reasonableness could become as a way of talking and thinking about the Fourth Amendment. Indeed the potential breadth and power of this new tool will no doubt trouble some. But it should surprise no one. For the Fourth Amendment, literally and in every other way, belongs at the center of the Bill of Rights and discussion about the Bill—in civil cases as well as criminal, on matters of both constitutional procedure and constitutional substance. By focusing on constitutional reasonableness, we restore the

Fourth to its rightful place. To be sure, the amendment is triggered only by a search or seizure, and to ignore these triggers is to rewrite the amendment into a global command of reasonableness. Yet a great many government actions can be properly understood as searches or seizures, especially when we remember that a person's "effects" may be intangible — as the landmark *Katz* case teaches us. Unlike the due process clause, in whose name so much has been done, the Fourth Amendment clearly speaks to substantive as well as procedural unfairness and openly proclaims a need to distinguish between reasonable and unreasonable government policy. For those who believe in a "substantive due process" approach to the Constitution, the Fourth Amendment thus seems a far more plausible textual base than the due process clause itself. For those who believe in general rationality review, the Fourth, here too, is more explicit than its current doctrinal alternative, the equal protection clause.

Remedies

Fixated on the exclusionary rule, the twentieth-century Supreme Court has, through acts of omission and commission, betrayed the traditional civil-enforcement model. What follows are illustrative but not exhaustive suggestions for refurbishing the traditional civil-enforcement model.

Entity Liability and Abolition of Immunity. Eighteenth-century common law allowed suit against the officers personally, but everyone understood that the real party in interest was the government itself, which would typically be forced to indemnify officials who were merely carrying out government policy. (Without indemnification, who would agree to work for the government?) . . .

In our century, however, judges for the first time have created wide zones of individual officer immunity for constitutional torts. Within these zones, the innocent citizen victim is in effect held liable and left to pay for the government's constitutional wrong. The Framers would have found the current remedial regime, in which a victim of constitutional tort can in many cases recover from neither the officer nor the government, a shocking violation of first principles, trumpeted in *Marbury v. Madison*, that for every right there must be a remedy.

The best way to dose this shocking remedial gap today would be to recognize direct liability of the government entity. (Of course, in keeping with Coase, the government could seek indemnification from, dock the pay of, or otherwise discipline, any officers who triggered the government's liability; this would most likely occur if officials were violating the entity's own internal policies.) If the search or seizure is ultimately deemed unreasonable, the government entity should pay. And the damages assessed will be a visible sign to legislators and the general public of the true costs of unreasonable government conduct.

Strict entity liability in the twentieth century makes perfect sense as the substitute for—indeed, the exact equivalent of—strict officer liability in the eighteenth century. The intervening years have brought us vastly increased bureaucratic density. The Framers' constables have become our police *departments*; their watchmen, our environmental protection *agencies*; and so on. The true locus of decision-making authority has shifted from the individual to the organization. The deterrence concept implicit in both the text and history of the amendment calls for placing (initial) liability at the level best suited to restructure government conduct to avoid future violations. For the Framers, that level was the constable; for us, the police department. . . .

Punitive Damages. Because only a fraction of unconstitutional searches and seizures will ever come to light for judicial resolution, merely compensatory damages in the litigated cases would generate systematic underdeterrence. The problem is hardly unique to the Fourth Amendment, and a widespread technique today is to use multipliers and punitive damages. As we have seen, the Framers were well aware of these techniques of "heavy" and "ruinous" damages. By 1789, punitive damages in search and seizure cases were "an invariable maxim." In fact, Lord Camden's explicit approval of punitive damages in *Wilkes v. Wood* and two companion search and seizure cases in the 1760s appears to mark the first clear acknowledgment in English case law of the very concept of punitive damages. *Wilkes's* lesson for us here is that modest and thoughtful remedial creativity *within the civil model* is in the truest spirit of the cases that gave birth to our Fourth Amendment. And in keeping with that spirit of modest remedial creativity, we should note an insight of modern tort theory: deterrence requires that the defendant must pay more than the plaintiff suffered, but not all this amount need go directly to the plaintiff. (This insight is actually implicit in Lord Camden's initial formulation, if read with care.) Perhaps some portion of punitive damages could flow to a "Fourth Amendment Fund" to educate Americans about the amendment and comfort victims of crime and police brutality, and thereby promote long term deterrence, compensation, and "security."

Class Actions, Presumed Damages, and Attorney's Fees. Large categories of unreasonable searches and seizures—street harassment, for example—will affect many persons, but each only a little. The offenses may be largely dignitary, and the citizen's out-of-pocket losses may be small or nonexistent. Here too, the problem is hardly unique to the Fourth Amendment, and modern law has developed general tools to address it. Class action aggregation techniques and minimum presumed damages are often the answer. Presumed damages are especially appropriate in Fourth Amendment cases, given Lord Camden's explicit embrace of an award of 300 pounds to a journeyman printer—a small fry of low "station and rank" caught up in the Wilkes affair—who had suffered in "mere personal injury only, perhaps 20 [pounds'] damages," but whose case raised a "great point of law touching the liberty" of "all the King's subjects."

In an isolated Fourth Amendment wrong involving a small dollar amount but large dignitary concerns, any plaintiff who proves a violation should receive reasonable attorney's fees, even if the fees bulk larger than the plaintiff's out-of-pocket damages, unless the government was willing to concede that a Fourth Amendment violation had indeed occurred.

Injunctive Relief. Early prevention is often better than after-the-fact remedy. The Fourth Amendment says its right "shall not be violated." When judges can prevent violations before they occur, they should do so—especially if after-the-fact damages could never truly make amends. Damages cannot bring back African-American males killed as a result of the unreasonable choke hold policy of the Los Angeles police department in the 1970s and 1980s. And yet in 1983 the Supreme Court in *Los Angeles v. Lyons* prevented federal courts from enjoining various forms of racially discriminatory police brutality. . . . *Lyons* was a sad entry in the annals of the Fourth Amendment. One can only wonder how much of the racial tragedy visited upon Los Angeles in recent years might have been avoided had the Supreme Court done the right thing in *Lyons* and sent a different signal to the LAPD.

Administrative Relief. The traditional judicial system is slow and cumbersome. Executive departments are typically the source of unconstitutional searches and seizures; is it too much to expect them to establish internal mechanisms to process citizen complaints quickly? Citizen review panels could serve a function akin to a traditional jury, and in many cases, victims of government unreasonableness might willingly forgo a judicial lawsuit in favor of a cheaper, less adversarial, quicker administrative solution that would vindicate their dignitary claims.

Regimes

At least four overlapping, reinforcing, and non-mutually exclusive enforcement regimes should exist to enforce the reasonableness norm.

Consider first a regime of *legislative* reasonableness. Legislatures are, and should be, obliged to fashion rules delineating the search and seizure authority of government officials. General rule of law, structural due process, and separation of powers principles frown on broad legislative abdications. In cases of borderline reasonableness, the less specifically the legislature has considered and authorized the practice in question, the less willing judges and juries should be to uphold the practice.

Now consider *executive/administrative* reasonableness. Professors John Kaplin, Anthony Amsterdam, and Kenneth Culp Davis and Judge Carl McGowan have generated thoughtful blueprints for this regime, and they deserve our most serious attention. Even if a search or seizure is broadly authorized by statute, administrators and agencies—including police departments—should promulgate implementing guidelines that publicly spell out more concrete search and seizure policies for recurring fact patterns. Advisory input from citizen panels may be particularly helpful here, but even if citizens do not participate in initial policy formation, public promulgation of agency guidelines will enable the citizenry to better assess things done in their name. Agencies should not only lay down substantive rules and standards but also implement these policies through good faith training programs and disciplinary mechanisms. Once again, judges and juries should be less willing to defer to official intrusions in borderline cases in which the agency fails to live up to this regime of reasonableness.

Next consider a regime of *judicial* reasonableness. Judges should continue to build up doctrine specifying certain actions that, as a matter of law, violate the Fourth Amendment. But unlike the current doctrinal mess, this new edifice would be built on the foundation of reason, not probability or warrant. Although no clear line divides common-sense reasonableness from constitutional reasonableness, judges should concentrate their doctrinal energies on the latter, especially in cases in which searches or seizures implicate constitutional principles beyond the Fourth Amendment, or in which judges have strong reasons to suspect unjustified jury insensitivity to certain claims or claimants. Although judicial preclearance may at times be appropriate, courts must strictly limit warrants. Civil litigation after the fact, with both citizen and government represented in the courtroom, would be far more deliberative and reviewable than the current system of practically unreviewable rubber-stamp magistrates acting ex parte.

Last, but not least, imagine a regime of *jury* reasonableness. Even when legislature, administrator, and judge have all accepted a search or seizure as reasonable, the government often should also be obliged to convince a civil jury of this. In the criminal context, the government may not prevail if the citizen can win over a jury under the Sixth Amendment. In the civil context, the parties' positions are reversed—the citizen is plaintiff, the government, the defendant—but a basic principle that governs the Sixth should inform the Seventh: the government should generally not prevail—at least on the issue of reasonableness—if the citizen can persuade a jury of her peers. Reasonableness is largely a matter of common sense, and the jury represents the common sense of common people.

20

Blind Spot: Racial Profiling, Meet Your Alter Ego:
Affirmative Action

RANDALL KENNEDY

*Randall Kennedy is a professor at Harvard Law School and previously
served as a law clerk to Justice Thurgood Marshall. In his book* Race,
Crime, and the Law *(1997) he criticized the Supreme Court's recent
rulings on the Fourth Amendment's guarantee against unreasonable searches
and seizures for encouraging police to target blacks and other minorities,
while also invalidating affirmative action programs and advancing of a
"colorblind Constitution" in its rulings on the equal protection of the law.
Here, he juxtaposes the controversies over racial profiling and affirmative
action in an article contributed to* The Atlantic Monthly *(2002).*

WHAT IS ONE to think about "racial profiling"? Confusion
abounds about what the term even means. It should be defined as the
policy or practice of using race as a factor in selecting whom to place
under special surveillance: if police officers at an airport decide to search
Passenger A because he is twenty-five to forty years old, bought a first-
class ticket with cash, is flying cross-country, and is apparently of Arab
ancestry, Passenger A has been subjected to racial profiling. But officials
often prefer to define racial profiling as being based solely on race; and
in doing so they are often seeking to preserve their authority to act against
a person partly on the basis of race. Civil-rights activists, too, often define
racial profiling as solely race-based; but their aim is to arouse their followers
and to portray law-enforcement officials in as menacing a light as possible.

The problem with defining racial profiling in the narrow manner of
these strange bedfellows is that doing so obfuscates the real issue confronting Americans. Exceedingly few police officers, airport screeners, or other
authorities charged with the task of foiling or apprehending criminals act
solely on the basis of race. Many, however, act on the basis of intuition,
using race along with other indicators (sex, age, patterns of past conduct)
as a guide. The difficult question, then, is not whether the authorities
ought to be allowed to act against individuals on the basis of race alone;
almost everyone would disapprove of that. The difficult question is

whether they ought to be allowed to use race at all in schemes of surveillance. If, indeed, it is used, the action amounts to racial discrimination. The extent of the discrimination may be relatively small when race is only one factor among many, but even a little racial discrimination should require lots of justification.

The key argument in favor of racial profiling, essentially, is that taking race into account enables the authorities to screen carefully and at less expense those sectors of the population that are more likely than others to contain the criminals for whom officials are searching. Proponents of this theory stress that resources for surveillance are scarce, that the dangers to be avoided are grave, and that reducing these dangers helps everyone — including, sometimes especially, those in the groups subjected to special scrutiny. Proponents also assert that it makes good sense to consider whiteness if the search is for Ku Klux Klan assassins, blackness if the search is for drug couriers in certain locales, and Arab nationality or ethnicity if the search is for agents of al Qaeda.

Some commentators embrace this position as if it were unassailable, but under U.S. law racial discrimination backed by state power is presumptively illicit. This means that supporters of racial profiling carry a heavy burden of persuasion. Opponents rightly argue, however, that not much rigorous empirical proof supports the idea of racial profiling as an effective tool of law enforcement. Opponents rightly contend, also, that alternatives to racial profiling have not been much studied or pursued. Stressing that racial profiling generates clear harm (for example, the fear, resentment, and alienation felt by innocent people in the profiled group), opponents of racial profiling sensibly question whether compromising our hard-earned principle of anti-discrimination is worth merely speculative gains in overall security.

A notable feature of this conflict is that champions of each position frequently embrace rhetoric, attitudes, and value systems that are completely at odds with those they adopt when confronting another controversial instance of racial discrimination — namely, affirmative action. Vocal supporters of racial profiling who trumpet the urgency of communal needs when discussing law enforcement all of a sudden become fanatical individualists when condemning affirmative action in college admissions and the labor market. Supporters of profiling, who are willing to impose what amounts to a racial tax on profiled groups, denounce as betrayals of "color blindness" programs that require racial diversity. A similar turn-about can be seen on the part of many of those who support affirmative action. Impatient with talk of communal needs in assessing racial profiling, they very often have no difficulty with subordinating the interests of individual white candidates to the purported good of the whole. Opposed to race consciousness in policing, they demand race consciousness in deciding whom to admit to college or select for a job.

The racial-profiling controversy — like the conflict over affirmative action — will not end soon. For one thing, in both cases many of the contestants are animated by decent but contending sentiments. Although exasperating, this is actually good for our society; and it would be even better if participants in the debates acknowledged the simple truth that their adversaries have something useful to say.

21

Homicide: A Year on the Killing Streets

DAVID SIMON

David Simon is a writer and a former reporter for the Baltimore Sun. *In 1988, he took a leave of absence and spent a year with a Baltimore homicide unit, chronicling their activities, practices, and procedures. Subsequently, in 1991 Simon published* Homicide: A Year on the Killing Streets. *In the excerpt here from that book, Simon describes a typical police interrogation of a suspect, and in the process, draws the reader into the experience of the suspect and the interrogator, especially regarding the* Miranda *ruling.*

YOU ARE A CITIZEN of a free nation, having lived your adult life in a land of guaranteed civil liberties, and you commit a crime of violence, whereupon you are jacked up, hauled down to a police station and deposited in a claustrophobic anteroom with three chairs, a table and no windows. There you sit for a half hour or so until a police detective — a man you have never met before, a man who can in no way be mistaken for a friend — enters the room with a thin stack of lined notepaper and a ball-point pen.

The detective offers a cigarette, not your brand, and begins an uninterrupted monologue that wanders back and forth for a half hour more, eventually coming to rest in a familiar place: *"You have the absolute right to remain silent."*

Of course you do. You're a criminal. Criminals always have the right to remain silent. At least once in your miserable life, you spent an hour in front of a television set, listening to this book-'em-Danno routine. You think Joe Friday was lying to you? You think Kojak was making this horseshit up? No way, bunk, we're talking sacred freedoms here, notably your Fifth Fucking Amendment protection against self-incrimination, and hey, it was good enough for Ollie North, so who are you to go incriminating yourself at the first opportunity? Get it straight: A police detective, a man who gets paid government money to put you in prison, is explaining your absolute right to shut up before you say something stupid.

"Anything you say or write may be used against you in a court of law."
Yo, bunky, wake the fuck up. You're now being told that talking to
a police detective in an interrogation room can only hurt you. If it could
help you, they would probably be pretty quick to say that, wouldn't they?
They'd stand up and say you have the right not to worry because what
you say or write in this godforsaken cubicle is gonna be used to your
benefit in a court of law. No, your best bet is to shut up. Shut up now.
*"You have the right to talk with a lawyer at any time—before any questioning,
before answering any questions, or during any questions."*
Talk about helpful. Now the man who wants to arrest you for violating
the peace and dignity of the state is saying you can talk to a trained
professional, an attorney who has read the relevant portions of the Maryland Annotated Code or can at least get his hands on some Cliffs Notes.
And let's face it, pal, you just carved up a drunk in a Dundalk Avenue
bar, but that don't make you a neurosurgeon. Take whatever help you
can get.
*"If you want a lawyer and cannot afford to hire one, you will not be asked
any questions, and the court will be requested to appoint a lawyer for you."*
Translation: You're a derelict. No charge for derelicts.
At this point, if all lobes are working, you ought to have seen enough
of this Double Jeopardy category to know that it ain't where you want
to be. How about a little something from Criminal Lawyers and Their
Clients for $50, Alex?
Whoa, bunk, not so fast.
"Before we get started, lemme just get through the paperwork," says
the detective, who now produces an Explanation of Rights sheet, BPD
Form 69. and passes it across the table
"EXPLANATION OF RIGHTS," declares the top line in bold block
letters The detective asks you to fill in your name, address, age, and
education, then the date and time. That much accomplished, he asks you
to read the next section. It begins, "YOU ARE HEREBY ADVISED
THAT:"
Read number one, the detective says. Do you understand number
one?
"You have the absolute right to remain silent."
Yeah, you understand. We did this already.
"Then write your initials next to number one. Now read number
two."
And so forth, until you have initialed each component of the *Miranda*
warning. That done, the detective tells you to write your signature on

the next line, the one just below the sentence that says, "I HAVE READ
THE ABOVE EXPLANATION OF MY RIGHTS AND FULLY UN-
DERSTAND IT."

You sign your name and the monologue resumes. The detective assures
you that he has informed you of these rights because he wants you to be
protected, because there is nothing that concerns him more than giving
you every possible assistance in this very confusing and stressful moment
in your life. If you don't want to talk, he tells you, that's fine. And if you
want a lawyer, that's fine, too, because first of all, he's no relation to the
guy you cut up, and second, he's gonna get six hours overtime no matter
what you do. But he wants you to know—and he's been doing this a lot
longer than you, so take his word for it—that your rights to remain silent
and obtain qualified counsel aren't all they're cracked up to be.

Look at it this way, he says, leaning back in his chair. Once you up
and call for that lawyer, son, we can't do a damn thing for you. No sir,
your friends in the city homicide unit are going to have to leave you
locked in this room all alone and the next authority figure to scan your case
will be a tie-wearing, three-piece bloodsucker—a no-nonsense prosecutor
from the Violent Crimes Unit with the official title of assistant state's
attorney for the city of Baltimore. And God help you then, son, because
a ruthless fucker like that will have an O'Donnell Heights motorhead like
yourself halfway to the gas chamber before you get three words out. Now's
the time to speak up, right now when I got my pen and paper here on
the table, because once I walk out of this room any chance you have of
telling your side of the story is gone and I gotta write it up the way it
looks. And the way it looks right now is first-fucking-degree murder.
Felony murder, mister, which when shoved up a man's asshole is a helluva
lot more painful than second-degree or maybe even manslaughter. What
you say right here and now could make the difference, bunk. Did I
mention that Maryland has a gas chamber? Big, ugly sumbitch at the
penitentiary on Eager Street, not twenty blocks from here. You don't
wanna get too close to that bad boy, lemme tell you.

A small, wavering sound of protest passes your lips and the detective
leans back in his chair, shaking his head sadly.

What the hell is wrong with you, son? You think I'm fucking with
you? Hey, I don't even need to bother with your weak shit. I got three
witnesses in three other rooms who say you're my man. I got a knife
from the scene that's going downstairs to the lab for latent prints. I got
blood spatter on them Air Jordans we took off you ten minutes ago. Why
the fuck do you think we took 'em? Do I look like I wear high-top
tennis? Fuck no. You got spatter all over 'em, and I think we both know

whose blood type it's gonna be. Hey, bunk, I'm only in here to make sure that there ain't nothing you can say for yourself before I write it all up.

You hesitate.

Oh, says the detective. You want to think about it. Hey, you think about it all you want, pal. My captain's right outside in the hallway, and he already told me to charge your ass in the first fuckin' degree. For once in your beshitted little life someone is giving you a chance and you're too fucking dumb to take it. What the fuck, you go ahead and think about it and I'll tell my captain to cool his heels for ten minutes. I can do that much for you. How 'bout some coffee? Another cigarette?

The detective leaves you alone in that cramped, windowless room. Just you and the blank notepaper and the Form 69 and . . . first-degree murder. First-degree murder with witnesses and fingerprints and blood on your Air Jordans. Christ, you didn't even notice the blood on your own fucking shoes. Felony murder, mister. First-fucking-degree. How many years, you begin to wonder, how many years do I get for involuntary manslaughter?

Whereupon the man who wants to put you in prison, the man who is not your friend, comes back in the room, asking if the coffee's okay.

Yeah, you say, the coffee's fine, but what happens if I want a lawyer?

The detective shrugs. Then we get you a lawyer, he says. And I walk out of the room and type up the charging documents for first-degree murder and you can't say a fucking thing about it. Look, bunk, I'm giving you a chance. He came at you, right? You were scared. It was self-defense.

Your mouth opens to speak.

He came at you, didn't he?

"Yeah," you venture cautiously, "he came at me."

Whoa, says the detective, holding up his hands. Wait a minute. If we're gonna do this, I gotta find your rights form. Where's the fucking form? Damn things are like cops, never around when you need 'em. Here it is, he says, pushing the explanation-of-rights sheet across the table and pointing to the bottom. Read that, he says.

"I am willing to answer questions and I do not want any attorney at this time. My decision to answer questions without having an attorney present is free and voluntary on my part."

As you read, he leaves the room and returns a moment later with a second detective as a witness. You sign the bottom of the form, as do both detectives.

The first detective looks up from the form, his eyes soaked with innocence. "He came at you, huh?"

"Yeah, he came at me."

Get used to small rooms, bunk, because you are about to be dropkicked into the lost land of pretrial detention. Because it's one thing to be a murdering little asshole from Southeast Baltimore, and it's another to be stupid about it, and with five little words you have just elevated yourself to the ranks of the truly witless.

End of the road, pal. It's over. It's history. And if that police detective wasn't so busy committing your weak bullshit to paper, he'd probably look you in the eye and tell you so. He'd give you another cigarette and say, son, you are ignorance personified and you just put yourself in for the fatal stabbing of a human being. He might even tell you that the other witnesses in the other rooms are too drunk to identify their own reflections, much less the kid who had the knife, or that it's always a long shot for the lab to pull a latent off a knife hilt, or that your $95 sneakers are as clean as the day you bought them. If he was feeling particularly expansive, he might tell you that everyone who leaves the homicide unit in handcuffs does so charged with first-degree murder, that it's for the lawyers to decide what kind of deal will be cut. He might go on to say that even after all these years working homicides, there is still a small part of him that finds it completely mystifying that anyone ever utters a single word in a police interrogation. To illustrate the point, he could hold up your Form 69, on which you waived away every last one of your rights, and say, "Lookit here, pistonhead, I told you twice that you were deep in the shit and that whatever you said could put you in deeper." And if his message was still somehow beyond your understanding, he could drag your carcass back down the sixth-floor hallway, back toward the sign that says Homicide Unit in white block letters, the sign you saw when you walked off the elevator.

Now think hard: Who lives in a homicide unit? Yeah, right. And what do homicide detectives do for a living? Yeah, you got it, bunk. And what did you do tonight? You murdered someone.

So when you opened that mouth of yours, what the fuck were you thinking?

Homicide detectives in Baltimore like to imagine a small, open window at the top of the long wall in the large interrogation room. More to the point, they like to imagine their suspects imagining a small, open window at the top of the long wall. The open window is the escape hatch, the Out. It is the perfect representation of what every suspect believes when he opens his mouth during an interrogation. Every last one envisions himself parrying questions with the right combination of alibi and excuse: every last one sees himself coming up with the right words, then crawling out the window to go home and sleep in his own bed. More often than not, a guilty man is looking for the Out from his first moments in the interrogation room: in that sense. the window is as much the suspect's fantasy as the detective's mirage.

The effect of the illusion is profound, distorting as it does the natural hostility between hunter and hunted, transforming it until it resembles a relationship more symbiotic than adversarial. That is the lie, and when the roles are perfectly performed, deceit surpasses itself, becoming manipulation on a grand scale and ultimately an act of betrayal. Because what occurs in an interrogation room is indeed little more than a carefully staged drama, a choreographed performance that allows a detective and his suspect to find common ground where none exists. There, in a carefully controlled purgatory, the guilty proclaim their malefactions, though rarely in any form that allows for contrition or resembles an unequivocal admission. . . .

For anyone with experience in the criminal justice machine, the point is driven home by every lawyer worth his fee. Repetition and familiarity with the process soon place the professionals beyond the reach of a police interrogation. Yet more than two decades after the landmark *Escobedo* and *Miranda* decisions, the rest of the world remains strangely willing to place itself at risk. As a result, the same law enforcement community that once regarded the 1966 *Miranda* decision as a death blow to criminal investigation has now come to see the explanation of rights as a routine part of the process—simply a piece of station house furniture, if not a civilizing influence on police work itself.

In an era when beatings and physical intimidation were common tools of an interrogation, the *Escobedo* and *Miranda* decisions were sent down by the nation's highest court to ensure that criminal confessions and statements were purely voluntary. The resulting *Miranda* warning was "a protective device to dispel the compelling atmosphere of the interrogation," as Chief Justice Earl Warren wrote in the majority opinion. Investigators would be required to assure citizens of their rights to silence and counsel, not only at the moment of arrest, but at the moment that they could reasonably be considered suspects under interrogation.

In answer to *Miranda*, the nation's police officials responded with a veritable jeremiad, wailing in unison that the required warnings would virtually assure that confessions would be impossible to obtain and conviction rates would plummet. Yet the prediction was soon proved false for the simple reason that those law enforcement leaders—and, for that matter, the Supreme Court itself—underestimated a police detective's ingenuity.

Miranda is, on paper, a noble gesture which declares that constitutional rights extend not only to the public forum of the courts, but to the private confines of the police station as well. *Miranda* and its accompanying decisions established a uniform concept of a criminal defendant's rights and effectively ended the use of violence and the most blatant kind of physical intimidation in interrogations. That, of course, was a blessing. But if the further intent of the *Miranda* decision was, in fact, an attempt to "dispel the compelling atmosphere" of an interrogation, then it failed miserably.

And thank God. Because by any standards of human discourse, a criminal confession can never truly be called voluntary. With rare exception, a confession is compelled, provoked and manipulated from a suspect by a detective who has been trained in a genuinely deceitful art. That is the essence of interrogation, and those who believe that a straightforward conversation between a cop and criminal—devoid of any treachery—is going to solve a crime are somewhere beyond naive. If the interrogation process is, from a moral standpoint, contemptible, it is nonetheless essential. Deprived of the ability to question and confront suspects and witnesses, a detective is left with physical evidence and in many cases, precious little of that. Without a chance for a detective to manipulate a suspect's mind, a lot of bad people would simply go free.

Yet every defense attorney knows that there can be no good reason for a guilty man to say anything whatsoever to a police officer, and any suspect who calls an attorney will be told as much, bringing the interrogation to an end. A court opinion that therefore requires a detective—the same detective working hard to dupe a suspect—to stop abruptly and guarantee the man his right to end the process can only be called an act of institutional schizophrenia. The *Miranda* warning is a little like a referee introducing a barroom brawl: The stern warnings to hit above the waist and take no cheap shots have nothing to do with the mayhem that follows.

Yet how could it be otherwise? It would be easy enough for our judiciary to ensure that no criminal suspect relinquished his rights inside a police station: The courts could simply require the presence of a lawyer at all times. But such a blanket guarantee of individual rights would effectively end the use of interrogation as an investigative weapon, leaving many more crimes unsolved and many more guilty men and women unpunished. Instead, the ideals have been carefully compromised at little cost other than to the integrity of the police investigator. . . .

The Baltimore department, like many others, uses a written form to confirm a suspect's acknowledgment of *Miranda*. In a city where nine out of ten suspects would otherwise claim they were never informed of their rights, the forms have proven essential. Moreover, the detectives have found that rather than drawing attention to the *Miranda*, the written form diffuses the impact of the warning. Even as it alerts a suspect to the dangers of an interrogation, the form co-opts the suspect, making him part of the process. It is the suspect who wields the pen, initialing each component of the warning and then signing the form; it is the suspect who is being asked to help with the paperwork. With witnesses, the detectives achieve the same effect with an information sheet that asks three dozen questions in rapid-fire succession. Not only does the form include information of value to the investigators—name, nickname, height, weight, complexion, employer, description of clothing at time of interview, relatives living in Baltimore, names of parents, spouse, boyfriend or girlfriend—but it acclimates the witness to the idea of answering questions before the direct interview begins.

Even if a suspect does indeed ask for a lawyer, he must—at least according to the most aggressive interpretation of *Miranda*—ask definitively: "I want to talk to a lawyer and I don't want to answer questions until I do."

Anything less leaves room for a good detective to maneuver. The distinctions are subtle and semantic:

"Maybe I should get a lawyer."

"Maybe you should. But why would you need a lawyer if you don't have anything to do with this?"

Or: "I think I should talk to a lawyer."

"You better be sure. Because if you want a lawyer then I'm not going to be able to do anything for you."

Likewise, if a suspect calls a lawyer and continues to answer questions until the lawyer arrives, his rights have not been violated. If the lawyer arrives, the suspect must be told that an attorney is in the building, but if he still wishes to continue the interrogation, nothing requires that the police allow the attorney to speak with his client. In short, the suspect can demand an attorney: a lawyer can't demand a suspect.

Once the minefield that is *Miranda* has been successfully negotiated, the detective must let the suspect know that his guilt is certain and easily established by the existing evidence. He must then offer the Out.

22

Gideon's Trumpet

ANTHONY LEWIS

Anthony Lewis is a prize-winning author and writer for the New York Times. *In the 1960s, as the* Times' *reporter covering the Supreme Court, Lewis chronicled the Warren Court's forging of the "due process revolution" by extending to the states, under the Fourteenth Amendment's due process clause, the guarantees of the rights of the accused in the Bill of Rights. One of the watershed rulings in that revolution that transformed American justice was* Gideon v. Wainwright *(1963), in which the Sixth Amendment's guarantee of a right to counsel was extended to individuals in state criminal proceedings, even if they are too poor to hire an attorney. The excerpts here are from Lewis's highly acclaimed 1964 book,* Gideon's Trumpet, *which tells the story of Clarence Earl Gideon's struggle to have an attorney appointed to defend him in a state criminal trial and how it led to the Supreme Court's landmark ruling in* Gideon v. Wainwright.

———

IN THE MORNING MAIL of January 8, 1962, the Supreme Court of the United States received a large envelope from Clarence Earl Gideon, prisoner No. 003826, Florida State Prison, P.O. Box 221, Raiford, Florida. Like all correspondence addressed to the Court generally rather than to any particular justice or Court employee, it went to a room at the top of the great marble steps so familiar to Washington tourists. There a secretary opened the envelope. As the return address had indicated, it was another petition by a prisoner without funds asking the Supreme Court to get him out of jail—another, in the secretary's eyes, because pleas from prisoners were so familiar a part of her work. . . .

. . . A federal statute permits persons to proceed in any federal court *in forma pauperis*, in the manner of a pauper, without following the usual forms or paying the regular costs. The only requirement in the statute is that the litigant "make affidavit that he is unable to pay such costs or give security therefor." . . .

Gideon was a fifty-one-year-old white man who had been in and out of prisons much of his life. He had served time for four previous felonies, and he bore the physical marks of a destitute life: a wrinkled, prematurely aged face, a voice and hands that trembled, a frail body, white hair. He had never been a professional criminal or a man of violence; he just could not seem to settle down to work, and so he had made his way by gambling and occasional thefts. Those who had known him, even the men who had arrested him and those who were now his jailers, considered Gideon a perfectly harmless human being, rather likeable, but one tossed aside by life. Anyone meeting him for the first time would be likely to regard him as the most wretched of men.

And yet a flame still burned in Clarence Earl Gideon. He had not given up caring about life or freedom; he had not lost his sense of injustice. Right now he had a passionate—some thought almost irrational—feeling of having been wronged by the State of Florida, and he had the determination to try to do something about it. . . .

Gideon's main submission was a five-page document entitled "Petition for a Writ of *Certiorari* Directed to the Supreme Court State of Florida." A writ of *certiorari* is a formal device to bring a case up to the Supreme Court from a lower court. In plain terms Gideon was asking the Supreme Court to hear his case.

What was his case? Gideon said he was serving a five-year term for "the crime of breaking and entering with the intent to commit a misdemeanor, to wit, petty larceny." He had been convicted of breaking into the Bay Harbor Poolroom in Panama City, Florida. Gideon said his conviction violated the due-process clause of the Fourteenth Amendment to the Constitution, which provides that "No state shall . . . deprive any person of life, liberty, or property, without due process of law." In what way had Gideon's trial or conviction assertedly lacked "due process of law"? For two of the petition's five pages it was impossible to tell. Then came this pregnant statement:

"When at the time of the petitioners trial he ask the lower court for the aid of counsel, the court refused this aid. Petitioner told the court that this Court made decision to the effect that all citizens tried for a felony crime should have aid of counsel. The lower court ignored this plea."

Five more times in the succeeding pages of his penciled petition Gideon spoke of the right to counsel. To try a poor man for a felony without giving him a lawyer, he said, was to deprive him of due process of law. There was only one trouble with the argument, and it was a problem Gideon did not mention. Just twenty years before, in the case of *Betts v. Brady*, the Supreme Court had rejected the contention that the due-process clause of the Fourteenth Amendment provided a flat guarantee of counsel in state criminal trials.

Betts v. Brady was a decision that surprised many persons when made and that had been a subject of dispute ever since. For a majority of six to three, Justice Owen J. Roberts said the Fourteenth Amendment provided no universal assurance of a lawyer's help in a state criminal trial. A lawyer was constitutionally required only if to be tried without one amounted to "a denial of fundamental fairness." . . .

Later cases had refined the rule of *Betts v. Brady*. To prove that he was denied "fundamental fairness" because he had no counsel, the poor man had to show that he was the victim of what the Court called "special circumstances." Those might be his own illiteracy, ignorance, youth, or mental illness, the complexity of the charge against him or the conduct of the prosecutor or judge at the trial.

But Gideon did not claim any "special circumstances." His petition made not the slightest attempt to come within the sophisticated rule of *Betts v. Brady*. Indeed, there was nothing to indicate he had ever heard of the case or its principle. From the day he was tried Gideon had had one idea: That under the Constitution of the United States he, a poor man, was flatly entitled to have a lawyer provided to help in his defense. . . .

Gideon was wrong, of course. The United States Supreme Court had not said he was entitled to counsel; in *Betts v. Brady* and succeeding cases it had said quite the opposite. But that did not necessarily make Gideon's petition futile, for the Supreme Court never speaks with absolute finality when it interprets the Constitution. From time to time—with due solemnity, and after much searching of conscience—the Court has overruled its own decisions. Although he did not know it, Clarence Earl Gideon was calling for one of those great occasions in legal history. He was asking the Supreme Court to change its mind. . . .

In the Circuit Court of Bay County, Florida, Clarence Earl Gideon had been unable to obtain counsel, but there was no doubt that he could have a lawyer in the Supreme Court of the United States now that it had agreed to hear his case. It is the unvarying practice of the Court to appoint a lawyer for any impoverished prisoner whose petition for review has been granted and who requests counsel.

Appointment by the Supreme Court to represent a poor man is a great honor. For the eminent practitioner who would never, otherwise, dip his fingers into the criminal law it can be an enriching experience, making him think again of the human dimensions of liberty. It may provide the first, sometimes the only, opportunity for a lawyer in some distant corner of the country to appear before the Supreme Court. It may also require great personal sacrifice. There is no monetary compensation of any kind—only the satisfaction of service. The Court pays the cost of the lawyer's transportation to Washington and home, and it prints the briefs, but there is no other provision for expenses, not even secretarial help or a hotel room. The lawyer donates that most valuable commodity, his own time. . . .

The next Monday the Court entered this order in the case of *Gideon*: . . .

"The motion for appointment of counsel is granted and it is ordered that Abe Fortas, Esquire, of Washington, D.C., a member of the Bar of this Court be, and he is hereby, appointed to serve as counsel for petitioner in this case." . . .

. . . A lawyer wants the smell of flesh and blood; he wants a human being for a client, not an abstract principle. And Fortas had been assigned to represent Clarence Earl Gideon, not an abstraction. There was always the chance that a closer examination of the facts in his case would show another reason for setting aside his conviction—a ground easier for the Supreme Court to accept than one that would require overruling of its own precedent. As one example, the trial record might disclose one of the "special circumstances" entitling a man to a free lawyer under the *Betts v. Brady* rule: Gideon might have been insane or hopelessly incompetent, or the judge might have shown prejudice, or the case against him might have been a particularly complicated or legally subtle one. If Gideon could win in the Supreme Court on any such ground, it was Fortas's duty to Gideon to argue that point, even though the result was to eliminate the case as a broad test of the right to counsel. There are few things Supreme Court justices like less than a lawyer who puts his client's interest aside in the zeal to make some great change in the law.

All of these considerations were in Fortas's mind. They presented what he called "a moral problem": Whether he should try to find out more about what had happened to Clarence Earl Gideon—in particular, whether he should get a transcript of his trial. "The real question," Fortas said, "was whether I should urge upon the Court the special-circumstances doctrine. As the record then stood, there was nothing to show that he had suffered from any special circumstances." . . .

When [the trial] transcript was read at Arnold, Fortas and Porter, there was no longer any question about the appropriateness of this case as the vehicle to challenge *Betts v. Brady*. Plainly Gideon was not mentally defective. The charge against him, and the proof, were not particularly complicated. The judge had tried to be fair; at least there was no overt bias in the courtroom. In short, Gideon had not suffered from any of the special circumstances that would have entitled him to a lawyer under the limited rule of *Betts v. Brady.* And yet it was altogether clear that a lawyer would have helped. The trial had been a rudimentary one, with a prosecution case that was fragmentary at best. Gideon had not made a single objection or pressed any of the favorable lines of defense. An Arnold, Fortas and Porter associate said later: "We knew as soon as we read that transcript that here was a perfect case to challenge the assumption of *Betts* that a man could have a fair trial without a lawyer. He did very well for a layman, he acted like a lawyer. But it was a pitiful effort really. He may have committed this crime, but it was never proved by the prosecution. A lawyer—not a great lawyer, just an ordinary, competent lawyer—could have made ashes of the case." . . .

Chief Justice Warren, as is the custom, called the next case by reading aloud its full title: Number 155, Clarence Earl Gideon, petitioner, versus H. G. Cochran, Jr., director, Division of Corrections, State of Florida. . . .

The lawyer arguing a case stands at a small rostrum between the two counsel tables, facing the Chief Justice. The party that lost in the lower court goes first, and so the argument in *Gideon v. Cochran* was begun by Abe Fortas. As he stood, the Chief Justice gave him the customary greeting, "Mr. Fortas," and he made the customary opening: "Mr. Chief Justice, may it please the Court. . . . "

This case presents "a narrow question," Fortas said—the right to counsel—unencumbered by extraneous issues. . . .

"This record does not indicate that Clarence Earl Gideon was a person of low intelligence," Fortas said, "or that the judge was unfair to him. But to me this case shows the basic difficulty with Betts versus Brady. It shows that no man, however intelligent, can conduct his own defense adequately." . . .

"I believe we can confidently say that overruling Betts versus Brady at this time would be in accord with the opinion of those entitled to an opinion. That is not always true of great constitutional questions. . . . We may be comforted in this constitutional moment by the fact that what we are doing is a deliberate change after twenty years of experience—a change that has the overwhelming support of the bench, the bar and even of the states." . . .

It was only a few days later, as it happened, that *Gideon v. Wainwright* was decided. There was no prior notice; there never is. The Court gives out no advance press releases and tells no one what cases will be decided on a particular Monday, much less how they will be decided. Opinion days have a special quality. The Supreme Court is one of the last American appellate courts where decisions are announced orally. The justices, who divide on so many issues, disagree about this practice, too. Some regard it as a waste of time; others value it as an occasion for descending from the ivory tower, however briefly, and communicating with the live audience in the courtroom. . . .

Then, in the ascending order of seniority, it was Justice Black's turn. He looked at his wife, who was sitting in the box reserved for the justices' friends and families, and said: "I have for announcement the opinion and judgment of the Court in Number One fifty-five, Gideon against Wainwright."

Justice Black leaned forward and gave his words the emphasis and the drama of a great occasion. Speaking very directly to the audience in the courtroom, in an almost folksy way, he told about Clarence Earl Gideon's case and how it had reached the Supreme Court of the United States.

"It raised a fundamental question," Justice Black said, "the rightness of a case we decided twenty-one years ago, Betts against Brady. When we granted *certiorari* in this case, we asked the lawyers on both sides to argue to us whether we should reconsider that case. We do reconsider Betts and Brady, and we reach an opposite conclusion."

By now the page boys were passing out the opinions. There were four—by Justices Douglas, Clark and Harlan, in addition to the opinion of the Court. But none of the other three was a dissent. A quick look at the end of each showed that it concurred in the overruling of *Betts v. Brady.* On that central result, then, the Court was unanimous. . . .

Resolution of the great constitutional question in *Gideon v. Wainwright* did not decide the fate of Clarence Earl Gideon. He was now entitled to a new trial, with a lawyer. Was he guilty of breaking into the Bay Harbor Poolroom? The verdict would not set any legal precedents, but there is significance in the human beings who make constitutional-law cases as well as in the law. And in this case there was the interesting question whether the legal assistance for which Gideon had fought so hard would make any difference to him. . . .

. . . After ascertaining that Gideon had no money to hire a lawyer of his own choice, Judge McCrary asked whether there was a local lawyer whom Gideon would like to represent him. There was: W. Fred Turner.

"For the record," Judge McCrary said quickly, "I am going to appoint Mr. Fred Turner to represent this defendant, Clarence Earl Gideon." . . .

The jury went out at four-twenty P.M., after a colorless charge by the judge including the instruction—requested by Turner—that the jury must believe Gideon guilty "beyond a reasonable doubt" in order to convict him. When a half-hour had passed with no verdict, the prosecutors were less confident. At five twenty-five there was a knock on the door between the courtroom and the jury room. The jurors filed in, and the court clerk read their verdict, written on a form. It was *Not Guilty.*

23

Search and Destroy: African-American Males in the Criminal Justice System

JEROME G. MILLER

Jerome G. Miller is co-founder and president of the National Center on Institutions and Alternatives, an organization devoted to promoting alternatives to incarceration. After receiving a Ph.D. in social work, he taught at Ohio State University and directed juvenile justice detention systems in Massachusetts and Illinois. The excerpt here is from his 1996 book, Search and Destroy: African-American Males in the Criminal Justice System, *in which Miller shows the disproportionate impact that the "war on drugs" has had on African-American males.*

———

AS JAIL MONITOR for the federal court in Duval County (Jacksonville), Florida, I learned that although African-American males made up only slightly more than 12% of the county's population, more than half of those brought to the jail each day were African-American. The criminal justice system had penetrated the black community of this predominantly white county deeply and widely. One in four of all the young African-American males (ages 18–34) who lived in the county were being jailed at least once each year. Approximately 75% of all 18-year-old black youths living there could expect to be jailed before reaching age 35. Because African-American males tended to fall at the lower end of the socioeconomic scale, they were often unable to make even the most modest of bail bonds. As a result, even those arrested on minor offenses were more likely to be kept in jail longer (hundreds for want of $200 and a bondsman). Consequently, though African-Americans made up about half of the arrestees, they constituted three-fourths of the average daily population of the jail. . . .

The matter of who ends up in the criminal justice system of any country has always carried racial and ethnic implications. While those who are confined in a country's jails or prisons are a rough measure of the types of criminal activity at a given time, they provide a sharper picture of who is at the bottom of the socioeconomic heap or on the political outs at that given time. Visit Berlin's jails and count the Turks.

Visit France's prisons and see the Algerians. Visit Canadian prisons in the English-speaking provinces and count the French-speaking and the Native populations. Visit American prisons and jails and see the blacks and Hispanics. The patterns are far from new. They give validity to the discomfiting comment of California sociologist John Irvin that the nation's jails exist less for purposes of crime control than as places of "rabble management."

During the social tumult and exploding crime rates that accompanied the waves of Irish, Italian, Greek, Portuguese, and Eastern European immigrants to the United States, these ethnic groups disproportionately filled the nation's prisons and jails. First-generation European immigrants had higher crime rates than "native-born" whites and were also overrepresented in America's jails, prisons, and reform schools of the late 19th and early 20th centuries. The percentage of second- and third-generation immigrants in the nation's criminal justice system was even higher. . . .

African-Americans: A Special Case

Although the disproportionate number of immigrants involved in crime moderated as immigrant families were assimilated into American culture, things were always different for African-Americans. As a group, they stood on the bottom rung—even when substantial percentages of first- and second-generation European ethnic populations were themselves very low on the socioeconomic ladder. Blacks were never assimilated in the ways primarily European whites had been. And when it came to blacks who had been labeled as "criminals," the differential treatment came with its own brutal history and vicious traditions. . . .

As sociologist Shirley Ann Vining-Brown noted: "In the South, both the facilities and the philosophy of prisons were tailor-made for Black convicts in the post-Civil War period . . . the crime problem in the South became equated with the 'Negro Problem' as Black prisoners began to outnumber White prisoners in all Southern prisons. . . . The sudden change in the racial composition of Southern prisons produced changes in various penal practices." Brown goes on to note that the most notable of these changes was the "prisoner lease system," whereby mostly black inmates were leased to local farmers and plantation owners as a way of making profit for the penal system and avoiding the costs of maintenance for the inmates. As one southerner of the times put it, "Before the war we owned the Negroes. . . . But these convicts we don't own 'em. One dies, get another." Brown concludes that "once a Black man was convicted in the South, he was viewed as incorrigible and any attempt to rehabilitate him was considered wasted money."

In its 1918 report *Negro Population: 1790–1915*, the Bureau of the Census noted that while blacks made up about 11% of the general population they constituted about one-fifth (21.9%) of the inmates in the prisons, penitentiaries, jails, reform schools, and workhouses of the states. They represented 56% of those held for "grave homicide" and about half of those held for "lesser homicide," and contributed slightly less than one-third of the commitments for robbery, burglary, and larceny. On the other hand, only about 16% of those held for drunkenness, disorderly conduct, or vagrancy were black. The authors of the 1918 report then posed the questions in terms that would be entirely familiar today:

While these figures . . . will probably be generally accepted as indicating that there is more criminality and law breaking among Negroes than among whites and while that conclusion is probably justified by the facts, . . . [i]t is a question whether the difference . . . may not be to some extent the result of discrimination in the treatment of white and Negro offenders on the part of the community and the courts. It must always be borne in mind that the amount of crime punished in different classes or communities may not bear a fixed or unvarying ratio to the amount of crime committed.

These comments on race and the justice system from nearly three-quarters of a century ago seem more measured than many contemporary assessments. Significantly, the report's relatively civil discussion of racial differences in reported crime and the possibility of discrimination makes no mention of the fact that, in the 30 years leading up to its publication, a black man was being lynched somewhere in the country on an average of every two or three days—public events often attended by hundreds and, in some cases, thousands of white citizens and frequently involving local law-enforcement officers—with the perpetrators virtually always listed as "unknown" and going unprosecuted. In the "informal" justice system in the United States, the most extreme punishments and unjust procedures for blacks were never beyond tacit support of a substantial proportion of the white population well into this century. Castration, lynching, and other vigilante-type actions were characteristically reserved for citizens of color and provided the backdrop and collective memory against which the formal criminal justice system functioned when it came to blacks.

These incidents numbered 3,224 (of those recorded) between 1889 and 1918. Although a few whites were lynched, the practice was virtually exclusively focused on young black males. As historian Richard Maxwell Brown noted, for a lynching to have the "maximum intimidative effect" on the black population of the surrounding area, ample notice had to be given. Indeed, railroads ran special trains and frequently assigned extra cars to regular trains to accommodate the demands of lynch-minded white crowds numbering as many as 15,000. The "macabre ritual" was less likely to be a hanging than one in which "the doomed victim was burned at the stake—a process that was prolonged for several hours, often as the black male was subjected to the excruciating pain of torture and mutilation . . . climaxed, ordinarily, by the hideous act euphemistically described as 'surgery below the belt.' " "Souvenirs" taken from the mutilated body were passed out, picture postcards of the proceedings were sold by enterprising photographers, and the leading participants were written up in the local newspapers. Yet the coroner's report inevitably concluded with a finding that the death of the victim was caused by "persons unknown."

Although it is not surprising that census researchers in 1918 would vacillate over whether racial discrimination existed in the justice system, the fact that the problem remains as mysterious to contemporary criminologists and sociologists is troubling. In his 1940s classic study of race, *An American Dilemma*, the Swedish anthropologist Gunnar Myrdal presented a devastating picture of what happened to black males in southern courts of that time. Historically, there was little argument that blacks had been handled differently from other minorities in the justice systems of most majority white nations. Indeed, until the late 1970s, most criminologists accepted the proposition that racial bias was an important element to be considered in studying the justice system. The prevailing view was perhaps best summarized by the journalist Haywood Burns: "The likelihood of the legal process being entirely uncontaminated by bias in any given case is small. Individual Blacks can and do win civil suits, and Individual Blacks can [be] and are acquitted of criminal charges, but in an institutional sense in almost all instances the law functions in a discriminatory and unfair manner when Blacks (and poor people) are involved."

While there was every reason to rejoice in the civil rights progress that African-Americans had made in the United States in the 1960s and 1970s, something else was quietly but inexorably building in the criminal justice system. Though the percentage of African-Americans in the national population had not grown appreciably over the past half-century (from 12% to 13%), the percentage of African-Americans going into state and federal prisons was steadily increasing, with the largest surge occurring simultaneously with the war on drugs. . . . In 1991, for example, the national incarceration rate in state and federal prisons was 310 per 100,000. For white males it was 352 per 100,000. For black males ages 25–29 it stood at an incredible 6,301. . . .

Feeding Stereotypes

It is probably no coincidence that as criminological research has grown more positivistic the stereotype of the African-American youth as "criminal" has grown more ubiquitous. This is not simply attributable to increased crime among black youths. Contemporary researchers also respond to the demands of their law-enforcement–oriented funders. Not surprisingly, when it comes to the problems of middle-class white youths, personal narrative (in the form of the psychiatric case record) continues to be the research modality of choice. As a result, very few white youths of means are subjected to the rigid categorizations demanded by the justice system. Even the bona fide delinquents among them are usually channeled into private psychiatric clinics and substance-abuse programs.

"Criminal behavior," says Washington University psychiatrist C. Robert Cloninger, "is essentially a disease." Dr. Cloninger's comment is but another example of the fact that the labels we choose to attach to those we define as social deviants are less likely to be born of scientific research than constructed to rationalize prevailing ideologies and consider social class. The researcher who intrudes upon this scene should therefore realize that he or she is there to provide what the late British psychiatrist Ronald Laing called a "social prescription"—a label that can be used to validate what we are already disposed to do for a host of reasons other than scientific.

Labeling becomes especially dicey when particular racial or ethnic groups find themselves unusually eligible for such diagnoses. The labels change with the times—from the late-19th century "moral imbecile," to the "constitutional psychopathic inferior" of the 1920s, the "psychopath" of the 1930s and 1940s, the "sociopath" or "person unresponsive to verbal conditioning" of the 1960s and 1970s—all attributions barely one step removed from a more atavistic nomenclature—"savages," "animals," and "monsters"—and, likewise, prescriptions for social neglect. Such labels are peculiarly "user-friendly" to the criminal justice system, in that they are mostly static, dichotomous categories that ignore individual, familial, social, and cultural history, minimize developmental conceptions of human behavior, and leave little room for nuance or individuality. They also lend a gloss of validity to racially charged decisions. The modern psychiatric diagnostic equivalent of the "insensible" criminal, the "antisocial personality" or "sociopath," is in fact suffused with racism.

Consequently, destructive terms like *psychopath* or *sociopath* are for the most part reserved for the poor and minorities. Unable to afford a more benign label, they fill youth detention centers and reform schools in inverse proportion to those troubled and troubling middle-class youths who occupy a surfeit of private mental hospitals, schools, and specialized treatment programs that guarantee a less debilitating diagnosis, while softening the woes and enhancing the social survival of those with sufficient insurance to substitute interminable therapy for long-term incarceration. Although some poorer white youths also end up in the justice system, they are usually afforded a disproportionate share of the meager "alternative" programs available under juvenile correctional auspices, particularly in those states in which professionally staffed private agencies care for delinquent youngsters.

The War on Drugs: Race Falls Out of the Closet

The "drug war" was a disaster-in-waiting for African-Americans from the day of its conception. Despite the fact that drug usage among various racial and ethnic groups in the 1970s and 1980s remained roughly equivalent to their representation in the society, from the first shot fired in the drug war African-Americans were targeted, arrested, and imprisoned in wildly disproportionate numbers. There was historical precedent for what happened. As the African-American writer Clarence Lusane has noted, although there was no evidence of disproportionate opiate use among blacks in the 19th and early 20th centuries (with studies in Florida and Tennessee at the time of World War I showing less opiate use proportionately among blacks than whites), law-enforcement agencies and the press at the time claimed that blacks were using cocaine at alarming levels. A *New York Times* article, entitled "Negro Cocaine Fiends Are a New Southern Menace," noted that southern sheriffs had switched from .32-caliber guns to .38-caliber pistols to protect themselves from drug-empowered blacks.

Although the first "war on drugs" was declared by President Nixon in 1970, federal and state budgets for this conflict grew slowly until the late 1980s. Then, in the wake of University of Maryland African-American basketball star Len Bias's death from cocaine overdose, President and Mrs. Reagan defined drug abuse as the major problem facing the nation and the "war" began in earnest. By 1992, the country was spending over $30 billion annually on the drug war. Though this war had been a failure in its own terms, it had inadvertently exposed the depth of racial bias in the justice system, making hitherto subtle discrimination boldly obvious. While African-Americans and Hispanics made up the bulk of those being arrested, convicted, and sentenced to prison for drug offenses, in 1992, the U.S. Public Health Service's Substance Abuse and Mental Health Services Administration estimated that 76% of the illicit drug users in the United States were white, 14% were black; and 8% were Hispanic. Patterns of cocaine use were only slightly different: two-thirds of cocaine users were white, 17.6% were black, and 15.9% Hispanic. Studies of those who consumed all illicit drugs showed slightly lower percentages of blacks and Latinos than whites in every age category. There was no evidence that the arresting patterns relative to African-Americans and Hispanics had stemmed cocaine use among these groups. The fact that drug dealing in the city, unlike that in the suburbs, often goes on in public areas guaranteed that law-enforcement efforts would be directed at young black and Hispanic men. . . .

Penalties followed the same trends. In 1991, 90% of the "crack" arrests nationally were of minorities, whereas three-fourths of the arrests for powder cocaine were of whites. However, sentences for possession of crack were usually three to four times harsher than those for possession of the same amount of powder cocaine. Blacks were sent to prison in unprecedented numbers and were kept there longer than whites. Ninety-two percent (92%) of all drug possession offenders sentenced to prison in New York were either black or Hispanic, and 71% in California. . . .

The racial discrimination endemic to the drug war wound its way through every stage of the processing—arrest, jailing, conviction, and sentencing. Among those sent to prison for drug offenses, African-Americans were less likely to be assigned to treatment programs than whites. In California, for example, whereas 70% of inmates sentenced for drug offenses were black, two-thirds of the drug-treatment slots went to whites. The situation was no different on the East Coast. A study done by a committee of the Monroe County (Rochester, New York) Bar Association revealed that, although drug use among ethnic and racial groups was roughly proportionate to their percentages in the general population, African-Americans were being arrested at 18 times the rate of whites. However, 75% of those who were afforded the few drug-treatment slots available were white. . . .

Off the Record

Having served in justice roles on the cabinets or personal staffs of governors of three major states—Massachusetts, Illinois, and Pennsylvania—I find it incredible that so many in the government and the judiciary deny the racism which is so much a part of the conversation and informal life of so many in the system. This was brought home to me while I was monitoring jail overcrowding for a federal court. I was taken aback, early in my tenure while sitting with the chief judge of the criminal court, to be told by him that the major reason for crime in the city was "Lyndon Johnson's Civil Rights Act." The judge then went on to explicate his embarrassing personal biases on black men and crime. When I mentioned the conversation later to other officials, the only response I got was, "Did he really say that?"—and the conversation turned quickly to other subjects. Meanwhile, hundreds of black males continued to have their cases heard in this judge's court. The same judge later "acquitted" himself with a local reporter (though the interview was not published for a number of months), by saying that the problems with blacks were not entirely their fault: "It's the fault of their mothers and their daddies and their ancestors and our fault. We have been too good to them." As a result, he concluded that "black youths have a tendency to fight and form gangs and have difficulty competing in public school where they molest teachers and commit rapes. . . . I would not date a black girl. I would not take one home. My mother would kill me. I wouldn't mistreat one. I would not want my children to marry a black or Asian or Chinese or a Puerto Rican."

The chief judge in Florida had committed the faux pas of speaking his mind. Unfortunately, what he said, in my opinion, was probably uncomfortably close to the quietly held attitudes that define the "social context" of justice for most young African-American males entering that judicial system. How else can we explain our increased reliance on imprisonment and harsher sentences as the skin color of arrestees and defendants grows ever darker?

This process, in turn, has had other unsavory effects. As the African-American sociologist Troy Duster put it: "If we are ignorant of recent history, and do not know that the incarceration rate and the coloring of our prisons is a function of dramatic changes in the last half century, we are far more vulnerable to the seduction of the genetic explanation . . . [the] astonishing pattern of incarceration rates by race . . . should give pause to anyone who would try to explain these incarcerated. . . . The gene pool among humans takes many centuries to change, but since 1933, the incarceration of African-Americans in relation to whites has gone up in a striking manner. In 1933, blacks were incarcerated as a race approximately three times the rate of incarceration for whites. In 1950, the ratio had increased to approximately 4 to 1; in 1960, it was 5 to 1, in 1970, it was 6 to 1, and in 1989, it was 7 to 1." Initially, the trends led to calls for new, higher levels of harsh punishment, which were to have their own set of unanticipated consequences. Ultimately, they set the political stage for resurrecting the genetic theories regarding the black criminal that had obsessed white criminologists 75 years earlier.

PART SIX

Capital Punishment

AMENDMENT 8
Excessive bail shall not be required,
nor excessive fines imposed,
nor cruel and unusual punishments inflicted.

24

Witness to Another Execution

SUSAN BLAUSTEIN

Susan Blaustein is a writer living in Washington, D.C. The selection here comes from her 1994 article appearing in Harper's *Magazine. In the late 1980s and early 1990s, the Supreme Court made it easier for states to impose capital punishment and cut back on appeals by death row inmates. As a result, the number of executions annually carried out is steadily rising. Texas has one of the largest death row populations, and in the 1990s, the number of executions more than tripled in its execution chamber in the federal prison in Huntsville, Texas. In the excerpt here, Blaustein recounts her visit to Huntsville and offers her observations on the town, its people, and her reflections on witnessing the execution of a death row inmate.*

———

THE ROAD FROM Austin to Huntsville, Texas, runs past oil rigs and tin-roofed homes whose ramshackle porches sag under the weight of old refrigerators and trailer parts, past red teams and white fences and hand-painted signs advertising Brahman Bulls and Suzie's Bar-B-Q, and on a quiet evening last August, following the road by a succession of tiny Baptist graveyards and watching the swifts dive and glide in the deepening blue, I noticed an anti-littering sign (DON'T MESS WITH TEXAS!) and remembered why I was driving northeast. After that night, at least one man wouldn't be messing with Texas any time soon, and I was going to witness his execution.

Outwardly a sleepy little Southern town, Huntsville is surrounded by seven prisons that house 11,800 inmates, 376 of them locked in five-by-nine-foot cells awaiting their carefully premeditated, supposedly painless, government-administered deaths. The Texas Department of Criminal Justice, known as the TDC, is Huntsville's principal industry, and during the busier seasons the state executes as many as two men a week, making the town the nation's capital of capital punishment. As a member of the press pool, I planned to attend the execution later that night of Carl Eugene "Bo" Kelly of Waco, Texas, who had spent twelve years under sentence of death for his part in the brutal murder of two young men. The series of efforts by Kelly's lawyers to get his execution stayed—on

the grounds that he had suffered brain damage as a result of severe childhood abuse; that he had been high on barbiturates, Valium, marijuana,
and alcohol at the time of his crime; that he was improperly compelled
by police to confess and sentenced more harshly than his accomplice; that
he had been heartwarmingly rehabilitated—had all failed. That morning,
in Austin, the governor's office had informed Kelly's lead attorney, Rob
Owen, that his client's chances of executive clemency were slim.

The town square was deserted, but beyond its one-block stretch of
quaintly renovated shops I found a glowing white Dairy Queen in which
two female prison guards, both of them in gray uniforms, were sharing
gossip and ice-cream sundaes. The DQ is just a block from the Walls
Unit, which houses the death chamber where, by state law, all executions
in Texas must be carried out, but neither guard knew that another convict
was scheduled to die later that night, "at any time," in the language of
the statute, "before the hour of sunrise." Nor did the crowd at Zach's, a
college hangout ten blocks away, where students from Sam Houston State
University (known locally as Sam) were eating nachos and shooting pool.
The university (the second largest business in town) is known nationally
for its fine criminal justice center, which graduates hundreds of "CJ"
majors and where active-duty TDC officials are trained. Like the prison
guards, the students at Zach's didn't much care that a man was going to
be executed in Huntsville that night, but a freshman dance major volun-
teered that an escaped convict had taken a female student hostage a few
weeks back. One bright eyed CJ major named Kevin Pooler said that
because two of his buddies had been murdered recently in Houston he
had no qualms about capital punishment.

"Burn 'em, fry 'em!" shrugged Pooler, who said he hoped to become
a prosecutor and then a Supreme Court justice. "So what if a few innocent
people slip through. That's better than having a lot of guilty people on
the street! If criminals start seeing people getting popped off after six
months, I'm sorry but that's going to change some minds."

The state of Texas apparently has taken its cue from citizens like
Pooler. A poll conducted in 1992 by a group of Texas newspapers found
that 79 percent of the state's citizens favor the death penalty. Since 1976,
when the Supreme Court ruled the death penalty constitutional (thereby
resurrecting execution in the United States after a four-year hiatus), sev-
enty-two men have been executed in Huntsville—more than twice as
many as in Florida, the next most productive state in the execution market,
and more than three times as many as in Virginia and Louisiana, which
rank third and fourth. In the last two years, the rate of Texas executions
has more than tripled, and the seventeen men executed in 1993 alone

constitute nearly a fourth of those put to death since executions resumed in Texas in 1982.

At 8:00 P.M. I called Kelly's lawyers, who told me that his petition had been denied by the U.S. Court of Appeals for the Fifth Circuit and that a new appeal had just been faxed to the Supreme Court. This, I knew, meant that Kelly's chances for a stay of execution had all but vanished, but, as it so happened, I didn't see him die. The wire services and the Texas press had filled the five available places in the media pool— that pale reminder of the once madding crowd that for centuries has reveled in witnessing the grim administration of justice. Prison officials assured me, however, that I wouldn't have to wait long for my turn, what with twenty-four more executions scheduled in the next eight weeks. When the death penalty was reactivated here, the first executions were mobbed. Now they have become so commonplace that few turn out for them. Nonetheless, I decided to post myself outside the Walls Unit, which was cordoned off to keep out possible rabble-rousers, to see who might show up to mark Carl Kelly's death.

Built in 1849 and by the turn of the century decked out with tropical atrium gardens, turrets, porticoes, and a clock tower that the whole town told time by, Texas's aptly named oldest prison is now a faceless brick bunker flanked by forty-foot walls topped by razor wire. A lone guard manned the corner tower, beneath which a dozen anti-death-penalty demonstrators, known locally as Amnesty people because of the affiliation some of them have with Amnesty International, had gathered for their sober candlelight vigil. By 11:20 prison officials learned that the Supreme Court had unanimously denied Kelly a stay. Shortly before midnight the official witnesses filed inside the Walls to the polite din of the protesters' pots, pans, and wooden flutes. Suddenly, two pickups roared into the parking lot, spewing out drunken college students who launched into raucous, inebriated choruses of "You're on the highway to hell" and "So long, farewell, auf wiedersehen, fuck you."

"Get a life!" a young woman hollered at the Amnesty people as she drove by. "We're trying to save one!" one demonstrator responded meekly. When one of the students asked who was being killed and why, and how the protesters would feel had the inmate's victim been their mother, he was quickly regaled with anti-death-penalty statistics; Carl Kelly's case never came up.

At 12:27 A.M. the witnesses emerged from the Walls, reporting that Kelly had been pronounced dead at 12:22; that he had requested wild game for his last meal but instead was given hamburgers, water, and fries (which he didn't eat); and that his last words were, "I'm an African warrior, born to bleed, born to die." (The mother of one of Kelly's victims was not impressed when I read his final words to her over the phone. "Oh yeah, right," she said. "What about the rest of us? When I heard he said that, any feelings I might have had for him just kinda snapped and I said, 'Okay, justice has been served.'")

Ask anyone in Huntsville and he or she will tell you that the rapid clip of executions has absolutely nothing to do with life there. "It's just not our issue," explained City Manager Gene Pipes. "This is the state carrying out a legal mandate that has nothing to do with the local community. It happens to be DATELINE, HUNTSVILLE, but it's just not what's being talked about on the square." . . .

Because Texas has no public-defender system, most death-row inmates are forced to rely on woefully incompetent, court-appointed counsel, and the churning of court-imposed execution dates and inmates' frantic appeals has meant that a number of inmates without any legal representation have come within minutes of being executed. Four death-row inmates in the last four years were found to be innocent and were released; at least four more have presented to the courts compelling claims of innocence. But their pleadings have been dismissed repeatedly because Texas law requires an inmate to produce new evidence of his innocence within thirty days of his conviction—an impossibly short time for a newly condemned person to procure trial transcripts (just preparing these often takes the court as long as thirty days), hire a new lawyer to reinvestigate the case, and file a motion for a new trial.

The thirty-day rule was upheld [in 1993] by the U.S. Supreme Court, much to the horror of Justice Harry A. Blackmun, who in his dissent warned his colleagues that "the execution of a person who can show that he is innocent comes perilously close to simple murder." The Court majority countered that those with technically inadmissible evidence can always fall back on executive clemency, "the 'fail-safe' in our criminal justice system." However, since 1976 not one appeal for clemency on the grounds of innocence has succeeded in Texas, where decisions are meted out by the governor and a parole board consisting of political appointees who follow no fixed set of procedures, are reluctant to second-guess the courts, and are accountable to no one.

As in many other death-penalty states, the dispensation of capital punishment in Texas is also tinged with racism. The disproportionate number of blacks on death row suggests that discriminatory practices continue to infect the state's police work, jury trials, and capital sentencing. Civil-rights groups have grown increasingly vocal on this issue. Meanwhile, violent crime continues, and frustrated white citizens, politicians, and law-enforcement officials have organized a slew of victims' rights groups that furiously condemn defense attorneys' "frivolous delaying tactics" and call for "justice now." . . .

"Death row is the loneliest place in the world," said Lester Leroy Bower, a white, forty-six-year-old inmate who edits one of the row's two newspapers, attends Bible classes, and studies Hebrew and Greek. "You have people around you all the time, but you have very few friends. There is too much dying on the row, so you don't build really true bonds. And the hardest," added this husband and father of two teenage girls, his voice suddenly subdued, "is separation from family — never being able to touch 'em, hold 'em."

Death-penalty proponents have little pity for such talk from convicted murderers. Bower, however, insists he is innocent of the four murders for which he was sentenced to death in 1984 and says he has strong evidence pointing to four other suspects. Because of the thirty-day rule, however, no Texas court has agreed to hear his story.

Bower believes he was framed by corrupt law-enforcement officials allegedly involved in drug transactions with at least one of the murder victims. All of the evidence gathered against Bower was circumstantial; potentially exculpatory evidence mysteriously disappeared before the trial. Although within days of his conviction witnesses began coming forward with new evidence supporting Bower's innocence, his lawyer, off on a Mexican vacation, failed to meet the thirty-day deadline. Bower's harrowing trial experience, followed by a decade spent studying the cases of his neighbors on the row, has persuaded him that inside Texas's sometimes Kafkaesque criminal-justice system, one's innocence can have astonishingly little bearing on one's fate.

"You can convict almost anybody in Texas," he told me. "I'm white, fairly well educated, moderately articulate, have taken paralegal courses, and now I even have a good lawyer. That puts me a step up on a lot of people — and that has nothing to do with my innocence! Say I'm black, poor, uneducated, inarticulate, have no lawyer, have been put through the mill: I haven't got a chance."

Yet most Huntsville residents are sure that those executed in their town are guilty. "If they were innocent, it would've been found out way back then," insisted Diamond Kornegay, a retiree who, like many of Huntsville's relative newcomers, fled crime-ridden Houston for a peaceful life in the country. "Just look at all these lawyers, all these witnesses and everything!" Diamond, a chatty lady whose "daddy" was a cotton farmer and who grew up close to Huntsville, said the executions never bothered her.

"It's not a big deal to me. When I was a little bitty girl, they used to open up the Walls and take the schoolchildren through there. I saw the electric chair, but I never did think about it; I just put that out of my mind. If anyone ended up getting killed, well, they just did a bad thing, and that's the law."

It wasn't hard to see how such attitudes have been forged. Each morning, shrill whistles at 6:00 A.M., 7:00 A.M., and noon (denoting times for head-counting, work detail, and more head-counting) make it impossible for those within earshot to forget that their neighbor is a bureaucracy run on involuntary labor. The reminders continue all day long: trusties in their prison whites performing menial tasks, the changing of the guards in gray, prison vans trucking manacled inmates from unit to unit, and the startling profusion of wisecracking sheriffs and wardens who gather from all over Texas for seminars at Sam's prestigious Criminal Justice Institute and who stroll through town resplendent in starched jeans, smart cowboy hats, boots, and huge silver belt buckles. . . .

On November 9, I learned that my turn had come and that I had been assigned to the media pool for the execution that night of Anthony Cook, a white thirty-two-year-old construction worker from nearby Crockett who had abducted and murdered a University of Texas law student in 1988. Cook was what is known in the trade as "a volunteer," meaning that he had waived his right to appeal and was ready to submit to his sentence, and it was a pretty sure bet that his execution would proceed on schedule. Until the last minute, attorney Elizabeth Cohen from the federally funded Texas Resource Center tried to persuade Cook to change his mind, but he was not to be swayed. Cook believed that he'd been saved by the Lord Jesus back in 1991 and that he was headed straight for the right hand of God.

Cook spent his last day with his family, who Cohen said were "not happy" about his decision and were "having a really hard time." At 4:00 P.M. he was moved to the Walls' holding cell, and after his double-meat-and-bacon cheeseburger, strawberry shake, and shower, he and Cohen sat within yards of the death chamber and talked about God.

"He's doing great, he can't wait," Cohen reported to me afterward. "He has no interest in changing his mind; he has more interest in bringing me to Christianity. He keeps praying for me, and he looks at me with tears in his eyes because I'm not saved." After Cohen left, Cook visited with his closest spiritual advisers, Baptist volunteer chaplains Jack and Irene Wilcox, who later told me Cook begged them to "follow up on" Cohen's conversion after his death.

Jack Wilcox had nothing but enthusiasm for the force of Cook's conversion. "We walk into the death house, and he says to me, 'Hey, Jack, I'm excited!' Two hours before he's going to die and he's excited? I say, 'Fantastic! That's great!' . . . This man saw prison five times, he committed a horrible kidnapping and murder . . . a sure loser!" exclaimed Jack, who himself had found the Lord after a life on the streets. "And then three years later, you be lookin' at a person prayin' to God."

We would have liked to have seen him continue with his appeals. because he was a great witness," Irene interrupted, "but he believed in the death penalty."

Jack jumped back in, impatient. "It's not for us to say. A lot of the men [on the row] are upset because he gave up his appeals. I say, 'Look, the man's been prayin' to God for two years—you don't get between a man and his prayers.' We wanna let God drive the car," he explained, and then asked whether I had yet let the Lord Jesus into my heart.

The evening of Cook's execution I attended a City Council meeting where neither the mayor, city manager, city councilmen, student body president, nor student-newspaper editor had any idea that Tony Cook had accepted with pleasure the state's invitation to be put to death later that night. Everyone came in talking about the day's big news: the Huntsville Hornets' star football coach was retiring after nineteen years. The main item on the City Council's agenda that evening was a hotly contested bid by Sam students and five bar owners to get drinking hours extended from midnight until 1:00 A.M. on weekdays and from 1:00 to 2:00 A.M. on Saturdays. The initiative lost by a wide margin—and not surprisingly: Huntsville is heavily Baptist and was dry until 1971. The students were up in arms at the outcome, and they stormed out of the meeting after threatening to unseat the councilmen in the upcoming January election (though only a few hundred Sam students ever bother to vote in local elections).

But I was thinking about that evening's execution. I'd never even seen anyone die, and here I was, about to witness a man's death, to observe it without objection. Already I felt sullied, voyeuristic. Yet this is the law, I told myself. What's more, this one should be easy: this man wants to die. And he did pump four bullets into that poor law student's head. I kept up this interior debate until it was time to report in at the TDC "Admin" building, just across from the Walls. I parked near the Dairy Queen and hurried through the foggy chill to the triple set of doors.

Several reporters had already gathered in the tiny Public Information Office. Two were chatting with assistant information director Brown about other executions they had attended; another, like me a first-time witness, was earnestly jotting down facts from his "Execution Information" briefing packet. Cook had requested no personal witnesses at his death, Brown told us; the family would not claim the body, which meant that Cook would be buried at state expense in the Colonel Joe Byrd Cemetery, named for the late assistant warden who not only supervised every execution from 1949 until his death in 1964 but also took it upon himself to tend the dead men's graves.

The phone rang at 11:56. Brown answered. "That's quick; they're ready to go," he said, getting up from his desk. We walked across the street to the Walls, some of us chatting, barely aware of a couple of protesters almost invisible in the fog. The Walls' handsome old clock face read 10:02. I wondered how many men had died inside the Walls since its clock last told the correct time.

Once we were inside the gates, an assistant warden led us across an interior courtyard with locked chain-link fences, down white corridors with white-tile floor, through one thick gray door after another, each opened with an enormous brass key. Brown was amazed by the different style of the new warden, Morris Jones, who was presiding tonight over his first execution. "I tell ya, this Jones, he's a new kind: quick, quick," he said. "No point in waiting I guess."

We then were marched single file to the death house. The other woman reporter must have seen the fearful look in my eyes. She told me that she couldn't sleep for three nights after her first execution. "Just attend to the business at hand," she advised. As we sat waiting to be admitted into the witness room. Reverend Pickett walked Cook the dozen-odd steps from his tiny holding cell with its bright orange bars, past a shower and toilet, and into the antiseptic death chamber, where he would he strapped down onto the chrome gurney while the warden and reverend stood by. I asked public-information officer David Nunnelee whether it made any difference to him when the men whose death he witnessed were volunteers.

"I appreciate that they accept what they did and want to pay the penalty," he said, without hesitation. "You gotta respect that."

Defense attorney Owen subsequently disparaged this view. "Actually, Cook was the perfectly rehabilitated prisoner," Owen said, then mused about the fine theological line between the insanity plea of an inmate who claims to hear voices, and is therefore not competent to be executed, and a volunteer such as Cook, whose execution was expedited because he had heard the voice of Jesus promising him a heavenly escape from death row.

We got our signal and were abruptly herded into the carpeted witness room, along with two large wardens in khaki jackets and a small dark man in an even darker suit, who, I was told, was the one assistant attorney general who never talked to the press. We stood behind bars and a pane of thick glass, which separated us from the actual death chamber.

The view was stunning. Cook lay spread-eagled on the gurney, ready, bound by six thick leather straps. Although the press briefing listed his height as only five foot six, he looked enormous. His eyes were only partly open; his strong chin pointed upward. He was balding, and his longish auburn hair looked blond beneath the chilling fluorescent light. Ace bandages covered both hands and IVs were inserted into both forearms, his thin, short-sleeved prison shirt revealing a blurry tattoo. He wore blue, standard-issue prison garb and his own Etonic sneakers, purchased, I later learned, in the prison commissary for $21.75.

Near Cook's head stood Warden Jones; near Cook's feet stood Reverend Pickett, his hands folded. Suddenly I saw movement in front of me and realized that on Cook's far side was a one-way mirror in which we all were reflected. It was our own movement, not that of the symmetrical threesome in the death chamber itself, that had been captured in the glass. The effect was eerie; not only would I witness an execution but I would witness myself witnessing it. Behind the mirror, in an adjacent room, stood the executioner (whether man or woman, or more than one, no one would tell me), who would, upon a signal from the warden, activate the death device and introduce into Cook's veins the $71.50 fix consisting of what prison officials term "those substances necessary to cause death": sodium thiopental, which is the lethal component, pancuronium bromide, to relax and anesthetize, and potassium chloride, to stop the heartbeat.

"Do you have anything to say?" the warden muttered at 12:08. Cook opened his eyes.

"Yessir," he said, speaking into a big black microphone hung just over his head. "I just want to tell my family that I love them and I thank the Lord Jesus for giving me another chance and for saving me."

With that, Cook shut his eyes. The warden gave a small, sharp nod toward the person or persons behind the mirror. We all stood rigid, frozen. The silence was absolute, a perfect vacuum. Within seconds Cook took a sudden deep breath, gagged once, and stiffened his chin upward, all in one gesture. His chest expanded tremendously when he breathed, as if he had eagerly inhaled his own death. His arms were still outstretched and bound; his mouth and eyes were slightly open; nothing else moved.

My eyes slowly traced the contours of his body—the ninety degrees from his shiny bald crown to the end of his outstretched left arm, down the length of his pants leg, across the white sneakers, and up the near side—searching for signs of life, a cough, a twitch, a moan, a second thought. None came. I waited for him to exhale. But the air he had so urgently seized a moment before remained trapped in Cook's chest. The show was over; the passage from life to death was horrifyingly invisible, a silent and efficient erasure.

We waited. Finally, the warden called in Dr. Darrell Wells, a bearded emergency-room physician who attends most of the prison's executions. Wells checked Cook's eyes with a flashlight and his heart with a stethoscope. The play had ended. At 12:15, within five minutes of Anthony Cook's last gasp, the doctor pronounced him dead.

We filed out the way we came, more quickly this time, with little conversation. When I reached the Public Information Office, one of the reporters was already calling his bureau.

"Hi, Harry. He's history," he greeted his editor. Another reporter filed his story by modem while press officer Brown invited us all to the opening of a new 2,250-bed prison later that morning.

"Cold, ain't it?" a thin young guard greeted me as I walked back to my car. The clock at the Walls still read 10:02. A yellow traffic light flashed in front of the closed, eternally lit Dairy Queen. Cook's death made the 1:00 A.M. news on CNN, flickering in the nation's consciousness but an instant.

By 7:30 that morning at the Huntsville Funeral Home (which handles the bodies of all executed men), Tony Cook's mother, stepfather, brother, sister, assorted in-laws, cousins, and the Wilcoxes were paying their last respects to his open casket. Cook looked smaller than he had on the gurney; he had pretty, long eyelashes and delicate hands, a slightly cleft chin, and the shadow of a beard. He was dressed now in a blue oxford shirt with white stripes, and his mother stood over him, gently caressing his thin hair, his cheek, his ear. "He feels like you could just squeeze him back to life," she said. He had called her two hours before his death to tell her how excited he was about dying. "He certainly was at peace with hisself," she said.

"No more cages," sighed his sister as she touched her brother's chest, arms, face. "He's free, free, free!" She clutched his hand again and again, then finally kissed his forehead good-bye. I tried to fathom what it must feel like, after five years of no physical contact, to be allowed to touch a son or brother only after he is dead.

We followed the hearse through town to the muddy cemetery, where the six inmates who had prepared the grave were warming themselves over an ashcan fire. The seventeen family members clustered together, held one another, and cried, while Reverend Pickett read some prayers. Chaplain Jack Wilcox, in a hot-pink tie with a bright paisley print, said he'd never heard Tony say a bad word about anybody and read us a statement that Cook had written for the occasion: "Someday you will read in the papers that I have died— don't you believe a word of it . . . "

After the service Chaplain Wilcox pointed to one of the hundreds of crosses in the cemetery. "That's one of Tony's best friends, right there," he said. Since the markers have only prison numbers and no names, I asked how he knew. "I buried him," he said. "Last June." I later asked Reverend Pickett why the crosses have no names.

"It makes it more accurate," he told me. "We have many at the prison with the same name. There'll be another Tony Cook, but there'll never be another number like that number."

The air was dank and cold as I drove out of town, and I hoped the day's sharp rawness would clear my numbed senses. I headed north out to farm route 980, past sallow fields, unkempt trailer clusters, and the occasional satellite dish. Suddenly I saw, strung from a ragged barbed-wire fence, what looked like a wild dog or wolf, hanging upside down by its right rear foot. Its tail was splayed in a lazy S; its other legs were beautifully poised as if the animal had been caught in mid-leap by a photographer's lens.

I sped by, stopped, then backed up to make sure I wasn't hallucinating. The animal had been shot in the right shoulder, and bloody organs were dribbling out. So far only a single fly had discovered the catch; long-tailed, white-bellied birds took no notice as they hopped along the fence and pecked at the unmowed field.

Like somebody's trophy, the animal hung there, far more dignified than its surroundings. It was a coyote, I was later told, a predator. Nothing to feel sorry for, in other words all crossbreeds were coyotes out here, and they ate the calves and young deer. It was hung there "as a warning to other coyotes," said one veteran hunter; another suggested it was hung "to let other farmers know they're doin' their part" in keeping the coyote population down. "That's just kinda the old way here in Texas," a former state game warden told me. Another old-timer, a man who'd mounted the rear end of a deer on the wall of his tiny living room wall, gave one more reason: "Somebody wants to show off that he killed somethin'," he said, then broke into a toothless grin.

All these explanations somehow made sense. But I wondered why I was so transfixed by this roadside display of a predator's comeuppance. Something about the crude, fresh death jarred me in a way that Cook's execution had not. That meticulous choreography had anesthetized me to the reality that a man was being killed before my eyes. But the flesh and blood of this handsome, dripping creature made both its death and its outlaw status immediately palpable.

From what I'd read about the stench of electrocution and the vividness of public hangings, I imagined that witnessing deaths by these means would have an immediacy that would preclude numbness. The lethal-injection method, first used in Texas in 1982 and now adopted by most death-penalty states as more humane, has turned dying into a still life, thereby enabling the state to kill without anyone involved feeling anything at all.

I wondered how viewing such a non-event could satisfy the desire for retribution so often expressed by death-penalty advocates and the families of victims. I wondered whether Huntsville's sterile, bloodless executions of the last twelve years might partly account for residents' wholesale disinterest and denial that what went on deep inside the Walls might have anything to do with them.

But it's not just here in Huntsville; we are all inured to such smooth exterminations. Any remaining glimmers of doubt—about whether the man received due process, about his guilt, about our right to take a life— cause us to rationalize these deaths with such catchwords as "heinous," "deserved," "deterrent," "justice," and "painless." We have perfected the art of institutional killing to the degree that it has deadened our natural, quintessentially human response to death.

25

For Capital Punishment: Crime and the Morality of the Death Penalty

WALTER BERNS

Walter Berns is a professor emeritus at Georgetown University and a constitutional scholar at the American Enterprise Institute (AEI). The AEI is a conservative think tank in Washington, D.C. Among his many books, Berns published For Capital Punishment: Crime and the Morality of the Death Penalty *(1979). In it, Berns defends capital punishment on the grounds that society needs to express its anger and exact retribution from those who commit particularly outrageous and wantonly vile crimes. Far from violating the Eighth Amendment's bar against "cruel and unusual punishment," Berns argues that the death penalty should be inflicted on those who commit heinously cruel and unusual crimes. His work has been cited as an authoritative source by Chief Justice William H. Rehnquist and provides a normative theory for the Supreme Court's rulings in the 1980s and 1990s, which have made it both easier to impose capital punishment and to carry out executions.*

ANGER IS EXPRESSED or manifested on those occasions when someone has acted in a manner that is thought to be unjust, and one of its bases is the opinion that men are responsible, and should be held responsible, for what they do. Thus, anger is accompanied not only by the pain caused by him who is the object of anger, but by the pleasure arising from the expectation of exacting revenge on someone who is thought to deserve it. We can become angry with an inanimate object (the door we run into and then kick in return) only by foolishly attributing responsibility to it, and we cannot do that for long, which is why we do not think of returning later to revenge ourselves on the door. For the same reason, we cannot be more than momentarily angry with an animate creature other than man; only a fool or worse would dream of taking revenge on a dog. And, finally, we tend to pity rather than to be angry with men who—because they are insane, for example—are not responsible for their acts. Anger, then, is a very human passion not only because only a human being can be angry, but also because it acknowledges the humanity of its objects: it holds them accountable for what they do. It is an expression of that element of the soul that is connected with the view that there is responsibility in the world; and in holding particular men responsible, it pays them that respect which is due them as men. Anger recognizes that only men have the capacity to be moral beings and, in so doing, acknowledges the dignity of human beings. Anger is somehow connected with justice, and it is this that modern penology has not understood; it tends, on the whole, to regard anger as merely a selfish passion. . . .

Criminals are properly the objects of anger, and the perpetrators of terrible crimes—for example, Lee Harvey Oswald and James Earl Ray—are properly the objects of great anger. They have done more than inflict an injury on an isolated individual; they have violated the foundations of trust and friendship, the necessary elements of a moral community, the only community worth living in. A moral community, unlike a hive of bees or a hill of ants, is one whose members are expected freely to obey the laws and, unlike a tyranny, are trusted to obey the laws. The criminal has violated that trust, and in so doing has injured not merely his immediate victim but the community as such. He has called into question the very possibility of that community by suggesting that men cannot be trusted freely to respect the property, the person, and the dignity of those with whom they are associated. If, then, men are not angry when someone else is robbed, raped, or murdered, the implication is that there is no moral community because those men do not care for anyone other than themselves. Anger is an expression of that caring, and society needs men who care for each other, who share their pleasures and their pains, and do so for the sake of the others. It is the passion that can cause us to act for reasons having nothing to do with selfish or mean calculation; indeed, when educated, it can become a generous passion, the passion that protects the community or country by demanding punishment for its enemies. It is the stuff from which heroes are made.

A moral community is not possible without anger and the moral indignation that accompanies it, which is why the most powerful attack on capital punishment was written by a man, Albert Camus, who denied the legitimacy of anger and moral indignation by denying the very possibility of a moral community in our time. The anger expressed in our world, he said, is nothing but hypocrisy. His famous novel *L'Etranger* (variously translated as *The Stranger* or *The Outsider*) is a brilliant portrayal of what he insisted is our world, a world deprived of God, as he put it. It is a world we would not choose to live in and, as we shall see, one which

Camus himself refused to live in. Nevertheless, the novel is a modern masterpiece, and Meursault, its antihero (for a world without anger can have no heroes), is a murderer. . . .

There is a sense in which punishment may be likened to dramatic poetry or the purpose of punishment to one of the intentions of a great dramatic poet (and Shakespeare is clearly the greatest in our language). The plots of Shakespeare's tragedies involve political men—Caesar the emperor, Coriolanus the general, Lear the king, Hamlet the son of a king, and others, including, of course, Macbeth who would be king—and this is not fortuitous, nor does it represent the prejudices of a poet who lived in an aristocratic age. He chose to write about such men because the moral problems can be made fully intelligible only in what they do or do not do and in the consequences of what they do or do not do. Dramatic poetry depicts men's actions because men are revealed in, or make themselves known through, their actions; and the essence of a human action consists in its being virtuous or vicious. Only a ruler or a contender for rule can act with the freedom and on a scale that allows the virtuousness or viciousness of human deeds to be fully displayed. Macbeth was such a man and in his fall, brought about by his own acts, and in the consequent suffering he endured, is revealed the meaning of morality. In *Macbeth* the majesty of the moral law is demonstrated to us; as I said, it teaches us the awesomeness of the commandment, thou shalt not kill. In a similar fashion, the punishments imposed by the legal order remind us of the reign of the moral order; not only do they remind us of it, but by enforcing its prescriptions, they enhance the dignity of the legal order in the eyes of moral men, in the eyes of those decent citizens who cry out "for gods who will avenge injustice." Reenforcing the moral order is especially important in a self-governing community, a community that gives laws to itself. . . .

The opponents of capital punishment had good reason to believe they would win their case in the Supreme Court. They had come close in 1972 when the Court held that the death penalty had been administered in so discriminatory, capricious, or arbitrary a manner as to be a cruel and unusual punishment, and two members of the five-man majority in those cases regarded the death penalty as unconstitutional no matter how administered. It is true that public and legislative opinion seemed to be moving against them, but if Arthur Koestler's characterization of the public support of the death penalty is accurate—that it is based on "ignorance, traditional prejudice and repressed cruelty"—then it was likely that the penalty would continue to be imposed discriminatorily, capriciously, or arbitrarily, and that a majority of the Court would, sooner or later, come to the conclusion that it could be imposed in no other manner. This may yet happen. In 1976, however, seven members of the Court not only voted to uphold the death penalty statutes of three states and the sentences imposed under them, but, in the course of doing so, gave the sanction of the Constitution to the principle that criminals should be paid back for their crimes.

It was this sanctioning of the retributive principle that especially disturbed Justice Marshall, one of the two dissenters. He would apparently be willing to allow executions if it could be shown that they serve some useful purpose—for example, that they serve to deter others from committing capital crimes (and he was not persuaded by Ehrlich's study suggesting that they do deter)—but to execute someone simply because society thinks he deserves to be executed is, he said, to deny him his "dignity and worth." Why it would not deprive a man of his dignity and worth to use him (by executing him) in order to influence the behavior of other men, Marshall did not say; apparently he would be willing to accept society's calculations but not its moral judgments. Be that as it may, it cannot be denied that he and other abolitionists have a point: to say that someone deserves to be executed is to make a godlike judgment with no assurance that it can be made with anything resembling godlike perspicacity. In the extreme case, and some abolitionists make much of its possibility, society may execute an innocent person, and no one can assure us that this has never happened or that it will never happen in the future. . . .

Not all murderers deserve to be executed; not even all first-degree murderers deserve to be executed, because not all first-degree murders are equally terrible. Yet, in reaction to the 1972 Supreme Court decisions, a number of states, determined to demonstrate that they could eliminate the injustice of arbitrary capital sentencing, enacted new statutes making death the mandatory sentence for persons convicted of first-degree murder. This is a mistake, and I think most of us know it. We can recognize the difference between the culpability of Jack Ruby, for example, the killer of Lee Harvey Oswald, and that of Lee Harvey Oswald himself (assuming, of course, that he was indeed the killer of President Kennedy); we could accept a prison term, perhaps even a relatively brief prison term, for Ruby because we could accept the prospect of his return to our community; but I doubt that we could accept the same sentence for Oswald or the prospect of *his* return to our community, even if he promised never again to assassinate a president. . . .

. . . The very awesomeness of condemning a man to death requires the punishment to be reserved for extraordinarily heinous crimes, but throughout most of modern history this has not been the case. The historical record is sprinkled with statements to the effect that no man's property will be safe unless death is the penalty for stealing it, even if the property is no more than that which is carried casually in a pocket and the theft is accomplished merely by picking that pocket. But retributive justice requires punishment to fit the crime, which requires a schedule of punishments, ranging from the most lenient through various degrees of severity to the most awful, death, because the moral sentiments of a just people recognize that crimes range from the most petty through various degrees of gravity to the most awful, which, as we understand these things, is the taking of a human life. The law cannot reinforce these moral sentiments (and its purpose is to do just that) if it executes the pickpocket or the shoplifter as well as the murderer; to do that is to equate petty theft with murder, and petty amounts of property with a human life, and to do that *is* to deny human dignity. The law that does it will lose, and will deserve to lose, the respect it must enjoy among the people, who will neither obey it nor, when serving on juries, enforce it. To reinforce the moral sentiments of a people, the criminal law must be made awful or awesome, and . . . the only way within our means to do that today is to impose the death sentence; but an execution cannot be awesome if it is associated with petty affairs or becomes a customary, familiar event. Thus, while the death penalty should not be seen as cruel, by the same token it should be seen as unusual, not in the techniques employed when carrying it out, but in the frequency with which it is carried out. It is this principle that should be embodied in statutes and impressed upon judge and jury; a properly drawn statute will allow the death penalty only for the most awful crimes: treason, some murders, and some particularly vile rapes. It is not beyond the skill of legislators to draft such a statute— for example, it could provide that the death sentence be imposed *only* for "outrageously or wantonly vile" offenses—one that defers to the jury's judgment in particular cases but, at the same time, impresses upon the jury the awesome character of the judgment it is asked to make. This is not incompatible with retributive sentencing; on the contrary, retribution, unlike deterrence, precisely because it derives from moral sensibilities, recognizes the justice of mercy, the injustice of punishing the irresponsible, and limits to the severity of punishment. (If the only purpose of punishment is deterrence, why not boil murderers in oil or chop off the hands of shoplifters?) It is also compatible with the purpose of capital punishment; only a relatively few executions are required to enhance the dignity of the criminal law, and that number is considerably smaller than the number of murderers and rapists. The other purpose of punishment can be more fully accomplished by a more rigorous enforcement of the other criminal statutes. . . .

There is, finally, the question of whether executions should be public. I have made much of the point that the anger that gives rise to the demand that criminals be paid back is not in principle selfish or otherwise reprehensible, and that it is a function of the law to tame that anger by satisfying and thereby justifying it. This it does when it punishes criminals; punishment, I have argued, serves to praise and reward law-abidingness even as it blames crime. But that anger has also to be tamed in the sense of being moderated. A proper criminal trial achieves this to some extent by forcing the jury to determine beyond a reasonable doubt that the accused is guilty as charged. In order further to calm or moderate that anger, and to impress upon the population the awesomeness of the moral order and the awful consequences of its breach, I think it necessary that executions be public. There are obvious objections to public executions, even when they are not the sort of spectacle Mandeville was describing in the eighteenth century. No ordinary citizen can be required to witness them, and it would be better if some people not be permitted to witness them—children, for example, and the sort of person who would, if permitted, happily join a lynch mob. Executions should not be televized, both because of the unrestricted character of the television audience and the tendency of television to make a vulgar spectacle of the most dignified event. Yet executions must be witnessed, and witnessed by the public, which means not hidden from the view of all but prison personnel and a few others. The solution to this problem is to be found where the framers of the Constitution found part of the solution to the problem of democracy, namely, in the principle of representation. In addition to prison personnel and the others now attending them, executions should be witnessed by representatives of the people. Since the process of selecting them could not be controlled sufficiently to ensure that decorum attend every aspect of this ceremony (and I use that word advisedly), the represen-tatives should not be specially selected for this purpose but should be those, or a part of those, already elected to the legislatures. They represent the people when they enact the statutes permitting the penalty of death, and they can represent the people when they witness its carrying out. As Madison said in the tenth *Federalist*, they are a "chosen body of citizens" who can be expected to "refine and enlarge the public views," and we have a right to expect them also to represent the public's moral indignation. If they cannot do this, they are not justified in enacting death penalty statutes. The abolitionists make this point and they are right. But execu-tions solemnly witnessed and carried out are not barbaric; on the contrary, they enhance the awesome dignity of the law and of the moral order it serves and protects.

26

*Capital Punishment: The Inevitability
of Caprice and Mistake*

CHARLES L. BLACK, JR.

*Charles L. Black, Jr., was a constitutional scholar at Yale Law School and
Columbia University Law School for 52 years. In 1974, he published a
now classic argument against capital punishment. In* Furman v. Georgia
*(1972), a plurality of the Supreme Court invalidated most death penalty
statutes at the time, but not on the ground that capital punishment is per
se unconstitutional; only Justices William J. Brennan, Jr., and Thurgood
Marshall took that position. Rather, in the words of concurring Justice Potter
Stewart: "These death sentences are cruel and unusual in the same way
that being struck by lightning is cruel and unusual." Building on that
insight, Black argues that the arbitrariness and capriciousness of the criminal
process and capital punishment system, as well as the inevitability of mistakes,
renders unconstitutional the imposition and execution of death sentences. In
his last term on the Supreme Court, one of the dissenters in* Furman,
*Justice Harry A. Blackmun, came to the same conclusion in his dissent
from the denial of review in* Callins v. Collins *(1994). The excerpt here
is from Black's book of the same name and lays out his main argument
against capital punishment.*

[T]HE CENTRAL THESIS . . . is that the problems of mistake and
caprice are ineradicable in the administration of the death penalty. . . .

I will skip over the preliminary decision on arrest, and go on to the
two-pronged decision made by the prosecutor. On the facts before him,
he must first decide whether to *charge* an offense carrying the penalty of
death, or a lesser offense. If he decides to charge the capital offense, he
must quite commonly decide whether to *accept a plea of guilty* to a lesser
(and therefore noncapital) offense, thus permitting the defendant to escape
at this early stage the possibility of execution, at the price of going to
prison without trial. . . .

If the *prosecutor*, having charged a capital crime, is nevertheless willing
to accept a plea of guilty to a lesser offense, then the *defendant* has in turn
the choice of accepting or rejecting this offer. This dreadful choice has

to be made by a man in custody, often disoriented and frightened, and hence dependent upon advice, and susceptible to following possibly bad advice; at this point, then, the choice is partly or wholly made by the *lawyer* for the defendant. With the best of intentions, this lawyer's decision is often a difficult one. . . .

If a "plea bargain" is not struck, then the defendant goes on trial for his life. At the end of this trial, the jury has a number of decisions or choices to make, most of them veiled by the secrecy of the jury-room. It must decide what the gross *physical* facts were: Did this defendant, for example, actually stab the deceased, or did somebody else do it? Did the defendant stab the victim at a time when the victim was trying to stab the defendant, or did he stab a man whose knife was sheathed? (I will now mention, not for the last time, that "mistake" as to these questions of physical fact seems to be what most people mean when they speak of "mistake" in criminal proceedings; I hope I shall be able to convince you that the range of possible "mistake" is much broader than that.) Having satisfied its mind as to the *physical* facts, the jury must then tackle the *psychological* facts. Did the defendant, who clearly (or admittedly) shot a man while that man was reaching for his handkerchief, *believe* that that man was reaching for a gun, or is the pretense that he so believed mere sham? Did the defendant *plan* this killing, or was it done in the heat of passion? Did he *intend* to kill at all?

The jury in a criminal case does not announce its decision on each of such points one by one. It simply comes in with a verdict of "not guilty," or "guilty of murder in the first degree," or of "manslaughter," or of some other offense known to the state's law. There is no question in the mind of anybody who has dealt with the criminal-law system that a jury sometimes comes in with a verdict of "guilty" of some offense lesser than the one strictly warranted by the evidence. All kinds of factors — sympathy, doubt of physical "guilt" in the narrow sense, doubt as to the other, less tangible factors going to make up "guilt," a feeling that extenuating circumstances exist, and so on — may motivate this behavior. But the pragmatic fact, visible from the outside, is that the jury, in finding a defendant guilty, let us say, of "second-degree" rather than of "first-degree" murder, is, for whatever reason and on whatever basis, *choosing* that this defendant not suffer death. . . .

If the jury, accepting the prosecutor's version of the facts and rejecting all defenses, convicts the defendant of an offense for which the death penalty is possible, the choice then has to be made as to *sentencing*. Under the old system, condemned in the 1972 *Furman* case, the usual procedure was for the jury, "in its discretion," to decide whether a death sentence was to be imposed. The form of words varied from state to state; sometimes the death sentence followed automatically unless the jury recommended mercy, while sometimes the affirmative recommendation of the jury was necessary for the sentence of death. Sometimes, indeed, the judge rather than the jury exercised this "discretion." In the newer statutes . . . a *second* hearing on sentencing often occurs, at the end of which, on the basis of mitigating or aggravating circumstances named in the new law, the sentence of death may or may not be imposed. In this initial survey, it is enough to note that this choice must usually be made. . . .

After conviction, sentencing, and appeal, we reach the possibility of executive clemency, or clemency exercised by a pardon board. In no state, as far as I know, is it the case that a death sentence, once imposed, must be carried out, without the possibility of there intervening an act of mercy by some authority. The national Constitution fixes this principle for federal crime, by giving the pardoning power to the President.

Now that is about the range, though some minor points may have been skipped, for later filling in. It becomes plainly visible that the choice of death as the penalty is the result not of just *one* choice—that of the trial judge or jury, dealt with in the *Furman* case—but of a *number* of choices, starting with the prosecutor's choice of a charge, and ending with the choice of the authority—the governor or a board—charged with the administration of clemency.

Regarding *each* of these choices, through all the range, one of two things, or perhaps both, may be true.

First, the choice made may be a *mistaken* one. The defendant may not have committed the act of which he is found guilty; the factors which ought properly to induce a prosecutor to accept a plea to a lesser offense may have been present, though he refused to do so; the defendant may have been "insane" in the way the law requires for exculpation, though the jury found that he was not. And so on.

Secondly, there may either be no legal standards governing the making of the choice, or the standards verbally set up by the legal system for the making of the choice may be so vague, at least in part of their range, as to be only *apparent* standards, in truth furnishing no direction and leaving the actual choice quite arbitrary.

These two possibilities have an interesting (and, in the circumstances, tragic) relationship. The concept of *mistake* fades out as the *standard* grows more and more vague and unintelligible. There is no vagueness problem about the question "Did Y hit Z on the head with a piece of pipe?" It is, for just that reason, easily possible to conceive of what it means to be "mistaken" in answering this question; one is "mistaken" if one answers it "yes" when in fact *Y* did not hit *Z* with the pipe. It is even fairly clear what it means to be "mistaken" in answering the question "Did *Y intend to kill Z?*" Conscious intents are facts; the difference here really is that, for obvious reasons, *mistake is more likely* in the second case than in the first, for it is hard or impossible to be confident of coming down on the right side of a question about past psychological fact.

It is very different when one comes to the question, "Was the action of which the defendant was found guilty performed in such a manner as to evidence an 'abandoned and malignant heart'?" (This phrase figures importantly in homicide law.) This question has the same grammatical form as a clearcut factual question; actually, through a considerable part of its range, it is not at all clear what it means. It sets up, in this range, not a standard but a *pseudo-standard*. One cannot, strictly speaking, be *mistaken* in answering it, at least within a considerable range, because to be mistaken is to be on the wrong side of a line, and there is no real line here. But that, in turn, means that the "test" may often be no test at all, but merely an invitation to arbitrariness and passion, or even to the influence of dark unconscious factors.

"Mistake" and "arbitrariness" therefore are reciprocally related. As a purported "test" becomes less and less intelligible, and hence more and more a cloak for arbitrariness, "mistake" becomes less and less possible — not, let it be strongly emphasized, because of any certainty of one's being right, but for the exactly contrary reason that there is no "right" or "wrong" discernible. . . .

. . . [The] decisions on charging, on acceptance of guilty plea, on determination of the offense for which conviction is warranted, on sentencing, and on clemency add up . . . to a process containing too much chance for mistake and too much standardless "discretion" for it to be decent for us to use it any longer as a means of choosing for death. We have to keep using it as a means of choosing for other punishment, even as we slowly try to make it better, but for the death of a person it will not do, and it cannot be reformed enough to do.

Suppose all the mistake-proneness and standardlessness I have laid out, step by step, were concentrated in the decision of one man. We would regard that as so evidently intolerable as to be undiscussable. But it might be better than what we have, for responsibility would at least be fixed. All our system does is to diffuse this same responsibility nearly to the point of its elimination, so that each participant in this long process, though perhaps knowing his own conclusions to be uncertain and inadequately based on lawful standards, can comfort himself with the thought, altogether false and vain, that the lack has been made up, or will be made up, somewhere else.

How have we allowed ourselves to get here? I suggest it is because of our seeing the whole process through the medium of a radically false mythology. We tend, I believe, to think of persons' being "clearly guilty" of crimes for which they ought to die. Then some of them, by acts of pure grace, are spared—by prosecutors' discretion, by jury leniency, by clemency. After all, who can complain at not receiving a pure favor? (There is here perhaps a touch of Calvinism—but to a true Calvinist a blasphemous touch, for the "grace" comes from humans all too human.)

The trouble is that the system may just as well be viewed, and with enormously higher accuracy, if numbers count, must be viewed, as one in which a few people are selected, without adequately shown or structured reason for their being selected, to die. The inevitable corollary of sparing some people through mere grace or favor is standardless condemnation of others. The thing that ought to impress us is the standardless condemnation; we have been looking too long at its mirror image; we should take courage and turn around.

One paragraph corrective of a possible misapprehension: When I condemn our capital punishment system as intolerably mistake-prone and standardless, I do not mean in any way to suggest corruptness or cruelty on the part of those who work it. The prosecutor must accept some pleas and reject others; I have no reason to think that most prosecutors do not try to exercise this function in a commonsense and humane manner. Juries *must* pronounce on the questions put them; if they are asked whether a particular murderer or rapist was "depraved" or "not depraved," they have to answer as best they can; if they are given an unintelligible "sanity" question to answer, they must do their best. Judges must pronounce on questions of law, whatever they may know as to their own fallibility. I have already given illustrations of the humane use of the clemency power by governors. All this is not to say, of course, that there are not some hanging prosecutors, hanging juries, hanging judges, and hanging governors. But, overwhelmingly, the trouble is not in the people but in the system—or nonsystem.

27

The Broken Machinery Of Death

ALAN BERLOW

After several decades of overwhelming support for capital punishment, recently public opinion appears to be shifting, in part because DNA testing has established that some death row inmates were actually innocent. Several Republican governors also imposed moratoriums on executions because of reports that substantial numbers of those sentenced to death were wrongly convicted. Alan Berlow, a reporter who frequently writes on the death penalty, places these developments and the current debate over the death penalty in historical and political perspective. This excerpt comes from The American Prospect *(2001).*

[O]N JULY 2, 1976, the U.S. Supreme Court voted 7-2 in *Gregg v. Georgia* to reinstate the death penalty after a brief official hiatus. Implicit in the *Gregg* decision was the optimistic belief that the many problems identified by a previous Supreme Court decision, *Furman v. Georgia*, could be fixed. In 1972 the *Furman* Court had struck down hundreds of state laws that the justices deemed "arbitrary and capricious." But the majority in *Gregg* argued that "clear and objective standards" would minimize juror caprice and reduce discrimination. In an age of science, a "maturing society" could have a death penalty to be proud of.

A quarter-century and more than 700 executions later—including, last month, the first two federal executions in four decades—the promise of *Gregg* seems preposterously naive. *Gregg's* ambition was to rationalize sentencing and ensure that death sentences would be applied more equitably and only to the most egregious offenders. It hasn't worked out that way. Today in the United States more than 3,700 men and women await execution on death row. The overwhelming number of those put to death will be poor, members of a minority, uneducated, or of questionable sanity, and they will have been represented by some of the worst lawyers available. Clearly, it was absurd to assume that the state legislatures that had crafted the multitude of unconstitutional abominations decried by the *Furman* decision would suddenly fix them.

The nation has made a few important improvements since 1976.

Concurrent with *Gregg*, the Supreme Court outlawed mandatory death sentences. The following year, it banned capital punishment in cases of nonhomicidal rape — a huge blow against one particularly racist aspect of the death penalty (between 1930 and 1972, of the 455 individuals executed in this country for rape, nine of every 10 were black). And all but three of the 38 death penalty states now offer "life without parole" as an alternative to the death sentence (although jurors frequently ignore the option, mistakenly believing that it doesn't work). During the past year, nearly half of the death penalty states have approved some sort of reform legislation, most often relating to DNA testing for prisoners who claim to be innocent. A few have also enacted new laws designed to improve the quality of representation provided to indigents, and five have approved bills banning execution of the mentally retarded.

Despite such efforts to "tinker with the machinery of death," as Justice Harry Blackmun once put it, growing numbers of Americans have begun to question the rationality of the system that executes people in their name. True, a majority of Americans support capital punishment and overwhelmingly supported the execution of Timothy McVeigh (including 58 percent of those who consider themselves death penalty opponents!). Yet recent polls reveal that 40 percent of the public also think that the penalty is not applied fairly and half think that there should be no more executions until a government commission thoroughly examines the system's fairness.

This growing skepticism stems from a combination of factors. First, 96 individuals since 1973 have been released from state death rows either because they were proved innocent (10 of them on the basis of DNA) or because courts found unconscionable due-process violations. Second, ample documentation has revealed how poorly the system works. Columbia Law School professor James S. Liebman's study *A Broken System: Error Rates in Capital Cases, 1973–1995* found such serious errors in 68 percent of death penalty cases that the death sentence or underlying conviction was overturned. Third, many people are anxiously aware that the man currently occupying the Oval Office presided with unnerving nonchalance over a record 152 executions while governor of Texas, including several cases in which there were real questions of innocence and due process. And finally, skepticism about the death penalty was given bipartisan legitimacy last year when Illinois Governor George Ryan, a Republican supporter of the death penalty, halted executions in his state after learning that 13 innocent persons had been found on its death row.

But while overall support for the death penalty has declined in recent years, it is still as strong as it was when *Gregg* was decided in 1976 (66 percent then, 67 percent in February of this year). And the moral-absolutist arguments that once gave strength to the abolitionist movement have receded. While the Catholic Church and other religious organizations continue to argue that taking a life is morally wrong, the most common line of resistance to the death penalty has become, in effect: "You can have your death penalty if you meet certain preconditions that will effectively guarantee that innocent people won't be put to death."

That was the approach represented in the American Bar Association's 1997 call for a nationwide freeze on capital punishment until states can ensure that "death penalty cases are administered fairly and impartially, in accordance with due process." To date, however, not a single state has fully embraced the ABA's standards (which specifically call for competent counsel, restoration of the right to litigate constitutional claims after conviction, reforms to eliminate racial discrimination, and outlawing execution of juveniles and the mentally retarded). Meanwhile, much of whatever progress individual states have made in increasing fairness has been rolled back by Supreme Court rulings and congressional actions that undermine the rights of defendants. . . .

Twenty-five years after *Gregg*, obvious racial discrimination in the administration of the death penalty remains routine—notwithstanding U.S. Attorney General John Ashcroft's recent denial of that fact. Nearly 90 percent of the federal inmates on death row are minorities. According to a Justice Department study released in September, 2000, more than 76 percent of the cases in which federal prosecutors had sought the death penalty during the previous five years involved a defendant who belonged to a minority group. In the same study, U.S. attorneys were nearly twice as likely to recommend death for a black defendant if the victim was nonblack than if the victim was black. (In North Carolina, death sentences were imposed three and a half times more frequently when the victim was white rather than black.)

Under the tenets established by *Gregg*, you might conclude that this would be unconstitutional. You would be wrong. In the *Gregg* decision, the Supreme Court said that a constitutional violation was established if a plaintiff demonstrated a "pattern of arbitrary and capricious sentencing." Since then, however, the Court appears to have abandoned this logic. In 1987, for example, it ruled in *McCleskey v. Kemp* that racial disparities are "an inevitable part of our criminal justice system." Thus, a defendant in a capital case now has a harder time demonstrating discrimination than someone arguing an employment discrimination case does. . . .

For most members of Congress, ensuring fairness in the death penalty process is less urgent than demonstrating that they're "tough on crime."

How else to explain Congress's decision to defund postconviction defender organizations that once provided a useful mechanism to check legally flawed death sentences? Or Congress's passage, one year after the Oklahoma City bombing, of the Anti-Terrorism and Effective Death Penalty Act, which decimated *habeas corpus* review not just for death row inmates but for everyone else as well?

Proponents of the Effective Death Penalty Act said that the law was needed to shorten the time between conviction and execution to as little as four to six years (the average is now 7.9 years). But it has taken 11 years, on average, to establish reversible error in capital cases. Among the 20 innocent people Florida has discovered on its death row was James Richardson, whose innocence was established only in 1989, after he'd spent 21 years in prison. And last year, after Frank Lee Smith died of cancer in his 14th year on Florida's death row, DNA tests established that another man had been guilty of the rape and murder of an eight-year-old girl for which Smith had been sentenced to die.

What is wrong with the death penalty system as it functions in this country today? Just about everything. But with more than 700 executions under our belts since 1976, the political difficulty of owning up to the fact that at least some of these people were unfairly executed — that the system is broken and has been for a long time — cannot be underestimated.

Nevertheless, with Democrats now in control of the Senate, it should be possible to gain passage of the Innocence Protection Act, which would impose a DNA-testing requirement, pressure states to improve counsel for indigent capital defendants, and address such other important issues as procedural barriers to *habeas corpus* review and the execution of juveniles and the mentally retarded. Meanwhile, the best near-term hope for reform of the nation's death penalty laws resides with state moratorium initiatives and in the seven states where special commissions have been set up to examine capital punishment. . . .

PART SEVEN

The Quest for Social Equality and Personal Liberty

AMENDMENT *9*
The enumeration in the Constitution,
of certain rights,
shall not be construed to deny or disparage
others retained by the people.

AMENDMENT *14*
Section 1 . . . No State shall make or enforce any law
which shall abridge the privileges or immunities
of citizens of the United States;
nor shall any State deprive any person of life, liberty, or property,
without due process of law;
nor deny to any person within its jurisdiction
the equal protection of the laws.

28

Simple Justice: The History of
Brown v. Board of Education

RICHARD KLUGER

Richard Kluger is an award-winning writer and author. The selection here is from his classic work, Simple Justice: The History of *Brown v.* Board of Education *and Black America's Struggle for Equality (1975). In it, Kluger highlights the importance of the Supreme Court's composition—specifically the death of Chief Justice Fred Vinson and Republican President Dwight D. Eisenhower's appointment of Earl Warren as chief justice—to that landmark school desegregation ruling. Kluger also illuminates how Chief Justice Warren forged consensus within the Court on reversing the doctrine of "separate but equal," announced in* Plessy v. Ferguson *(1896) and which legitimized racial discrimination and segregation.*

———

IN THE two AND A HALF years since they had last sat down to decide a major racial case, the Justices of the Supreme Court had not grown closer. Indeed, the philosophical and personal fissures in their ranks had widened since they had agreed—unanimously—to side with the Negro appellants in *Sweatt, McLaurin,* and *Henderson* in the spring of 1950. That had been a rare show of unanimity. By the 1952 Term, the Court was failing to reach a unanimous decision 81 percent of the time, nearly twice as high a percentage of disagreement as it had recorded a decade earlier. . . .

It was perhaps the most severely fractured Court in history—testament, on the face of it, to Vinson's failure as Chief Justice. Selected to lead the Court because of his skills as a conciliator, the low-key, mournful-visaged Kentuckian found that the issues before him were far different from, and far less readily negotiable than, the hard-edged problems he had faced as Franklin Roosevelt's ace economic troubleshooter and Harry Truman's Secretary of the Treasury and back-room confederate. . . .

What, then, could be expected of the deeply divided Vinson Court as it convened on the morning of December 13, 1952, to deliberate on the transcendent case of *Brown v. Board of Education*? The earlier racial cases—*Sweatt* and *McLaurin*—they had managed to cope with by chipping away at the edges of Jim Crow but avoiding the real question of *Plessy's* continued validity. The Court could no longer dodge that question, though it might continue to stall in resolving it. Hovering over the Justices were all the repressive bugaboos of the Cold War era. The civil rights of Negroes and the civil liberties of political dissenters and criminal defendants were prone to be scrambled together in the public mind, and every malcontent was a sitting target for the red tar of anti-Americanism. No sector of the nation was less hospitable to both civil-liberties and civil-rights claimants than the segregating states of the South, and it was the South with which the Justices had primarily to deal in confronting *Brown*. . . .

And so they were divided. But given the gravity of the issue, they were willing to take their time to try to reconcile their differences. They clamped a precautionary lid on all their discussions of *Brown* as the year turned and Fred Vinson swore in Dwight David Eisenhower as the thirty-fourth President of the United States. The Justices seemed to make little headway toward resolving the problem, but they all knew that a close vote would likely be a disaster for Court and country alike. The problem of welding the disparate views into a single one was obviously complicated by the ambivalence afflicting the Court's presiding Justice. As spring came and the end of the Court's 1952 Term neared, Fred Vinson seemed to be in increasingly disagreeable and edgy spirits. Says one of the people at the Court closest to him then: "I got the distinct impression that he was distressed over the Court's inability to find a strong, unified position on such an important case." . . .

During the last week of the term in June, the law clerks of all the Justices met in an informal luncheon session and took a two-part poll. Each clerk was asked how he would vote in the school-segregation cases and how he thought his Justice would vote. According to one of their number, a man who later became a professor of law: "The clerks, were almost unanimous for overruling *Plessy* and ordering desegregation, but, according to their impressions, the Court would have been closely divided if it had announced its decision at that time. Many of the clerks were only guessing at the positions of their respective Justices, but it appeared that a majority of the Justices would not have overruled *Plessy* but would have given some relief in some of the cases on the ground that the separate facilities were not in fact equal." . . .

All such bets on the alignment of the Court ended abruptly a few days later when the single most fateful judicial event of that long summer occurred. In his Washington hotel apartment, Fred M. Vinson died of a heart attack at 3:15 in the morning of September 8. He was sixty-three.

All the members of the Court attended Vinson's burial in Louisa,

Kentucky, his ancestral home. But not all the members of the Court grieved equally at his passing. And one at least did not grieve at all. Felix Frankfurter had not much admired Fred Vinson as judge or man. And he was certain that the Chief Justice had been the chief obstacle to the Court's prospects of reaching a humanitarian and judicially defensible settlement of the monumental segregation cases. In view of Vinson's passing just before the *Brown* reargument, Frankfurter remarked to a former clerk, "This is the first indication I have ever had that there is a God."

Fred Vinson was not yet cold in his grave when speculation rose well above a whisper as to whom President Eisenhower would pick to heal and lead the Supreme Court as it faced one of its most momentous decisions in the segregation cases. . . .

Dwight Eisenhower's principal contribution to the civil rights of Americans would prove to be his selection of Earl Warren as Chief Justice—a decision Eisenhower would later say had been a mistake. The President was on hand, at any rate, on Monday, October 5, when just after noon the clerk of the Supreme Court read aloud the commission of the President that began, "Know ye: That reposing special trust and confidence in the wisdom, uprightness and learning of Earl Warren of California, I do appoint him Chief Justice of the United States. . . . " Warren stood up at the clerk's desk to the side of the bench and read aloud his oath of office. At the end, Clerk Harold Willey said to him, "So help you God." Warren said. "So help me God." Then he stepped quickly behind the velour curtains and re-emerged a moment later through the opening in the center to take the presiding seat. His entire worthy career to that moment would be dwarfed by what followed. . . .

At the reargument, Earl Warren had said very little. The Chief Justice had put no substantive questions to any of the attorneys. Nor is it likely that he had given any indication of his views to the other Justices before they convened at the Saturday-morning conference on December 12. But then, speaking first, he made his views unmistakable.

Nearly twenty years later, he would recall, "I don't remember having any great doubts about which way it should go. It seemed to me a comparatively simple case. Just look at the various decisions that had been eroding *Plessy* for so many years. They kept chipping away at it rather than ever really facing it head-on. If you looked back—to *Gaines*, to *Sweatt*, to some of the interstate-commerce cases—you saw that the doctrine of separate-but-equal had been so eroded that only the *fact* of segregation itself remained unconsidered. On the merits, the natural, the logical, and practically the only way the case could be decided was clear. The question was *how* the decision was to be reached."

At least two sets of notes survive from the Justices' 1953 conference discussion of the segregation cases—extensive ones by Justice Burton and exceedingly scratchy and cryptic ones by Justice Frankfurter. They agree on the Chief Justice's remarks. The cases had been well argued, in his judgment, Earl Warren told the conference, and the government had been very frank in both its written and its oral presentations. He said he had of course been giving much thought to the entire question since coming to the Court, and after studying the briefs and relevant history and hearing the arguments, he could not escape the feeling that the Court had "finally arrived" at the moment when it now had to determine whether segregation was allowable in the public schools. Without saying it in so many words, the new Chief Justice was declaring that the Court's policy of delay, favored by his predecessor, could no longer be permitted.

The more he had pondered the question, Warren said, the more he had come to the conclusion that the doctrine of separate-but-equal rested upon the concept of the inferiority of the colored race. He did not see how *Plessy* and its progeny could be sustained on any other theory—and if the Court were to choose to sustain them, "we must do it on that basis," he was recorded by Burton as saying. He was concerned, to be sure, about the necessity of overruling earlier decisions and lines of reasoning, but he had concluded that segregation of Negro schoolchildren had to be ended. The law, he said in words noted by Frankfurter, "cannot in 'this day and age' set them apart." The law could not say, Burton recorded the Chief as asserting, that Negroes were "not entitled to *exactly same* treatment of all others." To do so would go against the intentions of the three Civil War amendments. . . .

Unless any of the other four Justices who had indicated a year earlier their readiness to overturn segregation—Black, Douglas, Burton, and Minton—had since changed his mind, Warren's opening remarks meant that a majority of the Court now stood ready to strike down the practice.

But to gain a narrow majority was no cause for exultation. A sharply divided Court, no matter which way it leaned, was an indecisive one, and for Warren to force a split decision out of it would have amounted to hardly more constructive leadership on this transcendent question than Fred Vinson had managed. The new Chief Justice wanted to unite the Court in *Brown*. . . .

He recognized that a number of Court precedents of long standing would be shattered in the process of overturning *Plessy*, and he regretted that necessity. It was the sort of reassuring medicine most welcomed by Burton and Minton, the least judicially and intellectually adventurous members of the Court.

He recognized that the Court's decision would have wide repercussions, varying in intensity from state to state, and that they would all therefore have to approach the matter in as tolerant and understanding a way as possible. Implicit in this was a call for flexibility in how the Court might frame its decree.

But overarching all these cushioning comments and a tribute to both his compassion as a man and his persuasive skills as a politician was the moral stance Earl Warren took at the outset of his remarks. Segregation, he had told his new colleagues, could be justified only by belief in the inferiority of the Negro; any of them who wished to perpetuate the practice, he implied, ought in candor to be willing to acknowledge as much. These were plain words, and they did not have to be hollered. They cut across all the legal theories that had been so endlessly aired and went straight to the human tissue at the core of the controversy. . . .

The Warren opinion was "finally approved" at the May 15 conference, Burton noted in his diary. The man from California had won the support of every member of the Court.

Not long before the Court's decision in *Brown* was announced, Warren told *Ebony* magazine twenty years later, he had decided to spend a few days visiting Civil War monuments in Virginia. He went by automobile with a black chauffeur.

At the end of the first day, the Chief Justice's car pulled up at a hotel, where he had made arrangements to spend the night. Warren simply assumed that his chauffeur would stay somewhere else, presumably at a less expensive place. When the Chief Justice came out of his hotel the next morning to resume his tour, he soon figured out that the chauffeur had spent the night in the car. He asked the black man why.

"Well, Mr. Chief Justice," the chauffeur began, "I just couldn't find a place—couldn't find a place to . . . "

Warren was stricken by his own thoughtlessness in bringing an employee of his to a town where lodgings were not available to the man solely because of his color. "I was embarrassed, I was ashamed," Warren recalled. "We turned back immediately. . . . "

In the press room on the ground floor, reporters filing in at the tail end of the morning were advised that May 17, 1954, looked like a quiet day at the Supreme Court of the United States. . . .

... [A]s the first three routine opinions were distributed, it looked, as predicted, like a very quiet day at the Court. But then, as Douglas finished up, Clerk of the Court Harold Willey dispatched a pneumatic message to Banning E. Whittington, the Court's dour press officer. Whittington slipped on his suit jacket, advised the press-room contingent, "Reading of the segregation decisions is about to begin in the courtroom," added as he headed out the door that the text of the opinion would be distributed in the press room afterward, and then led the scrambling reporters in a dash up the marble stairs.

"I have for announcement," said Earl Warren, "the judgment and opinion of the Court in No. 1 — *Oliver Brown et al. v. Board of Education of Topeka.*" It was 12:52 p.m. In the press room, the Associated Press wire carried the first word to the country: "Chief Justice Warren today began reading the Supreme Court's decision in the public school segregation cases. The court's ruling could not be determined immediately." The bells went off in every news room in America. The nation was listening.

It was Warren's first major opinion as Chief Justice. He read it, by all accounts, in a firm, clear, unemotional voice. If he had delivered no other opinion but this one, he would have won his place in American history. . . .

Without in any way becoming technical and rhetorical, Warren then proceeded to demonstrate the dynamic nature and adaptive genius of American constitutional law. . . . Having declared its essential value to the nation's civic health and vitality, he then argued for the central importance of education in the private life and aspirations of every individual. . . . That led finally to the critical question: "Does segregation of children in public schools solely on the basis of race . . . deprive the children of the minority group of equal educational opportunities?"

To this point, nearly two-thirds through the opinion, Warren had not tipped his hand. Now, in the next sentence, he showed it by answering that critical question: "We believe that it does." . . .

This finding flew directly in the face of *Plessy.* And here, finally, Warren collided with the 1896 decision. . . .

The balance of the Chief Justice's opinion consisted of just two paragraphs. The first began: "We conclude" — and here Warren departed from the printed text before him to insert the word "unanimously," which sent a sound of muffled astonishment eddying around the courtroom — "that in the field of public education the doctrine of 'separate but equal' has no place. Separate educational facilities are inherently unequal." The plaintiffs and others similarly situated — technically meaning Negro children within the segregated school districts under challenge — were therefore being deprived of the equal protection of the laws guaranteed by the Fourteenth Amendment.

The concluding paragraph of the opinion revealed Earl Warren's political adroitness both at compromise and at the ready use of the power of his office for ends he thought worthy. "Because these are class actions, because of the wide applicability of this decision, and because of the great variety of local conditions," he declared, "these cases present problems of considerable complexity. . . . In order that we may have the full assistance of the parties in formulating decrees," the Court was scheduling further argument for the term beginning the following fall. The attorneys general of the United States and all the states requiring or permitting segregation in public education were invited to participate. In a few strokes, Warren thus managed to (1) proclaim "the wide applicability" of the decision and make it plain that the Court had no intention of limiting its benefits to a handful of plaintiffs in a few outlying districts; (2) reassure the South that the Court understood the emotional wrench desegregation would cause and was therefore granting the region some time to get accustomed to the idea; and (3) invite the South to participate in the entombing of Jim Crow by joining the Court's efforts to fashion a temperate implementation decree—or to forfeit that chance by petulantly abstaining from the Court's further deliberations and thereby run the risk of having a harsh decree imposed upon it. It was such dexterous use of the power available to him and of the circumstances in which to exploit it that had established John Marshall as a judicial statesman and political tactician of the most formidable sort. The Court had not seen his like since. Earl Warren, in his first major opinion, moved now with that same sure purposefulness

It was 1:20 p.m. The wire services proclaimed the news to the nation. Within the hour, the Voice of America would begin beaming word to the world in thirty-four languages: In the United States, schoolchildren could no longer be segregated by race. The law of the land no longer recognized a separate equality. No Americans were more equal than any other Americans. Jim Crow was on the way to the burial ground.

29

Dismantling Desegregation: The Quiet Reversal of Brown v. Board of Education

GARY ORFIELD
SUSAN E. EATON

Gary Orfield is a professor and co-director of the Civil Rights Project at the University of California, Los Angeles, School of Law. A prolific author, Orfield is one of the country's leading authorities on school desegregation. The excerpt here is from his book, written with Susan E. Eaton, a journalist. In Dismantling Desegregation: The Quiet Reversal of Brown v. Board of Education (1996), *Orfield examines the consequences of the Rehnquist Court's rulings in the 1990s on judicial supervision of integration efforts and contends that they, along with contemporary housing patterns, are returning the country to increasingly segregated schools.*

———◆———

FOUR DECADES AFTER the civil rights revolution began with the Supreme Court's unanimous 1954 school desegregation decision, *Brown v. Board of Education*, the Supreme Court reversed itself in the 1990s, authorizing school districts to return to segregated and unequal public schools. The cases were part of a general reversal of civil rights policy, which included decisions against affirmative action and voting rights. After decades of bitter political, legal, and community struggles over civil rights, there was surprisingly little attention to the new school resegregation policies spelled out in the Court's key 1990s decisions in *Board of Education of Oklahoma City v. Dowell, Freeman v. Pitts,* and *Missouri v. Jenkins.* The decisions were often characterized as belated adjustments to an irrelevant, failed policy: But in fact, these historic High Court decisions were a triumph for the decades-long powerful, politicized attacks on school desegregation. The new policies reflected the victory of the conservative movement that altered the federal courts and turned the nation from the dream of *Brown* toward accepting a return to segregation.

Dowell, Pitts, and *Jenkins,* spelled out procedures for court approval of the dismantling of school desegregation plans—plans that, despite the well-publicized problems in some cities—have been one of the few legally enforced routes of access and opportunity for millions of African American and Latino schoolchildren in an increasingly polarized society. Though now showing clear signs of erosion, the school desegregation *Brown v. Board of Education* made possible had weathered political attacks better than many had predicted it would.

But *Dowell, Pitts,* and *Jenkins* established legal standards to determine when a local school district had repaid what the Court defined as a historic debt to its black students, a debt incurred during generations of intentional racial segregation and discrimination by state and local policies and practices. Under these decisions, districts that, in the eyes of a court, had obeyed their court orders for several years could send students back to neighborhood schools, even if those schools were segregated and inferior. With the 1995 *Jenkins* decision, the Court further narrowed educational remedies.

This is a troubling shift. *Brown* rested on the principle that intentional public action to support segregation was a violation of the U.S. Constitution. Under *Dowell* and *Pitts*, however, public decisions that re-create segregation, sometimes even more severe than before desegregation orders, are now deemed acceptable. These new resegregation decisions legitimate a deliberate return to segregation. As long as school districts temporarily maintain some aspects of desegregation for several years and do not express an intent to discriminate, the Court approves plans to send minority students back to segregation.

Dowell and *Pitts* embrace new conceptions of racial integration and school desegregation. These decisions view racial integration not as a goal that segregated districts should strive to attain, but as a merely temporary punishment for historic violations, an imposition to be lifted after a few years. After the sentence of desegregation has been served, the normal, "natural" pattern of segregated schools can be restored. In just two years in the early 1990s, *Dowell* and *Pitts* had reduced the long crusade for integrated education to a formalistic requirement that certain rough indicators of desegregation be present briefly.

These resegregation decisions received little national attention, in part because their most dramatic impact was on the South, the region that became the most integrated after *Brown*. The Supreme Court's 1974 *Milliken* decision had already rendered *Brown* almost meaningless for most of the metropolitan North by blocking desegregation plans that would integrate cities with their suburbs. Resegregation decisions made no difference to Washington and New York City since there were no desegregation plans in place.

In this chapter, we analyze the effects of the *Dowell, Pitts,* and *Jenkins* decisions and describe the social and political forces that shaped their underlying philosophy. These three cases largely displace the goal of rooting out the lingering damage of racial segregation and discrimination with the twin goals of minimizing judicial involvement in education and restoring power to local and state governments, whatever the consequences.

The Supreme Court handed down the first of the three resegregation decisions in 1991. *Board of Education of Oklahoma City v. Dowell* outlined circumstances under which courts have authority to release school districts from their obligation to maintain desegregated schools. A previously illegally segregated district whose desegregation plan was being supervised by a court could be freed from oversight if the district had desegregated its students and faculty, and met for a few years the other requirements laid out in the Supreme Court's 1968 *Green v. School Board of New Kent County* decision. *Green* ordered "root and branch" eradication of segregated schooling and specified several areas of a school system—such as students, teachers, transportation, and facilities—in which desegregation was mandatory. Under *Dowell*, a district briefly taking the steps outlined in *Green* can be termed "unitary" and is thus freed from its legal obligation to purge itself of segregation. Unitary might best be understood as the opposite of a "dual" system, in which a school district, in essence, operates two separate systems, one black and one white. A unitary district is assumed to be one that has repaired the damage caused by generations of segregation and overt discrimination.

Under *Brown*, proof of an intentionally segregated dual system triggers desegregation mandates. But once the formerly dual system becomes unitary, according to the decisions of the 1990s, minority students no longer have the special protection of the courts, and school districts no longer face any requirement to maintain desegregation or related education programs.

In 1992, a year after *Dowell*, the *Freeman v. Pitts* decision went even further, holding that various requirements laid out in *Green* need not be present at the same time. This meant, for example, that a once-segregated system could dismantle its student desegregation plan without ever having desegregated its faculty or provided equal access to educational programs.

The Court's 5–4 decision in the 1995 case, *Missouri v. Jenkins*, found the Court's majority determined to narrow the reach of the "separate but equal" remedies provided in big cities after the Supreme Court blocked city-suburban desegregation in 1974. Its 1995 decision prohibited efforts to attract white suburban and private school students *voluntarily* into city schools through excellent programs. Kansas city spent more than a billion dollars upgrading a severely deteriorated school system. The goal here was to create desegregation by making inner city schools so attractive that private school and suburban students would choose to transfer to them. Because possible desegregation was limited within the city system by a lack of white students, the emphasis was put on upgrading the schools. When the district court said that it would examine test scores to help ensure that the remedy actually helped the black children who had been harmed by segregation, the Supreme Court said no, emphasizing the limited role of the courts and the need to restore state and local authority quickly, regardless of remaining inequalities. Ironically, the conservative movement that claimed it would be more productive to emphasize choice and "educational improvement" over desegregation, won a constitutional decision in *Jenkins* that pushed desegregation in big cities toward simple, short-term racial balancing within a city, even where the African American and Latino majority is so large that little contact with whites is possible.

Under *Dowell, Pitts* and *Jenkins*, school districts need not prove actual racial equality, nor a narrowing of academic gaps between the races. Desegregation remedies can even be removed when achievement gaps between the races have widened, or even if a district has never fully implemented an effective desegregation plan. Formalistic compliance for a time with some limited requirements was enough, even if the roots of racial inequality were untouched.

This profound shift of judicial philosophy is eerily compatible with philosophies espoused by the Nixon, Reagan, and Bush administrations. This should not be much of a surprise, since the Supreme Court appointees of these presidents generally shared conservative assumptions about race, inequality, and schooling with the presidents who appointed them. Furthermore, under the Reagan and Bush administrations, even the federal civil rights agencies actively undermined desegregation while embracing a "separate but equal" philosophy. Clarence Thomas, first named by President Reagan to begin dismantling enforcement activities in the civil rights office at the Education Department, was appointed by President Bush to the Supreme Court and became the deciding vote on the Supreme Court in the 1995 *Jenkins* decision.

Civil rights groups, represented by only a handful of lawyers, had little money to resist powerful dismantling efforts by local school districts and their legal teams. The fiscal and organizational crises that in the 1990s plagued the NAACP, the most visible and important civil rights organization, compounded the problem. Local school boards seeking to dismantle their desegregation plans were allied in court not only with powerful state officials but also, in the 1980s, with the U.S. Department of Justice.

After *Dowell* and *Pitts*, many educational leaders thought that, with courts out of the way, racial issues might be set aside and attention would shift from the divisiveness of imposed desegregation plans to educational improvement for all children. With this idea in mind, many school systems, including some of the nation's largest, have filed or are now considering filing motions for unitary status that will make it easier for them to return to neighborhood schools. Living under antidesegregation rhetoric and loosening desegregation standards, still other school districts have adopted policies based on "separate but equal" philosophies. Such policies pledge to do what *Brown* said could not be done—provide equality within segregated schools. Some have tried new and fashionable approaches that focused less and less on desegregation and incorrectly view segregation and its accompanying concentration of poverty as irrelevant to educational quality. . . .

The 1990s' Definition of Unitary Status

The Court expressed its philosophical shift away from *Brown*'s principles most clearly by redefining the legal term "unitary status." In doing so, the Court managed to invent a kind of judicial absolution for the sins of segregation. Under the new resegregation decisions, if a court declared a school district "unitary," that school district could knowingly re-create segregated schools with impunity.

This new use of unitary status represented an important change. Ironically, unitary status had been first used by the Court in its 1968 *Green* decision as a standard that segregated school districts should strive to attain. *Green* posited a unitary school system with equitable interracial schools as a long-term, permanent goal, viewing any school board action that worked against or ignored the goal of total desegregation, to be impermissible.

By 1990, unitary status in that sense—discrimination-free, racially integrated education—was no longer the objective; it became merely a method of getting out of racial integration. The Court rejected not only the ideal of lasting integration, but also the idea that elements of a desegregation plan were part of an inseparable package necessary to break down the dual school system and create desegregated education.

Thus unitary status decisions now have profound consequences for racial integration in U.S. schools. A court-supervised district that has never been declared unitary is obligated under the law to avoid actions that create segregated and unequal schools. But after a declaration of unitary status, the courts presume any government action creating racially segregated schools to be innocent, unless a plaintiff proves that the school officials intentionally decided to discriminate. This burden of proof is nearly impossible to meet, as contemporary school officials can easily formulate plausible alternative justifications. They certainly know better than to give overtly racist reasons for the policy change. With local authorities expressing innocence and the courts inclined to accept any professed educational justification regardless of consequences, minority plaintiffs face overwhelming legal obstacles when they try to prevent resegregation and other racial inequalities. Many of the very same actions that were illegal prior to a unitary status declaration become perfectly legal afterward.

The unitary status ruling assumes two things: that segregation does not have far-reaching effects and that a few years of desegregation, no matter how ineffective, could miraculously erase residual "vestiges" or effects of segregation. In this way, the courts implied that generations of discrimination and segregation could be quickly overcome through formal compliance with *Green* requirements for just one-tenth or one-twentieth as much time as the segregation and discrimination had been practiced.

Many courts do not even investigate whether or not vestiges of segregation are ever remedied. For example, under *Pitts, Dowell,* and *Jenkins,* school districts do not need to show that education gains or opportunities are equal between minority and white children. Nor do courts require solid evidence that discriminatory attitudes and assumptions growing out of a history of segregation have been purged from the local educational system.

In practice, the shift in the burden of proof that results from the unitary status declaration may be the key difference that allows a system to resegregate its schools. For example, after an Austin, Texas Independent School District was declared unitary in 1983, the federal district court relinquished jurisdiction completely in 1986; one year later, the school board redrew attendance zones to create segregated neighborhood schools. By 1993, nearly one-third of the elementary schools had minority enrollments of more than 80 percent nonwhite in a district that still had a white majority. The judge allowed this segregation, though the student reassignments created the segregation in fourteen of the nineteen imbalanced schools. Since the school district had been officially proclaimed unitary, actions that created segregation were assumed to be nondiscriminatory as long as the school leaders claimed an educational justification for the new plans. In contrast, an attendance plan in Dallas, then a nonunitary system, was rejected because it would have created too many one-race schools. . . .

The Growth of Segregation

Segregation grew in the early 1990s. For the first time since the Supreme Court overturned segregation laws in 1954, southern public schools returned to greater segregation. Southern segregation grew significantly from 1988 to 1991 and segregation of African American students across the United States also increased. Latino students remained in an unbroken pattern of increasing segregation dating to the time national data was first collected in the late 1960s. These trends surfaced even before the Supreme Court opened the door to large-scale resegregation. Those decisions were likely to accelerate the trend.

National data show that most segregated African American and Latino schools are dominated by poor children but that 96 percent of white schools have middle-class majorities. The extremely strong relationship between racial segregation and concentrated poverty in the nation's schools is a key reason for the educational differences between segregated and integrated schools. One of the most consistent findings in research on education has been the powerful relationship between concentrated poverty and virtually every measure of school-level academic results. Schools with large numbers of impoverished students tend to have much lower test scores, higher dropout rates, fewer students in demanding classes, less well-prepared teachers, and a low percentage of students who will eventually finish college. Low-income families and communities can provide much less for children and their schools have much weaker links with colleges and good jobs. Segregated schools are far more likely to face intense social and personal problems related to poverty.

Such problems include: low levels of competition and expectation, less qualified teachers who leave as soon as they get seniority, deteriorated schools in dangerous neighborhoods, more limited curricula, peer pressure against academic achievement and supportive of crime and substance abuse, high levels of teen pregnancy, few connections with colleges and employers who can assist students, little serious academic counseling or preparation for college, and powerless parents who themselves failed in school and do not know how to evaluate or change schools.

Poor children face a variety of family problems that make their way into the classroom every day and deeply affect the school environment. Poor families are more likely to move frequently for lack of rent money, disrupting school continuity. Children of jobless parents are more likely to encounter violence, alcoholism, abuse, divorce, and desertion related to joblessness and poverty. Poor children are much more likely to come to school sick, sometimes with severe long-term problems that limit their ability to see or hear in school. Students in concentrated poverty communities and schools often grow up without experience preparing them to function effectively in the middle-class settings of college or well-paying jobs.

In contemporary debates, desegregation plans are often ridiculed as reflecting a belief that there is "something magic about sitting next to whites." In fact, however, a student moving from a segregated African American or Latino school to a white school is usually moving from a school of concentrated poverty with many social and educational short-comings to a school with fewer burdens and better resources to prepare students for college or jobs. Attendance at an integrated rather than a segregated city high school greatly increases the probability that an African American or Latino student will finish college, even if both students start college with the same test scores. Black disenchantment is most likely when the desegregation plan is not able to provide access to strong middle-class schools for black children, a particular problem in plans in older central cities with few remaining middle-class families—cities that have been cut off from suburbia by *Milliken I*.

Resegregation in the Late 1980s

The proportion of black students in schools with more than half minority students rose from 1986 to 1991, to the level that had existed before the Supreme Court's first busing decision in 1971. The share of black students in intensely segregated (90–100 percent minority) schools, which had actually declined during the 1980s, also rose. The consistent trend toward greater segregation of Latino students continued unabated on both measures. . . .

Why These Trends?

The huge changes in the racial composition of American public schools and the segregation of African American and Latino students over the past half century have often been misunderstood. The great increase in the proportion of nonwhite students has not been a consequence of "white flight" from public to private schools, but rather of basic changes in birth rates and immigration patterns. In fact, there has been no significant redistribution between public and private schools. During the period from 1970 to 1984, there was a small increase in the share of students in private schools, but between 1984 and 1991 public enrollment grew 7 percent while private enrollment dropped 9 percent. U.S. Department of Education projections indicate that between 1994 and 2004 public school enrollment would climb 12 percent while private enrollment would rise 11 percent. Even as many Americans believe there is flight from public schools, many believe that desegregation is something that was tried a generation ago but did not last. Both beliefs reflect the political rhetoric of the 1980s, not what actually happened in the society.

According to the Census Bureau, the number of black students in public schools in the United States increased 3 percent from 1972 to 1992, the first two decades of widespread busing plans. In contrast, Latino enrollments soared 89 percent and white enrollments fell 14 percent. These trends led to many claims that whites were abandoning public education because of resistance to integration. The decline was not, however, the result of whites leaving public schools.

The white drop was not balanced by growth in white private school enrollment. The Census Bureau reports that there were 18 percent fewer white students in private elementary schools and 13 percent fewer whites in private high schools than two decades ago. The proportion of whites in public schools was actually increasing. The underlying cause, of course, was a dramatic drop in the white birth rate. Contrary to many claims by politicians, these overall changes had nothing to do with desegregation. Public schools were actually holding a growing share of a declining group of school-age white children.

In 1992, 89 percent of whites, 95 percent of blacks, and 92 percent of Latinos attended public schools at the elementary level. Even among upper-income whites, only one-sixth of the children were in private schools. At the high school level, 92 percent of American children were in public schools, including 92 percent of whites, 95 percent of Latinos, and 97 percent of blacks. Private high schools were more popular among affluent whites, but served only one-eighth of their children.

White and middle-class enrollments have been shrinking in all of the largest central city school districts for decades. In fact, the total number of white students in the United States fell sharply from 1968 to 1986 as a result of plummeting white birth rates. In 1986, the nation's twenty-five largest urban school districts served only 3 percent of whites. In metropolitan Atlanta, for example, 98 percent of the area's white high school students attended suburban schools by 1986.

There is no evidence that these trends will reverse or that changes in school desegregation plans will reverse these patterns. Middle-class suburbanization is continuing. Census Bureau studies of migration patterns between 1985 and 1990 show that each year "central cities lost 1.6 to 3.0 million residents while their suburbs . . . gained 1.9 to 3.2 million persons." The overwhelming majority of those who left central cities for the suburbs were white and/or middle class. Central cities were left with increasing concentrations of minority and low-income families. The growth of minority middle-class population is now largely suburban as well, though the suburbs are also segregated, especially for blacks. It would be ironic if *Milliken I*, a decision that was intended to protect the suburbs from unwanted racial change, ended up undermining the ability to cope successfully with vast demographic changes sweeping across the entire nation.

The loss of white and middle-class families and students in central cities occurred in cities that always had neighborhood schools and even in cities that abandoned desegregation orders. Atlanta, for example, decided against a busing plan in 1973 but experienced one of the most drastic losses in white students; similarly, the rapid decline in Los Angeles in the number of white students did not end or reverse itself after elimination of all mandatory desegregation in 1981. The largest cities that never had a mandatory busing plan but experienced large white declines include New York, Chicago, and Houston. Los Angeles bused children for only eighteen months at the middle school level before it returned to neighborhood schools in search of a stability that has not materialized. American cities were changing rapidly long before busing and continue to change where busing stops. Certain kinds of mandatory city-only plans may accelerate the change; others may slow it.

The Feasibility of Desegregation Strategies

. . . As segregation grows in the country, demographic trends and divisions among school districts point to increasing separation by race and poverty. This isolation is deeply and systemically linked to educational inequality, both in educational experiences and results. It is not likely to be self-correcting since the most troubled are also those with the fewest resources, organizational skills, and political power. Teacher recruitment and assignment practices are likely to increase rather than diminish this gap. To try to provide equal opportunities within segregated schools and districts, school officials would have to set up mechanisms to provide the most resources to the most disadvantaged, who happen to be the most powerless. Given the operation of local and state school politics there is no probability that such money, resources, special programs would stay in place. The depth and severity of the inequalities and their self-perpetuating character help explain why desegregation cases continue to seek ways to reconstruct the basic structures of educational segregation.

30

The Equality Crisis: Some Reflections on Culture, Courts, and Feminism

WENDY W. WILLIAMS

Wendy W. Williams is a professor at the Georgetown University Law Center in Washington, D.C. Among her many publications on women's rights and feminist issues is an article, excerpted here, from the Women's Rights Law Reporter *(1982). In the excerpt selected here, Williams reviews the Supreme Court's application of the Fourteenth Amendment's equal protection clause to claims of gender discrimination and, then, offers her reflections on courts, feminism, and American culture.*

TO SAY THAT courts are not and never have been the source of radical social change is an understatement. They reflect, by and large, mainstream views, mostly after those views are well established, although very occasionally (as in *Brown v. Board of Education,* the great school desegregation case) the Court moves temporarily out ahead of public opinion. What women can get from the courts—what we have gotten in the past decade—is a qualified guarantee of equal treatment. We can now expect, for the most part, that courts will rule that the privileges the law explicitly bestows on men must also be made available to women.

Because courts, as institutions of circumscribed authority, can only review in limited and specific ways the laws enacted by elected representatives, their role in promoting gender equality is pretty much confined to telling legislators what they cannot do, or extending the benefit of what they have done, to women. In an important sense, then, courts will do no more than measure women's claim to equality against legal benefits and burdens that are an expression of white male middle-class interests and values. This means, to rephrase the point, that women's equality as delivered by the courts can only be an integration into a pre-existing, predominantly male world. To the extent that women share those predominant values or aspire to share that world on its own terms, resort to the courts has, since the early 1970s, been the most efficient, accessible, and reliable mode of redress. But to the extent that the law of the public world must be reconstructed to reflect the needs and values of both sexes, change must be sought from legislatures rather than the courts. And women, whose separate experience has not been adequately registered in the political process, are the ones who must seek the change.

Nonetheless, I am going to talk about courts because what they do— what the Supreme Court does—is extremely important, for a number of reasons. (1) The way courts define equality, within the limits of their sphere, does indeed matter in the real world. (2) Legal cases have been and continue to be a focal point of debate about the meaning of equality; our participation in that debate and reflection upon it has enabled us to begin to form coherent overall theories of gender equality that inform our judgments about what we should seek from legislatures as well as courts. (3) The cases themselves, the participation they attract and the debate they engender, tell us important things about societal norms, cultural tensions, indeed, cultural limits concerning gender and sexual roles.

My thesis is that we (feminists) are at a crisis point in our evaluation of equality and women and that perhaps one of the reasons for the crisis is that, having dealt with the easy cases, we (feminists and courts) are now trying to cope with issues that touch the hidden nerves of our most profoundly embedded cultural values. . . .

A Brief History of Gender Equality and the Supreme Court

Just before the American Revolution, Blackstone, in the course of his comprehensive commentary on the common law, set forth the fiction that informed and guided the treatment of married women in the English law courts. When a woman married, her legal identity merged into that of her husband; she was civilly dead. She couldn't sue, be sued, enter into contracts, make wills, keep her own earnings, control her own property. She could not even protect her own physical integrity—her husband had the right to chastise her (although only with a switch no bigger than his thumb), restrain her freedom, and impose sexual intercourse upon her against her will.

Beginning in the middle of the nineteenth century, the most severe civil disabilities were removed in this country by state married women's property acts. Blackstone's unities fiction was for the most part replaced by a theory that recognized women's legal personhood but which assigned her a place before the law different and distinct from that of her husband. This was the theory of the separate spheres of men and women, under which the husband was the couple's representative in the public world and its breadwinner; the wife was the center of the private world of the family. Because it endowed women with a place, role, and importance of their own, the doctrine of the separate spheres was an advance over the spousal unities doctrine. At the same time, however, it preserved and promoted the dominance of male over female. The public world of men was governed by law while the private world of women was outside the law, and man was free to exercise his prerogatives as he chose.

Perhaps the best-known expression of the separate spheres ideology is Justice Bradley's concurring opinion in an 1873 Supreme Court case, *Bradwell v. Illinois*, which begins with the observation that "Civil law, as well as nature herself, has always recognized a wide difference in the respective spheres and destinies of man and women" end concludes, in ringing tones, that the "paramount destiny and mission of woman are to fulfill the noble and benign offices of wife and mother." The separate spheres ideology was used in *Bradwell* to uphold the exclusion of women from legal practice. Thirty-five years later, in *Muller v. Oregon*, it became the basis for upholding legislation governing the hours women were permitted to work in the paid labor force. Women's special maternal role, said the Court, justified special protections in the workplace. As late as 1961, in a challenge by a criminal defendant, the Court upheld a statute creating an automatic exemption from jury duty for all women who failed to volunteer their names for the jury pool, saying, "[W]oman is still re-garded as the center of home and family life. We cannot say that it is constitutionally impermissible for a State . . . to conclude that a woman should be relieved from the civil duty of jury service unless she herself determines that such service is consistent with her own special responsi-bilities."

The separate spheres ideology was repudiated by the Supreme Court only in the last twelve years. The engine of destruction was, as a technical matter, the more rigorous standard of review that the Court began applying to sex discrimination cases beginning in 1971. By 1976 the Court was requiring that sex-based classifications bear a "substantial" relationship to an "important" governmental purpose. This standard, announced in *Craig v. Boren*, was not as strong as that used in race cases, but it was certainly a far cry from the rational basis standard that had traditionally been applied to sex-based classifications.

As a practical matter, what the Court did was strike down sex-based classifications that were premised on the old breadwinner-homemaker, master-dependent dichotomy inherent in the separate spheres ideology. Thus, the Supreme Court insisted that women wage earners receive the same benefits for their families under military, social security, welfare, and worker's compensation programs as did male wage earners; that men receive the same child care allowance when their spouses died as women did; that the female children of divorce be entitled to support for the same length of time as male children, so that they too could get the education necessary for life in the public world; that the duty of support through alimony not be visited exclusively on husbands; that wives as well as husbands participate in the management of the community property; and that wives as well as husbands be eligible to administer their deceased relatives' estates.

All this happened in the little more than a decade that has elapsed since 1971. The achievement is not an insubstantial one. Yet it also seems to me that in part what the Supreme Court did was simply to recognize that the real world outside the courtroom had already changed. Woman were in fact no longer chiefly housewife-dependents. The family wage no longer existed; for a vast number of two-parent families, two wage earners were an economic necessity. In addition, many families were headed by a single parent. It behooved the Court to account for this new reality and it did so by recognizing that the breadwinner-homemaker dichotomy was an outmoded stereotype. . . .

Women's Culture: Mother of Humanity

. . . What does the culture identify as quintessentially female? Where does our pride and self-identity lie? Most probably, I think, somewhere in the realm of behaviors and concerns surrounding maternity. . . .

Let me start again with a Supreme Court case. As discussed earlier, before 1971, the ideology of the separate spheres informed Supreme Court opinions; it allowed the courts to view men and women as basically on different life tracks and therefore never really similarly situated. That fundamentally dichotomous view which characterized man as breadwinner, woman as homemaker-childrearer, foreclosed the possibility that the courts could successfully apply an equality model to the sexes.

Once the Supreme Court took on the task of dismantling the statutory structure built upon the separate spheres ideology, it had to face the question of how to treat pregnancy itself. Pregnancy was, after all, the centerpiece, the linchpin, the essential feature of women's separate sphere. The stereotypes, the generalizations, the role expectations were at their zenith when a woman became pregnant. Gender equality would not be possible, one would think, unless the Court was willing to examine, at least as closely as other gender-related rulemaking, those prescriptions concerning pregnancy itself. On the other hand, the capacity to bear a child is a crucial, indeed definitional, difference between women and men. While it is obvious that the sexes can be treated equally with respect to characteristics that they share, how would it be possible to apply the equality principle to a characteristic unique to women?

So what did the Court do? It drew the line at pregnancy. *Of course* it would take a more critical look at sex discrimination than it had in the past—but, it said, discrimination on the basis of pregnancy is not sex discrimination. Now here was a simple but decisive strategy for avoiding the doctrinal discomfort that inclusion of pregnancy within the magic circle of stricter review would bring with it. By placing pregnancy altogether outside that class of phenomena labeled sex discrimination, the Court need not apply to classifications related to pregnancy the level of scrutiny it had already reserved, in cases such as *Reed v. Reed* and *Frontiero v. Richardson*, for gender classifications. Pregnancy classifications would henceforth be subject only to the most casual review.

The position was revealed for the first time in 1974 in *Geduldig v. Aiello*, a case challenging under the equal protection clause exclusion of pregnancy-related disabilities from coverage by an otherwise comprehensive state disability insurance program. The Court explained, in a footnote, that pregnancy classifications were not sex-based but were, instead, classifications based upon a physical condition and should be treated accordingly.

The California insurance program does not exclude anyone from benefit eligibility because of gender *but merely remove one physical condition*—pregnancy—*from the list of compensable disabilities.* While it is true that only women can become pregnant, it does not follow that every legislative classification concerning pregnancy is a sex-based classification . . . Normal pregnancy is an objectively identifiable physical condition with unique characteristics . . . [L]awmakers are constitutionally free to include or exclude pregnancy from the coverage of legislation such as this on any reasonable basis, *just as with respect to any other physical condition.*

The second time the Supreme Court said pregnancy discrimination is not sex discrimination was in *General Electric Company v. Gilbert*, decided in 1976. *Gilbert* presented the same basic facts—exclusion of pregnancy-related disabilities from a comprehensive disability program—but this case was brought under Title VII rather than the equal protection clause. The Court nonetheless relied on *Geduldig*, saying that when Congress prohibited "sex discrimination," it didn't mean to include within the definition of that term pregnancy discrimination.

There was, however, an additional theory available in *Gilbert* because it was a Title VII case that was not available in the equal protection case. That theory was that if an employer's rule has a disparate *effect* on women, even though there is no intent to discriminate, it might also violate Title

VII. And did the Court find that the exclusion of pregnancy-related disabilities had a disparate effect on women? It did not. Men and women, said Justice Rehnquist, received coverage for the disabilities they had in common. Pregnancy was an *extra* disability, since only women suffered it. To compensate women for it would give them more than men got. So here there was no disparate effect—the exclusion of pregnancy merely insured the basic equality of the program.

The remarkable thing about this statement, like Rehnquist's later assertion in *Michael M. v. Superior Court* that only men can "cause" pregnancy, is its peculiarly blinkered male vision. After all, men received coverage under General Electric's disability program for disabilities they did not have in common with women, including disabilities linked to exclusively male aspects of the human anatomy. Thus, the only sense in which one can understand pregnancy to be "extra" is in some reverse-Freudian psychological fashion. Under Freud's interpretation, women were viewed by both sexes as inadequate men (men *minus*) because they lacked penises. In Rehnquist's view, woman is now man *plus*, because she shares all his physical characteristics except that she also gets pregnant. Under either of these extravagantly skewed views of the sexes, however, man is the measure against which the anatomical features of woman are counted and assigned value, and when the addition or subtraction is complete, woman comes out behind.

The corollary to *Gilbert* appeared in *Nashville Gas Co. v. Satty*, decided in 1977. There the Court finally found a pregnancy rule that violated Title VII. The rule's chief characteristic was its gratuitously punitive effect. It provided that a woman returning from maternity leave lost all of the seniority she acquired *prior* to her leave. Here, said Rehnquist, we have a case where women are not seeking extra benefits for pregnancy. Here's a case where a woman, now back at work and no longer pregnant, has actually had something taken away from her—her pre-pregnancy seniority—and she therefore suffers a burden that men don't have to bear. This rule therefore has a disproportionate impact on women.

Roughly translated, *Gilbert* and *Satty* read together seemed to stand for the proposition that insofar as a rule deprives a woman of benefits for actual pregnancy, that rule is lawful under Title VII. If, on the other hand, it denies her benefits she had earned while not pregnant (and hence like a man) and now seeks to use upon return to her non-pregnant (male-like) status, it has a disproportionate effect on women and is not lawful.

In summary, then, the Court seems to be of the view that discrimination on the basis of pregnancy isn't sex discrimination. The Court achieves this by, on the one hand, disregarding the "ineluctible link" between gender and pregnancy, treating pregnancy as just another physical condition that the employer or state can manipulate on any arguably rational basis, and on the other hand, using woman's special place in "the scheme of human existence" as a basis for treating her claim to benefits available to other disabled workers as a claim not to equal benefits but to extra benefits, not to equal treatment but to special treatment. The equality principle, according to the Court, cannot be bent to such ends.

In reaction to *Gilbert* and, to a lesser extent, to *Satty*, Congress amended the definitions section of Title VII to provide that discrimination on the basis of pregnancy, childbirth, and related medical conditions was, for purposes of the Act, sex discrimination. The amendment, called the Pregnancy Discrimination Act (PDA), required a rather radical change in approach to the pregnancy issue from that adopted by the Court. In effect, Title VII creates a general presumption that men and women are alike in all relevant respects and casts the burden on the employer to show otherwise in any particular case. The PDA, likewise, rejects the presumption that pregnancy is so unique that special rules concerning it are to be treated as prima facie reasonable. It substitutes the contrary presumption that pregnancy, at least in the workplace context, is like other physical conditions which may affect workers. As with gender classifications in general, it places the burden of establishing pregnancy's uniqueness in any given instance on the employer. The amendment itself specifies how this is to be done:

[W]omen affected by pregnancy, childbirth, or related medical conditions shall be treated the same for all employment-related purposes, including receipt of benefits under fringe benefit programs, as other persons not so affected but similar in their ability or inability to work. . . .

Under the PDA, employers cannot treat pregnancy less favorably than other potentially disabling conditions, but neither can they treat it more favorably. And therein lies the crisis.

At the time the PDA was passed, all feminist groups supported it. Special treatment of pregnancy in the workplace had always been synonymous with unfavorable treatment; the rules generally had the effect of forcing women out of the work force and back into the home when they became pregnant. By treating pregnancy discrimination as sex discrimination, the PDA required that pregnant women be treated as well as other wage earners who became disabled. The degree to which this assisted women depended on the generosity of their particular employers' sick leave or disability policy, but anything at all was better than what most pregnant women had had before.

The conflict within the feminist community arose because some states had passed legislation which, instead of placing pregnant women at a disadvantage, gave them certain positive protections. Montana, for example, passed a law forbidding employers to fire women who became pregnant and requiring them to give such women reasonable maternity leave. The Miller-Wohl Company, an employer in that state, had a particularly ungenerous sick leave policy. Employees were entitled to *no* sick leave in their first year of employment and five days per year thereafter. On August 1, 1979, the company hired a pregnant woman who missed four or five days over the course of the following three weeks because of morning sickness. The company fired her. She asserted her rights under the Montana statute. The company sought declaratory relief in federal court, claiming that Montana's special treatment statute was contrary to the equality principle mandated by the PDA and was therefore invalid under the supremacy clause of the constitution.

Feminists split over the validity of the Montana statute. Some of us felt that the statute was, indeed, incompatible with the philosophy of the PDA. Others of us argued that the PDA was passed to *help* pregnant women, which was also the objective of the Montana statute. Underneath are very different views of what women's equality means; the dispute is therefore one of great significance for feminists.

The Montana statute *was* meant to help pregnant women. It was passed with the best of intentions. The philosophy underlying it is that pregnancy is central to a woman's family role and that the law should take special account of pregnancy to protect that role for the working wife. And those who supported the statute can assert with great plausibility that pregnancy is a problem that men don't have, an extra source of workplace disability, and that women workers cannot adequately be protected if pregnancy is not taken into account in special ways. They might also add that procreation plays a special role in human life, is viewed as a fundamental right by our society, and therefore is appropriately singled out on social policy grounds. The instinct to treat pregnancy as a special case is deeply imbedded in our culture, indeed in every culture. It seems natural, and *right*, to treat it that way.

Yet, at a deeper level, the Supreme Court in cases like *Gilbert*, and the feminists who seek special recognition for pregnancy, are starting from the same basic assumption, namely, that women have a special place in the scheme of human existence when it comes to maternity. Of course, one's view of how that basic assumption cuts is shaped by one's perspective.

What businessmen, Supreme Court Justices, and feminists make of it is predictably quite different. But the same doctrinal approach that permits pregnancy to be treated *worse* than other disabilities is the same one that will allow the state constitutional freedom to create special *benefits* for pregnant women. The equality approach to pregnancy (such as that embodied in the PDA) necessarily creates not only the desired floor under the pregnant woman's rights but also the ceiling which the *Miller-Wohl* case threw into relief. If we can't have it both ways, we need to think carefully about which way we want to have it.

My own feeling is that, for all its problems, the equality approach is the better one. The special treatment model has great costs. First, as discussed above, is the reality that conceptualizing pregnancy as a special case permits unfavorable as well as favorable treatment of pregnancy. Our history provides too many illustrations of the former to allow us to be sanguine about the wisdom of urging special treatment.

Second, treating pregnancy as a special case divides us in ways that I believe are destructive in a particular political sense as well as a more general sense. On what basis can we fairly assert, for example, that the pregnant woman fired by Miller-Wohl deserved to keep her job when any other worker who got sick for any other reason did not? Creating special privileges of the Montana type has, as one consequence, the effect of shifting attention away from the employer's inadequate sick leave policy or the state's failure to provide important protections to all workers and focusing it upon the unfairness of protecting one class of worker and not others.

Third, as our experience with single-sex protective legislation earlier in this century demonstrated, what appear to be special "protections" for women often turn out to be, at best, a double-edged sword. It seems likely, for example, that the employer who wants to avoid the inconveniences and costs of special protective measures will find reasons not to hire women of childbearing age in the first place.

Fourth, to the extent the state (or employers as proxies for the state) can lay claim to an interest in women's special procreational capacity for "the future well-being of the race," as *Muller v. Oregon* put it in 1908, our freedom of choice about the direction of our lives is more limited than that of men in significant ways. This danger is hardly a theoretical one today. The Supreme Court has recently shown an increased willingness to permit restrictions on abortion in deference to the state's interest in the "potential life" of the fetus, and private employers are adopting policies of exclusion of women of childbearing capacity in order to protect fetuses from exposure to possibly hazardous substances in the workplace.

More fundamentally, though, this issue, like the others I discussed earlier, has everything to do with how, in the long run, we want to define women's and men's places and roles in society.

Implicit in the PDA approach to maternity issues is a stance toward parenthood and work that is decidedly different from that embodied in the special-treatment approach to pregnancy. For many years, the prototype of the enlightened employer maternity policy was one which provided for a mandatory unpaid leave of absence for the woman employee commencing four or five months before and extending for as long as six months after childbirth. Such maternity leaves were firmly premised on that aspect of the separate spheres ideology which assigned motherhood as woman's special duty and prerogative; employers believed that women should be treated as severed from the labor force from the time their pregnancies became apparent until their children emerged from infancy. Maternity leave was always based upon cultural constructs and ideologies rather than upon biological necessity, upon role expectations rather than irreducible differences between the sexes.

The PDA also has significant ideological content. It makes the prototypical maternity leave policy just described illegal. In its stead, as discussed above, is a requirement that the employer extend to women disabled by pregnancy the same disability or sick leave available to other workers. If the employer chooses to extend the leave time beyond the disability period, it must make such leaves available to male as well as to female parents. Title VII requires sex neutrality with respect to employment practices directed at parents. It does not permit the employer to base policies on the separate spheres ideology. Accordingly, the employer must devise its policies in such a way that women and men can, if they choose, structure the allocation of family responsibilities in a more egalitarian fashion. It forecloses the assumption that women are necessarily and inevitably destined to carry the dual burden of homemaker and wage earner. . . .

Conclusion: Confronting Yin and Yang

The human creature seems to be constructed in such a way as to be largely culture bound. . . .At this point, we need to think as deeply as we can about what we want the future of women and men to be. Do we want equality of the sexes—or do we want justice for two kinds of human beings who are fundamentally different? If we gain equality, will we lose the special sense of kinship that grows out of experiences central to our lives and not shared by the other sex? Are feminists defending a separate women's culture while trying to break down the barriers created by men's separate culture? Could we, even if we wanted to, maintain the one while claiming our place within the other? . . . I for one suspect a deep but sometimes nearly invisible set of complementarities, a yin-yang of sex-role assumptions and assignments so complex and interrelated that we cannot successfully dismantle any of it without seriously exploring the possibility of dismantling it all.

31

Speaking in a Judicial Voice: Reflections on Roe v. Wade

JUSTICE RUTH BADER GINSBURG

Justice Ruth Bader Ginsburg is the second woman to sit on the high bench and the Supreme Court's 107th justice. After graduating from Columbia University School of Law and unable to find a law firm that would hire a female attorney, Ginsburg served for several years as a research associate at Columbia Law School and then joined Rutgers University School of Law, where she rose to the rank of full professor before becoming the first female professor at Columbia Law School. In the 1970s Ginsburg continued to teach, but also served as the director of the American Civil Liberties Union's Women's Rights Project. There, she argued six (winning five) important gender-based discrimination cases before the Supreme Court. In 1980 she was appointed to the Court of Appeals for the District of Columbia Circuit, and in 1993 she was named to the Supreme Court by President Bill Clinton. Shortly before her appointment to the Court, Ginsburg delivered the Madison Lecture at New York University Law School, which appeared in the 1992 New York University Law Review. *In the excerpt here from that lecture, Ginsburg offers some reflections on the watershed rulings on a woman's right to choose an abortion in* Roe v. Wade *(1973) and* Planned Parenthood Association of Southeastern Pennsylvania v. Casey *(1992) and places them within the broader context of the evolving equal protection doctrine of the Fourteenth Amendment.*

———

IN THE *FEDERALIST* No. 78, Alexander Hamilton said that federal judges, in order to preserve the people's rights and privileges, must have authority to check legislation and acts of the executive for constitutionality. But he qualified his recognition of that awesome authority. The judiciary, Hamilton wrote, from the very nature of its functions, will always be "the least dangerous" branch of government, for judges hold neither the sword nor the purse of the community; ultimately, they must depend upon the political branches to effectuate their judgments. Mindful of that reality, the effective judge, I believe and will explain why in these remarks, strives to persuade, and not to pontificate. She speaks in "a moderate and restrained" voice, engaging in a dialogue with, not a diatribe against, co-equal departments of government, state authorities, and even her own colleagues. . . .

Moving from the style to the substance of third branch decisionmaking, I will stress in the remainder of these remarks that judges play an interdependent part in our democracy. They do not alone shape legal doctrine but, as I suggested at the outset, they participate in a dialogue with other organs of government, and with the people as well. "Judges do and must legislate," Justice Holmes "recognized without hesitation," but "they can do so," he cautioned, "only interstitially; they are confined from molar to molecular motions." Measured motions seem to me right, in the main, for constitutional as well as common law adjudication. Doctrinal limbs too swiftly shaped, experience teaches, may prove unstable. The most prominent example in recent decades is *Roe v. Wade.* To illustrate my point, I have contrasted that breathtaking 1973 decision with the Court's more cautious dispositions, contemporaneous with *Roe*, in cases involving explicitly sex-based classifications, and will further develop that comparison here.

The seven to two judgment in *Roe v. Wade* declared "violative of the Due Process Clause of the Fourteenth Amendment" a Texas criminal abortion statute that intolerably shackled a woman's autonomy; the Texas law "excepted from criminality only a life-saving procedure on behalf of the pregnant woman." Suppose the Court had stopped there, rightly declaring unconstitutional the most extreme brand of law in the nation, and had not gone on, as the Court did in *Roe*, to fashion a regime blanketing the subject, a set of rules that displaced virtually every state law then in force. Would there have been the twenty-year controversy we have witnessed, reflected most recently in the Supreme Court's splintered decision in *Planned Parenthood v. Casey*? A less encompassing *Roe*, one that merely struck down the extreme Texas law and went no further on that day, I believe and will summarize why, might have served to reduce rather than to fuel controversy.

In the 1992 *Planned Parenthood* decision, the three controlling Justices accepted as constitutional several restrictions on access to abortion that could not have survived strict adherence to *Roe*. While those Justices did not closely consider the plight of women without means to overcome the restrictions, they added an important strand to the Court's opinions on abortion—they acknowledged the intimate connection between a woman's "ability to control her reproductive life" and her "ability . . . to participate equally in the economic and social life of the Nation." The idea of the woman in control of her destiny and her place in society was less prominent in the *Roe* decision itself, which coupled with the rights of the pregnant woman the free exercise of her physician's medical judgment. The *Roe* decision might have been less of a storm center had it both homed in more precisely on the women's equality dimension of the issue and, correspondingly, attempted nothing more bold at that time than the mode of decisionmaking the Court employed in the 1970s gender classification cases.

In fact, the very term *Roe* was decided, the Supreme Court had on its calendar a case that could have served as a bridge, linking reproductive choice to disadvantageous treatment of women on the basis of their sex. The case was *Struck v. Secretary of Defense*; it involved a captain the Air Force sought to discharge in Vietnam War days. Perhaps it is indulgence in wishful thinking, but the *Struck* case, I believe, would have proved extraordinarily educational for the Court and had large potential for advancing public understanding. Captain Susan Struck was a career officer. According to her commanding officer, her performance as a manager and nurse was exemplary. Captain Struck had avoided the drugs and the alcohol that hooked many service members in the late 1960s and early 1970s, but she did become pregnant while stationed in Vietnam. She undertook to use, and in fact used, only her accumulated leave time for childbirth. She declared her intention to place, and in fact placed, her child for adoption immediately after birth. Her religious faith precluded recourse to abortion.

Two features of Captain Struck's case are particularly noteworthy. First, the rule she challenged was unequivocal and typical of the time. It provided: "A woman officer will be discharged from the service with the least practicable delay when a determination is made by a medical officer that she is pregnant." To cover any oversight, the Air Force had a back-up rule: "The commission of any woman officer will be terminated with the least practicable delay when it is established that she . . . has given birth to a living child while in a commissioned officer status."

A second striking element of Captain Struck's case was the escape route available to her, which she chose not to take. Air Force regulations current at the start of the 1970s provided: "The Air Force Medical Service is not subject to State laws in the performance of its functions. When medically indicated or for reasons involving medical health, pregnancies may be terminated in Air Force hospitals . . . ideally before 20 weeks gestation."

Captain Struck argued that the unwanted discharge she faced unjustifiably restricted her personal autonomy and dignity; principally, however, she maintained that the regulation mandating her discharge violated the equal protection of the laws guarantee implicit in the fifth amendment's due process clause. She urged that the Air Force regime differentiated invidiously by allowing males who became fathers, but not females who became mothers, to remain in service and by allowing women who had undergone abortions, but not women who delivered infants, to continue their military careers. Her pleas were unsuccessful in the lower courts, but on October 24, 1972, less than three months before the *Roe* decision, the Supreme Court granted her petition for *certiorari*.

At that point the Air Force decided it would rather switch than fight. At the end of November 1972, it granted Captain Struck a waiver of the once unwaivable regulation and permitted her to continue her service as an Air Force officer. The Solicitor General promptly and successfully suggested that the case had become moot.

Given the parade of cases on the Court's full calendar, it is doubtful that the Justices trained further attention on the Struck scenario. With more time and space for reflection, however, and perhaps a female presence on the Court, might the Justices have gained at least these two insights? First, if even the military, an institution not known for avant-garde policy, had taken to providing facilities for abortion, then was not a decision of *Roe*'s muscularity unnecessary? Second, confronted with Captain Struck's unwanted discharge, might the Court have comprehended an argument, or at least glimpsed a reality, it later resisted — that disadvantageous treatment of a woman because of her pregnancy and reproductive choice is a paradigm case of discrimination on the basis of sex? What was the assumption underlying the differential treatment to which Captain Struck was exposed? The regulations that mandated her discharge were not even thinly disguised. They declared, effectively, that responsibility for children disabled female parents, but not male parents, for other work — not for biological reasons, but because society had ordered things that way.

Captain Struck had asked the Court first to apply the highest level of scrutiny to her case, to hold that the sex-based classification she encountered was a "suspect" category for legislative or administrative action. As a fallback, she suggested to the Court an intermediate standard of review, one under which prescriptions that worked to women's disadvantage would gain review of at least heightened, if not the very highest, intensity. In the course of the 1970s, the Supreme Court explicitly acknowledged that it was indeed applying an elevated, labeled "intermediate," level of review to classifications it recognized as sex-based. . . .

Until 1971, women did not prevail before the Supreme Court in any case charging unconstitutional sex discrimination. In the years from 1971 to 1982, however, the Court held unconstitutional, as violative of due process or equal protection constraints, a series of state and federal laws that differentiated explicitly on the basis of sex.

The Court ruled in 1973, for example, that married women in the military were entitled to the housing allowance and family medical care benefits that Congress had provided solely for married men in the military. Two years later, the Court held it unconstitutional for a state to allow a parent to stop supporting a daughter once she reached the age of eighteen, while requiring parental support for a son until he turned twenty-one. In 1975, and again in 1979, the Court declared that state jury-selection systems could not exclude or exempt women as a class. In decisions running from 1975 to 1980, the Court deleted the principal explicitly sex-based classifications in social insurance and workers' compensation schemes. In 1981, the Court said nevermore to a state law designating the husband "head and master" of the household. And in 1982, in an opinion by Justice O'Connor, the Court held that a state could not limit admission to a state nursing college to women only.

The backdrop for these rulings was a phenomenal expansion, in the years from 1961 to 1971, of women's employment outside the home, the civil rights movement of the 1960s and the precedents set in that struggle, and a revived feminist movement, fueled abroad and in the United States by Simone de Beauvoir's remarkable 1949 publication, *The Second Sex*. In the main, the Court invalidated laws that had become obsolete, retained into the 1970s by only a few of the states. In a core set of cases, however, those dealing with social insurance benefits for a worker's spouse or family, the decisions did not utterly condemn the legislature's product. Instead, the Court, in effect, opened a dialogue with the political branches of government. In essence, the Court instructed Congress and state legislatures: rethink ancient positions on these questions. Should you determine that special treatment for women is warranted, i.e., compensatory legislation because of the sunken-in social and economic bias or disadvantage women encounter, we have left you a corridor in which to move. But your classifications must be refined, adopted for remedial reasons, and not rooted in prejudice about "the way women (or men) are." In the meantime, the Court's decrees removed no benefits; instead, they extended to a woman worker's husband, widower, or family benefits Congress had authorized only for members of a male worker's family.

The ball, one might say, was tossed by the Justices back into the legislators' court, where the political forces of the day could operate. The Supreme Court wrote modestly, it put forward no grand philosophy; but by requiring legislative reexamination of once customary sex-based classifications, the Court helped to ensure that laws and regulations would "catch up with a changed world."

Roe v. Wade, in contrast, invited no dialogue with legislators. Instead, it seemed entirely to remove the ball from the legislators' court. In 1973, when *Roe* issued, abortion law was in a state of change across the nation. As the Supreme Court itself noted, there was a marked trend in state legislatures "toward liberalization of abortion statutes." That movement for legislative change ran parallel to another law revision effort then underway—the change from fault to no-fault divorce regimes, a reform that swept through the state legislatures and captured all of them by the mid-1980s.

No measured motion, the *Roe* decision left virtually no state with laws fully conforming to the Court's delineation of abortion regulation still permissible. Around that extraordinary decision, a well-organized and vocal right-to-life movement rallied and succeeded, for a considerable time, in turning the legislative tide in the opposite direction.

Constitutional review by courts is an institution that has been for some two centuries our nation's hallmark and pride. Two extreme modes of court intervention in social change processes, however, have placed stress on the institution. At one extreme, the Supreme Court steps boldly in front of the political process, as some believe it did in *Roe*. At the opposite extreme, the Court in the early part of the twentieth century found—or thrust—itself into the rearguard opposing change, striking down, as unconstitutional, laws embodying a new philosophy of economic regulation at odds with the nineteenth century's laissez-faire approach. Decisions at both of these poles yielded outcries against the judiciary in certain quarters. The Supreme Court, particularly, was labeled "activist" or "imperial," and its precarious position as final arbiter of constitutional questions was exposed.

I do not suggest that the Court should never step ahead of the political branches in pursuit of a constitutional precept. *Brown v. Board of Education*, the 1954 decision declaring racial segregation in public schools offensive to the equal protection principle, is the case that best fits the bill. Past the midpoint of the twentieth century, apartheid remained the law-enforced system in several states, shielded by a constitutional interpretation the Court itself advanced at the turn of the century—the "separate but equal" doctrine.

In contrast to the legislative reform movement in the states, contemporaneous with *Roe*, widening access to abortion, prospects in 1954 for state legislation dismantling racially segregated schools were bleak. That was so, I believe, for a reason that distances race discrimination from discrimination based on sex. Most women are life partners of men; women bear and raise both sons and daughters. Once women's own consciousness was awakened to the unfairness of allocating opportunity and responsibility on the basis of sex, education of others—of fathers, husbands, sons as well as daughters—could begin, or be reinforced, at home. When blacks were confined by law to a separate sector, there was no similar prospect for educating the white majority.

It bears emphasis, however, that *Brown* was not an altogether bold decision. First, Thurgood Marshall and those who worked with him in the campaign against racial injustice, carefully set the stepping stones leading up to the landmark ruling. Pathmarkers of the same kind had not been installed prior to the Court's decision in *Roe*. Second, *Brown* launched no broadside attack on the Jim Crow system in all its institutional manifestations. Instead, the Court concentrated on segregated schools; it left the follow-up for other days and future cases. A burgeoning civil rights movement—which *Brown* helped to propel—culminating in the Civil Rights Act of 1964, set the stage for the Court's ultimate total rejection of Jim Crow legislation.

Significantly, in relation to the point I just made about women and men living together, the end of the Jim Crow era came in 1967, thirteen years after *Brown*: the case was *Loving v. Virginia*, the law under attack, a state prohibition on interracial marriage. In holding that law unconstitutional, the Court effectively ruled that, with regard to racial classifications, the doctrine of "separate but equal" was dead—everywhere and anywhere within the governance of the United States.

The framers of the Constitution allowed to rest in the Court's hands large authority to rule on the Constitution's meaning; but the framers, as I noted at the outset, armed the Court with no swords to carry out its pronouncements. President Andrew Jackson in 1832, according to an often-told legend, said of a Supreme Court decision he did not like: "The Chief Justice has made his decision, now let him enforce it." With prestige to persuade, but not physical power to enforce, with a will for self-preservation and the knowledge that they are not "a bevy of Platonic Guardians," the Justices generally follow, they do not lead, changes taking place elsewhere in society. But without taking giant strides and thereby risking a backlash too forceful to contain, the Court, through constitutional adjudication, can reinforce or signal a green light for a social change. In most of the post-1970 gender-classification cases, unlike *Roe*, the Court functioned in just that way. It approved the direction of change through a temperate brand of decisionmaking, one that was not extravagant or divisive. *Roe*, on the other hand, halted a political process that was moving in a reform direction and thereby, I believe, prolonged divisiveness and deferred stable settlement of the issue. The most recent *Planned Parenthood* decision notably retreats from *Roe* and further excludes from the High Court's protection women lacking the means or the sophistication to surmount burdensome legislation. The latest decision may have had the sanguine effect, however, of contributing to the ongoing revitalization in the 1980s and 1990s of the political movement in progress in the early 1970s, a movement that addressed not simply or dominantly the courts but primarily the people's representatives and the people themselves. That renewed force, one may hope, will—within a relatively short span—yield an enduring resolution of this vital matter in a way that affirms the dignity and equality of women.

32

Sex, Death, and the Courts

RONALD DWORKIN

Ronald Dworkin is a Professor of Jurisprudence at Oxford University and a professor both in the Law School and Philosophy Department at New York University. He is one of the world's preeminent liberal legal theorists. Among his many books are Taking Rights Seriously *(1977) and* Law's Empire *(1986). In the selection here, excerpted from an article published in 1996 in the* New York Review of Books, *Dworkin reflects on two of the most vexing contemporary controversies, namely, those over the so-called "right to die" and claims to homosexual rights and freedom from discrimination under the Fourteenth Amendment's due process and equal protection clauses. In* Cruzan v. Director, Missouri Department of Health *(1990), the Supreme Court acknowledged the "fundamental liberty" of a terminally-ill patient to have life-support systems withdrawn. Subsequently, in March 1996 the Court of Appeals for the Ninth Circuit extended that ruling by finding the right of privacy, under the Fourteenth Amendment's due process clause, to include the right of terminally ill patients to physician-assisted suicide, in* Compassion in Dying v. Washington. *A month later in* Quill v. Vacco, *the Court of Appeals for the Second Circuit struck down New York's law outlawing physician-assisted suicide on the ground that the state's distinction between the right of terminally ill patients to withdraw from life-support systems and the claim of terminally ill patients to physician-assisted suicide ran afoul of the Fourteenth Amendment's guarantee for the equal protection of the law. On appeal, both of those decisions were reversed by the Supreme Court in two 1997 rulings,* Washington v. Glucksberg *and* Vacco v. Quill, *which rejected (but did not entirely rule out) claims to a constitutionally protected right to physician-assisted suicide. Dworkin, nonetheless, defends the results reached by the appellate courts as a matter of constitutional principle. For the same reason, Dworkin sharply criticizes the Supreme Court's 1986 decision in* Bowers v. Hardwick, *upholding Georgia's law criminalizing private, consensual sodomy and defends the Court's 1996 ruling in* Romer v. Evans, *striking down a Colorado constitutional amendment that forbid localities from enacting laws prohibiting discrimination against homosexuals.*

MILLIONS OF PEOPLE think that doctors are murderers if they help patients, even those dying slowly in great pain, to kill themselves; the American Medical Association has just confirmed its longstanding opposition to euthanasia, and most states have made assisting suicide a crime. But [in March 1996], in a decision that would have seemed incredible a few years ago, the Ninth Circuit of the US Court of Appeals declared that Washington State's law forbidding assisted suicide was unconstitutional, and a month later the Second Circuit held New York's similar law unconstitutional as well. . . .

In May the Supreme Court considered a different social problem: how far states are free to discriminate against homosexuals. Colorado voters had enacted a sweeping amendment to that state's constitution, declaring that no law protecting homosexuals from discrimination hitherto or henceforth enacted in the state or any part of it would be valid. That struck many constitutional experts as an appalling interference with normal political practice—why shouldn't homosexuals be as free as other groups to campaign for laws protecting their interests in local and state legislatures?—but the experts were doubtful that the Supreme Court would invalidate what Colorado had done. The Court had itself declared, in *Bowers* v. *Hardwick* in 1986, that states could make homosexual sex a crime, even between consenting adults. How could it now declare that a lesser and more speculative burden, which only prevented special legislation in favor of homosexuals, was unconstitutional? But in a 6–3 decision it did so declare, and Justice Scalia, in an outraged dissent, accused it of taking sides in a "*Kulturkampf*," or culture war, that it had no business joining.

A common issue runs through these three recent decisions. May a "moral majority" limit the liberty of other citizens on no better ground than that it disapproves of the personal choices they make? That was the central question in the assisted suicide cases. Though almost all Americans agree that human life is sacred in some way, they disagree about whether it follows that people must never kill themselves, even to avoid terrible pain or crippling indignity and even when they will soon die anyway. Some think it degrades life to end it prematurely, even in those circumstances; others think it degrading not to die in dignity when further life would be appalling. Should that decision be made individually, each person deciding for his own life out of his own conviction? Or should it be made collectively, so that the convictions of the majority are imposed even on those whose most basic beliefs are thereby compromised?

Sexual morality is also central to people's lives and personalities. Should adults be free to make their own decisions about sex when these decisions have no direct impact on others? If so, how far should others then be free, as private persons, to express their disapproval of those decisions in their own choice of employees, associates, or teachers for their children? Americans have accepted that some forms of private discrimination are matters of public concern, and that the law should guarantee equality of treatment in many spheres for blacks, women, and the handicapped. Why not for homosexuals as well? Does it matter that sexual behavior, unlike race or gender or handicap, is finally a matter of choice? Scientists disagree about how far genetic factors fix sexuality, although it seems undeniable that they have at least a significant role. In any case, abstaining from homosexual sex would mean no sex at all for many people, or living a lie. Should society allow discrimination against people who refuse to make a choice with such costs?

These great questions of personal and political morality arise in any modern society, and lawmakers must confront them. In the United States—and in many other nations and international communities that have followed our lead in establishing constitutional rights—judges must face those issues as well. The American Constitution contains two pertinent provisions, and they both played a prominent part in the three recent cases. The Fourteenth Amendment provides that no state may constrain any citizen's liberty without "due process of law." The same amendment requires states to extend to everyone "the equal protection of the laws." The essential difference between the two clauses lies in their rationale. The due process clause forbids compromising certain basic rights altogether except for a particularly compelling reason. The equal protection clause is less stringent: it requires only that states not discriminate unfairly in the liberties and other privileges it chooses to allow.

But both clauses are exceedingly abstract. How should judges decide which liberties the due process clause treats as basic, and what kinds of discriminations the equal protection clause treats as unfair? For over a century two sharply opposed views have been fighting a constitutional War of the Roses, with first one side and then the other achieving temporary dominion. One party anxious to restrict the power of judges to adjudicate moral issues, insists that the due process and equal protection clauses give legal protection only to a limited list of rights that have been recognized and enforced during America's post–Civil-War history. In the *Bowers* v. *Hardwick* decision, Justice Byron White set out this view of the due process clause in a passage that has become a talisman for the party of history. He said that the clause protects only those rights that meet one of two tests that he treated as identical: the right must be such that "neither liberty nor justice would exist if [it] were sacrificed," or it must be "deeply rooted in this Nation's history and tradition." He said it was a decisive argument against the alleged right of homosexuals to be free to practice sodomy that until 1961 all fifty American states outlawed that act; the suggestion that "a right to engage in such conduct" meets either of the two tests is therefore, he said, at best "facetious."

On this view of constitutional interpretation, which has had immense influence on American law, logic and consistency in principle play little part in identifying constitutional rights. The fact that the Court has recognized one right—a right to abortion, for example—provides no argument why it should also recognize any other right—the right of homosexuals to sexual freedom or of dying patients to control their own deaths, for instance—even if no principled reason can be given why people should have the former right but not the latter ones. The only issue is whether the particular right in question has been historically recognized, and that test must be applied independently to each suggested right, one by one. Only by such a procedure, as Judge White made plain, can the power of judges to expand constitutional rights in the name of consistency be curtailed. "Nor are we inclined," he said, "to take a more expansive view of our authority to discover new fundamental rights imbedded in the Due Process Clause . . . Otherwise, the Judiciary necessarily takes to itself further authority to govern the country without express constitutional authority." It is better, on this view to tolerate inconsistency in the rights the Court recognizes than to expand the list of those rights.

The opposite party in the constitutional wars—the party of principle—denies that order of priority. It insists on "integrity" in constitutional law: it argues that the abstract constitutional rights acknowledged for one group be extended to others if no moral ground distinguishes between them. In 1961, a conservative justice—John Harlan—offered one of the strongest judicial statements of this view, and just as White's formulation in *Bowers* has become central for the party of history, Harlan's has become central for the party of principle. The liberty protected by the due process clause, Harlan said, "is not a series of isolated points. . . . It is a rational continuum which, broadly speaking, includes a freedom from all substantial arbitrary imposition and purposeless restraints. Though Harlan made that statement in a dissenting opinion, it has often been cited in later decisions of the Court. Justices Kennedy, O'Connor, and Souter relied on it, for example, in their crucial plurality opinion of 1992, in *Planned Parenthood v. Casey*, to explain why the Supreme Court was right to recognize a right to abortion in *Roe v. Wade*, even though most states had outlawed abortion for decades before that decision. . . .

Judges characteristically decide due process challenges to legislation by asking two questions. First, does the law compromise a "liberty interest"—that is, a right that the Constitution in principle protects from state action? Second, if so, are the purposes and effects of the statute so important that they justify a state in nevertheless restricting that liberty interest? The first is the question that divides the parties of history and principle in the way I described. The second, which arises only if a constitutional right is recognized, requires a balance. A court must assess the strength of that right and consider whether the state's alleged interests are sufficiently strong to justify compromising a right of that strength.

In 1990, in the *Cruzan* case, a majority of the Supreme Court agreed that citizens have a liberty interest in deciding for themselves when medical treatment that prolongs their lives, including respirators and other life support systems, should be terminated. And though the actual decision held that Missouri had a competing interest strong enough to require proof that a vegetative patient had made an unambiguous choice in advance, a majority made plain that a state could not deny the right altogether. Many commentators have assumed, however, that the question in the *Compassion* case in Washington State—whether the Constitution protects, even in principle, a dying patient's right to the assistance of a willing doctor in suicide—is a distinct one, because both medical practice and ordinary moral opinion draw a sharp distinction between stopping treatment a patient does not want and administering drugs with the sole purpose of killing him. A right to prevent or stop treatment is part of a more general constitutionally protected right not to suffer unwanted invasions of one's body. But that more general right does not include a right that invasions the patient desires, like lethal pills or injections, be provided—otherwise it would include a constitutional right for everyone to take narcotic drugs, for example. . . .

The Fourteenth Amendment language forbidding states to deny any person "the equal protection of the laws" might conceivably have been understood to impose only a very weak requirement on states: that they could only discriminate among their citizens if they first enacted laws describing and authorizing that discrimination. But that banal reading would leave a state free to create a caste system in which blacks (for example) were denied any civil or legal rights, so long as it did so through explicit legislation. Since the Fourteenth Amendment was enacted after the Civil War, with the expectation of preventing the most blatant forms of racial discrimination, that reading is unacceptable.

So is the opposite reading, however, which would declare that states must never enact laws that discriminate in any way among groups of citizens, awarding advantages to some at cost to others. For almost every national or state law has precisely that effect—the NAFTA treaty worked against the interests of some workers and in favor of others; environmental legislation injures some industries though not others; and state banking, securities, and professional regulations help some people but disadvantage others. So the Supreme Court has developed a more sophisticated interpretation of the equal protection clause that avoids either of these extreme and unacceptable readings. It has done this through a set of doctrinal rules and distinctions which, taken together, are calculated to serve an underlying rationale of political morality.

That underlying rationale is a theory which distinguishes between circumstances in which a democracy is working well, so that those who lose out in a political contest cannot complain of procedural inequality or unfairness, and when it is defective, so that losses to some groups cannot be accepted as fair. In the normal circumstances of ordinary politics, groups that lose—as the timber industry, for example, might lose through environmental legislation—have had a fair opportunity to present their case and exert an influence on the result in rough proportion to their numbers and the strength of their interests. The Court will therefore scrutinize ordinary legislation challenged on equal protection grounds only in a "relaxed" way. It will declare such legislation unconstitutional only if it finds that the distinction it draws, between those it benefits and those it harms, is plainly irrational, which means that those attacking it can show that it does not serve, even in a speculative or problematical way, any legitimate purpose of government. So the Court has approved, for example, a law subjecting oculists and optometrists to different regulatory schemes, even though no very impressive reason could be given why they should be treated differently. Only rarely, in fact, has any statute been found to violate this "relaxed" test of rationality.

In some circumstances, however, the general presumption that the political process has worked in a fair way is doubtful. That presumption cannot rescue legislation that deprives some group of the very political rights it needs in order to participate in the process on fair terms—when the legislation reduces the voting power of some group, for example, so that its political impact is made less than its numbers would otherwise justify. The Court has therefore created a different, "strict" or "heightened," level of scrutiny for laws that have that effect. It declares such laws unconstitutional, even if they are rationally related to some legitimate state purpose, unless they can be shown to be necessary to prevent some grievous result that cannot be avoided in any other reasonable way. The Court relied on the strict test, for example, in its series of "reapportionment" decisions in which it struck down state schemes for drawing boundaries of electoral districts whose effect was to deny equal electoral impact, citizen by citizen, on a one-person, one-vote basis. Just as the "relaxed" test is rarely failed, so this "strict" test is rarely passed.

The presumption of a fair political process is also doubtful when the group that loses is one that has historically been the victim of a prejudice or stereotype that makes it likely that its interests will be discounted by other voters. Blacks have often lost out in politics, for example, not because their own interests were outweighed by those of others in a fair contest, but for one or both of two other reasons: because they were economically depressed and socially without influence, and lacked the training and means needed to command the attention of politicians and other voters, or because many white citizens voted for discriminatory laws not just to protect their own competing personal interests but because they held blacks in contempt and wanted them subjugated.

So the Court has created another special category attracting "heightened" scrutiny: it declared that blacks form a "suspect" class, and that any legislation that works to their special disadvantage must be struck down unless it can be defended as serving some absolutely compelling purpose. That strict test, too, has rarely been met. The Court has added other groups to the list of "suspect" classes deserving special protection: ethnic minorities and immigrants. It has, moreover, created a further category of "quasi-suspect" classes—these now include women and illegitimate children—and declared that legislation working against them will also receive "heightened" (but not as "strict" as in the case of fully "suspect" classes) scrutiny.

We must consider Judge Miner's claim in *Quill* v. *Vacco*—that laws forbidding assisted suicide deny equal protection—against that complex doctrinal background. The judge could not plausibly hold that dying patients form a suspect or quasi-suspect class—such patients are objects of sympathy, not prejudice—and *Bowers* prevented him, he said, from supposing that such patients have a fundamental right to a willing doctor's aid in killing themselves. So he conceded that only relaxed scrutiny was appropriate, but he claimed that even on that test New York failed, because no rational ground could justify allowing some patients to terminate life support but not allowing others, who need a different kind of help in dying, to have it.

It is true that some of the grounds that have been urged for that distinction are dubious. It is sometimes said that doctors who do not use life-saving equipment are only failing to act to save life, while those who prescribe pills are positively helping patients to die. But though the distinction between acts and omissions is often valid—there is a moral difference between killing and failing to contribute to a life-saving charity—that distinction does not seem important in this context. On the contrary, it may seem more humane for a doctor to give a patient a lethal injection that kills at once than to terminate life support and allow a patient to suffocate or starve to death. In any case, moreover, removing life-support systems already in place, which the *Cruzan* case said states must allow, is as positive an act as an injection.

The relaxed-scrutiny standard requires only that there be some speculative ground for a distinction, however, and I have already mentioned one that seems strong enough to pass that weak test. A patient's right to decline life support, or to order the removal of life support already in place, can plausibly be thought part of people's undoubted right to control invasions of their own bodies. A right to a lethal injection or a lethal dose of pills cannot. So the State of New York can argue that its distinction is perfectly rational. It wants to preserve life in whatever way it can, and therefore to prevent as much suicide as is legally possible. It cannot forbid people from terminating their life support, because they have the right just described. But (if Miner is right in his judgment that patients have no independent liberty interest in assisted suicide) it can forbid them lethal injections or pills. So it does.

The Second Circuit's argument, understood as a classic equal protection argument, is therefore fragile. It is much stronger, however, if we read it as the due-process argument Miner denied he was making—not the argument that New York must allow assisted suicide to one group of patients only because it allows others to direct that life support be removed, but the more fundamental argument that New York must respect a right that applies with equal force in both cases and could not be denied in either or both: the basic right of citizens to decide for themselves whether to die at once or after prolonged agony. For the most powerful passages in Miner's opinion are not those in which he argues that New York cannot rationally distinguish between the two forms of hastening death, but those in which he denies that New York could have any legitimate interest in opposing either form. "But what interest can the state possibly have in requiring the prolongation of a life that is all but ended?" he asked. "And what business is it of the state to require the continuation of agony when the result is imminent and inevitable?" He then quoted exactly the passage from the plurality *Casey* opinion on which Judge Rothstein and the Ninth Circuit had relied, which asserted a due process "right to define [one's] own concept of existence, of meaning, of the universe, and of the mystery of human life."

Though press reports have emphasized that the Ninth and the Second Circuits relied on different constitutional provisions in striking down statutes forbidding assisted suicide, the difference was, in fact, only one of candor. The Ninth Circuit was able to justify its *Compassion* decision naturally—and persuasively—by refusing to follow the philosophy of *Bowers*. The Second Circuit, because it tried to defer to that philosophy, offered a bad argument first, and then, in thin disguise, the same argument the Ninth Circuit had offered openly.

Many Americans have become concerned about the legal, economic, and social disadvantages that homosexuals still suffer in this country, and in recent decades they have supported laws and industrial and academic regulations prohibiting or limiting such discrimination. The Colorado cities of Aspen, Boulder, and Denver recently enacted legislation that protected homosexuals, along with minority races and women, from discrimination in housing, education, employment, and health and welfare services. Other Colorado voters were outraged, however, by the suggestion, implicit in such legislation, that homosexuality is a legitimate way of life. In a 1992 statewide referendum, they adopted "Amendment 2" to their state constitution, which was titled, "No Protected Status Based on Homosexual, Lesbian, or Bisexual Orientation." It declared that:

Neither the State of Colorado, through any of its branches or departments, nor any of its agencies, political subdivisions, municipalities or school districts, shall enact, adopt or enforce any statute, regulation, ordinance or policy whereby homosexual, lesbian or bisexual orientation, conduct, practices or relationships shall constitute or otherwise be the basis of or entitle any person or class of persons to have or claim any minority status, quota, preferences, protected status or claim of discrimination.

This provision, if valid, would have a catastrophic effect on the political situation of homosexuals in Colorado. It would annihilate the protection that some cities had already given, and forbid any political subdivision of the state, and indeed the state itself, from enacting any protective legislation in the future. Homosexuals could thereafter secure anti-discrimination legislation only by further amending the state constitution itself, to repeal or amend Amendment 2.

That struck many people, within the state and outside it, as monstrously unfair. They assumed that there must be some ground on which Amendment 2 violated the national constitution, and a group of Colorado homosexuals and others sued in a Denver court, in the case of *Romer* v. *Evans*, asking for a ruling to that effect. Many constitutional lawyers were dubious, however, that they could win. The doctrinal background I have already described, governing due process and equal protection, made it seem doubtful that Amendment 2 violated either of those clauses, and no other constitutional provision was pertinent.

For the *Bowers* precedent was now directly applicable. Justice White had explicitly declared that homosexuals do not have a "liberty interest" in freedom of sexual conduct that can prevent states from declaring homosexual sex a crime. It therefore seemed impossible to argue that they have a liberty interest that would bar the less serious disadvantage of Amendment 2, which merely prevents them from obtaining special legislation in their favor. . . .

The equal protection clause might seem a more promising basis for objection, because Amendment 2 denied homosexuals a political opportunity—to attempt to secure local legislation protecting their basic interests—open to other groups. But, as we have seen, an equal protection challenge to any legislation must show either some reason why "heightened scrutiny" of that legislation is appropriate, or that the legislation is irrational because it does not bear even a speculative relation to a legitimate governmental purpose. Heightened scrutiny is appropriate if the group that is disadvantaged counts as a "suspect" or "quasi-suspect" class, and homosexuals are certainly targets of prejudice and irrational hatred. In the years following the *Bowers* decision, however, several federal courts held that homosexuals nevertheless do *not* count as a suspect or quasi-suspect class, for a reason it is important to explain. Suspect groups are those that lack the political power necessary to make the political process a fair and democratic one for them. But a group might lack that power for either of two different reasons that I distinguished, earlier, in discussing the case of blacks.

First, it might be so disadvantaged financially, socially, and politically that it lacks the means to attract the attention of politicians and other voters to its interests, and so cannot wield the power at the polls, or in alliances or horse-trading compromises with other groups, that its numbers could otherwise be expected to produce. Second, it might be the victim of bias, prejudice, hatred, or stereotype so serious that a majority wants it constrained or punished for that reason, even when this does not serve any other, more respectable or legitimate, interests of other groups.

Blacks and the other groups the Supreme Court has hitherto treated as suspect or quasi-suspect suffer from both these disabilities. But (at least in the view of the judges who have spoken on the issue) homosexuals suffer only from the second. Justice Scalia in his *Evans* dissent, insisted that homosexuals have at least the political power their numbers would warrant: "Because those who engage in homosexual conduct," he said, tend to reside in disproportionate numbers in certain communities, have high disposable income, and of course care about homosexual-rights issues much more ardently than the public at large, they possess political power much greater than their numbers, both locally and statewide.

If a state like Colorado rejects the homosexuals' case, he said, it is not because they have not had a chance to organize their political efforts, or to speak effectively to their fellow citizens, but because, in spite of the fact that they have had those opportunities, the majority has decided against them.

It is therefore crucial to decide whether the second disadvantage — the prejudice and contempt of a potential majority — is an independent defect in the proper functioning of a democracy, a defect that is sufficiently serious to justify heightened scrutiny of legislation that harms those who suffer from such prejudice. The *Bowers* decision answered that question negatively. The groups who challenged the Georgia anti-sodomy law in that case argued that a state has no right to enact criminal legislation when its only reason is that the majority morally disapproves of those it makes criminals. Justice White replied that "the law, however, is constantly based on notions of morality, and if all laws representing essentially moral choices are to be invalidated under the Due Process Clause, the courts will be very busy indeed."

White's comment missed the point. Of course most of the criminal laws that a community enacts express a moral choice: laws against murder express a moral condemnation of that activity. The groups challenging the Georgia anti-sodomy law argued only for the narrower principle that a criminal law is unconstitutional if it is enacted only to condemn some people morally, and not to protect anyone else's direct interests. Laws against murder do more than denounce murderers: they protect the most basic interests of innocent people. Making consensual adult sodomy a crime, on the other hand, serves no interests that are independent of the moral condemnation, and those who challenged Georgia's anti-sodomy law argued that that is not a legitimate justification for a criminal penalty.

White clearly meant to reject that narrower principle as well, however, and *Bowers* therefore stands for the principle that it is permissible for government to prohibit freedom of choice in private sexual behavior even if that behavior harms no one in any direct way, so long as the condemnation expresses popular morality. Since the *Bowers* decision, judges have therefore uniformly rejected the suggestion that homosexuals form a suspect or quasi-suspect class for equal protection purposes, and every judge who expressed a clear opinion on that issue during the litigation of the *Evans* v. *Romer* case agreed.

There is, however, another kind of legislation that also attracts the "heightened scrutiny" test, as we noticed: legislation that compromises a fundamental political right. The claim that Amendment 2 violated a fundamental political right does not depend on supposing that homosexuals are a suspect or quasi-suspect class. On the contrary, it could be sustained only by showing that it would be unconstitutional to treat any group of citizens—people who rent houses, for example, as opposed to owning them—as Amendment 2 treated homosexuals. But, just for that reason, it is enormously difficult to define what the right in question is.

The Denver trial judge who first considered the case, H. Jeffrey Bayless, decided that the amendment did violate a fundamental right: the right "not to have the State endorse and give effect to private biases." But that is exactly the right that Justice White, in *Bowers*, said that no one has. So when Colorado appealed the trial judge's decision to the Colorado Supreme Court, that court upheld the trial judge's decision but cited a different fundamental right—the right of all groups to "participate equally in the political process."

There is an evident difficulty in that suggestion as well, however. Amendment 2 did not diminish or dilute anyone's voting power. It did mean that one group—homosexuals—would have to amend the state constitution again to secure legislation of particular concern to it. But no group has a right not to have to amend the constitution to obtain legislation it favors or believes it needs. It would not be unconstitutional, in principle, for Colorado's constitution to forbid municipalities to adopt rent-control legislation, for example, even though that would pose special problems for people who rent. Indeed, the US Constitution has parallel disabilities: groups who fervently want prayer back in their schools would have to repeal the First Amendment before petitioning the local school board.

Many lawyers were therefore fearful, when Colorado appealed from its own supreme court to the national one, that even if a majority of the justices wanted to strike down Amendment 2, they would not find room to do so within the network of doctrine and precedents they had themselves constructed. But a group of some of America's most distinguished constitutional law scholars submitted an ingenious brief, as *amici curiae*, or friends of the court, which pointed a way out of these doctrinal difficulties. The academic brief bypassed the elaborate structure of categories and distinctions I described, about suspect classes, fundamental rights, and different levels of scrutiny, by insisting that it is an automatic (or "*per se*") violation of equal protection for the state to declare that *any* group of citizens is simply ineligible for any protection whatever from any form of the harm of discrimination. Such a declaration, the brief said, in effect *outlaws* the group, and it was the central point of the equal protection clause to prevent that kind of caste distinction.

This argument, the brief insisted, assumes nothing about homosexuals being a suspect class. A state constitutional provision would violate equal protection, it said, if it forbade any legislation protecting any group of citizens against any form of discrimination. It offered this example: a state constitution would deny equal protection for people who rent homes (surely not a suspect class) if it provided that any local or state legislation that protects renters from *any* imaginable harm or loss is invalid. But this comparison reveals how limited an argument the brief was making, and how carefully it had tailored that argument to the facts of this particular case. It made the unconstitutionality of Amendment 2 depend on its great breadth and, as the example of home renters shows, that argument would permit a state to pass a narrower but still destructive constitutional amendment aimed at homosexuals.

The brief conceded, for example, that it would not be a *per se* violation of equal protection for a state constitution to forbid local rent-control legislation, even if such a law were necessary to protect renters from unjustified and oppressive rent increases. So, by a parity of reasoning, it would not be a *per se* violation for a constitution to forbid a single form of anti-discrimination legislation—local laws from banning discrimination against homosexuals in hiring, for example, or in hospital admissions. We might be tempted to say that these are different matters: a provision forbidding rent control might express an economic theory, while one forbidding even a specific and limited form of help to homosexuals would express only bias. But the academic brief's argument was careful, for reasons I have tried to make clear, not to rely on that distinction, because that would have been tantamount to declaring homosexuals a suspect class, or to affirming the right Judge Bayless had cited but the state supreme court had feared to endorse—a right to be free from legislation motivated by bias or hatred.

When the Supreme Court delivered its long-awaited verdict in May, Justice Kennedy's opinion for the six-justice majority was surprisingly bold—bolder than the opinions of either of the lower courts and bolder than even the academic brief. (As Justice Scalia wryly noted, the Court has the luxury, as other judges and lawyers do not, of ignoring its own precedents.) Kennedy did accept, in general terms, the argument of the academic brief. He emphasized, as that brief did, that Amendment 2 was wholly novel in the sheer breadth of the potential damage it worked on homosexuals, by depriving them of any possible opportunity to secure protection, except by constitutional amendment, against any form of discrimination no matter how harmful or wrongful.

But, perhaps understanding the limitations of that argument, he also made a much broader and potentially more reforming claim whose significance the press has not adequately reported. He said that Amendment 2 violates even the most relaxed form of scrutiny under equal protection doctrine, because it is not even rational. "In the ordinary case," Kennedy said, "a law will be sustained if it can be said to advance a legitimate government interest, even if the law seems unwise or works to the disadvantage of a particular group, or if the rationale for it seems tenuous." But, he said, "Amendment 2's sheer breadth is so discontinuous with the reasons offered for it that the amendment seems inexplicable by anything but animus toward the class that it affects; it lacks a rational relationship to legitimate state interests."

That statement is of crucial importance, because it flatly contradicts Justice White's pivotal assumption in *Bowers*. White, you recall, declared that it is legitimate for a state to impose a disadvantage on a particular group just to express the majority's moral contempt for that group's practices, even when no other proper purpose, such as protecting anyone's economic or security interests, is served. Kennedy, in the passage just quoted, said that this is not legitimate. It is true that White spoke in terms of moral disapproval and Kennedy in terms of "animus." But there can be no difference in what these words mean in this context. For Colorado could certainly declare, in perfect good faith, that the amendment's "sheer breath" was justified by the depth of its citizens' moral disapproval of homosexuality. Nothing less than a complete ban on any law that suggests that homosexuality is an acceptable form of sexual union, it might say, would be enough to express the profoundness of the majority's rejection of that moral opinion. By describing that justification as one appealing to "animus," and declaring it illegitimate, Kennedy reached back to Judge Bayless's original judgment in the trial court, and drew the sting from *Bowers* without even mentioning it.

Kennedy's reasoning would apply even to a much narrower constitutional provision than Amendment 2, and to many other discriminatory laws as well. He did not put homosexuals in as secure a position as they would enjoy if they were designated a suspect or quasi-suspect class. They have the burden of proof in showing that a particular rule or law that harms them serves no legitimate purpose, but only the illegitimate one of expressing "animus," and they might find that burden difficult to sustain in many cases—in challenging the military's opposition to retaining openly homosexual soldiers, for example. But they would presumably not find it difficult to show that the outright criminalization of all homosexual sex serves no purpose beyond that illegitimate one.

Scalia was right, in his biting dissent, that the combination of the result in *Evans* and the result in *Bowers* is ludicrous: practicing homosexuals can be jailed but not put at an electoral disadvantage—having to amend a constitution to get legislation they want—that many other groups, including people who favor prayer in schools, suffer. But the inevitable resolution of that conflict may not be the one he would prefer. The members of the majority in *Romer* v. *Evans* may have done more than simply ignore *Bowers*: they may have begun the process of isolating and finally overruling it altogether, an event that would have an enormous impact not only on the civil liberties of homosexuals but, as I have tried to show throughout this essay, on constitutional theory generally.

33

Sexual Harassment and the Ironies of the 1964 Civil Rights Act

DAVID M. O'BRIEN

David M. O'Brien is a professor of politics at the University of Virginia and author of numerous books on the Supreme Court, constitutional law, and judicial politics. This selection focuses on the ironies and unanticipated consequences of how the 1964 Civil Rights Act's prohibition against discrimination on the basis of gender was designed to defeat passage of the act, but in the hands of federal agencies and the courts came to apply to sexual harassment — heterosexual and homosexual harassment — in the workplace. The excerpt is from his contribution to Congress and the Politics of Emerging Rights *(2002), edited by Colton C. Campbell and John F. Stack, Jr.*

THE SUPREME COURT handed down three rather remarkable statutory rulings at the end of its October 1997–98 term. Together, they extended the protection of Title VII of the Civil Rights Act of 1964 to make employers liable for same-sex harassment of workers and for tolerating "hostile-workplace sexual harassment." These rulings not only were sweeping and significant in their impact on employers' liability but also serve to illustrate how congressional legislation frequently has unanticipated (and occasionally even ironic) consequences. . . .

[W]riting for a unanimous Court in *Oncale v. Sundowner Offshore Services* (1998), one of the most conservative justices — Justice Antonin Scalia — held that Title VII applies to same-sex harassment of workers by coworkers no less than to the harassment of employees by supervisors of different sexes or sexual orientations in the workplace. In *Faragher v. City of Boca Raton* (1998), the Court reaffirmed that employers are subject to liability for hostile-environment or workplace sexual harassment created by supervisors. Furthermore, in his opinion for the Court, Justice David H. Souter ruled that employees need not show that employers knew or should have known about the sexual harassment and failed to stop it. Even if employees do not suffer the loss of promotion or employment, suits may be brought if the harassment or abuse was severe or pervasive, although employers may offer as defenses that they took reasonable care to prevent or correct the sexually harassing behavior and that employees unreasonably failed to take advantage of corrective opportunities offered by the employer. Here, Justice Souter concluded that Boca Raton, Florida, failed to exercise reasonable care in protecting its female lifeguards from a hostile environment of sexual harassment. In that case only Justices Scalia and Clarence Thomas dissented, as they did in the third ruling. Delivering the opinion for the Court in the third decision, *Burlington Industries v. Ellerth* (1998), Justice Anthony Kennedy ruled that employers are liable under Title VII for hostile-environment sexual harassment by supervisors unless they demonstrate (a) reasonable care to prevent or correct promptly the harassing behavior and (b) that the allegedly harassed employee unreasonably failed to take advantage of grievance procedures offered by the employer in order to avoid harm. . . .

Purposes and Paradoxes of the Civil Rights Act

Looking back almost forty years after the passage of the Civil Rights Act of 1964 gives one pause when considering how much law and politics has changed in the country. The Civil Rights Act of 1964 remains the most significant and comprehensive civil rights legislation since the Reconstruction era after the Civil War. It was the product of the long, bitter, and occasionally violent struggles of the civil rights movement. More specifically, in 1963 the "sit-in" movement to dramatize segregation in the South resulted in a change in the national political climate as a consequence of televised coverage of the ugly use of police dogs and fire hoses against peaceful protesters in Birmingham, Alabama. That violent episode moved the administration of Democratic President John F. Kennedy (JFK) to make a commitment to the advancement of civil rights. Congress, though, remained unmoved until after JFK's assassination. His successor, and notably a former very powerful Senate leader, President Lyndon B. Johnson (LBJ) and his Democratic supporters pushed the act through Congress as a kind of memorial to JFK. . . .

From LBJ's special message to Congress on June 19, 1963, proposing the legislation throughout the acrimonious debates in Congress, attention was almost exclusively given to the problem of racial discrimination. Indeed, LBJ's message focused solely on discrimination based on "race, color, religion, or national origin." Likewise, the congressional debates and committee reports of both the House of Representatives and the Senate focused overwhelmingly on the problems of racial segregation and discrimination.

Ironies abound in the legislative history and politics of how "sex" came to be included in Title VII and other provisions of the Civil Rights Act. Not until the bill that would become the Civil Rights Act was finally debated on the floor of the House was the "sex amendment" introduced by Virginia's Democratic Representative Howard W. Smith. Smith was an eighty-year-old segregationist and former judge who had served in the House for almost three decades. As the powerful chair of the House Rules Committee, he was known for manipulating procedures to obstruct the passage of civil rights legislation.

When introducing the "sex amendment" on the floor, Representative Smith explained:

This amendment is offered to prevent discrimination against another minority group, the women, but a very essential minority group, in the absence of which the majority group would not be here today. . . . I do not think it can do any harm to this legislation; maybe it can do some good. I think it will do some good for the minority sex. I think we all recognize and it is indisputable fact that all throughout industry women are discriminated against in that just generally speaking they do not get as high compensation for their work as do the majority sex. . . .

Representative Smith . . . brought the proverbial "house down" (recall, too, that the House of Representatives at the time was dominated by white males). Quickly playing to the laughter in the House, Smith reminded the House of the seriousness of the matter since, as he claimed again with tongue in cheek, half of the voters in the country were female. "I am serious about this thing," he concluded disingenuously, "What harm can you do this bill that was so perfect yesterday?"

The "pandemonium" on the floor, as Charles and Barbara Whalen nicely recount in their book *The Longest Debate: A Legislative History of the 1964 Civil Rights Act*, was eventually broken by the Democratic House leadership. New York's liberal Democratic Representative Emanuel Celler and Oregon's Democratic Representative Edith S. Green, who was also a member of the president's Commission on the Status of Women, both spoke out against adoption of the amendment. They feared, exactly as Smith hoped, that the amendment would defeat passage of the entire bill. . . .

Ultimately, Smith's amendment was approved by a vote of 168 to 133. Two days later the act passed the House on a 290 to 130 vote. Subsequently, the Senate eventually concluded an incredible five-hundred-hour-long filibuster and passed the bill on a vote of 73 to 27. Throughout the debate in the Senate, which also focused almost exclusively on the problem of racial discrimination and federalism concerns, there was virtually no attention paid to the Smith amendment.

Outside of Congress, even the press and media gave Smith's amendment scant attention. It was largely portrayed for what it was—a tactical move to derail the strongest civil rights legislation since the Reconstruction Amendments (the Thirteenth, Fourteenth, and Fifteenth Amendments) to the U.S. Constitution, not as a major step forward in the struggle for women's rights.

Putting Title VII into Practice

In light of the terse legislative history and the fact that the Title VII prohibition against gender discrimination in employment originated as a kind of mischievous joke aimed at derailing the enactment of the Civil Rights Act, perhaps inevitably the Equal Employment Opportunity Commission (EEOC), which was entrusted with its enforcement, initially treated it as a joke as well. The EEOC's first executive director, Herman Edelsberg, for instance, publicly called it a "fluke," "conceived out of wedlock". . . .

Given its inauspicious origins and in spite of its potential legal and political significance, the prohibition on gender discrimination in Title VII continued to invite jokes in the press. It did, though, spark a controversy that many likewise thought was a laughing matter in late 1965. The controversy centered on whether newspapers had to stop their traditional gender discrimination in the placement of classified advertisements. The mere suggestion that gender-classified ads might be discriminatory moved, for instance, a 1965 *Wall Street Journal* article to ask "its readers to picture, if they could, 'a shapeless, knobby-kneed male bunny' serving drinks to a group of stunned businessmen in a Playboy Club' or a 'matronly vice-president' chasing a male secretary around her desk."

Remember that forty years ago it was common for "Help Wanted" advertisements to be separate for males and females. Admittedly, a few newspapers had begun to integrate their ads even before Title VII went into effect. But others, including the *New York Times*, declined to do so. They sought to protect themselves by citing the First Amendment's guarantee for freedom of the press and, as permitted by the EEOC at the time, with the disclaimer that separate columns for male and female positions was for "the convenience of readers and not intended as an unlawful limitation or discrimination based on sex". . . .

. . . [N]ot until December 1, 1968, did the EEOC finally move to bar gender-based classified advertisements. Some newspapers still resolutely refused to comply. And they did not comply until after the Supreme Court handed down its 1973 ruling in *Pittsburgh Press v. Pittsburgh Commission on Human Rights.* There, over the dissent of conservative Chief Justice Warren E. Burger and the Court's leading liberal, Justice William O. Douglas, the high bench laid to rest claims by newspapers to First Amendment protection for gender-segregated advertisements. Writing for the majority in *Pittsburgh Press,* Justice Lewis F. Powell Jr. found no impairment of editorial freedom. And he emphasized what should have been clear and noncontroversial from the outset, namely: "The advertisements, as embroidered by their placement, signal that the advertisers were likely to show an illegal sex preference in their hiring decisions."

In fairness, admittedly the EEOC initially had very weak enforcement authority. That was the result of compromises and deals struck in the halls of Congress during the passage of the Civil Rights Act. Provisions that would have authorized the EEOC to bring litigation on behalf of employees and to enforce Title VII were eliminated in the final act. Hence, the EEOC had no independent enforcement authority to bring litigation. When responding to complaints of employment discrimination, the EEOC could investigate them. But, if the EEOC determined that they were well grounded, it only had the power to try to persuade employers to abandon their discriminatory practices. If that failed, the EEOC was in a position only to refer cases for litigation to the Civil Rights Division of the Department of Justice (DOJ).

By 1970, however, the EEOC confronted a growing backlog of complaints. Congress gave some consideration in 1971 to empowering the EEOC to issue cease and desist orders to employers with discriminatory employment policies. Yet, the proposal was defeated by the combined opposition of some Republicans and Southern Democrats. Instead, a year later Congress passed the Equal Employment Opportunity Act of 1972. Under that legislation the EEOC was authorized to bring suits against employers who refused to abandon discriminatory practices. Subsequently, a full decade after the passage of the Civil Rights Act, in 1974 the authority to file "pattern and practice" lawsuits — lawsuits challenging systemic discrimination on a company-wide or industry-wide basis — was transferred from the DOJ's Civil Rights Division to the EEOC. Besides thereby reinforcing and expanding the EEOC's power, the commission's jurisdiction was broadened to include federal, state, county, and municipal employees within the scope of Title VII. Nonetheless, the EEOC continued drawing criticism from some women's groups for failing to sue more offending employers.

The EEOC's power was yet again broadened under Democratic President Jimmy Carter's Reorganization Plan Number 1. As of July 1, 1979, the EEOC was reorganized as the "lead agency" in enforcing employment discrimination law. The EEOC's authority and the statutory basis for bringing gender-discrimination employment lawsuits was also gradually reinforced by lower federal court and Supreme Court rulings in the 1970s and early 1980s (*Griggs vs. Duke Power Company* [1971], *McDonnell Douglas v. Green* [1973], *Albemarle Paper Company v. Moody* [1975], *Dothard v. Rawlison* [1977], and *Texas Department of Community Affairs v. Burdine* [1981]).

But, following the 1980 election of Republican President Ronald Reagan, the direction of the EEOC changed in 1982 under Clarence Thomas, Reagan's EEOC chairman, who was later named by President George H. W. Bush to the Court of Appeals for the District of Columbia Circuit and, then, to the Supreme Court in 1991. Under Thomas, the EEOC abandoned its policy of bringing class action lawsuits and shifted to concentrating on cases of individualized discrimination. Although drawing sharp criticisms from women's groups and others, Thomas defended his approach as "more methodical, more cautious and certainly less noisy" than that of his predecessors. Still, by the 1980s the EEOC's authority concerning gender-discrimination in employment litigation, as noted above, was finally firmly established. . . .

From Discrimination to Sexual Harassment in Employment

Recall that not until the 1970s and 1980s was there a political and legal movement, as an outgrowth of the "women's movement," to recognize claims of "sexual harassment" in employment — or, in other words, to develop categories and a legal basis for reconstructing the social reality of the workplace. The battles waged over acknowledging sexual harassment in the workplace culminated, improbably, in a kind of dramatic way, played out with no little irony, during the 1991 nationally televised hearings before the Senate Judiciary Committee on Clarence Thomas's nomination to the Supreme Court.

The Senate's confirmation of Justice Thomas was almost defeated by the allegations of law school professor Anita Hill that, almost a decade earlier, when she served as an assistant to the then chair of the EEOC, Thomas had sexually harassed her. Hill testified that Thomas had repeatedly asked for dates, frequently talked about pornographic movies, and created a hostile work environment. Thomas in turn categorically denied the accusations and angrily protested that the confirmation process had become "a cricus" and "a high tech lynching for uppity blacks."

The nasty drama of "she said, he said" failed to resolve the immediate questions about the veracity of either Hill or Thomas; nor could it have resolved their and others' conflicting perceptions of sexual harassment in the workplace. Still, the episode served to underscore how much public perception of sexual harassment in the workplace had changed (and was continuing to change) as a result of the legal and political battles of the preceding two decades.

Before the mid-1970s there was virtually no reliable empirical data on sexual harassment in the workplace. But that changed with a series of surveys documenting complaints by women about sexual harassment. In addition, by the mid-1970s individual women and women's groups began filing sexual harassment lawsuits, and feminist legal scholars were advancing arguments and theories for recognizing legal claims to sexual harassment.

In her pioneering 1979 book, *Sexual Harassment of Working Women*, law professor and leading feminist theorist Catherine MacKinnon distinguished between two kinds of sexual harassment claims in advocating their legal recognition: *Quid pro quo harassment*, on the one hand, involves an employer or supervisor demanding sexual favors in exchange for employment advantages, such as a promotion or simply not being laid off. On the other hand, MacKinnon distinguished "condition of work harassment," or what the EEOC and the courts eventually come to term "hostile workplace harassment" and "hostile-environment sexual harassment." That arises when employees are subjected to sexual comments, insults, or demands for favors, but there are not adverse employment consequences. In MacKinnon's words:

[U]nwanted sexual advances, made simply because she has a woman's body, can be a daily part of a woman's work life. She may be constantly felt or pinched, visually undressed and stared at, surreptitiously kissed, commented upon, manipulated into being found alone, and generally taken advantage of at—but never promised or denied anything explicitly connected with her job.

As a feminist theorist, MacKinnon viewed sexual harassment principally as the expression of male dominance over females. Yet, on a different theoretical basis, as courts in the 1990s eventually acknowledged, both categories of sexual harassment — quid pro quo and hostile environment harassment — would apply (and now do apply) to females harassing males and to same-sex harassment (*Oncale v. Sundowner Offshore Services* [1998]).

Initially, courts neither distinguished between *quid pro quo* and hostile environment harassment, nor were they very receptive to claims of sexual harassment. The first workplace harassment suit was brought successfully by a Hispanic worker, in *Rogers v. EEOC* (1971). Other harassment claims based on race, religion, and national origins followed. By contrast, although federal courts proved willing to uphold claims to *quid pro quo* sexual harassment in the late 1970's, it was not until 1981 that a claim to workplace sexual harassment proved successful (*Bundy v. Jackson* [1981]). . . .

One measure of the difficulty of successfully bringing early sexual harassment suits is that between 1974 and 1977 just five such suits in federal district courts were decided. Not only was the number small, reflecting the novelty of the claims, but three courts held that Title VII did not apply to sexual harassment.

Another court ruled that, while Title VII did not apply in the case before it, the statute might apply in other cases and circumstances. Moreover, that court also warned of the potential for widespread and abusive Title VII sexual harassment litigation, observing that "it would not be difficult to foresee a federal challenge based on alleged sex motivated considerations of the complainant's superior in every case of a lost promotion, transfer, demotion or dismissal."

In only one suit, *Williams v. Saxbe* (1976), was a sexual harassment claim successful; indeed, it was the first to succeed in a federal district court. Diane Williams, a Department of Justice public information officer, sued when she was fired less than two weeks after refusing her supervisor's sexual advances. In holding that Title VII's prohibition did apply, the district court rejected as a defense that sexual demands could be made to both sexes and, thus, fell outside of the scope of the structure. And it concluded that the actions of supervisors "created an artificial barrier to employment which was placed before one gender and not the other."

Nevertheless, each of the three district court decisions that had expressly rejected Title VII sexual harassment claims were subsequently reversed by federal appellate courts. Notably, the Court of Appeals for the Third Circuit held squarely that Title VII is violated when a supervisor "makes sexual advances or demands towards a subordinate employee . . . and the employer does not take prompt and appropriate remedial action" (*Tomkins v. Public Service Electric and Gas* [1977]).

The Court of Appeals for the Ninth Circuit in *Miller v. Bank of America* (1979), likewise, affirmed employers' liability under Title VII for its supervisory employees' harassment of coworkers, reasoning by analogy that:

It would be shocking to most of us if a court should hold, for example, that a taxi company is not liable to a pedestrian caused by the negligence of one of its drivers because the company has a safety training program and strictly forbids negligent driving. Nor would the taxi company be exonerated even if the taxi driver, in the course of his employment, became enraged at a jaywalking pedestrian and intentionally ran him down. (215)

On the basis of that analogy the Ninth Circuit concluded, as had the Third Circuit and some other appellate courts, that Congress did not intend in Title VII to exempt employers from standard rules for employer liability.

In light of the lower federal appellate court rulings interpreting Title VII to extend to sexual harassment claims and to impose liability on employers for their employees' harassing behavior, the Carter administration's controversial and outspoken EEOC chair, Eleanor Holmes Norton, moved in 1980 to issue guidelines, based on the emerging Title VII federal case law, as amendments to EEOC Guidelines on Discrimination Based on Sex. After a sixty-day public comment period, the guidelines were released on November 10, 1980.

The EEOC's 1980 guidelines built on and in some respects further extended and refined the developing Title VII case law. In particular, they provided a comprehensive definition of "sexual harassment," distinguishing between *quid pro quo* and hostile workplace harassment, as well as expanded employer liability. The guidelines specified provided that,

Unwelcome sexual advances, requests for sexual favors, and other verbal or physical conduct of a sexual nature constitute sexual harassment when (1) submission to such conduct is made either explicitly or implicitly a term or condition of an individual's employment (2) submission to or rejection of such conduct by an individual is used as a basis for employment decisions affecting such individual, or (3) such conduct has the purpose or effect of unreasonably interfering with an individual's work performance or creating an intimidating hostile, or offensive working environment.

In addition, the guidelines recommended holding companies strictly liable — that is, always liable — and made no distinction in this regard between *quid pro quo* and hostile workplace harassment when supervisors are involved. However, when coworkers harass coworkers, the guidelines did recommend holding employers liable only if they knew or should have known about the harassing behavior and failed to do anything about it. . . .

. . . [W]ithin a year the influential Court of Appeals for the District of Columbia Circuit upheld a hostile workplace sexual harassment claim in light of the EEOC's new guidelines, in *Bundy v. Jackson* (1981). It did so when reversing a 1979 district court decision that had, prior to the EEOC's guidelines, dismissed the claim.

Sandra Bundy, a Department of Corrections employee, charged that her supervisor's sexual advances constituted workplace harassment and a hostile environment, even though she was neither fired nor denied benefits for refusing the advances. The district court, which in retrospect appears "out of tune with the times," dismissed her claim upon concluding that, in its words, "the making of improper sexual advances to female employees [was] standard operating procedure, a fact of life, a normal condition of employment in the office."

The district court's language and reasoning appears antiquated in light of the developing Title VII case law and the EEOC's 1980 guidelines, and accordingly the Court of Appeals for the District of Columbia Circuit reversed the decision. On appeal, in *Bundy v. Jackson* (1981) the appellate court emphasized that developing case law had found "Title VII violations where an employer created or condoned a substantially discriminatory work *environment*, regardless of whether the complaining employees lost any tangible job benefits as a result of the discrimination." . . .

While *Bundy v. Jackson* was pending in the lower federal courts, another lawsuit was moving up through the federal judiciary and would eventually result in the Supreme Court's watershed ruling on Title VII sexual harassment claims in *Meritor Savings Bank, FBD v. Vinson* (1986). After four years of working as a bank teller-trainee, teller, and finally as an assistant manager, Mechelle Vinson filed a lawsuit against her supervisor, Sidney Taylor, and her employer, at the time Capital City Federal Savings and Loan Association, but later known as Meritor Savings Bank, FBD. Vinson did so after notifying Taylor in September 1978 that she was taking indefinite sick leave and, then, the bank discharged her for taking excessive leave. In her suit, Vinson claimed that during the preceding four years she had "constantly been subject to sexual harassment" by Taylor in violation of Title VII.

At an eleven-day trial, Vinson testified that Taylor was initially "fatherly" but soon asked her out to dinner, whereupon he suggested going to a motel for sex. While Vinson at first refused, she ultimately agreed out of fear of losing her job. After that Taylor allegedly repeatedly made demands for sexual favors and Vinson testified to having intercourse with him some forty to fifty times over the next several years. For his part, Taylor denied all of Vinson's allegations and countered that her accusations stemmed from a business dispute.

The federal district court ruled that Vinson had failed to substantiate a Title VII claim and, furthermore, held that, since the bank had a policy against gender discrimination and Vinson had failed to complain, the bank was not liable for Taylor's behavior, even if true.

On appeal, the Court of Appeals for the District of Columbia Circuit reversed. Relying on its own decision in *Bundy*, the appellate court asserted that it was not established that *quid pro quo* harassment was impermissible under Title VII. In addition, the appellate court ruled that the EEOC's 1980 guidelines also made a "persuasive" argument for applying Title VII to the second category of "hostile workplace harassment." And the circuit court remanded the case to the district court in order to determine whether Taylor's behavior had created a hostile environment in violation of Title VII.

The circuit court rejected as well the district court's view of employer liability, which the lower court had set aside because Vinson had not filed a grievance with her supervisor, Taylor. The appellate court deemed that arrangement unacceptable and impractical under the circumstances, as well as reasoned that Title VII applies to both the employer *and* its agents. Furthermore, on a theory of vicarious liability, the court concluded that Taylor's violation of Title VII was also attributable to the bank, regardless of its knowledge of the behavior (*Vinson v. Taylor* [1985]).

Meritor Savings Bank appealed the District of Columbia Circuit's decision to the Supreme Court. And the justices unanimously affirmed the appellate court's decision to remand the case back to the district court on Vinson's complaint of hostile workplace harassment in violation of Title VII. Besides legitimating the basis for claims of hostile workplace harassment under Title VII, no less importantly the Court rejected the contention of Meritor Savings Bank that Title VII applied only to gender discrimination that imposes "tangible, economic barriers."

Notably, in so ruling in his opinion for the Court in *Meritor Savings Bank*, Justice Rehnquist relied on, and affirmed, the EEOC's 1980 guidelines that extended Title VII to complaints of a hostile workplace environment. Justice Rehnquist did so because, as he noted in summarizing the origins of the "sex amendment," there "was little legislative history to guide [the Court] in interpreting the [Civil Rights] Act's prohibition against discrimination based on 'sex.'" Although affirming the EEOC's interpretation of Title VII, Justice Rehnquist cautioned that "not all workplace conduct that may be described as 'harassment' affects a 'term, condition, or privilege' of employment within the meaning of Title VII." And he stressed that, "For sexual harassment to be actionable, it must be sufficiently severe or pervasive 'to alter the condition of [the alleged victim's] employment and create an abusive working environment.'" . . .

Conclusion

. . . The ways in which the prohibition in Title VII on gender discrimination came to be enforced remains doubly ironic, given both the origins of its inclusion in the Civil Rights Act of 1964 in the first place and the subsequent extension to claims — claims not merely unanticipated but virtually unimaginable — of same-sex harassment.

Statutory language, of course, is rarely unambiguous, and this case study serves to underscore the enormous influence that federal agencies and courts may have on the application of civil rights legislation. Beyond that, though, the development of Title VII sexual harassment law demonstrates the power of ideas and social forces in pressuring Congress to enact legislation and, then, pushing federal agencies and courts to enforce that legislation, at times in directions completely unforeseen by Congress.

34

Rethinking the Civil Rights and
Civil Liberties Revolution

MICHAEL J. KLARMAN

Michael J. Klarman is a professor of law at Harvard Law School. The excerpt here is from his 1996 article in the Virginia Law Review. *In it and in his other writings, Professor Klarman challenges the "conventional wisdom" that the post-1937 Supreme Court has played a countermajoritarian role as a guardian of civil rights and civil liberties. Like political scientist, Gerald N. Rosenberg, in his 1991 book* Hollow Hope: Can Courts Bring About Social Change?, *Professor Klarman contends that the Court has not brought about major social changes. Instead of forging "countermajoritarian revolutions" with its rulings on civil rights and liberties, according to Professor Klarman, the Court has largely followed societal changes and the dominant national political coalition. He elaborated the themes here in his 2004 book* From Jim Crow to Civil Rights: The Supreme Court and the Struggle for Racial Equality.

IT IS COMMON wisdom that a fundamental purpose of judicial review is to protect minority rights from majoritarian overreaching. Supreme Court justices themselves have frequently propagated this view. Most famously, Justice Stone wrote in his *Carolene Products* footnote that the Court should invalidate legislation that reflects "prejudice against discrete and insular minorities . . . which tends seriously to curtail the operation of those political processes ordinarily to be relied upon to protect minorities." Justice Black once declared that courts stand "as havens of refuge for those who might otherwise suffer because they are helpless, weak, outnumbered, or because they are nonconforming victims of prejudice and public excitement." Justice Jackson proclaimed in his celebrated opinion in the second flag salute case that "the very purpose of a Bill of Rights was to withdraw certain subjects from the vicissitudes of political controversy, to place them beyond the reach of majorities." And in his famous concurring opinion in *Whitney v. California,* Justice Brandeis wrote that one function of judicial review is to protect against "the occasional tyrannies of governing majorities."

This understanding of judicial review—which I shall call the Court's heroic countermajoritarian function—exercises a powerful hold over our constitutional discourse. The rhetoric of heroic countermajoritarianism is, for example, prominently on display at the confirmation hearings of Supreme Court justices. On the occasion of the fortieth anniversary of *Brown v. Board of Education*, pundits' celebration of the Court's momentous contribution to the transformation of American race relations testified to the force the conventional wisdom exercises over our nation's opinion molders.

The legal academy's reception of this popular understanding of the Court's countermajoritarian capacity has been more mixed. Many scholars appear wholeheartedly to embrace this conception of judicial review. For example, Michael Perry defends noninterpretive judicial review on the ground that without it, there would be no basis for objecting "to laws authorizing torture, establishing slavery, or even instituting another Holocaust"; Perry thus implies that judicial review could prevent such atrocities. Judith Baer writes that without judicial review "there would be little hope for rights or for equality" and that individual rights in America "have never gotten very far without appeals to the Court." Ken Karst declares that courts "restrain the majority's worst excesses, in the name of the constitutional values that define our national community." Alpheus Mason opines that judicial review "advances the cause of peaceful change" by preventing the "oppression of individuals and minorities" that might encourage resort to the right of revolution. Laurence Tribe writes that the function of the judicial branch "is to protect dissenters from a majority's tyranny." Paul Murphy argues that without judicial review the populace would be "at the mercy of legislative majorities," and he observes that since 1931 courts have protected "formerly helpless Americans" in their exercise of constitutionally protected free speech rights.

Other scholars, it is true, have challenged this conventional wisdom, denying that the Court possesses any substantial capacity to protect minority rights from majoritarian overreaching. In a classic article, political theorist Robert Dahl observes that, given any reasonable set of assumptions about the nature of the political process, "it would appear to be somewhat naive to assume that the Supreme Court either would or could play the role of Galahad." Dahl's article is a distinguished contribution to a long tradition of scholarly and judicial writing that questions the Court's capacity to engage in countermajoritarian heroics. For present purposes, the most noteworthy feature of this impressive corpus of skeptical scholarship is that its principal contributions were composed before 1960—that is, before *Brown* had achieved iconic status and before the Warren Court had produced its constitutional rights revolution. Thus, Leonard Levy begins his mid-1960s reevaluation of judicial review by noting with apparent approval the skeptical assessments of the Court's countermajoritarian capacity provided in classic articles by Henry Steele Commager in the 1940s and John Frank in the 1950s. But Levy, one of the past generation's most eminent constitutional historians, goes on to observe that under Chief Justice Warren the constitutional law of civil liberties "has enjoyed a golden age in our history." He concludes that First Amendment freedoms and civil rights "have flourished and prospered in the pages of the [Warren] Court's opinions, with considerable fall-out in the world beyond." . . .

In any event, my purpose here is neither to deny that some scholars appreciate the overblown nature of the countermajoritarian hero image nor to dispute that the Court does occasionally play a limited countermajoritarian function. Both the countermajoritarian capacity of the Court and scholars' assessment of that capacity are measured along a continuum. My claim is only that the Court's capacity to protect minority rights is more limited than most justices or scholars allow. . . . Rather than viewing the Court as protecting minority rights from oppressive majorities, as the conventional wisdom holds, I suggest that the Court's decisions are better understood as comprising two categories. Frequently the Court takes a strong national consensus and imposes it on relatively isolated outliers. Infrequently the Court resolves a genuinely divisive issue that rends the nation in half; on these occasions, roughly half the country supports the Court's determination. Neither of these roles, it seems to me, is accurately characterized as providing "havens of refuge for those who . . . are helpless, weak, outnumbered, or . . . are non-conforming victims of prejudice." . . .

The Supreme Court does not play the strong countermajoritarian role in defense of individual liberties that popular wisdom ascribes to it. The conventional view probably exerts its greatest force in the area of race discrimination, and more specifically with regard to *Brown v. Board of Education*. *Brown*, according to the usual story line, represents a paradigmatic example of the Supreme Court intervening to protect an oppressed minority from majoritarian overreaching. Without the Court's timely intervention, according to this view, there would have been, at least in the near term, no civil rights movement, no landmark civil rights legislation, and no dramatic transformation in American race relations.

This understanding of *Brown*'s significance is distorted. *Brown* is better understood as the product of a civil rights movement spawned by World War II than as the principal cause of the 1960s civil rights movement. The many scholars who have treated *Brown* as the inaugural event in the modern civil rights movement have difficulty accounting for the

momentous civil rights developments of the late 1940s and early 1950s—
the landmark report of President Truman's civil rights committee, the
executive orders desegregating the federal military and civil service, the
integration of major league baseball, the exponential increase in Southern
black voter registration, the enactment of a plethora of Northern antidis-
crimination laws, the incipient crumbling of Jim Crow's outer facade in
many Southern cities (for example, initial steps taken toward the desegregation of Southern police forces, juries, and public accommodations), and
the emergence of a general war-related civil rights consciousness among
African-Americans.

Perhaps even more devastating to the traditional understanding of
Brown as a heroically countermajoritarian decision are the opinion polls
showing that by the time of the Court's intervention roughly half of
the country supported racial integration in public schools. The justices
themselves, moreover, repeatedly expressed astonishment in their private
discussions of the school segregation cases at the rapidity with which race
relations had been changing. Had the Supreme Court decided *Brown*
twenty (perhaps even only ten) years earlier, the result would have been
dramatically counter—majoritarian. Yet the Court declined more than
one opportunity to render such a decision.

The Court's rulings in another important equal protection context—
sex discrimination—reveal an even more limited countermajoritarian
bent. The Supreme Court did not invalidate a single law on sex discrimination grounds until 1971—that is, not until after the explosion in social
and political support for the women's movement in the late 1960s. Well
into the postwar period, the Court continued to reject equal protection
challenges to laws excluding women from traditionally male occupations
or defining jury service obligations differently for men and women. The
Court began to disfavor legislative classifications based on sex at almost
precisely the same time that Congress, by the requisite supermajorities,
passed a constitutional amendment to accomplish essentially the same
objective. Most of the sex discrimination cases of the 1970s and early
1980s, moreover, involved legislation employing antiquated sex stereotypes
that even most opponents of the Equal Rights Amendment would have
been unwilling to defend. The Court in these cases was doing little more
than chopping down some dead legislative wood. Moreover, when the
Court in 1981 finally encountered a sex classification that retained substantial support in public opinion—the exclusion of women from military
combat positions and the draft—it declined to interfere. Thus, the sex
discrimination cases do little to confirm the view of the Court as countermajoritarian defender of historically oppressed groups.

The point just made about the race and sex components of equal protection is also true of the Court's modern substantive due process jurisprudence, which principally involves the rights to privacy and sexual autonomy. None of the Court's decisions in this area corroborates the popular conception of the Court as countermajoritarian savior. When the justices in *Griswold v. Connecticut* first articulated a constitutional right to privacy and invalidated a state ban on the use of contraceptives as applied to married couples, only two states in the nation (two of the three with the highest percentage Roman Catholic populations) had such laws. *Griswold* is best understood as the Court constitutionalizing a dominant national consensus and using it to suppress a local outlier. Certainly this decision can be seen as protecting minority rights in a certain sense—the rights of a minority within Connecticut—but this is hardly the heroic countermajoritarian role claimed for judicial review by proponents of the conventional wisdom. Congress, after all, can force local outliers to abide by national norms as well as the Court can.

At first blush *Roe v. Wade*, which constitutionalized a right to abortion, seems to fit the conventional wisdom better. That decision, after all, had the effect of invalidating abortion laws in at least forty-six states. Yet even with regard to *Roe*, the extent of the Court's countermajoritarianism is easily exaggerated. By the time *Roe* was decided in 1973, public opinion on the abortion issue had already been dramatically transformed, primarily as a result of the burgeoning women's movement. Seventeen states had recently passed legislation liberalizing their abortion regulations. Opinion polls conducted soon after the decision revealed that slender pluralities or majorities of the public endorsed the Court's ruling. *Roe* could have been dramatically countermajoritarian only if it had been decided years earlier—say, in 1964, when the abortion issue first appeared on the ACLU agenda, or even in 1967, when Planned Parenthood and the National Organization for Women still found themselves deeply divided over whether to call for repeal of abortion statutes. Yet it seems safe to say that the justices would not have dreamed of invalidating abortion restrictions even as few as a half dozen years before *Roe*.

The limited scope of the Court's countermajoritarian capacity is also evidenced by its most recent privacy/sexual autonomy case—*Bowers v. Hardwick*. Let us suppose that Justice Lewis Powell had changed his mind about the outcome when it still mattered, as we know he almost did, and together with the four dissenters in *Bowers* had produced a majority opinion recognizing at least a limited due process right for consenting adults to engage in private, homosexual activity. Would such a result have corroborated the view of the Court as heroic defender of minority rights from majoritarian oppression? I think not. The justices would not have contemplated constitutionalizing a sexual orientation right before the emergence of a powerful social and political gay rights movement in the 1970s and 1980s. One can easily imagine *Bowers* coming out differently in 1986, but a contrary result is virtually unimaginable, say, in 1966—the year the American Civil Liberties Union first formally endorsed the principle of constitutional protection for sexual orientation and several years before the American Psychiatric Association ceased labeling homosexuality a mental illness. Had the Court decided *Bowers* the other way in 1986, contemporaneous opinion polls reveal that roughly half the country would have endorsed the ruling. No minority rights savior here. . . .

To sum up, then, a quick review of some of the Court's leading individual rights decisions of the modern era fails to corroborate the conventional image of the Court as countermajoritarian hero. Apparently the justices possess neither the inclination, nor the power, to play such a role. Rather, the modern Court's individual rights jurisprudence can be usefully distilled into two general categories. First, constitutional adjudication frequently involves the justices' seizing upon a dominant national consensus and imposing it on resisting local outliers. Cases illustrating this pattern include *Griswold v. Connecticut* (striking down a state ban on contraceptive use, as applied to married couples); *Gideon v. Wainwright* (requiring state-appointed defense counsel in all felony cases); *Pierce v. Society of Sisters* (invalidating a state law barring children from attending private schools); *Harper v. Virginia Bd. Of Elections* (invalidating a poll tax); *Coker v. Georgia* (forbidding imposition of the death penalty for the crime of rape); and *Moore v. City of East Cleveland* (invalidating legislation denying certain blood relatives the right to live in a single household). Second, less frequently and far more controversially, the Court intervenes on issues where the nation is narrowly divided—racial segregation in 1954, the death penalty in 1972, abortion in 1973, affirmative action in 1978, and (with the shift of a single vote) sexual orientation in 1986. On these occasions, the justices seem, whether consciously or not, to be endeavoring to predict the future. Obviously their efforts have been more successful on some occasions than others. For present purposes, however, the significant point is that with regard to neither of these two categories of decisions— suppressing outliers on the basis of a dominant national consensus or intervening "at the margin" on narrowly divided issues—can the Court accurately be portrayed as providing a "haven of refuge" for minorities suffering persecution from overreaching majorities.

To risk putting the point somewhat cynically, the Court identifies and protects minority rights only when a majority or near majority of the community has come to deem those rights worthy of protection. Judicial review operates only within the parameters established by the social, political, and ideological context within which judges function. Thus it was possible for the Court to invalidate racial segregation in public schools in 1954, not 1944; sex discrimination in 1971, not 1961; abortion restrictions in 1973, not 1963; and restrictions on radical political affiliation and speech in 1965, not 1955.

None of this, of course, is to deny that judicial review possesses some countermajoritarian capacity. Striking down local laws on the basis of a national consensus—which is what most constitutional adjudication is about—does protect local minorities. And on rare occasions the Court does frustrate the will of a slender national majority. Interestingly, neither of the two epochal decisions of the postwar period—*Brown* and *Roe*—fits this description, as the Court on both occasions probably had a narrow majority, or at least a plurality, of the nation on its side.

35

Constitutional Futurology, or What Are Courts Good For?

JEFFREY ROSEN

*Courts better serve the country by promoting a constitutional dialogue with
the President, Congress, and American people over civil rights and civil
liberties, rather than asserting judicial supremacy or unilateralism. So argues
the author, Professor Jeffrey Rosen, who teaches at George Washington
University Law School and serves as the legal affairs editor at* The New
Republic. *The selection here excerpts his* The Most Democratic Branch:
How Courts Serve America *(2006).*

———

THE SUPREME COURT has followed the public's views about
constitutional questions throughout its history, and, on the rare occasions
that it has been even modestly out of line with popular majorities, it has
gotten into trouble. Paradoxically, the federal courts, often considered the
least democratic branch of government, have maintained their legitimacy
over time when they have been deferential to the constitutional views of
the country as a whole.

But will—and should—this historical pattern continue to hold in the
future? For much of American history, liberals and conservatives were
united around the importance of judicial deference to democratic outcomes. Over the next few decades, that may be less likely as activists on
both sides of the political spectrum are insisting that only judges will have
the expertise and stature to resolve the complex technological and scientific
disputes that the future may bring. In fact, however, the issues that divide
the country in coming years will continue to be political and moral, far
more than they are technological, and can only be resolved by political
debate. If the Court tries unilaterally to impose the views of either progressive or social conservative minorities in the face of public resistance,
it may provoke social turmoil. In the future, in other words, both the
temptations and the costs of judicial unilateralism may continue to grow.

Although constitutional futurology is hardly an exact science, let's try
to imagine the kinds of disputes that might arise over the next few decades
and how the courts might best serve the country in confronting them.

Controversies might arise in areas such as genetic selection and enhancement; high-tech brain mapping that can identify criminal suspects with a propensity to violence; the demand for personalized drug and gene therapies; and efforts to patent novel forms of human life. As Congress and the states pass legislation to address these combustible issues, the laws will inevitably be challenged in court, raising novel questions about how to interpret our constitutional rights to privacy, autonomy, equality, and private property. Let's consider each in turn.

In the wake of terrorist attacks after September 11, 2001, the New York subway system implemented random bag searches, and the London Underground imposed the equivalent of electronic strip searches by high-tech body scanners that use millimeter waves to peer through clothing. In the coming years, if technology and the threat of terror continue to advance, Western democracies may confront ever more sophisticated and intrusive forms of surveillance, many of which will be challenged in court as a violation of rights to privacy and equality. It's easy to imagine, for example, the increasing use of data-mining computer programs to identify potentially suspicious individuals. As biometric camera systems become more accurate, they will be able to take pictures of people's faces, link the face to databases full of personal information, and generate a threat index based on how suspicious the individual appears. Marc Rotenberg of the Electronic Privacy Information Center, a civil liberties group in Washington, D.C., imagines a young man walking around the Washington Monument for thirty minutes while waiting for a friend. Cameras might record his face and zoom in on, for example, the Koran he was carrying under his arm. The link between his face and his travel records and magazine subscriptions, maintained by a commercial database, might generate a threat index score that suggests further investigation. Based on his low trustworthiness score, and the copy of the Koran, the young man might be stopped by the police, who might open his backpack and find marijuana. Would the examination of the backpack be an unconstitutional search or seizure?

On the current Supreme Court, a challenge to terrorist threat indices generated by computer algorithms would face an uphill battle. In 2005, the Court upheld the dog sniff of a driver who had been stopped for speeding. (When the dog barked, the cops opened the trunk and found marijuana.) In preferring mass technological searches to police discretion, the conservative justices were joined by liberal justices such as Stephen Breyer, who has voted to uphold group drug tests of high school students as a way of avoiding the dangers of racial profiling. The only dissenters were David Souter and Ruth Bader Ginsburg, who worried that the

Court had cleared the way for the police to turn drug-sniffing dogs on large groups of innocent citizens without cause to suspect illegal activity. But even Ginsburg and Breyer said there might be nothing wrong with the use of bomb-detection dogs if they were effective in identifying potential terrorists.

If polls about the U.S.A Patriot Act are correct (only 22 percent of Americans say it goes too far in restricting civil liberties to fight terrorism, while 69 percent are happy with it or think it doesn't go far enough) many citizens may not object to data-mining technology that claims to identify potential terrorists. But if the war against terror escalates, the government may deploy even more controversial forms of electronic surveillance, such as neuroimaging technologies that can detect the presence of electrochemical signals in the brain. The promoters of this "brain fingerprinting," which uses Functional Magnetic Resonance Imaging, or fMRI, say that it can detect brain waves that are consistent with particular kinds of recollection. In a murder case in Iowa, for example, a convicted murderer introduced an fMRI scan that suggested his brain did not contain information about the murder but did contain information consistent with his alibi. Similar scans could be used in the future to interrogate enemy combatants, for example, whom officials suspect of having trained in Afghanistan. They could be shown pictures of the battlefield, and, if they have been there before, the device would detect a brain wave.

It is an open question, under the Supreme Court's current cases, whether the fMRI scans, used as a glorified, high-tech lie detector, would be considered a form of compulsory self-incrimination that violates the Fifth Amendment. If the justices viewed an involuntary brain scan as no more intrusive than a blood or urine sample or an ordinary fingerprint, there wouldn't be any Fifth Amendment problem. But if the Court decides that the fMRI scans are looking not merely for physical evidence but also for a suspect's memories and substantive consciousness, the justices might conclude that his mental privacy is being invaded, and he is being forced to testify against his will in a way that raises constitutional concerns.

There is also the possibility that police or counterterror experts may eventually search suspects for brain waves that suggest a propensity toward violence — a sort of cognitive profiling. These fMRI scans can show that the parts of the brain responsible for impulse control and empathy are underactive and those responsible for aggression and more animalistic, violent activities are overactive. In the future, suspects who show a propensity for violence might be detained indefinitely as enemy combatants, even though they have committed no crimes. Cognitive terrorist profiling seems more intrusive than brain fingerprinting deployed as a high-tech lie detector test and might put pressure in the future on the Court's traditional understanding of privacy, which has tended to focus on information that people go out of their way to conceal from the world. Brain-scan technology can access personal information that is neither actively hidden from view nor meant to be exposed to the public. Still, it's not clear under current doctrine that even cognitive profiling violates the Fourth or Fifth Amendments, as conventionally understood. This means that the fate of fMRI technology — and in particular the difficult question of whether citizens or aliens can be detained based on their propensity to commit future crimes — should be debated and at least initially decided by elected representatives in Congress and the states.

In addition to battles over the scope of privacy protected by the Fourth and Fifth Amendments, there will also be battles over the scope of personal autonomy protected by the Fourteenth Amendment. In *Roe v. Wade,* the Court said that the Fourteenth Amendment includes a right to privacy broad enough to protect a woman's decision to terminate her pregnancy. Regardless of whether *Roe* remains on the books in coming decades, America's political and legal disputes about reproduction may well have moved far beyond efforts to balance the interest of a fetus against the interests of a pregnant mother. Instead, the country will likely be debating the use of sophisticated technologies involving genetic manipulation and reproductive cloning outside the womb — controversial procedures that may prompt restrictions or bans by state legislatures or Congress.

Already, scientists are able to analyze the genetic makeup of embryos created through in vitro fertilization, using that information to help aspiring parents implant in the woman's womb only those embryos that display a specified range of desired characteristics — including not only sex but also, perhaps someday, traits like intelligence, eye color, and height. Not all the traits that parents demand will be conventionally desirable: in a recent case in the United States, a deaf lesbian couple attracted attention (and criticism) by deliberately choosing a deaf man as a sperm donor in order to increase their chances of having a deaf child. And if scientists ever learn to identify a genetic predisposition to homosexuality with a high degree of certainty, genetic screening might be used to select for those embryos or to weed them out.

The political response to so-called designer babies might create strange bedfellows. "As we increasingly come to see our children as commodities to be chosen, like consumer products, they will be devalued in ways that we will come as a society to regret," says the feminist leader Judy Norsigian, co-author of *Our Bodies Ourselves.* "This kind of sex selection would create a sex imbalance, and it would reinforce preferential attitudes toward male children." Social conservatives would also oppose these efforts, but out of concern for the rights of the fertilized embryo: in 2005, in fact, a Republican state legislator in Maine introduced a bill to ban abortions based on the sexual orientation of the unborn child.

How would the Supreme Court view the constitutionality of a state law banning sex selection? In 1992, when it reaffirmed *Roe* in *Planned Parenthood v. Casey,* the court held that the Constitution protects a right of personal autonomy. The scope of this right will be at the heart of disputes over genetic technologies in the future. At the moment, the expansive vision of personal autonomy is most vigorously defended by John A. Robertson, a law professor who argues that the right to have offspring (or not), recognized in the Fourteenth Amendment and in *Roe v. Wade,* necessarily entails some right to select the characteristics of the offspring. The liberal notion of autonomy over reproduction includes some right of selectivity that logically could extend to nonmedical traits, he suggests.

But surely the Supreme Court should not attempt unilaterally to draw the line between those traits that parents can select for and those traits they cannot. Even justices who agree that the Fourteenth Amendment protects a certain right of personal autonomy might share a reluctance to decide, by judicial fiat, the mysterious point at which screening for genetic disabilities becomes screening for genetic enhancement. For example, genetic screening by prospective parents for Down's syndrome is already widely accepted, and couples in the future may naturally insist that if they are permitted to screen for genes associated with a low IQ they should also be allowed to screen for those associated with a high IQ. But judicial decrees about the scope of privacy rights will not settle this debate. Rather than presuming to define the boundary between therapy and enhancement on the basis of its understanding of privacy doctrine, the Court might serve the country better by leaving that agonizing decision — which has confounded our leading scientists and philosophers — to democratically accountable legislatures. . . .

In avoiding judicial unilateralism, it goes without saying, the Court should defer to the national majority's constitutional views, not its political views. Confident that free expression is a nationally accepted constitutional value, for example, the justices are free to interpret it in ways that may clash with the policy preferences of current national majorities. If majorities are indifferent about the technological restrictions of digital rights management, similarly the justices should be free to interpret the free expression guarantees of the copyright clause or the First Amendment in a way that recognizes some right to tinker.

. . . I have argued that Courts in the past have maintained their legitimacy — in both a political and principled sense — by avoiding judicial unilateralism. And these futuristic scenarios suggest that avoiding unilateralism will remain the best way for Courts to maintain their legitimacy in the future. But although maintaining legitimacy may be good for the judiciary, an obvious question arises: legitimacy for what? How can the Courts serve democracy in a positive sense, not only handing down decisions that national majorities will accept as principled but also defending constitutional values in the face of political assaults?

Some of the most distinguished defenders of judicial restraint have argued that Courts have a unique ability to predict the constitutional future, anticipating constitutional transformations before they have occurred. Alexander Bickel, for example, insisted that the Supreme Court was the only institution of government equipped to be the "pronouncer and guardian" of our "enduring values." Comparing the justices to teachers in a national seminar, Bickel wrote that "[t]heir insulation and the marvelous mystery of time give courts the capacity to appeal to men's better natures, to call forth their aspirations, which may have been forgotten in the moment's hue and cry." Bickel noted with approval a story told by the legal scholar Charles Black about a French intellectual who arrived in New York harbor and exclaimed: "It is wonderful to breathe the sweet air of legitimacy!" What really intoxicated the Frenchman, Black suggested, with uncharacteristic grandiosity, was the "sweet odor of the Supreme Court of the United States." Such a precious suggestion would be inconceivable today, because the idea of a fragrant Supreme Court intoxicating deferential observers is no longer plausible. American Courts have interjected themselves too deeply into politics to have their verdicts accepted with good grace by political losers.

Those who accept the purely political vision of the Supreme Court's legitimacy — that is, those who agree that the Court's decisions are most likely to be accepted by the country when the justices accurately predict the future — may agree with Bickel that justices should try to anticipate a constitutional consensus before it occurs, as long as they guess right. But judges are often inept at constitutional futurology, and the backlashes that wrong guesses tend to provoke may delay the constitutional transformation the judges are attempting to predict. For this reason, if judges are inclined to anticipate the future, they should confine themselves to gentle nudges rather than dramatic shoves.

Rather than trying to anticipate a constitutional consensus that has not yet occurred, judges often serve a more constructive role when they try to preserve a constitutional consensus that has become contested but has not yet been repudiated by a majority of the country. At important moments in history, Courts may also have an opportunity to enforce a constitutional principle that neither the president nor Congress are willing enthusiastically to embrace as long as there is no danger of active resistance. The failure to declare railroad segregation unconstitutional in *Plessy v. Ferguson* (1896) may be such a missed opportunity: only nine southern states had formally embraced railroad segregation at the time, and the Court might have claimed that it was merely bringing state outliers into a national consensus about the unconstitutionality of segregation with respect to fundamental civil rights such as the right to travel, embodied in the Fourteenth Amendment itself. Although there would have been little enthusiasm on the part of the president or Congress for vigorous enforcement of a decision banning railroad segregation, the Court might have issued a symbolic challenge to Jim Crow that, in small ways, might have slowed its expansion or perhaps even hastened its demise. In the face of congressional ambivalence, the Court has opportunities to influence constitutional debates at the margins.

Rather than trying to anticipate the future on its own, the Court can also play a constructive role by encouraging the president and Congress to reach a bilateral consensus on constitutional issues, rather than trying to monopolize the field of constitutional interpretation. . . .

In addition to encouraging a constitutional dialogue between the president and Congress, courts are good at identifying constitutional principles that have emerged from that dialogue and enforcing them in a principled fashion as fundamental law. The First Amendment is the most obvious example: although representatives in Congress since the nineteenth century insisted that principles of free expression prohibited the government from banning speech unless it was likely to cause imminent harm, the claim remained politically contested until the postwar period. After the Courts in the 1960s acknowledged the constitutional status of the principle, citizens could take its judicial enforcement for granted. Once the Court embraced the principle, justices of all political persuasions were willing to enforce it, even in the face of congressional attacks. The Supreme Court and lower federal courts are good, in other words, at forcing Congress to abide by principles that Congress itself has helped to define and whose constitutional status has been accepted by the country as beyond dispute. . . .

Today, on the right and the left, there are similarly combative declarations about the importance of defending constitutional principle regardless of the political consequences. By embracing judicial unilateralism as a mark of their devotion to principle, the extremists on both sides risk dooming themselves to electoral failure. If the courts embrace the invitation to unilateralism, they risk a backlash that could imperil their effectiveness and legitimacy in ways that will make the current attacks on judges look like shadowboxing. The courts can best serve the country in the future as they have served it in the past: by reflecting and enforcing the constitutional views of the American people.

PERMISSIONS AND ACKNOWLEDGMENTS

1. Alexander Hamilton (Publius), *The Federalist, No. 78* (1788).
2. From "Constitutional Interpretation: A Contemporary Ratification," a lecture delivered by Justice William J. Brennan, Jr., at the Text and Teaching Symposium at Georgetown University (1985).
3. Excerpted from Justice Antonin Scalia's William Howard Taft Constitutional Law Lecture, "Originalism: The Lesser Evil" (16 September 1988), in 57 *University of Cincinnati Law Review* 849 (1989). Copyright © 1989 by University of Cincinnati Law Review. Reprinted by permission.
4. Excerpted from Justice Stephen Breyer's James Madison Lecture, "Our Democratic Constitution," at New York University School of Law in 77 *New York University Law Review* 245 (2002). Copyright © 2002 by New York University Law Review. Reprinted by permission.
5. Excerpts from Walton H. Hamilton, "The Path of Due Process of Law," 47 *Ethics*, (April, 1938), 269–96. Copyright © 1938, renewed 1965, by Ethics. Reprinted by permission of the University of Chicago.
6. Excerpts from Robert G. McCloskey, "Economic Due Process and the Supreme Court: An Exhumation and Reburial," in Philip B. Kurland, ed., *The Supreme Court Review 1962* (Chicago: University of Chicago Press, 1962), 34–62. Copyright © 1962 by the University of Chicago. Reprinted by permission of the publisher.
7. Excerpts from Richard C. Cortner, *The Supreme Court and the Second Bill of Rights: The Fourteenth Amendment and the Nationalization of Civil Liberties* (Madison: University of Wisconsin Press, 1981), 279–94, 298–301. Copyright © 1981 by the Board of Regents of the University of Wisconsin System. Reprinted by permission of the University of Wisconsin Press.
8. Excerpts from David A. Strauss, "Due Process, Government Inaction, and Private Wrongs," in Gerhard Casper and Dennis J. Hutchinson, eds., *The Supreme Court Review 1989* (Chicago: University of Chicago Press, 1989), 53–87. Copyright © 1962 by the University of Chicago. Reprinted by permission of the publisher.
9. From *The System of Freedom of Expression* by Thomas I. Emerson. Copyright © 1970 by Thomas I. Emerson. Used by permission of Random House, Inc.
10. Reprinted from Erwin N. Griswold, *Ould Fields, New Corne: The Personal Memoirs of a Twentieth Century Lawyer*, 296–309. Copyright © 1992 by West Publishing. Reprinted by permission of Thomson Reuters.

26. Excerpted from *Capital Punishment: The Inevitability of Caprice and Mistake*, Second Edition. Augmented by Charles L. Black, Jr. Copyright © 1981, 1974 by W. W. Norton & Company. Inc. Copyright © 1977, 1978 by Charles L. Black, Jr. Reprinted by permission of W. W. Norton & Company, Inc.

27. From "The Broken Machinery of Death" by Alan Berlow reprinted by permission of *The American Prospect*, Volume 12, Issue 13, July 30, 2001. Copyright © 2001, *The American Prospect*, 5 Broad Street, Boston, MA 02109. All rights reserved.

28. From *Simple Justice* by Richard Kluger, copyright © 1975 and renewed 2003 by Richard Kluger. Reprinted by permission of Alfred A. Knopf, Inc., a division of Random House, Inc.

29. Copyright © 1996 *Dismantling Desegregation: The Quiet Reversal of* Brown v. Board of Education edited by Gary Orfield and Susan E. Eaton. Reprinted by permission of The New Press. www.thenewpress.com.

30. Excerpted from Wendy W. Williams, "The Equality Crisis: Some Reflections on Culture, Courts, and Feminism," 7 *Women's Rights Law Reporter* (1982), 175–79, 190–98, 200. Copyright © by Wendy W. Williams. Reprinted by permission of the Women's Rights Law Reporter.

31. Excerpted from Ruth Bader Ginsburg, "Speaking in a Judicial Voice," *New York University Law Review*, 67 (1992), 1185. Copyright © 1992 by Ruth Bader Ginsburg. Reprinted by permission of the *New York University Law Review*.

32. Excerpted from Ronald Dworkin, "Sex, Death, and the Courts," *New York Review of Books* (August 8, 1996), 44–50. Reprinted with permission from *The New York Review of Books*. Copyright © 1996, NYREV, Inc.

33. From "Sexual Harassment and the Ironies of the 1964 Civil Rights Act," by David M. O'Brien, in Colton C. Campbell and John F. Stack, Jr., eds., *Congress and the Politics of Emerging Rights*. Copyright © 2002 by Colton C. Campbell and John F. Stack. Reprinted by permission of Rowman and Littlefield.

34. Excerpted from Michael J. Klarman, "Rethinking the Civil Rights and Civil Liberties Revolution," *Virginia Law Review* 82 (1996), 1. Copyright © 1996 by Michael J. Klarman. Reprinted by permission of Virginia Law Review Association.

35. Excerpted from Jeffrey Rosen, *The Most Democratic Branch: How the Courts Serve America*, 185–210. Copyright © 2006 by Oxford University Press. Reprinted by permission of the publisher.